Ultimate Recipes

Italian

Ultimate Recipes

Italian

p

This is a Parragon Book
This edition published in 2001

Parragon
Queen Street House
4 Queen Street
Bath BA1 1HE, UK

ISBN 0-75256-641-5

Printed in China

Produced by Haldane Mason, London

Notes
Use all metric or all imperial quantities, as the two are not interchangeable.
Cup measurements in this book are for American cups. Tablespoons are assumed to be 15 ml.
Unless otherwise stated, milk is assumed to be full fat, eggs are medium and pepper is freshly
ground black pepper.

The nutritional information provided for each recipe is per serving or per portion.
Optional ingredients, variations or serving suggestions have not been included in the
calculations. The times given for each recipe are an approximate guide only as the
preparation times may differ as a result of the type of oven used.

Contents

Introduction 10

Soups

Starters

Snacks & Light Meals

Snacks & Light Meals (continued)

Fish & Seafood

Meat

Poultry & Game

Vegetables

Salads

Salads (continued)

Pasta

Rice & Grains

Pizzas & Breads

Desserts

Introduction

Italian food, including the many pasta dishes, pizzas and risottos, as well as the decadent desserts, are enjoyed all around the world. This inspirational cookbook aims to bring a little bit of Italy into your kitchen!

Glorious sunlight, spectacular beaches, luscious countryside, rugged mountains, world-famous museums and art galleries, elegant designer shops, picturesque villages and magnificent cities – if this were not enough, Italy also boasts one of the longest and finest culinary traditions in the whole of Europe.

The ancient Romans loved good food and plenty of it, vying with each other to produce increasingly lavish and outlandish banquets. One of the earliest cookbooks written by Apicius, a gourmet in the first century, includes an appalling recipe for dormouse stuffed with walnuts! Overseas trade as the Roman Empire expanded brought new ingredients, and agriculture began to flourish at home. However, even then, wine production was just as prodigious as it is today.

With the collapse of the Roman Empire, the diet returned to plainer fare, relying on the wealth of cereals, fruit and vegetables that could be cultivated on the fertile plains. However, with the Renaissance, an interest in and enthusiasm for fine food revived and, once again, there were wealthy families who presided over extravagant banquets.

Italian pastry cooks were valued throughout the courts of Europe and were generally acknowledged as the best in the world. When Catherine de' Medici went to Paris to marry the future King Henri II, she took an army of Italian cooks with her and changed French culinary traditions irrevocably. A new middle class developed who also took an interest in eating well, creating a bourgeois cuisine characterized by fresh flavours and simple, unsauced dishes. The poor, of course, continued with a peasant subsistence.

The very finest produce and freshest ingredients still characterize Italian cuisine as a whole.

Introduction

Although modern transportation makes it possible for more exotic ingredients to travel across the world, Italian cooking still centres on home-grown produce. Over 60 per cent of the land is devoted to crops and pasture. With a climate that ranges from very cold in the Alps and Apennines to semi-tropical along the coast of the Ligurian Sea, the range of produce is extensive: olives, oranges, lemons, figs, grapes pomegranates, almonds, wheat, potatoes, tomatoes, sugar beet, maize and rice.

Livestock includes cattle and buffalo, sheep, goats, pigs and chickens. In a single year, Italy produces nearly 6.5 million tonnes of wine, nearly 2.5 million tonnes of olives, about 500,000 tonnes of olive oil, over 4.5 million tonnes of tomatoes and 120 million chickens. An impressive amount, you'll agree!

The introduction to this book continues to explore Italy, region by region, to discover the different types of food that is identified with a specific area of the country. Seasonal ingredients are also examined to provide the reader with as much insight into the type of produce used by the very discerning people of Italy.

Ragu Sauce

3 tbsp olive oil

45 g/1½ oz butter

2 large onions, chopped

4 celery stalks, sliced thinly

175 g/6 oz streaky bacon, chopped

2 garlic cloves, chopped

500 g/1 lb 2 oz minced (ground) lean beef

2 tbsp tomato purée (paste)

1 tbsp flour

400 g/14 oz can chopped tomatoes

150 ml/¼ pint /⅔ cup beef stock

150 ml/¼ pint /⅔ cup red wine

2 tsp dried oregano

½ tsp freshly grated nutmeg

salt and pepper

1 Heat the oil and butter in a pan over a medium heat. Add the onions, celery and bacon and fry for 5 minutes, stirring.

2 Stir in the garlic and minced (ground) beef and cook, stirring until the meat has lost its redness. Lower the heat and cook for 10 minutes, stirring.

3 Increase the heat to medium, stir in the tomato purée (paste) and the flour and cook for 1-2 minutes. Stir in the tomatoes, stock and wine and bring to the boil, stirring. Season and stir in the oregano and nutmeg. Cover and simmer for 45 minutes, stirring. The sauce is now ready to use.

Regional Cooking

To talk about Italian cuisine is somewhat misleading, as it is not a single entity. The country has been united only since 17 March, 1861 and Italians still have a powerful sense of their regional identity.

Regional cuisine is a source of pride and considerable competition. Sicilians are dismissed as *mangimaccaroni* (pasta eaters), while they express their contempt for Neapolitan cooking with the term *mangiafoglie* (vegetable eaters). Each region bases its cuisine on local ingredients, so the best ham comes from the area where pigs are raised, fish and seafood feature in coastal regions, butter is used in dishes from the north of Italy where there is dairy farming, while olive oil is characteristic of southern recipes.

Abruzzi & Molise

This was once a single region and although it has now been divided into two separate provinces, they remain closely associated. Located in northern Italy to the east of Rome, the area is well-known for its high-quality cured meats and cheese. The cuisine is traditional and also features lamb and fish and seafood in the coastal areas. Peperoncino a tiny, fiery hot, dried red chilli is from Abruzzi.

Basilicata

If the Italian peninsula looks like a boot, Basilicata is located on the arch of the foot. The landscape is rugged and inhospitable, with much of the region being over 2,000 metres/6,500 feet above sea level.

Regional Cooking

It is hardly surprising, therefore, that the cuisine is warming and filling, featuring substantial soups in particular. Cured meats, pork, lamb and game are typical ingredients and freshwater fish are abundant in the more mountainous areas.

Calabria

In the south, on Italy's toe, Calabria is a region of dramatic contrasts – superb beaches and towering mountains. Excellent fish and seafood typify the local cuisine, which is well known for its swordfish and tuna dishes. Fruit and vegetables are abundant, particularly oranges, lemons, aubergines (eggplants) and olives. Like other southern regions, desserts are a speciality, often based on local figs, honey or almonds.

Campania

Naples on the west coast is the home of pizza, now known across the world from Sydney to New York and the region bases many of its other dishes on the wonderful sun-ripened tomatoes grown locally. Fish and seafood feature strongly in the Neapolitan diet and robust herb-flavoured stews, redolent with garlic, are popular. Pastries and fruit desserts are also characteristic.

Emilia-Romagna

A central Italian province, Emilia-Romagna's capital is the beautiful medieval city of Bologna, nicknamed *la grassa*, the fat city, and home to some of the best restaurants in the country. A gourmet paradise, the region is famous for Parmesan cheese and Parma ham from Parma, balsamic vinegar from the area around Modena, cotechino, mortadella and other cured meats and, of course, *spaghetti alla bolognese*. Butter, cream and other dairy products feature

in the fine food of the region and a wide range of pasta dishes is popular.

Lazfio

Capital of the region and the country, Rome is a cosmopolitan and sophisticated city with some of the best restaurants – and ice cream parlours – in Europe. Fruit and vegetables are abundant and lamb and veal dishes are characteristic of the region, which is famous for *saltimbocca*, which literally means "jump in the mouth". Here, they have perfected the art of preparing high-quality ingredients in simple, but delicious ways that retain the individual flavours. A Roman speciality is *supplì al telefono* – "telephone wires" – mozzarella cheese wrapped in balls of cooked rice and deep-fried. The mozzarella is stringy, hence the name of the dish.

Liguria

A northern province with a long coastline, Liguria is well known for its superb fish and seafood. It is also said to produce the best basil in the whole of Italy and it is where pesto sauce was first invented. Th ancient port of Genoa was one of the first places in Europe to import Asian spices and highly seasoned dishes are still particularly characteristic of this area.

Lombardy

An important rice-growing region in north-west Italy, this is the home of risotto and there are probably as many variations of this dish as there are cooks. Dairy produce features in the cuisine and Lombardy is credited with the invention of butter, as well as mascarpone cheese. Vegetable soups, stews and pot roasts are characteristic of this region. Bresaola, cured raw beef, is a local

Regional Cooking

speciality that is often served wrapped around soft goat's cheese.

Marche

With its long coastline and high mountains, this region is blessed with both abundant seafood and game. Pasta, pork and olives also feature and methods of preparation are even more elaborate than those of neighbouring Umbria.

Piedmont

On the borders of France and Switzerland, Piedmont in the north-west is strongly influenced by its neighbours. A fertile, arable region, it is well known for rice, polenta and gnocchi and is said to grow the finest onions in Italy. Gorgonzola, one of the world's greatest cheeses, comes from this region although, sadly, the little village that gave it its name has now

been subsumed by the urban sprawl of Milan. Piedmontese garlic is said to be the best in Italy and the local white truffles are a gourmet's dream.

Puglia

On the heel of Italy, this region produces excellent olives, herbs, vegetables and fruit, particularly melons and figs. Fish and seafood are abundant and the region is known for its oyster and mussel dishes. Calzone, a sort of inside out pizza, was invented here.

Sardinia

This Mediterranean island is famous for its luxurious desserts and extravagant pastries, many of them featuring honey, nuts and home-grown fruit. Hardly surprisingly, fish and seafood – tuna, eel, mullet, sea

bass, lobster and mussels – are central to Sardinian cuisine and spit-roasted suckling pig is the national dish served on feast days. *Sardo* is a mild-tasting pecorino cheese produced in Sardinia.

Sicily

Like their southern neighbours, Sicilians have a sweet tooth, which they indulge with superb cakes, desserts and ice cream, often incorporating locally grown almonds, pistachios and citrus fruits. Pasta dishes are an important part of the diet and fish and seafood, including tuna, swordfish and mussels, feature prominently.

Trentino Alto-Adage

A mountainous region in the north-east, Trentino has been strongly influenced by its Austrian neighbour. Smoked sausage and dumplings are characteristic of the cuisine, which is also well known for its filled pasta.

Tuscany

The fertile plains of Tuscany are ideal for farming and the region produces superb fruit and vegetables. Cattle are raised here and both steak and veal dishes feature on the Tuscan menu, together with a wide range of game. Tripe is a local speciality and *Panforte di Siena*, a traditional Christmas cake made with honey and nuts, comes from the city of Siena. A grain known as *farro* is grown almost exclusively in Tuscany, where it is used to make a nourishing soup.

Umbria

Pork, lamb, game and freshwater fish, prepared and served simply but deliciously, characterize the excellent cuisine of the region. Fragrant black truffles are a feature and Umbrian cooking makes good use of its high-quality olive oil. Umbria is also famous for *imbrecciata*, a hearty soup made with lentils, chick-peas (garbanzo beans) and haricot (navy) beans.

Veneto and Friuli

An intensively farmed area in the north-east of Italy, this region produces cereals and almost 20 per cent of the country's wine.

Polenta and risotto feature in the cuisine, as well as an extensive range of fish and seafood. *Risi e bisi*, rice and peas, is a traditional dish which was served every year at the Doge's banquet in Venice to honour the city's patron saint, Mark.

Ingredients

Whatever regional variations there may be, all the cuisines of Italy have one thing in common – the use of the freshest and highest-quality seasonal ingredients. Choosing and buying meat, fish, vegetables and fruit are as important as the way they are prepared and cooked.

Cheese

Bel Paese

Its name means "beautiful country" and it is a very creamy, mild-flavoured cheese with a waxy yellow rind. It maybe eaten on its own or used for cooking.

Dolcelatte

This is a very creamy, delicate-tasting type of Gorgonzola. Its name means "sweet milk".

Fontina

A mild, nutty-tasting cheese with a creamy texture, genuine fontina is produced from the unpasteurized milk of cattle grazed on alpine herbs and grass in the Val d'Aosta. When fresh, it is delicious eaten on its own and the mature cheese is excellent for cooking.

Gorgonzola

Strictly speaking, this cheese should be called Stracchino Gorgonzola. It is a creamy cheese with green-blue veining and its flavour can range from mild to strong. Delicious on its own, it can also be used in pasta sauces and stirred into polenta.

Mascarpone

This is a triple cream cheese from Lombardy that can be used for making cheesecakes and other desserts. It also adds richness to risotto and pasta sauces.

Mozzarella

No Italian kitchen would be complete without a supply of this moist, white, egg-shaped cheese. Traditionally made from buffalo milk, it is the ideal cheese for cooking and is also used in salads with tomatoes and fresh basil. It originated in the area around Naples, which still produces the best mozzarella, but it is now made throughout Italy, often from cow's milk.

Parmesan

Probably the best-known Italian cheese, Parmesan is extensively used in cooking. Parmigiano Reggiano is produced under strictly controlled conditions in a closely defined area. It is always aged for a minimum of two years, but this may be extended up to seven years. A cow's milk cheese, it is hard with a granular, flaky texture and a slightly nutty flavour. It is best bought in a single piece and grated as required.

Pecorino

A hard or semi-hard ewe's milk cheese, pecorino is widely used in cooking. It has a sharp flavour and a granular texture rather like Parmesan. Pecorino pepato from Sicily is studded with black peppercorns.

Provolone

Eaten on its own when fresh, provolone is also perfect for cooking, as it has a stringy texture when melted. It is made from different types of milk – the strongest being made from goat's milk. Buffalo milk is often used in the south of Italy. Cylindrical or oval, it varies considerably in size and is often seen hanging from the ceiling in Italian delicatessens.

Ricotta

Literally translated as "recooked", ricotta is a soft white curd cheese originally made from goat's or ewe's milk. It is more often made from cow's milk these days. It is widely used for both savoury and sweet dishes and is classically paired with spinach.

Cured Meats

Bresaola

This salt-cured, air-dried beef is usually served in thin slices as an antipasto. It is similar to prosciutto in flavour, but not so salty.

Mortadella

Considered to be one of the finest Italian sausages, mortadella is also the largest with a diameter that may reach 45 cm/18 inches. It has a smooth texture and a fairly bland flavour. It is usually eaten in

Ingredients

sandwiches or as an antipasto, but may also be added to risottos or pasta sauces shortly before the end of the cooking time.

Pancetta

Made from belly of pork, this resembles unsmoked bacon. It is very fatty and is used in a wide variety of dishes, particularly spaghetti alla carbonara. Smoked pancetta is also available.

Prosciutto

This salted, air-dried ham does not need any cooking. The drying process may take up to two years. Prosciutto di Parma, also known as Parma ham, is produced under strictly controlled conditions in a closely defined area between Taro and Baganza from pigs fed on the whey from the process of making Parmesan cheese. San Daniele is a leaner prosciutto with a very distinctive flavour that is produced in Friuli. Prosciutto cotto is a cooked ham, often flavoured with herbs. Prosciutto is traditionally served with melon or figs as an antipasto, but is also used in veal dishes, risottos and pasta sauces.

Salami

Salami are all made from pork, but there is an almost infinite variety of types which vary according to how finely or coarsely the meat is minced, the proportion of lean meat to fat, the seasoning and spices and length of drying time. Some of the best known varieties are salame milano, salame sardo, a hotly spiced sausage from Sardinia, salame napoletano, flavoured with black and red pepper, salame fiorentina, a coarse-cut Tuscan salame flavoured with fennel seeds and pepper, and salame di Felino from the Emilia-Romagna, a very lean salame flavoured with garlic and white wine.

Sausages

Most Italian sausages are made from pork, but both venison and wild boar are sometimes used. There must be hundreds of different varieties from every region of the country. Cotechino is a large, lightly spiced sausage, weighing about 1 kg/2¼ lb It is usually boiled and served hot with lentils or beans. Luganega is a mildly spiced, long, coiled sausage that is sold by the metre. Zampone is a pig's trotter stuffed with minced pork. Traditionally, it is boiled, sliced into rings and served with lentils. It is one of the classic ingredients of bollito misto.

Mushrooms

Collecting wild mushrooms is a national pastime and pharmacies throughout the country will identify species if there is any doubt whether they are edible varieties.

Caesar's mushrooms

These are large mushrooms with orange caps and were once the favourites of Roman emperors. They are difficult to find outside Italy.

Chanterelles

These slightly frilly, orange-yellow mushrooms have a delicate flavour and aroma. They are now cultivated and are widely available in supermarkets.

Porcini

Also known as ceps or boletus mushrooms, these have a superb flavour. They can grow to be huge, weighing as much as 500 g/1 lb 2 oz each. Young mushrooms may be eaten raw and larger specimens are delicious grilled. Dried porcini are available from Italian delicatessens and although they are very expensive, you need only a small quantity.

Pasta

Plain & filled pasta

There are hundreds of different types of pasta and new shapes are being produced all the time. Basic pasta is made from hard durum wheat flour and water, while pasta all'uova is enriched with eggs. Additional ingredients, such as spinach, tomatoes and squid ink, are used to flavour and colour it.

It is worth buying fresh pasta, called maccheroni, in Italy, if you have access to a good Italian delicatessen, and the stuffed varieties available in supermarkets are often quite good. Otherwise, commercially available, fresh, unfilled pasta is not really any better than the dried variety. There is no definitive list of names and the same shape may be called different things in various regions. Some have delightfully descriptive names: capelli d'angelo (angel's hair), dischi volante (flying saucers), linguine di passeri (sparrows' tongues) and strozzapreti (priest strangler), for example.

There are no hard-and-fast rules about which pasta should be served with which sauce. As a guide, long, thin types of pasta, such as fettuccine, tagliatelle, spaghetti and taglioni, are best for delicate, olive-oil-based and seafood sauces. Short, fat pasta shapes, such as lumache, conchiglie and penne, or curly shapes, such as farfalle and fusilli,

Ingredients

are best for meat sauces, as they trap the pieces. Tomato-based sauces go with virtually any pasta shape. Tiny pasta shapes, such as stellete, pepe bucato and risi, are used for soups.

Pasta may be stuffed with cheese, meat, fish, chicken, sun-dried tomatoes and any number of other fillings. Traditionally, ravioli are square, tortelli are round and tortelloni resemble the shape of Venus's navel! Flat pasta is used to make baked dishes, such as lasagne al forno.

Gnocchi

These are rather like little dumplings and are served as a first course in a similar way to pasta, either in soup or with a sauce. They are made from a variety of ingredients: milled durum wheat, potatoes, flour or spinach and ricotta. They are available from Italian delicatessens and are easy to make at home.

Basic Pasta Dough

Making your own pasta dough is time consuming but immensely satisfying. You will need plenty of space for the rolled-out dough, and somewhere to hang it to dry.

SERVES 4

INGREDIENTS

125 g/4½ oz/1 cup strong plain (all-purpose) flour, plus extra for dusting

125 g/4½ oz/⅔ cup fine semolina

1 tsp salt

1 tbsp olive oil

2 eggs

2–3 tbsp hot water

1 Sieve the flour, semolina and salt into a bowl and make a well in the centre. Pour in half of the oil and add the eggs. Add 1 tablespoon of hot water and, using your fingertips, work to form a smooth dough. Sprinkle on a little more water if necessary to make the dough pliable.

2 Lightly dust a board with flour, turn the dough out and knead it until it is elastic and silky. This could take 10–15 minutes. Dust the dough with more flour if your fingers become too sticky.

3 Alternatively, put the eggs, 1 tablespoon hot water and the oil in the bowl of a food processor and process for a few seconds. Add the flour, semolina and salt and process until smooth. Sprinkle on a little more hot water if necessary to make the dough pliable. Transfer to an electric mixer and knead using the dough hook for 2–3 minutes.

4 Divide the dough into 2 equal pieces. Cover a work surface (counter) with a clean cloth or tea towel (dish cloth) and dust it liberally with flour. Place one portion of the dough on the floured cloth and roll it out as thinly and evenly as possible, stretching the dough gently until the pattern of the weave shows through. Cover it with a cloth and roll out the second piece in a similar way.

5 Use a ruler and a sharp knife blade to cut long, thin strips for noodles, or small confectionery cutters to cut rounds, stars or an assortment of other decorative shapes.

6 Cover the dough shapes with a clean cloth and leave them in a cool place (not the refrigerator) for 30–45 minutes to become partly dry. To dry ribbons, place a tea towel (dish cloth) over the back of a chair and hang the ribbons over it.

Olive Oil

Arguably the best olive oil in the world comes from Italy and each region produces an oil with a different flavour. The oil is made by pressing the pulp of ripe olives. The first pressing, with no additional processing, produces extra virgin olive oil. This is the highest quality and is carefully regulated. It is the best oil to use for salad dressings.

The next quality, virgin olive oil, may also be used for dressings and is good for cooking. It has slightly higher level of acidity than extra virgin, but still has a good flavour.

Other types of olive oil are usually refined and may have been heat-treated. They can be used for cooking, but should not be used in dressings.

Rice & Grains

Polenta

A kind of cornmeal, polenta is a staple in northern Italy. There, it is available in an astonishing range of degrees of coarseness, but elsewhere there are two main types – coarse and fine. It is boiled to make a kind of porridge and can then be cooled and left to set, before being grilled (broiled), fried or baked. It is very versatile and can be used for both savoury and sweet dishes. Traditionally, polenta was cooked in a large copper pan and had to be stirred for at least 1 hour. Nowadays, quick-cook polenta is available.

Rice

Italy produces a wide range of types of rice in greater quantities than any other European country. Superfino rice is a round grain type used for risottos. It can absorb a large amount of liquid, swelling to three times its size during cooking, while still retaining its shape and texture. This is what gives the dish its unique and characteristic creaminess. Carnaroli, arborio and vialone nano are especially fine varieties. Semifino rice is used for soups and salads. Italians never serve food on a bed of rice, but may sometimes serve plain boiled rice with butter and cheese as a separate dish.

Vegetables & Pulses

Artichokes

Globe artichokes are cultivated throughout Italy and grow wild on Sicily. Naples is credited with the first cultivation and, nowadays, they are regarded as a Roman speciality, being served twice deep-fried. Tiny plants may be eaten raw or braised

Ingredients

with olive oil and fresh herbs. Larger artichokes are boiled and served with a dressing or stuffed.

Aubergines (Eggplants)

Originally regarded with great suspicion, aubergines (eggplants) are now integral to Italian cooking, especially in the southern part of the country. They may be cooked in a wide of variety of ways and add depth of flavour and colour to many dishes.

Beans

Haricot (navy), cannellini, borlotti, black-eyed (known as fagioli coll'occhio), broad beans, chick peas and other pulses are eaten all over Italy, although Tuscans are renowned for being bean-eaters. They are incorporated in substantial stews and soups or may be served as a simple side dish dressed with a little olive oil.

Courgettes (Zucchini)

Widely used in northern Italian cooking, courgettes (zucchini) combine well with many other typically Mediterranean ingredients, such as tomatoes and aubergines (eggplants). They may be served cold as an antipasto, stuffed or deep-fried. They are often sold with their flowers still attached.

Fennel

Also known as Florence fennel, this aniseed-flavoured bulb is one the most important ingredients in Italian cooking. It is served raw with a vinaigrette or with cheese at the end of a meal and may be cooked in a variety of ways, including sautéing, braising and baking.

Onions

Sweet red onions are delicious raw and add colour to cooked dishes.

White onions have a stronger flavour and yellow onions are mild-tasting. Baby white onions are traditionally cooked in a sour-sweet sauce – agrodolce – and usually served as an antipasto.

(Bell) Peppers

Capsicums or sweet (bell) peppers are invariably sun-ripened in Italy and, while they do not always have the uniform shape of greenhouse-grown (bell) peppers, they have a depth of flavour that is unsurpassed. They are served raw or roasted as an antipasto and roasted or stuffed as a hot dish. They are classically partnered with anchovies, aubergines (eggplants), capers, olives or tomatoes.

Radicchio

This bitter-tasting, red-leafed member of the chicory family is nearly always cooked in Italy, rather than being included in salads. It may be grilled (broiled) or stuffed and baked and is quite often used as a pizza topping.

Rocket

Now enjoying a rediscovered popularity in Britain and America, rocket has never lost favour in Italy, where it grows wild. It is also cultivated, but the home-grown variety has a better flavour. It is usually served in salads or on its own with a dressing of balsamic vinegar and olive oil. It is sometimes cooked like spinach, but tends to lose its pungency.

Spinach

Spinach and its close relatives Swiss chard and spinach beet are used in a wide variety of Italian dishes. Anything described as alla fiorentina is likely to contain it. Young leaves are eaten raw in salads and spinach is typically paired with ricotta in pasta and pancake fillings. It is also classically combined with eggs, fish, chicken and veal.

Squash

A huge variety of squashes, from tiny butternuts to massive pumpkins, are used in northern Italian cooking for both savoury and sweet dishes, including soups, risottos, stuffed pasta and dessert tarts. Deep-fried pumpkin flowers in batter are also served.

Tomatoes

Many different varieties of tomatoes have been grown throughout Italy since the sixteenth century and it is difficult to imagine an Italian kitchen without them. Plum tomatoes are probably the most familiar and they have a firm texture that is less watery than other varieties, which makes them ideal for cooking. They may be served raw, typically partnering mozzarella cheese and fresh basil in an insalata tricolore, and are used to add both colour and flavour to a range of dishes. Italian tomatoes are always sun ripened and have a truly unmistakable flavour.

Sun-dried tomatoes have an intense flavour and are sold dry in packets or preserved in oil. These days, commercially produced sun-dried tomatoes have, in fact, been air-dried by machine, although sometimes it is possible to obtain the genuine article. If they are to be used for cooking, they should be soaked in hot water first.

Passata is a pulp made from sieved tomatoes. It has a strong flavour and may be fine or coarse. It is useful for soups and sauces and can be used as substitute for fresh tomatoes in slow-cooked dishes. Tomato purée is a paste made from tomatoes which has a less intense flavour than passata.

Basic Recipes

These recipes form the basis of several of the dishes contained throughout this book. Many of these basic recipes can be made in advance and stored in the refrigerator until required.

Basic Tomato Sauce

2 tbsp olive oil

1 small onion, chopped

1 garlic clove, chopped

400 g/14 oz can chopped tomatoes

2 tbsp chopped parsley

1 tsp dried oregano

2 bay leaves

2 tbsp tomato purée (paste)

1 tsp sugar

salt and pepper

1 Heat the oil in a pan over a medium heat and fry the onion for 2–3 minutes or until translucent. Add the garlic and fry for 1 minute.

2 Stir in the chopped tomatoes, parsley, oregano, bay leaves, tomato purée (paste), sugar, and salt and pepper to taste.

3 Bring the sauce to the boil, then simmer, uncovered, for 15–20 minutes or until the sauce has reduced by half. Taste the sauce and adjust the seasoning if necessary. Discard the bay leaves just before serving.

Béchamel Sauce

300 ml/½ pint/1¼ cups milk

2 bay leaves

3 cloves

1 small onion

60 g/2 oz/¼ cup butter, plus extra for greasing

45 g/1½ oz/6 tbsp flour

300 ml/½ pint/1¼ cups single (light) cream

large pinch of freshly grated nutmeg

salt and pepper

1 Pour the milk into a small pan and add the bay leaves. Press the cloves into the onion, add to the pan and bring the milk to the boil. Remove the pan from the heat and set aside to cool.

2 Strain the milk into a jug and rinse the pan. Melt the butter in the pan and stir in the flour. Stir for 1 minute, then gradually pour on the milk, stirring constantly. Cook the sauce for 3 minutes, then pour on the cream and bring it to the boil. Remove from the heat and season with nutmeg, salt and pepper to taste.

Lamb Sauce

2 tbsp olive oil

1 large onion, sliced

2 celery stalks, thinly sliced

500 g/1 lb 2 oz lean lamb, minced (ground)

3 tbsp tomato purée (paste)

150 g/5½ oz bottled sun-dried tomatoes, drained and chopped

1 tsp dried oregano

1 tbsp red wine vinegar

150 ml/¼ pint/⅔ cup chicken stock

salt and pepper

1 Heat the oil in a frying pan (skillet) over a medium heat and fry the onion and celery until the onion is translucent, about 3 minutes. Add the lamb and fry, stirring frequently, until it browns.

2 Stir in the tomato purée (paste), sun-dried tomatoes, oregano, vinegar and stock. Season with salt and pepper to taste.

3 Bring to the boil and cook, uncovered, for 20 minutes or until the meat has absorbed the stock. Taste and adjust the seasoning if necessary.

Cheese Sauce

25 g/1 oz/2 tbsp butter

1 tbsp flour

250 ml/9 fl oz/1 cup milk

2 tbsp single (light) cream

pinch of freshly grated nutmeg

45 g/1½ oz mature (sharp) Cheddar, grated

1 tbsp freshly grated Parmesan

salt and pepper

1 Melt the butter in a pan, stir in the flour and cook for 1 minute. Gradually pour on the milk, stirring all the time. Stir in the cream and season the sauce with nutmeg, salt and pepper to taste.

2 Simmer the sauce for 5 minutes to reduce, then remove it from the heat and stir in the cheeses. Stir until the cheeses have melted and blended into the sauce.

Espagnole Sauce

2 tbsp butter

25 g/1 oz/¼ cup plain (all-purpose) flour

1 tsp tomato purée (paste)

250 ml/9 fl oz/1⅛ cups hot veal stock

1 tbsp Madeira

1½ tsp white wine vinegar

2 tbsp olive oil

25 g/1 oz bacon, diced

25 g/1 oz carrot, diced

25 g/1 oz onion, diced

15 g/½ oz celery, diced

15 g/½ oz leek, diced

15 g/½ oz fennel, diced

1 fresh thyme sprig

1 bay leaf

1 Melt the butter in a pan, add the flour and cook, stirring, until lightly coloured. Add the tomato purée (paste), then stir in the hot veal stock, Madeira and white wine vinegar and cook for 2 minutes.

2 Heat the oil in a separate pan, add the bacon, carrot, onion, celery, leek, fennel, thyme sprig and bay leaf and fry until the vegetables have softened. Remove the vegetables from the pan with a slotted spoon and drain thoroughly. Add the vegetables to the sauce and leave to simmer for 4 hours, stirring occasionally. Strain the sauce before using.

Italian Red Wine Sauce

150 ml/¼ pint /⅝ cup Brown Stock (see page 30)

150 ml/¼ pint /⅔ cup Espagnole Sauce (see left)

125 ml/4 fl oz/½ cup red wine

2 tbsp red wine vinegar

4 tbsp shallots, chopped

1 bay leaf

1 thyme sprig

pepper

1 First make a demi-glace sauce. Put the Brown Stock and Espagnole Sauce in a pan and heat for 10 minutes, stirring occasionally.

2 Meanwhile, put the red wine, red wine vinegar, shallots, bay leaf and thyme in a pan, bring to the boil and reduce by three-quarters.

3 Strain the demi-glace sauce and add to the pan containing the Red Wine Sauce and leave to simmer for 20 minutes, stirring occasionally. Season with pepper to taste and strain the sauce before using.

Basic Recipes

Italian Cheese Sauce

2 tbsp butter

25 g/1 oz/¼ cup plain (all-purpose) flour

300 ml/½ pint/1¼ cups hot milk

pinch of nutmeg

pinch of dried thyme

2 tbsp white wine vinegar

3 tbsp double (heavy) cream

60 g/2 oz/½ cup grated Mozzarella cheese

60 g/2 oz/½ cup Parmesan cheese

1 tsp English mustard

2 tbsp soured cream

salt and pepper

1 Melt the butter in a pan and stir in the flour. Cook, stirring, over a low heat until the roux is light in colour and crumbly in texture. Stir in the hot milk and cook, stirring, for 15 minutes until thick and smooth.

2 Add the nutmeg, thyme, white wine vinegar and season to taste. Stir in the cream and mix well.

3 Stir in the cheeses, mustard and cream and mix until the cheeses have melted and blended into the sauce.

Fish Stock

900 g/2 lb non-oily fish pieces, such as heads, tails, trimmings and bones

150 ml/¼ pint/⅔ cup white wine

1 onion, chopped

1 carrot, sliced

1 celery stick (stalk), sliced

4 black peppercorns

1 bouquet garni

1.75 litres/3 pints/7 ½ cups water

1 Put the fish pieces, wine, onion, carrot, celery, black peppercorns, bouquet garni and water in a large pan and leave to simmer for 30 minutes, stirring occasionally. Strain and blot the fat from the surface with kitchen paper (towels) before using.

Garlic Mayonnaise

2 garlic cloves, crushed

8 tbsp mayonnaise

chopped parsley

salt and pepper

1 Put the mayonnaise in a bowl. Add the garlic, parsley and salt and pepper to taste and mix together well.

Brown Stock

900 g/ 2 lb veal bones and shin of beef

1 leek, sliced

1 onion, chopped

1 celery stick (stalk), sliced

1 carrot, sliced

1 bouquet garni

150 ml/¼ pint/⅔ cup white wine vinegar

1 thyme sprig

1.75 litres/3 pints/7 ½ cups cold water

1 Roast the veal bones and shin of beef in their own juices in the oven for 40 minutes.

2 Transfer the bones to a large pan and add the leeks, onion, celery, carrots, bouquet garni, white wine vinegar and thyme and cover with the cold water. Leave to simmer over a very low heat for about 3 hours. Strain and blot the fat from the surface with kitchen paper (towels) before using.

How to Use This Book

Each recipe contains a wealth of useful information, including a breakdown of nutritional quantities, preparation and cooking times, and level of difficulty. All of this information is explained in detail below.

This amount of time represents the actual cooking time.

The nutritional information provided for each recipe is per serving or per portion. Optional ingredients, variations or serving suggestions have not been included in the calculations.

The number of chef's hats represents the difficulty of each recipe, ranging from easy (1 chef's hat) to difficult (5 chef's hats).

This amount of time represents the preparation of ingredients, including cooling, chilling and soaking times.

The ingredients for each recipe are listed in the order that they are used.

The method is illustrated with step-by-step photographs, making the recipe easy to follow.

A full-colour photograph of the finished dish.

Variations and cook's tips provide useful information regarding ingredients or cooking techniques.

The method is clearly explained with step-by-step instructions that are easy to follow.

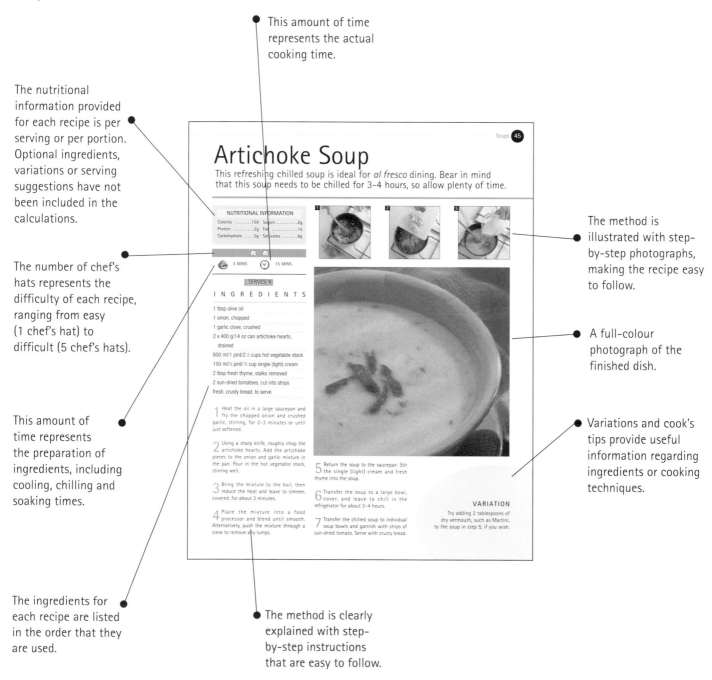

Soups 45

Artichoke Soup

This refreshing chilled soup is ideal for *al fresco* dining. Bear in mind that this soup needs to be chilled for 3-4 hours, so allow plenty of time.

NUTRITIONAL INFORMATION

Calories ....159 Sugars 2g
Protein ....2g Fat 15
Carbohydrate ....5g Saturates 6g

5 MINS   15 MINS

SERVES 4

INGREDIENTS

1 tbsp olive oil
1 onion, chopped
1 garlic clove, crushed
2 x 400 g/14 oz can artichoke hearts, drained
600 ml/1 pint/2 ½ cups hot vegetable stock
150 ml/¼ pint/⅔ cup single (light) cream
2 tbsp fresh thyme, stalks removed
2 sun-dried tomatoes, cut into strips
fresh, crusty bread, to serve

1 Heat the oil in a large saucepan and fry the chopped onion and crushed garlic, stirring, for 2-3 minutes or until just softened.

2 Using a sharp knife, roughly chop the artichoke hearts. Add the artichoke pieces to the onion and garlic mixture in the pan. Pour in the hot vegetable stock, stirring well.

3 Bring the mixture to the boil, then reduce the heat and leave to simmer, covered, for about 3 minutes.

4 Place the mixture into a food processor and blend until smooth. Alternatively, push the mixture through a sieve to remove any lumps.

5 Return the soup to the saucepan. Stir the single (light) cream and fresh thyme into the soup.

6 Transfer the soup to a large bowl, cover, and leave to chill in the refrigerator for about 3-4 hours.

7 Transfer the chilled soup to individual soup bowls and garnish with strips of sun-dried tomato. Serve with crusty bread.

VARIATION

Try adding 2 tablespoons of dry vermouth, such as Martini, to the soup in step 5, if you wish.

Soups

Soups are an important part of the Italian cuisine. They vary in consistency from light and delicate to hearty main meal soups. Texture is always apparent – Italians rarely serve smooth soups. Some may be partially puréed but the identity of the ingredients is never entirely obliterated. There are regional characteristics, too. In the north, soups

are often based on rice, while in Tuscany, thick bean- or bread-based soups are popular. Tomato, garlic and pasta soups are typical of the south. Minestrone is known world-wide but the best-known version probably comes from Milan. However, all varieties are full of vegetables and are delicious and satisfying. Fish soups also abound in one guise or another, and most of these are village specialities, so the variety is unlimited and always tasty.

Tuscan Onion Soup

This soup is best made with white onions, which have a mild flavour. If you cannot get hold of them, try using large Spanish onions instead.

NUTRITIONAL INFORMATION

Calories	390	Sugars	.........0g
Protein	.........9g	Fat	..........33g
Carbohydrate	...15g	Saturates	......14g

5–10 MINS | 40–45 MINS

SERVES 4

INGREDIENTS

50 g/1¾ oz pancetta ham, diced

1 tbsp olive oil

4 large white onions, sliced thinly into rings

3 garlic cloves, chopped

850 ml/1½ pints/3½ cups hot chicken or ham stock

4 slices ciabatta or other Italian bread

50 g/1¾ oz/3 tbsp butter

75 g/2¾ oz Gruyère or Cheddar

salt and pepper

1 Dry fry the pancetta in a large saucepan for 3–4 minutes until it begins to brown. Remove the pancetta from the pan and set aside until required.

2 Add the oil to the pan and cook the onions and garlic over a high heat for 4 minutes. Reduce the heat, cover and cook for 15 minutes or until the onions are lightly caramelized.

3 Add the stock to the saucepan and bring to the boil. Reduce the heat and leave the mixture to simmer, covered, for about 10 minutes.

4 Toast the slices of ciabatta on both sides, under a preheated grill (broiler), for 2–3 minutes or until golden. Spread the ciabatta with butter and top with the Gruyère or Cheddar cheese. Cut the bread into bite-size pieces.

5 Add the reserved pancetta to the soup and season with salt and pepper to taste.

6 Pour into 4 soup bowls and top with the toasted bread.

COOK'S TIP

Pancetta is similar to bacon, but it is air- and salt-cured for about 6 months. Pancetta is available from most delicatessens and some large supermarkets. If you cannot obtain pancetta use unsmoked bacon instead.

Pumpkin Soup

This thick, creamy soup has a wonderful, warming golden colour.
It is flavoured with orange and thyme.

NUTRITIONAL INFORMATION

Calories	111	Sugars	........4g
Protein	.........2g	Fat	.......6g
Carbohydrate	....5g	Saturates	.......2g

 10 MINS   35–40 MINS

SERVES 4

I N G R E D I E N T S

2 tbsp olive oil

2 medium onions, chopped

2 cloves garlic, chopped

900 g/2 lb pumpkin, peeled and cut into
2.5 cm/1 inch chunks

1.5 litres /2 ¾ pints/6 ¼ cups boiling
vegetable or chicken stock

finely grated rind and juice of 1 orange

3 tbsp fresh thyme, stalks removed

150 ml/¼ pint/⅔ cup milk

salt and pepper

crusty bread, to serve

1 Heat the olive oil in a large saucepan. Add the onions to the pan and cook for 3–4 minutes or until softened. Add the garlic and pumpkin and cook for a further 2 minutes, stirring well.

2 Add the boiling vegetable or chicken stock, orange rind and juice and 2 tablespoons of the thyme to the pan. Leave to simmer, covered, for 20 minutes or until the pumpkin is tender.

3 Place the mixture in a food processor and blend until smooth. Alternatively, mash the mixture with a potato masher until smooth. Season to taste.

4 Return the soup to the saucepan and add the milk. Reheat the soup for 3–4 minutes or until it is piping hot but not boiling.

5 Sprinkle with the remaining fresh thyme just before serving.

6 Divide the soup among 4 warm soup bowls and serve with lots of fresh crusty bread.

COOK'S TIP

Pumpkins are usually large vegetables. To make things a little easier, ask the greengrocer to cut a chunk off for you. Alternatively, make double the quantity and freeze the soup for up to 3 months.

Cream of Artichoke Soup

A creamy soup with the unique, subtle flavouring of Jerusalem artichokes and a garnish of grated carrots for extra crunch.

NUTRITIONAL INFORMATION

Calories 19	Sugars 0g
Protein 0.4g	Fat 2g
Carbohydrate ...0.7g	Saturates 0.7g

10–15 MINS | 55–60 MINS

SERVES 6

INGREDIENTS

750 g/1 lb 10 oz Jerusalem artichokes

1 lemon, sliced thickly

60 g/2 oz/¼ cup butter or margarine

2 onions, chopped

1 garlic clove, crushed

1.25 litres/2¼ pints/5½ cups chicken or
  vegetable stock

2 bay leaves

¼ tsp ground mace or ground nutmeg

1 tbsp lemon juice

150 ml/¼ pint/⅔ cup single (light) cream or
  natural fromage frais

salt and pepper

TO GARNISH

coarsely grated carrot

chopped fresh parsley or coriander
  (cilantro)

1 Peel and slice the artichokes. Put into a bowl of water with the lemon slices.

2 Melt the butter or margarine in a large saucepan. Add the onions and garlic and fry gently for 3–4 minutes until soft but not coloured.

3 Drain the artichokes (discarding the lemon) and add to the pan. Mix well and cook gently for 2–3 minutes without allowing to colour.

4 Add the stock, seasoning, bay leaves, mace or nutmeg and lemon juice. Bring slowly to the boil, then cover and simmer gently for about 30 minutes until the vegetables are very tender.

5 Discard the bay leaves. Cool the soup slightly then press through a sieve (strainer) or blend in a food processor until smooth. If liked, a little of the soup may be only partially puréed and added to the rest of the puréed soup, to give extra texture.

6 Pour into a clean pan and bring to the boil. Adjust the seasoning and stir in the cream or fromage frais. Reheat gently without boiling. Garnish with grated carrot and chopped parsley or coriander (cilantro).

Vegetable & Bean Soup

This wonderful combination of cannellini beans, vegetables and vermicelli is made even richer by the addition of pesto and dried mushrooms.

NUTRITIONAL INFORMATION

Calories 294	Sugars 2g
Protein 11g	Fat 16g
Carbohydrate . . .30g	Saturates 2g

30 MINS   30 MINS

SERVES 4

INGREDIENTS

1 small aubergine (eggplant)

2 large tomatoes

1 potato, peeled

1 carrot, peeled

1 leek

425 g/15 oz can cannellini beans

850 ml/1½ pints/3¾ cups hot vegetable or
   chicken stock

2 tsp dried basil

15 g/½ oz dried porcini mushrooms,
   soaked for 10 minutes in enough warm
   water to cover

50 g/1¾ oz/¼ cup vermicelli

3 tbsp pesto (see page 53 or use shop
   bought)

freshly grated Parmesan cheese, to serve
   (optional)

1 Slice the aubergine (eggplant) into rings about 1 cm/½ inch thick, then cut each ring into 4.

2 Cut the tomatoes and potato into small dice. Cut the carrot into sticks, about 2.5 cm/1 inch long and cut the leek into rings.

3 Place the cannellini beans and their liquid in a large saucepan. Add the aubergine (eggplant), tomatoes, potatoes, carrot and leek, stirring to mix.

4 Add the stock to the pan and bring to the boil. Reduce the heat and leave to simmer for 15 minutes.

5 Add the basil, dried mushrooms and their soaking liquid and the vermicelli

and simmer for 5 minutes or until all of the vegetables are tender.

6 Remove the pan from the heat and stir in the pesto.

7 Serve with freshly grated Parmesan cheese, if using.

Chick-pea (Garbanzo Bean) Soup

A thick vegetable soup which is a delicious meal in itself. Serve with Parmesan cheese and warm sun-dried tomato-flavoured ciabatta bread.

NUTRITIONAL INFORMATION

Calories 297   Sugars 0g
Protein ....11g   Fat 18g
Carbohydrate ...24g   Saturates 2g

 5 MINS   15 MINS

SERVES 4

INGREDIENTS

2 tbsp olive oil

2 leeks, sliced

2 courgettes (zucchini), diced

2 garlic cloves, crushed

2 x 400 g/14 oz cans chopped tomatoes

1 tbsp tomato purée (paste)

1 fresh bay leaf

850 ml/1 ½ pints/3 ¾ cups chicken stock

400 g/14 oz can chick-peas (garbanzo
    beans), drained and rinsed

225 g/8 oz spinach

salt and pepper

TO SERVE

Parmesan cheese

sun-dried tomato bread

COOK'S TIP

Chick-peas (garbanzo beans) are used extensively in North African cuisine and are also found in Italian, Spanish, Middle Eastern and Indian cooking. They have a deliciously nutty flavour with a firm texture and are an excellent canned product.

1 Heat the oil in a large saucepan, add the leeks and courgettes (zucchini) and cook briskly for 5 minutes, stirring constantly.

2 Add the garlic, tomatoes, tomato purée (paste), bay leaf, stock and chick-peas (garbanzo beans). Bring to the boil and simmer for 5 minutes.

3 Shred the spinach finely, add to the soup and cook for 2 minutes. Season.

4 Remove the bay leaf from the soup and discard.

5 Serve the soup with freshly grated Parmesan cheese and sun-dried tomato bread.

Potato & Pesto Soup

Fresh pesto is a treat to the taste buds and very different in flavour from that available from supermarkets. Store fresh pesto in the refrigerator.

NUTRITIONAL INFORMATION

Calories 548   Sugars 0g
Protein ....11g   Fat 52g
Carbohydrate ...10g   Saturates 18g

 5–10 MINS   50 MINS

SERVES 4

I N G R E D I E N T S

3 slices rindless, smoked, fatty bacon

450 g/1 lb floury potatoes

450 g/ 1 lb onions

2 tbsp olive oil

25 g/1 oz/2 tbsp butter

600 ml/1 pint/2 ½ cups chicken stock

600 ml/1 pint/2 ½ cups milk

100 g/3 ½ oz/ ¾ cup dried conchigliette

150 ml/ ¼ pint/ ⅝ cup double (heavy) cream

chopped fresh parsley

salt and pepper

freshly grated Parmesan cheese and garlic
　bread, to serve

P E S T O   S A U C E

60 g/2 oz/1 cup finely chopped fresh
　parsley

2 garlic cloves, crushed

60 g/2 oz/ ⅔ cup pine nuts (kernels),
　crushed

2 tbsp chopped fresh basil leaves

60 g/2 oz/ ⅔ cup freshly grated Parmesan
　cheese

white pepper

150 ml/ ¼ pint/ ⅝ cup olive oil

1 To make the pesto sauce, put all of the ingredients in a blender or food processor and process for 2 minutes, or blend by hand using a pestle and mortar.

2 Finely chop the bacon, potatoes and onions. Fry the bacon in a large pan over a medium heat for 4 minutes. Add the butter, potatoes and onions and cook for 12 minutes, stirring constantly.

3 Add the stock and milk to the pan, bring to the boil and simmer for 10 minutes. Add the conchigliette and simmer for a further 10-12 minutes.

4 Blend in the cream and simmer for 5 minutes. Add the parsley, salt and pepper and 2 tbsp pesto sauce. Transfer the soup to serving bowls and serve with Parmesan cheese and fresh garlic bread.

Creamy Tomato Soup

This quick and easy creamy soup has a lovely fresh tomato flavour. Basil leaves complement tomatoes perfectly.

NUTRITIONAL INFORMATION

Calories 218   Sugars 10g
Protein . . . . .3g   Fat 19g
Carbohydrate . . .10g   Saturates 11g

 5 MINS   25–30 MINS

SERVES 4

I N G R E D I E N T S

50 g/1 ¾ oz/3 tbsp butter

700 g/1 lb 9 oz ripe tomatoes, preferably
    plum, roughly chopped

850 ml/1 ½ pints/3 ¾ hot vegetable stock

50 g/1 ¾ oz/¼ cup ground almonds

150 ml/¼ pint/⅔ cup milk or single (light)
    cream

1 tsp sugar

2 tbsp shredded basil leaves

salt and pepper

1 Melt the butter in a large saucepan. Add the tomatoes and cook for 5 minutes until the skins start to wrinkle. Season to taste with salt and pepper.

2 Add the stock to the pan, bring to the boil, cover and simmer for 10 minutes.

3 Meanwhile, under a preheated grill (broiler), lightly toast the ground almonds until they are golden-brown. This will take only 1-2 minutes, so watch them closely.

4 Remove the soup from the heat and place in a food processor and blend the mixture to form a smooth consistency. Alternatively, mash the soup with a potato masher until smooth.

5 Pass the soup through a sieve to remove any tomato skin or pips.

6 Place the soup in the pan and return to the heat. Stir in the milk or cream, toasted ground almonds and sugar. Warm the soup through and add the shredded basil leaves just before serving.

7 Transfer the creamy tomato soup to warm soup bowls and serve hot.

COOK'S TIP

Very fine breadcrumbs can be used instead of the ground almonds, if you prefer. Toast them in the same way as the almonds and add with the milk or cream in step 6.

Calabrian Mushroom Soup

The Calabrian Mountains in southern Italy provide large amounts of wild mushrooms that are rich in flavour and colour.

NUTRITIONAL INFORMATION

Calories	452	Sugars	. . . . .5g
Protein	. . . . .15g	Fat	. . . . .26g
Carbohydrate	. . .42g	Saturates	. . . . . .12g

 5 MINS   25–30 MINS

SERVES 4

INGREDIENTS

2 tbsp olive oil

1 onion, chopped

450g/1 lb mixed mushrooms, such as ceps, oyster and button

300 ml/ ½ pint/1 ¼ cup milk

850 ml/1 ½ pints/3 ¾ cups hot vegetable stock

8 slices of rustic bread or French stick

2 garlic cloves, crushed

50 g/1 ¾ oz/3 tbsp butter, melted

75 g/2 ¾ oz Gruyère cheese, finely grated

salt and pepper

1 Heat the oil in a large frying pan (skillet) and cook the onion for 3–4 minutes or until soft and golden.

2 Wipe each mushroom with a damp cloth and cut any large mushrooms into smaller, bite-size pieces.

3 Add the mushrooms to the pan, stirring quickly to coat them in the oil.

4 Add the milk to the pan, bring to the boil, cover and leave to simmer for about 5 minutes. Gradually stir in the hot vegetable stock and season with salt and pepper to taste.

5 Under a preheated grill (broiler), toast the bread on both sides until golden.

6 Mix together the garlic and butter and spoon generously over the toast.

7 Place the toast in the bottom of a large tureen or divide it among 4 individual serving bowls and pour over the hot soup. Top with the grated Gruyère cheese and serve at once.

COOK'S TIP

Mushrooms absorb liquid, which can lessen the flavour and affect cooking properties. Therefore, carefully wipe them with a damp cloth rather than rinsing them in water.

Green Soup

This fresh-tasting soup with green (dwarf) beans, cucumber and watercress can be served warm, or chilled on a hot summer day.

NUTRITIONAL INFORMATION

Calories	121	Sugars	........2g
Protein	.........2g	Fat	..........8g
Carbohydrate	...10g	Saturates	.......1g

5 MINS   25–30 MINS

SERVES 4

INGREDIENTS

1 tbsp olive oil

1 onion, chopped

1 garlic clove, chopped

200 g/7 oz potato, peeled and cut into
2.5 cm/1 inch cubes

700 ml/1 ¼ pints/scant 3 cups vegetable or
chicken stock

1 small cucumber or ½ large cucumber, cut
into chunks

80 g/3 oz bunch watercress

125 g/4 ½ oz green (dwarf) beans, trimmed
and halved lengthwise

salt and pepper

VARIATION

Try using 125 g/4½ oz mange tout (snow peas) instead of the beans, if you prefer.

1 Heat the oil in a large pan and fry the onion and garlic for 3–4 minutes or until softened.

2 Add the cubed potato and fry for a further 2–3 minutes.

3 Stir in the stock, bring to the boil and leave to simmer for 5 minutes.

4 Add the cucumber to the pan and cook for a further 3 minutes or until the potatoes are tender. Test by inserting the tip of a knife into the potato cubes – it should pass through easily.

5 Add the watercress and allow to wilt. Then place the soup in a food processor and blend until smooth. Alternatively, before adding the watercress, mash the soup with a potato masher and push through a sieve, then chop the watercress finely and stir into the soup.

6 Bring a small pan of water to the boil and steam the beans for 3–4 minutes or until tender.

7 Add the beans to the soup, season and warm through.

Bean & Pasta Soup

A dish with proud Mediterranean origins, this soup is a winter warmer.
Serve with warm, crusty bread and, if you like, a slice of cheese.

NUTRITIONAL INFORMATION

Calories	463	Sugars	.........5g
Protein	........13g	Fat	..........33g
Carbohydrate	...30g	Saturates	.......7g

5–10 MINS   1¼ HOURS

SERVES 4

INGREDIENTS

225 g/8 oz/generous 1 cup dried haricot
  (navy) beans, soaked, drained and rinsed

4 tbsp olive oil

2 large onions, sliced

3 garlic cloves, chopped

400 g/14 oz can chopped tomatoes

1 tsp dried oregano

1 tsp tomato purée (paste)

850 ml/1 ½ pints/3 ½ cups water

90 g/3 oz small pasta shapes, such as fusilli
  or conchigliette

125 g/4 ½ oz sun-dried tomatoes, drained
  and sliced thinly

1 tbsp chopped coriander (cilantro),
  or flat-leaf parsley

2 tbsp freshly grated Parmesan

salt and pepper

1 Put the soaked beans into a large pan,
cover with cold water and bring them
to the boil. Boil rapidly for 15 minutes to
remove any harmful toxins. Drain the
beans in a colander.

2 Heat the oil in a pan over a medium
heat and fry the onions until they are
just beginning to change colour. Stir in the
garlic and cook for 1 further minute. Stir

in the chopped tomatoes, oregano and the
tomato purée (paste) and pour on the
water. Add the beans, bring to the boil and
cover the pan. Simmer for 45 minutes or
until the beans are almost tender.

3 Add the pasta, season the soup with
salt and pepper to taste and stir in the
sun-dried tomatoes. Return the soup to

the boil, partly cover the pan and continue
cooking for 10 minutes, or until the pasta
is nearly tender.

4 Stir in the chopped coriander
(cilantro) or parsley. Taste the soup
and adjust the seasoning if necessary.
Transfer to a warmed soup tureen to serve.
Sprinkle with the cheese and serve hot.

Tomato & Pasta Soup

Plum tomatoes are ideal for making soups and sauces as they have denser, less watery flesh than rounder varieties.

NUTRITIONAL INFORMATION

Calories 503   Sugars 16g
Protein . . . . .9g   Fat 28g
Carbohydrate . . .59g   Saturates 17g

 5 MINS   50–55 MINS

SERVES 4

INGREDIENTS

60 g/2 oz/4 tbsp unsalted butter

1 large onion, chopped

600 ml/1 pint/2 ½ cups vegetable stock

900 g/2 lb Italian plum tomatoes, skinned
   and roughly chopped

pinch of bicarbonate of soda (baking soda)

225 g/8 oz/2 cups dried fusilli

1 tbsp caster (superfine) sugar

150 ml/¼ pint/⅔ cup double (heavy) cream

salt and pepper

fresh basil leaves, to garnish

1 Melt the butter in a large pan, add the onion and fry for 3 minutes, stirring. Add 300 ml/½ pint/1¼ cups of vegetable stock to the pan, with the chopped tomatoes and bicarbonate of soda (baking

soda). Bring the soup to the boil and simmer for 20 minutes.

2 Remove the pan from the heat and set aside to cool. Purée the soup in a blender or food processor and pour through a fine strainer back into the saucepan.

3 Add the remaining vegetable stock and the fusilli to the pan, and season to taste with salt and pepper.

4 Add the sugar to the pan, bring to the boil, then lower the heat and simmer for about 15 minutes.

5 Pour the soup into a warm tureen, swirl the double (heavy) cream around the surface of the soup and garnish with fresh basil leaves. Serve immediately.

VARIATION

To make orange and tomato soup, simply use half the quantity of vegetable stock, topped up with the same amount of fresh orange juice and garnish the soup with orange rind.

Artichoke Soup

This refreshing chilled soup is ideal for *al fresco* dining. Bear in mind that this soup needs to be chilled for 3-4 hours, so allow plenty of time.

NUTRITIONAL INFORMATION

Calories	159	Sugars 2g
Protein	.........2g	Fat 15
Carbohydrate	....5g	Saturates 6g

 5 MINS   15 MINS

SERVES 4

INGREDIENTS

1 tbsp olive oil

1 onion, chopped

1 garlic clove, crushed

2 x 400 g/14 oz can artichoke hearts, drained

600 ml/1 pint/2 ½ cups hot vegetable stock

150 ml/¼ pint/⅔ cup single (light) cream

2 tbsp fresh thyme, stalks removed

2 sun-dried tomatoes, cut into strips

fresh, crusty bread, to serve

1 Heat the oil in a large saucepan and fry the chopped onion and crushed garlic, stirring, for 2–3 minutes or until just softened.

2 Using a sharp knife, roughly chop the artichoke hearts. Add the artichoke pieces to the onion and garlic mixture in the pan. Pour in the hot vegetable stock, stirring well.

3 Bring the mixture to the boil, then reduce the heat and leave to simmer, covered, for about 3 minutes.

4 Place the mixture into a food processor and blend until smooth. Alternatively, push the mixture through a sieve to remove any lumps.

5 Return the soup to the saucepan. Stir the single (light) cream and fresh thyme into the soup.

6 Transfer the soup to a large bowl, cover, and leave to chill in the refrigerator for about 3–4 hours.

7 Transfer the chilled soup to individual soup bowls and garnish with strips of sun-dried tomato. Serve with crusty bread.

VARIATION

Try adding 2 tablespoons of dry vermouth, such as Martini, to the soup in step 5, if you wish.

Minestrone & Pasta Soup

Italian cooks have created some very heart-warming soups and this is the most famous of all.

NUTRITIONAL INFORMATION

Calories 231   Sugars 3g
Protein . . . . .8g   Fat 16g
Carbohydrate . . .14g   Saturates 7g

10 MINS   1¾ HOURS

SERVES 10

I N G R E D I E N T S

3 garlic cloves

3 large onions

2 celery sticks

2 large carrots

2 large potatoes

100 g/3½ oz French (green) beans

100 g/3½ oz courgettes (zucchini)

60 g/2 oz/4 tbsp butter

50 ml/2 fl oz/¼ cup olive oil

60 g/2 oz rindless fatty bacon, finely diced

1.5 litres/2¾ pints/6⅞ cups vegetable or
   chicken stock

1 bunch fresh basil, finely chopped

100 g/3½ oz chopped tomatoes

2 tbsp tomato purée (paste)

100 g/3½ oz Parmesan cheese rind

90 g/3 oz dried spaghetti, broken up

salt and pepper

freshly grated Parmesan cheese, to serve

1 Finely chop the garlic, onions, celery, carrots, potatoes, beans and courgettes (zucchini).

2 Heat the butter and oil together in a large saucepan, add the bacon and cook for 2 minutes.

3 Add the garlic and onion and fry for 2 minutes, then stir in the celery, carrots and potatoes and fry for a further 2 minutes.

4 Add the beans to the pan and fry for 2 minutes. Stir in the courgettes (zucchini) and fry for a further 2 minutes. Cover the pan and cook all the vegetables, stirring frequently, for 15 minutes.

5 Add the stock, basil, tomatoes, tomato purée (paste) and cheese rind and season to taste. Bring to the boil, lower the heat and simmer for 1 hour. Remove and discard the cheese rind.

6 Add the spaghetti to the pan and cook for 20 minutes. Serve in large, warm soup bowls; sprinkle with freshly grated Parmesan cheese.

Red Bean Soup

Beans feature widely in Italian soups, making them hearty and tasty. The beans need to be soaked overnight, so prepare well in advance.

NUTRITIONAL INFORMATION

Calories 184	Sugars 5g	
Protein 4g	Fat 11g	
Carbohydrate ...19g	Saturates 2g	

 5–10 MINS 3¾ HOURS

SERVES 6

INGREDIENTS

175 g/6 oz/scant 1 cup dried red kidney
    beans, soaked overnight

1.7 litres/3 pints/7 ½ cups water

1 large ham bone or bacon knuckle

2 carrots, chopped

1 large onion, chopped

2 celery stalks, sliced thinly

1 leek, trimmed, washed and sliced

1–2 bay leaves

2 tbsp olive oil

2–3 tomatoes, peeled and chopped

1 garlic clove, crushed

1 tbsp tomato purée (paste)

60 g/2 oz/4½ tbsp arborio or Italian rice

125–175 g/4–6 oz green cabbage,
    shredded finely

salt and pepper

1 Drain the beans and place them in a saucepan with enough water to cover. Bring to the boil, then boil for 15 minutes to remove any harmful toxins. Reduce the heat and simmer for 45 minutes.

2 Drain the beans and put into a clean saucepan with the water, ham bone or knuckle, carrots, onion, celery, leek, bay leaves and olive oil. Bring to the boil, then cover and simmer for 1 hour or until the beans are very tender.

3 Discard the bay leaves and bone, reserving any ham pieces from the bone. Remove a small cupful of the beans and reserve. Purée or liquidize the soup in a food processor or blender, or push through a coarse sieve (strainer), and return to a clean pan.

4 Add the tomatoes, garlic, tomato purée (paste), rice and season. Bring

back to the boil and simmer for about 15 minutes or until the rice is tender.

5 Add the cabbage and reserved beans and ham, and continue to simmer for 5 minutes. Adjust the seasoning and serve very hot. If liked, a piece of toasted crusty bread may be put in the base of each soup bowl before ladling in the soup. If the soup is too thick, add a little boiling water or stock.

Brown Lentil & Pasta Soup

In Italy, this soup is called *Minestrade Lentiche*. A *minestra* is a soup cooked with pasta; here, farfalline, a small bow-shaped variety, is used.

NUTRITIONAL INFORMATION

Calories 225	Sugars 1g
Protein 13g	Fat 8g
Carbohydrate ...27g	Saturates 3g

 5 MINS   25 MINS

SERVES 4

INGREDIENTS

4 rashers streaky bacon, cut into small
squares

1 onion, chopped

2 garlic cloves, crushed

2 sticks celery, chopped

50 g/1 ¾ oz/ ¼ cup farfalline or spaghetti,
broken into small pieces

1 x 400 g/14 oz can brown lentils, drained

1.2 litres/2 pints/5 cups hot ham or
vegetable stock

2 tbsp chopped, fresh mint

1 Place the bacon in a large frying pan (skillet) together with the onions, garlic and celery. Dry fry for 4–5 minutes, stirring, until the onion is tender and the bacon is just beginning to brown.

2 Add the pasta to the pan (skillet) and cook, stirring, for about 1 minute to coat the pasta in the oil.

3 Add the lentils and the stock and bring to the boil. Reduce the heat and leave to simmer for 12–15 minutes or until the pasta is tender.

4 Remove the pan (skillet) from the heat and stir in the chopped fresh mint.

5 Transfer the soup to warm soup bowls and serve immeditely.

COOK'S TIP

If you prefer to use dried lentils, add the stock before the pasta and cook for 1–1¼ hours until the lentils are tender. Add the pasta and cook for a further 12–15 minutes.

Minestrone Soup

Minestrone translates as 'big soup' in Italian. It is made all over Italy, but this version comes from Livorno, a port on the western coast.

NUTRITIONAL INFORMATION

Calories	311	Sugars	.........8g
Protein	........12g	Fat	..........19g
Carbohydrate	...26g	Saturates	.......5g

 10 MINS   30 MINS

SERVES 4

INGREDIENTS

1 tbsp olive oil

100 g/3 ½ oz pancetta ham, diced

2 medium onions, chopped

2 cloves garlic, crushed

1 potato, peeled and cut into 1 cm/
   ½ inch cubes

1 carrot, peeled and cut into chunks

1 leek, sliced into rings

¼ green cabbage, shredded

1 stick celery, chopped

450 g/1 lb can chopped tomatoes

200 g/7 oz can flageolet (small navy)
   beans, drained and rinsed

600 ml/1 pint/2 ½ cups hot ham or chicken
   stock, diluted with 600 ml/1 pint/2 ½ cups
   boiling water

bouquet garni (2 bay leaves, 2 sprigs
   rosemary and 2 sprigs thyme, tied
together)

salt and pepper

freshly grated Parmesan cheese, to serve

1 Heat the olive oil in a large saucepan. Add the diced pancetta, chopped onions and garlic and fry for about 5 minutes, stirring, or until the onions are soft and golden.

2 Add the prepared potato, carrot, leek, cabbage and celery to the saucepan. Cook for a further 2 minutes, stirring frequently, to coat all of the vegetables in the oil.

3 Add the tomatoes, flageolet (small navy) beans, hot ham or chicken stock and bouquet garni to the pan, stirring to mix. Leave the soup to simmer, covered, for 15–20 minutes or until all of the vegetables are just tender.

4 Remove the bouquet garni, season with salt and pepper to taste and serve with plenty of freshly grated Parmesan cheese.

Spinach & Mascarpone Soup

Spinach is the basis for this delicious soup, but use sorrel or watercress instead for a pleasant change.

NUTRITIONAL INFORMATION

Calories 537	Sugars 2g
Protein 6g	Fat 53g
Carbohydrate 9g	Saturates 29g

5 MINS   35 MINS

SERVES 4

INGREDIENTS

60 g/2 oz/¼ cup butter

1 bunch spring onions (scallions), trimmed
   and chopped

2 celery sticks, chopped

350 g/12 oz/3 cups spinach or sorrel, or
   3 bunches watercress

850 ml /1 ½ pints/3 ½ cups vegetable stock

225 g/8 oz/1 cup Mascarpone cheese

1 tbsp olive oil

2 slices thick-cut bread, cut into cubes

½ tsp caraway seeds

salt and pepper

sesame bread sticks, to serve

1 Melt half the butter in a very large saucepan. Add the spring onions (scallions) and celery and cook gently for about 5 minutes, or until softened.

2 Pack the spinach, sorrel or watercress into the saucepan. Add the vegetable stock and bring to the boil; then reduce the heat and simmer, covered, for 15–20 minutes.

3 Transfer the soup to a blender or food processor and blend until smooth, or pass through a sieve. Return to the saucepan.

4 Add the Mascarpone cheese to the soup and heat gently, stirring, until smooth and blended. Taste and season with salt and pepper.

5 Heat the remaining butter with the oil in a frying pan (skillet). Add the bread cubes and fry in the hot oil until golden brown, adding the caraway seeds towards the end of cooking, so that they do not burn.

6 Ladle the soup into 4 warmed bowls. Sprinkle with the croûtons and serve at once, accompanied by the sesame bread sticks.

VARIATIONS

Any leafy vegetable can be used to make this soup to give variations to the flavour. For anyone who grows their own vegetables, it is the perfect recipe for experimenting with a glut of produce. Try young beetroot (beet) leaves or surplus lettuces for a change.

Tuscan Bean Soup

A thick and creamy soup that is based on a traditional Tuscan recipe. If you use dried beans, the preparation and cooking times will be longer.

NUTRITIONAL INFORMATION

Calories 250   Sugars 4g
Protein . . . . .13g   Fat 10g
Carbohydrate . . .29g   Saturates 2g

 2 MINS   10 MINS

SERVES 4

I N G R E D I E N T S

225 g/8 oz dried butter beans, soaked
    overnight, or 2 x 400 g/14 oz can butter
    beans

1 tbsp olive oil

2 garlic cloves, crushed

1 vegetable or chicken stock cube,
    crumbled

150 ml/¼ pint/⅔ cup milk

2 tbsp chopped fresh oregano

salt and pepper

1 If you are using dried beans that have been soaked overnight, drain them thoroughly. Bring a large pan of water to the boil, add the beans and boil for 10 minutes. Cover the pan and simmer for a further 30 minutes or until tender. Drain the beans, reserving the cooking liquid. If you are using canned beans, drain them thoroughly and reserve the liquid.

2 Heat the oil in a large frying pan (skillet) and fry the garlic for 2–3 minutes or until just beginning to brown.

3 Add the beans and 400 ml/14 fl oz/1⅔ cup of the reserved liquid to the pan (skillet), stirring. You may need to add a little water if there is insufficient liquid. Stir in the crumbled stock cube. Bring the

mixture to the boil and then remove the pan from the heat.

4 Place the bean mixture in a food processor and blend to form a smooth purée. Alternatively, mash the bean mixture to a smooth consistency. Season

to taste with salt and pepper and stir in the milk.

5 Pour the soup back into the pan and gently heat to just below boiling point. Stir in the chopped oregano just before serving.

Ravioli alla Parmigiana

This soup is traditionally served at Easter and Christmas in the province of Parma.

 4½–5 HOURS   25 MINS

SERVES 4

INGREDIENTS

285 g/10 oz Basic Pasta Dough (see page 24)

1.2 litres/2 pints/5 cups veal stock

freshly grated Parmesan cheese, to serve

FILLING

125 ml/4 fl oz/½ cup Espagnole Sauce (see page 29)

100 g/3½ oz/1 cup freshly grated Parmesan cheese

100 g/3½ oz/1⅔ cup fine white breadcrumbs

2 eggs

1 small onion, finely chopped

1 tsp freshly grated nutmeg

1. Make the Basic Pasta Dough (see page 24) and the Espagnole Sauce (see page 29).

2. Carefully roll out 2 sheets of the pasta dough and cover with a damp tea towel (dish cloth) while you make the filling for the ravioli.

3. To make the filling, place the freshly grated Parmesan cheese, fine white breadcrumbs, eggs, Espagnole Sauce, finely chopped onion and the freshly grated nutmeg in a large mixing bowl, and mix together well.

4. Place spoonfuls of the filling at regular intervals on 1 sheet of pasta dough. Cover with the second sheet of pasta dough, then cut into squares and seal the edges.

5. Bring the veal stock to the boil in a large saucepan.

6. Add the ravioli to the pan and cook for about 15 minutes.

7. Transfer the soup and ravioli to warm serving bowls and serve, generously sprinkled with Parmesan cheese.

COOK'S TIP

It is advisable to prepare the Basic Pasta Dough (see page 24) and the Espagnole Sauce (see page 29) well in advance, or buy ready-made equivalents if you are short of time.

Minestrone with Pesto

This version of minestrone contains cannellini beans – these need to be soaked overnight, so prepare in advance.

NUTRITIONAL INFORMATION

Calories ....604 Sugars 3g
Protein ....26g Fat 45g
Carbohydrate ...24g Saturates 11g

 10-15 MINS 1¾ HOURS

SERVES 6

INGREDIENTS

175 g/6 oz/scant 1 cup dried cannellini
   beans, soaked overnight

2.5 litres/4 ½ pints/10 cups water or stock

1 large onion, chopped

1 leek, trimmed and sliced thinly

2 celery stalks, sliced very thinly

2 carrots, chopped

3 tbsp olive oil

2 tomatoes, peeled and chopped roughly

1 courgette (zucchini), trimmed and
   sliced thinly

2 potatoes, diced

90 g/3 oz elbow macaroni (or other small
   macaroni)

salt and pepper

4–6 tbsp freshly grated Parmesan, to serve

PESTO

2 tbsp pine kernels (nuts)

5 tbsp olive oil

2 bunches basil, stems removed

4–6 garlic cloves, crushed

90 g /3 oz/ ½ cup Pecorino or Parmesan,
   grated

1 Drain the beans, rinse and put in a pan with the water or stock. Bring to the boil, cover and simmer for 1 hour.

2 Add the onion, leek, celery, carrots and oil. Cover and simmer for 4–5 minutes.

3 Add the tomatoes, courgette (zucchini), potatoes, macaroni and seasoning. Cover again and continue to simmer for about 30 minutes or until very tender.

4 Meanwhile, make the pesto. Fry the pine kernels (nuts) in 1 tablespoon of the oil until pale brown, then drain. Put the basil into a food processor or blender with the nuts and garlic. Process until well chopped. Alternatively, chop finely by hand and pound with a pestle and mortar. Gradually add the remaining oil until smooth. Turn into a bowl, add the cheese and seasoning, and mix thoroughly.

5 Stir 1½ tablespoons of the pesto into the soup until well blended. Simmer for a further 5 minutes and adjust the seasoning. Serve very hot, sprinkled with the cheese.

Fish Soup

There are many varieties of fish soup in Italy, some including shellfish. This one, from Tuscany, is more like a chowder.

NUTRITIONAL INFORMATION

Calories 305	Sugars 3g	
Protein 47g	Fat 7g	
Carbohydrate 11g	Saturates 1g	

 5–10 MINS   1 HOUR

SERVES 6

INGREDIENTS

1 kg/2 lb 4 oz assorted prepared fish
  (including mixed fish fillets, squid, etc.)

2 onions, sliced thinly

2 celery stalks, sliced thinly

a few sprigs of parsley

2 bay leaves

150 ml/ ¼ pint/ ⅔ cup white wine

1 litre/1 ¾ pints/4 cups water

2 tbsp olive oil

1 garlic clove, crushed

1 carrot, chopped finely

400 g/14 oz can peeled tomatoes, puréed

2 potatoes, chopped

1 tbsp tomato purée (paste)

1 tsp chopped fresh oregano or ½ tsp
  dried oregano

350 g/12 oz fresh mussels

175 g/6 oz peeled prawns (shrimp)

2 tbsp chopped fresh parsley

salt and pepper

crusty bread, to serve

1 Cut the fish into slices and put into a pan with half the onion and celery, the parsley, bay leaves, wine and water. Bring to the boil, cover and simmer for 25 minutes.

2 Strain the fish stock and discard the vegetables. Skin the fish, remove any bones and reserve.

3 Heat the oil in a pan. Fry the remaining onion and celery with the garlic and carrot until soft but not coloured, stirring occasionally. Add the puréed canned tomatoes, potatoes, tomato purée (paste), oregano, reserved stock and seasoning. Bring to the boil and simmer for about 15 minutes or until the potato is almost tender.

4 Meanwhile, thoroughly scrub the mussels. Add the mussels to the pan with the prawns (shrimp) and leave to simmer for about 5 minutes or until the mussels have opened (discard any that remain closed).

5 Return the fish to the soup with the chopped parsley, bring back to the boil and simmer for 5 minutes. Adjust the seasoning.

6 Serve the soup in warmed bowls with chunks of fresh crusty bread, or put a toasted slice of crusty bread in the bottom of each bowl before adding the soup. If possible, remove a few half shells from the mussels before serving.

Mussel & Potato Soup

This quick and easy soup would make a delicious summer lunch, served with fresh crusty bread.

NUTRITIONAL INFORMATION

Calories ....804 Sugars 3g
Protein ....17g Fat 68g
Carbohydrate ...32g Saturates 38g

🍲 10 MINS   🕙 35 MINS

SERVES 4

INGREDIENTS

750 g/1 lb 10 oz mussels

2 tbsp olive oil

100 g/3 ½ oz/7 tbsp unsalted butter

2 slices rindless fatty bacon, chopped

1 onion, chopped

2 garlic cloves, crushed

60 g/2 oz/ ½ cup plain (all-purpose) flour

450 g/1 lb potatoes, thinly sliced

100 g/3 ½ oz/ ¾ cup dried conchigliette

300 ml/ ½ pint/1 ¼ cups double (heavy)
   cream

1 tbsp lemon juice

2 egg yolks

salt and pepper

TO GARNISH

2 tbsp finely chopped fresh parsley

lemon wedges

1 Debeard the mussels and scrub them under cold water for 5 minutes. Discard any mussels that do not close immediately when sharply tapped.

2 Bring a large pan of water to the boil, add the mussels, oil and a little pepper. Cook until the mussels open. (discard any mussels that remain closed.

3 Drain the mussels, reserving the cooking liquid. Remove the mussels from their shells.

4 Melt the butter in a large saucepan, add the bacon, onion and garlic and cook for 4 minutes. Carefully stir in the flour. Measure 1.2 litres/2 pints/5 cups of the reserved cooking liquid and stir it into the pan.

5 Add the potatoes to the pan and simmer for 5 minutes. Add the conchigliette and simmer for a further 10 minutes.

6 Add the cream and lemon juice, season to taste with salt and pepper, then add the mussels to the pan.

7 Blend the egg yolks with 1-2 tbsp of the remaining cooking liquid, stir into the pan and cook for 4 minutes.

8 Ladle the soup into 4 warm individual soup bowls, garnish with the chopped fresh parsley and lemon wedges and serve immediately.

Italian Fish Stew

This robust stew is full of Mediterranean flavours. If you do not want to prepare the fish yourself, ask your local fishmonger to do it for you.

NUTRITIONAL INFORMATION

Calories 236   Sugars 4g
Protein ....20g   Fat 7g
Carbohydrate ...25g   Saturates 1g

5–10 MINS   25 MINS

SERVES 4

INGREDIENTS

2 tbsp olive oil

2 red onions, finely chopped

1 garlic clove, crushed

2 courgettes (zucchini), sliced

400 g/14 oz can chopped tomatoes

850 ml/1 ½ pints/3 ½ cups fish or vegetable
   stock

90 g/3 oz dried pasta shapes

350 g/12 oz firm white fish, such as cod,
   haddock or hake

1 tbsp chopped fresh basil or oregano or
   1 tsp dried oregano

1 tsp grated lemon rind

1 tbsp cornflour (cornstarch)

1 tbsp water

salt and pepper

sprigs of fresh basil or oregano, to garnish

1 Heat the oil in a large saucepan and fry the onions and garlic for 5 minutes. Add the courgettes (zucchini) and cook for 2–3 minutes, stirring often.

2 Add the tomatoes and stock to the saucepan and bring to the boil. Add the pasta, cover and reduce the heat. Simmer for 5 minutes.

3 Skin and bone the fish, then cut it into chunks. Add to the saucepan with the basil or oregano and lemon rind and cook gently for 5 minutes until the fish is opaque and flakes easily (take care not to overcook it).

4 Blend the cornflour (cornstarch) with the water and stir into the stew. Cook gently for 2 minutes, stirring, until thickened. Season with salt and pepper to taste and ladle into 4 warmed soup bowls. Garnish with basil or oregano sprigs and serve at once.

Italian Seafood Soup

This colourful mixed seafood soup would be superbly complemented by a dry white wine.

NUTRITIONAL INFORMATION

Calories	668	Sugars	.........3g
Protein	........48g	Fat	..........43g
Carbohydrate	...21g	Saturates	......25g

5 MINS   55 MINS

SERVES 4

I N G R E D I E N T S

60 g/2 oz/4 tbsp butter

450 g/1 lb assorted fish fillets, such as red mullet and snapper

450 g/1 lb prepared seafood, such as squid and prawns (shrimp)

225 g/8 oz fresh crabmeat

1 large onion, sliced

25 g/1 oz/¼ cup plain (all-purpose) flour

1.2 litres/2 pints/5 cups fish stock

100 g/3½ oz/¾ cup dried pasta shapes, such as ditalini or elbow macaroni

1 tbsp anchovy essence (extract)

grated rind and juice of 1 orange

50 ml/2 fl oz/¼ cup dry sherry

300 ml/½ pint/1¼ cups double (heavy) cream

salt and pepper

crusty brown bread, to serve

1 Melt the butter in a large saucepan, add the fish fillets, seafood, crabmeat and onion and cook gently over a low heat for 6 minutes.

2 Add the flour to the seafood mixture, stirring thoroughly to avoid any lumps from forming.

3 Gradually add the stock, stirring, until the soup comes to the boil. Reduce the heat and simmer for 30 minutes.

4 Add the pasta to the pan and cook for a further 10 minutes.

5 Stir in the anchovy essence, orange rind, orange juice, sherry and double (heavy) cream. Season to taste with salt and pepper.

6 Heat the soup until completely warmed through.

7 Transfer the soup to a tureen or to warm soup bowls and serve with crusty brown bread.

Lemon & Chicken Soup

This delicately flavoured summer soup is surprisingly easy to make, and tastes delicious.

NUTRITIONAL INFORMATION

Calories 506	Sugars 4g
Protein 19g	Fat 31g
Carbohydrate ...41g	Saturates 19g

 5-10 MINS 1¼ HOURS

SERVES 4

I N G R E D I E N T S

60 g/2 oz/4 tbsp butter

8 shallots, thinly sliced

2 carrots, thinly sliced

2 celery sticks (stalks), thinly sliced

225 g/8 oz boned chicken breasts,
  finely chopped

3 lemons

1.2 litres/2 pints/5 cups chicken stock

225 g/8 oz dried spaghetti, broken into
  small pieces

150 ml/¼ pint/⅝ cup double (heavy) cream

salt and white pepper

TO GARNISH

fresh parsley sprig

3 lemon slices, halved

COOK'S TIP

You can prepare this soup up to the end of step 3 in advance, so that all you need do before serving is heat it through before adding the pasta and the finishing touches.

1 Melt the butter in a large saucepan. Add the shallots, carrots, celery and chicken and cook over a low heat, stirring occasionally, for 8 minutes.

2 Thinly pare the lemons and blanch the lemon rind in boiling water for 3 minutes. Squeeze the juice from the lemons.

3 Add the lemon rind and juice to the pan, together with the chicken stock. Bring slowly to the boil over a low heat and simmer for 40 minutes, stirring occasionally.

4 Add the spaghetti to the pan and cook for 15 minutes. Season to taste with salt and white pepper and add the cream. Heat through, but do not allow the soup to boil or it will curdle.

5 Pour the soup into a tureen or individual bowls, garnish with the parsley and half slices of lemon and serve immediately.

Chicken & Pasta Broth

This satisfying soup makes a good lunch or supper dish and you can use any vegetables you like. Children will love the tiny pasta shapes.

NUTRITIONAL INFORMATION

Calories 185	Sugars 5g	
Protein 17g	Fat 5g	
Carbohydrate ...20g	Saturates 1g	

 5 MINS   15-20 MINS

SERVES 6

INGREDIENTS

350 g/12 oz boneless chicken breasts

2 tbsp sunflower oil

1 medium onion, diced

250 g/9 oz/1 ½ cups carrots, diced

250 g/9 oz cauliflower florets

850 ml/1 ½ pints/3 ¾ cups chicken stock

2 tsp dried mixed herbs

125 g/4 ½ oz small pasta shapes

salt and pepper

Parmesan cheese (optional) and crusty
   bread, to serve

1 Using a sharp knife, finely dice the chicken, discarding any skin.

2 Heat the oil in a large saucepan and quickly sauté the chicken, onion, carrots and cauliflower until they are lightly coloured.

3 Stir in the chicken stock and dried mixed herbs and bring to the boil.

4 Add the pasta shapes to the pan and return to the boil. Cover the pan and leave the broth to simmer for 10 minutes, stirring occasionally to prevent the pasta shapes from sticking together.

5 Season the broth with salt and pepper to taste and sprinkle with Parmesan cheese, if using. Serve the broth with fresh crusty bread.

COOK'S TIP

You can use any small pasta shapes for this soup – try conchigliette or ditalini or even spaghetti broken up into small pieces. To make a fun soup for children you could add animal-shaped or alphabet pasta.

Chicken & Bean Soup

This hearty and nourishing soup, combining chick-peas (garbanzo beans) and chicken, is an ideal starter for a family supper.

NUTRITIONAL INFORMATION

Calories ....347 Sugars 2g
Protein ....28g Fat 11g
Carbohydrate ...37g Saturates 4g

 5 MINS   1¾ HOURS

SERVES 4

INGREDIENTS

25 g/1 oz/2 tbsp butter

3 spring onions (scallions), chopped

2 garlic cloves, crushed

1 fresh marjoram sprig, finely chopped

350 g/12 oz boned chicken breasts, diced

1.2 litres/2 pints/5 cups chicken stock

350 g/12 oz can chick-peas (garbanzo
   beans), drained

1 bouquet garni

1 red (bell) pepper, diced

1 green (bell) pepper, diced

115 g/4 oz/1 cup small dried pasta shapes,
   such as elbow macaroni

salt and white pepper

croûtons, to serve

COOK'S TIP

If you prefer, you can use dried chick-peas (garbanzo beans). Cover with cold water and set aside to soak for 5–8 hours. Drain and add the beans to the soup, according to the recipe, and allow an additional 30 minutes–1 hour cooking time.

1 Melt the butter in a large saucepan. Add the spring onions (scallions), garlic, sprig of fresh marjoram and the diced chicken and cook, stirring frequently, over a medium heat for 5 minutes.

2 Add the chicken stock, chick-peas (garbanzo beans) and bouquet garni and season with salt and white pepper.

3 Bring the soup to the boil, lower the heat and simmer for about 2 hours.

4 Add the diced (bell) peppers and pasta to the pan, then simmer for a further 20 minutes.

5 Transfer the soup to a warm tureen. To serve, ladle the soup into individual serving bowls and serve immediately, garnished with the croûtons.

Tuscan Veal Broth

Veal plays an important role in Italian cuisine and there are dozens of recipes for all cuts of this meat.

NUTRITIONAL INFORMATION

Calories	420	Sugars	.........5g
Protein	........54g	Fat	...........7g
Carbohydrate	...37g	Saturates	.......2g

 2¼ HOURS 4¾ HOURS

SERVES 4

INGREDIENTS

60 g/2 oz/⅓ cup dried peas, soaked for 2 hours and drained

900 g/2 lb boned neck of veal, diced

1.2 litres/2 pints/5 cups beef or brown stock (see Cook's Tip)

600 ml/1 pint/2 ½ cups water

60 g/2 oz/⅓ cup barley, washed

1 large carrot, diced

1 small turnip (about 175 g/6 oz), diced

1 large leek, thinly sliced

1 red onion, finely chopped

100 g/3 ½ oz chopped tomatoes

1 fresh basil sprig

100 g/3 ½ oz/¾ cup dried vermicelli

salt and white pepper

1 Put the peas, veal, stock and water into a large pan and bring to the boil over a low heat. Using a slotted spoon, skim off any scum that rises to the surface.

2 When all of the scum has been removed, add the barley and a pinch of salt to the mixture. Simmer gently over a low heat for 25 minutes.

3 Add the carrot, turnip, leek, onion, tomatoes and basil to the pan, and season with salt and pepper to taste. Leave to simmer for about 2 hours, skimming the surface from time to time to remove any scum. Remove the pan from the heat and set aside for 2 hours.

4 Set the pan over a medium heat and bring to the boil. Add the vermicelli and cook for 12 minutes. Season with salt and pepper to taste; remove and discard the basil. Ladle into soup bowls and serve immediately.

COOK'S TIP

The best brown stock is made with veal bones and shin of beef roasted with dripping (drippings) in the oven for 40 minutes. Transfer the bones to a pan and add sliced leeks, onion, celery and carrots, a bouquet garni, white wine vinegar and a thyme sprig and cover with cold water. Simmer over a very low heat for 3 hours; strain before use.

Veal & Wild Mushroom Soup

Wild mushrooms are available commercially and an increasing
range of cultivated varieties is now to be found in many supermarkets.

NUTRITIONAL INFORMATION

Calories 413   Sugars 3g
Protein . . . . .28g   Fat 22g
Carbohydrate . . .28g   Saturates 12g

 5 MINS   3¼ HOURS

SERVES 4

INGREDIENTS

450 g/1 lb veal, thinly sliced

450 g/1 lb veal bones

1.2 litres/2 pints/5 cups water

1 small onion

6 peppercorns

1 tsp cloves

pinch of mace

140 g/5 oz oyster and shiitake mushrooms,
    roughly chopped

150 ml/¼ pint/⅔ cup double (heavy) cream

100 g/3½ oz/¾ cup dried vermicelli

1 tbsp cornflour (cornstarch)

3 tbsp milk

salt and pepper

COOK'S TIP

You can make this soup
with the more inexpensive
cuts of veal, such as breast or
neck slices. These are lean and the
long cooking time ensures that the
meat is really tender.

1 Put the veal, bones and water into a large saucepan. Bring to the boil and lower the heat. Add the onion, peppercorns, cloves and mace and simmer for about 3 hours, until the veal stock is reduced by one-third.

2 Strain the stock, skim off any fat on the surface with a slotted spoon, and pour the stock into a clean saucepan. Add the veal meat to the pan.

3 Add the mushrooms and cream, bring to the boil over a low heat and then leave to simmer for 12 minutes, stirring occasionally.

4 Meanwhile, cook the vermicelli in lightly salted boiling water for 10 minutes or until tender, but still firm to the bite. Drain and keep warm.

5 Mix the cornflour (cornstarch) and milk to form a smooth paste. Stir into the soup to thicken. Season to taste with salt and pepper and just before serving, add the vermicelli. Transfer the soup to a warm tureen and serve immediately.

Veal & Ham Soup

Veal and ham is a classic combination, complemented here with the addition of sherry to create a richly-flavoured Italian soup.

NUTRITIONAL INFORMATION

Calories 501	Sugars 10g	
Protein 38g	Fat 18g	
Carbohydrate . . .28g	Saturates 10g	

 5 MINS   3¼ HOURS

SERVES 4

I N G R E D I E N T S

60 g/2 oz/4 tbsp butter

1 onion, diced

1 carrot, diced

1 celery stick (stalk), diced

450 g/1 lb veal, very thinly sliced

450 g/1 lb ham, thinly sliced

60 g/2 oz/½ cup plain (all-purpose) flour

1 litre/1¾ pints/4⅜ cups beef stock

1 bay leaf

8 black peppercorns

pinch of salt

3 tbsp redcurrant jelly

150 ml/¼ pint/⅝ cup cream sherry

100 g/3½ oz/¾ cup dried vermicelli

garlic croûtons (see Cook's Tip), to serve

1 Melt the butter in a large pan. Add the onions, carrot, celery, veal and ham and cook over a low heat for 6 minutes.

2 Sprinkle over the flour and cook, stirring constantly, for a further 2 minutes. Gradually stir in the stock, then add the bay leaf, peppercorns and salt. Bring to the boil and simmer for 1 hour.

3 Remove the pan from the heat and add the redcurrant jelly and cream sherry, stirring to combine. Set aside for about 4 hours.

4 Remove the bay leaf from the pan and discard. Reheat the soup over a very low heat until warmed through.

5 Meanwhile, cook the vermicelli in a saucepan of lightly salted boiling water for 10-12 minutes. Stir the vermicelli into the soup and transfer to soup bowls. Serve with garlic croûtons.

COOK'S TIP

To make garlic croûtons, remove the crusts from 3 slices of day-old white bread. Cut the bread into 5 mm/¼ inch cubes. Heat 3 tbsp oil over a low heat and stir-fry 1–2 chopped garlic cloves for 1–2 minutes. Remove the garlic and add the bread. Cook, stirring frequently, until golden. Remove with a slotted spoon and drain.

Starters

Starters are known as antipasto in Italy which is translated as meaning 'before the main course'. Antipasti usually come in three categories: meat, fish and vegetables. There are many varieties of cold meats, including ham, invariably sliced paper-thin. All varieties of fish are popular in Italy, including inkfish, octopus and cuttlefish. Seafood is also

highly prized, especially huge prawns (shrimp), mussels and fresh sardines. Numerous vegetables feature in Italian cuisine and are an important part of the daily diet. They are served as a starter, as an accompaniment to main dishes, or as a course on their own. In Italy, vegetables are cooked only until 'al dente' and still slightly crisp. This ensures that they retain more nutrients and the colours remain bright and appealing.

Roasted (Bell) Peppers

These (bell) peppers can be used as an *antipasto*, as a side dish or as a relish to accompany meat and fish.

NUTRITIONAL INFORMATION

Calories 98   Sugars 13g
Protein . . . . .3g   Fat 4g
Carbohydrate . . .15g   Saturates 1g

5 MINS   40 MINS

SERVES 4

INGREDIENTS

2 each, red, yellow and orange (bell)
   peppers

4 tomatoes, halved

1 tbsp olive oil

3 garlic cloves, chopped

1 onion, sliced in rings

2 tbsp fresh thyme

salt and pepper

1 Halve and deseed the (bell) peppers. Place them, cut-side down, on a baking tray (cookie sheet) and cook under a preheated grill (broiler) for 10 minutes.

2 Add the tomatoes to the baking tray (cookie sheet) and grill (broil) for 5 minutes, until the skins of the (bell) peppers and tomatoes are charred.

COOK'S TIP

Preserve (bell) peppers in the refrigerator by placing them in a sterilized jar and pouring olive oil over the top to seal. Or, heat 300 ml/½ pint/¼ cup white wine vinegar with a bay leaf and 4 juniper berries and bring to the boil. Pour over the (bell) peppers and set aside until cold. Pack into sterilized jars.

3 Put the (bell) peppers into a polythene bag for 10 minutes to sweat, which will make the skin easier to peel.

4 Remove the tomato skins and chop the flesh. Peel the skins from the (bell) peppers and slice the flesh into strips.

5 Heat the oil in a large frying pan (skillet) and fry the garlic and onion, stirring occasionally, for 3–4 minutes or until softened.

6 Add the (bell) peppers and tomatoes to the frying pan (skillet) and cook for 5 minutes. Stir in the fresh thyme and season to taste with salt and pepper.

7 Transfer to serving bowls and serve warm or chilled.

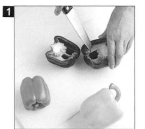

Sweet & Sour Baby Onions

This typical Sicilian dish combines honey and vinegar to give a sweet and sour flavour. Serve hot as an accompaniment or cold with cured meats.

NUTRITIONAL INFORMATION

Calories	131	Sugars	. . . . .11g
Protein	. . . . .2g	Fat	. . . . .6g
Carbohydrate	. . .19g	Saturates	. . . . . . .1g

   2 MINS   15 MINS

SERVES 4

I N G R E D I E N T S

350 g/12 oz baby or pickling onions

2 tbsp olive oil

2 fresh bay leaves, torn into strips

thinly pared rind of 1 lemon

1 tbsp soft brown sugar

1 tbsp clear honey

4 tbsp red wine vinegar

1 Soak the onions in a bowl of boiling water – this will make them easier to peel. Using a sharp knife, peel and halve the onions.

2 Heat the oil in a large frying pan (skillet). Add the bay leaves and onions to the pan and cook for 5–6 minutes over a medium-high heat or until browned all over.

3 Cut the lemon rind into thin matchsticks. Add to the frying pan (skillet) with the sugar and honey. Cook for 2-3 minutes, stirring occasionally, until the onions are lightly caramelized.

4 Add the red wine vinegar to the frying pan (skillet), being careful because it will spit. Cook for about 5 minutes, stirring, or until the onions are tender and the liquid has all but disappeared.

 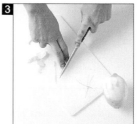 

5 Transfer the onions to a serving dish and serve at once.

COOK'S TIP

Adjust the piquancy of this dish to your liking by adding extra sugar for a sweeter, more caramelized taste or extra red wine vinegar for a sharper, tarter flavour.

Aubergine (Eggplant) Rolls

Thin slices of aubergine (eggplant) are fried in olive oil and garlic, and then topped with pesto sauce and finely sliced Mozzarella.

NUTRITIONAL INFORMATION

Calories	278	Sugars	.........2g
Protein	.........4g	Fat	.........28g
Carbohydrate	....2g	Saturates	.......7g

15–20 MINS   20 MINS

SERVES 4

INGREDIENTS

2 aubergines (eggplant), sliced thinly
   lengthways

5 tbsp olive oil

1 garlic clove, crushed

4 tbsp pesto

175 g/6 oz/1½ cups Mozzarella, grated

basil leaves, torn into pieces

salt and pepper

fresh basil leaves, to garnish

1 Sprinkle the aubergine (eggplant) slices liberally with salt and leave for 10–15 minutes to extract the bitter juices. Turn the slices over and repeat. Rinse well with cold water and drain on paper towels.

2 Heat the olive oil in a large frying pan (skillet) and add the garlic. Fry the aubergine (eggplant) slices lightly on both sides, a few at a time. Drain them on paper towels.

3 Spread the pesto on to one side of the aubergine (eggplant) slices. Top with the grated Mozzarella and sprinkle with the torn basil leaves. Season with a little salt and pepper. Roll up the slices and secure with wooden cocktail sticks (toothpicks).

4 Arrange the aubergine (eggplant) rolls in a greased ovenproof baking dish. Place in a preheated oven, 180°C/ 350°F/Gas Mark 4, and bake for 8–10 minutes.

5 Transfer the aubergine (eggplant) rolls to a warmed serving plate. Scatter with fresh basil leaves and serve at once.

Leek & Tomato Timbales

Angel-hair pasta, known as cappellini, is mixed with fried leeks, sun-dried tomatoes, fresh oregano and beaten eggs, and baked in ramekins.

NUTRITIONAL INFORMATION

Calories 331   Sugars 10g
Protein . . . . .10g   Fat 21g
Carbohydrate . . .26g   Saturates 9g

 5–10 MINS   50 MINS

SERVES 4

I N G R E D I E N T S

90 g/3 oz angel-hair pasta (cappellini)

25 g/1 oz/2 tbsp butter

1 tbsp olive oil

1 large leek, sliced finely

60 g/2 oz/½ cup sun-dried tomatoes in oil,
    drained and chopped

1 tbsp chopped fresh oregano
    or 1 tsp dried oregano

2 eggs, beaten

100 ml/3½ fl oz/generous ⅓ cup
    single (light) cream

1 tbsp freshly grated Parmesan

salt and pepper

sprigs of oregano, to garnish

lettuce leaves, to serve

S A U C E

1 small onion, chopped finely

1 small garlic clove, crushed

350 g/12 oz tomatoes, peeled and chopped

1 tsp mixed dried Italian herbs

4 tbsp dry white wine

1 Cook the pasta in plenty of boiling salted water for about 3 minutes until 'al dente' (just tender). Drain and rinse with cold water to cool quickly.

2 Meanwhile, heat the butter and oil in a frying pan (skillet). Gently fry the leek until softened, about 5–6 minutes. Add the sun-dried tomatoes and oregano, and cook for a further 2 minutes. Remove from the heat.

3 Add the leek mixture to the pasta. Stir in the beaten eggs, cream and Parmesan. Season with salt and pepper. Divide between 4 greased ramekin dishes or dariole moulds (molds).

4 Place the dishes in a roasting tin (pan) with enough warm water to come halfway up their sides. Bake in a preheated oven, 180°C/350°F/Gas Mark 4, for about 30 minutes, until set.

5 Meanwhile, make the tomato sauce. Fry the onion and garlic in the remaining butter and oil until softened. Add the tomatoes, herbs and wine. Cover and cook gently for about 20 minutes until pulpy. Blend in a food processor until smooth, or press through a sieve.

6 Run a knife or small spatula around the edge of the ramekins, then turn out the timbales on to 4 warm serving plates. Pour over a little sauce and garnish with oregano. Serve with the lettuce leaves.

Baked Fennel Gratinati

Fennel is a common ingredient in Italian cooking. In this dish its distinctive flavour is offset by the smooth Béchamel Sauce.

NUTRITIONAL INFORMATION

Calories	426	Sugars	........9g
Protein	........13g	Fat	.........35g
Carbohydrate	...16g	Saturates	......19g

5–10 MINS   45 MINS

SERVES 4

I N G R E D I E N T S

4 heads fennel

25 g/1 oz/ 2 tbsp butter

150 ml/¼ pint/½ cup dry white wine

Béchamel Sauce (see page 28),
   enriched with 2 egg yolks

25 g/1 oz/½ cup fresh white breadcrumbs

3 tbsp freshly grated Parmesan

salt and pepper

fennel fronds, to garnish

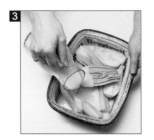

1 Remove any bruised or tough outer stalks of fennel and cut each head in half. Put into a saucepan of boiling salted water and simmer for 20 minutes until tender, then drain.

2 Butter an ovenproof dish liberally and arrange the drained fennel in it.

3 Mix the wine into the Béchamel Sauce and season with salt and pepper to taste. Pour over the fennel.

4 Sprinkle evenly with the breadcrumbs and then the Parmesan.

5 Place in a preheated oven, 200°C/ 400°F/Gas Mark 6, and bake for 20 minutes until the top is golden. Serve garnished with fennel fronds.

Stewed Artichokes

This is a traditional Roman dish. The artichokes are stewed in olive oil with fresh herbs.

NUTRITIONAL INFORMATION

Calories	129	Sugars	.........0g
Protein	.........4g	Fat	...........8g
Carbohydrate	...10g	Saturates	.......1g

  5 MINS   50 MINS

SERVES 4

I N G R E D I E N T S

4 small globe artichokes

olive oil

4 garlic cloves, peeled

2 bay leaves

finely grated rind and juice of 1 lemon

2 tbsp fresh marjoram

lemon wedges, to serve

1 Using a sharp knife, carefully peel away the tough outer leaves surrounding the artichokes. Trim the stems to about 2.5 cm/1 inch.

2 Using a knife, cut each artichoke in half and scoop out the choke (heart).

3 Place the artichokes in a large heavy-based pan. Pour over enough olive oil to half cover the artichokes in the pan.

4 Add the garlic cloves, bay leaves and half of the grated lemon rind.

5 Start to heat the artichokes gently, cover the pan and continue to cook over a low heat for about 40 minutes. It is important that the artichokes should be stewed in the oil, not fried.

6 Once the artichokes are tender, remove them with a perforated spoon

and drain thoroughly. Remove the bay leaves and discard.

7 Transfer the artichokes to warm serving plates. Garnish the artichokes with the remaining grated lemon rind, fresh marjoram and a little lemon juice. Serve with lemon wedges.

COOK'S TIP

To prevent the artichokes from oxidizing and turning brown before cooking, brush them with a little lemon juice. In addition, use the oil used for cooking the artichokes for salad dressings – it will impart a lovely lemon and herb flavour.

Aubergine (Eggplant) Bake

This dish combines layers of aubergine (eggplant), tomato sauce, Mozzarella and Parmesan cheese to create a very tasty starter.

NUTRITIONAL INFORMATION

Calories 232	Sugars 8g
Protein 10g	Fat 18g
Carbohydrate 8g	Saturates 6g

🍲 5 MINS   🕐 45 MINS

SERVES 4

I N G R E D I E N T S

3–4 tbsp olive oil

2 garlic cloves, crushed

2 large aubergines (eggplants)

100 g/3½ oz Mozzarella cheese,
  sliced thinly

200 g/7 oz passata (tomato purée)

50 g/1¾ oz Parmesan cheese, grated

1 Heat 2 tablespoons of the olive oil in a large frying pan (skillet). Add the garlic and sauté for 30 seconds.

2 Slice the aubergines (eggplants) lengthwise. Add the slices to the pan and cook in the oil for 3–4 minutes on each side or until tender. (You will probably have to cook them in batches, so add the remaining oil as necessary.)

3 Remove the aubergines (eggplants) with a perforated spoon and drain on absorbent kitchen paper.

4 Place a layer of aubergine (eggplant) slices in a shallow ovenproof dish. Cover the aubergines (eggplants) with a layer of Mozzarella and then pour over a third of the passata (tomato purée). Continue layering in the same order, finishing with a layer of passata (tomato purée) on top.

5 Generously sprinkle the grated Parmesan cheese over the top and bake in a preheated oven at 200°C/400°F/Gas Mark 6 for 25–30 minutes.

6 Transfer to serving plates and serve warm or chilled.

(Bell) Pepper Salad

Colourful marinated Mediterranean vegetables make a tasty starter.
Serve with fresh bread or Tomato Toasts (see below).

NUTRITIONAL INFORMATION

Calories 234   Sugars 4g
Protein ....6g   Fat 17g
Carbohydrate ...15g   Saturates 2g

5–10 MINS   35 MINS

SERVES 4

INGREDIENTS

1 onion

2 red (bell) peppers

2 yellow (bell) peppers

3 tbsp olive oil

2 large courgettes (zucchini), sliced

2 garlic cloves, sliced

1 tbsp balsamic vinegar

50 g/1¾ oz anchovy fillets, chopped

25 g/1 oz/¼ cup black olives,
    halved and pitted

1 tbsp chopped fresh basil

salt and pepper

TOMATO TOASTS

small stick of French bread

1 garlic clove, crushed

1 tomato, peeled and chopped

2 tbsp olive oil

1 Cut the onion into wedges. Core and deseed the (bell) peppers and cut into thick slices.

2 Heat the oil in a large heavy-based frying pan (skillet). Add the onion, (bell) peppers, courgettes (zucchini) and garlic and fry gently for 20 minutes, stirring occasionally.

3 Add the vinegar, anchovies, olives and seasoning to taste, mix thoroughly and leave to cool.

4 Spoon on to individual plates and sprinkle with the basil.

5 To make the tomato toasts, cut the French bread diagonally into 1 cm/ ½ inch slices.

6 Mix the garlic, tomato, oil and seasoning together, and spread thinly over each slice of bread.

7 Place the bread on a baking tray (cookie sheet), drizzle with the olive oil and bake in a preheated oven, 220°C/425°F/Gas Mark 7, for 5–10 minutes until crisp. Serve the Tomato Toasts with the (Bell) Pepper Salad.

Black Olive Pâté

This pâté is delicious served as a starter on Tomato Toasts (see page 73). It can also be served as a cocktail snack on small rounds of fried bread.

NUTRITIONAL INFORMATION

Calories . . . . . . .149 Sugars 1g
Protein . . . . .2g Fat 14g
Carbohydrate . . . .4g Saturates 6g

 5 MINS 5 MINS

SERVES 4

I N G R E D I E N T S

225 g/8 oz/1½ cups pitted
   juicy black olives

1 garlic clove, crushed

finely grated rind of 1 lemon

4 tbsp lemon juice

25 g/1 oz/½ cup fresh breadcrumbs

60 g/2 oz/¼ cup full fat soft cheese

salt and pepper

lemon wedges, to garnish

TO SERVE

thick slices of bread

mixture of olive oil and butter

1 Roughly chop the olives and mix with the garlic, lemon rind and juice, breadcrumbs and soft cheese. Pound the mixture until smooth, or place in a food processor and work until fully blended. Season to taste with salt and freshly ground black pepper.

2 Store the pâté in a screw-top jar and chill for several hours before using – this allows the flavours to develop.

3 For a delicious cocktail snack, use a pastry cutter to cut out small rounds from a thickly sliced loaf.

4 Fry the bread rounds in a mixture of olive oil and butter until they are a light golden brown colour. Drain thoroughly on paper towels.

5 Top each round with a little of the pâté, garnish with lemon wedges and serve immediately. This pâté will keep chilled in an airtight jar for up to 2 weeks.

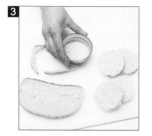

Stuffed Globe Artichokes

This specific recipe has been designed for microwave cooking. Use conventional cooking methods if you prefer.

NUTRITIONAL INFORMATION

Calories	189	Sugars 5g
Protein	.........5g	Fat 11g
Carbohydrate	...17g	Saturates 1g

  15 MINUTES · 1 HOUR

SERVES 4

I N G R E D I E N T S

4 globe artichokes

8 tbsp water

4 tbsp lemon juice

1 onion, chopped

1 garlic clove, crushed

2 tbsp olive oil

225 g/8 oz/2 cups button mushrooms, chopped

40 g/1 ½ oz pitted black olives, sliced

60 g/2 oz/ ¼ cup sun-dried tomatoes in oil, drained and chopped (reserve the oil for drizzling)

1 tbsp chopped fresh basil

60 g/2 oz/1 cup fresh white breadcrumbs

25 g/1 oz/ ¼ cup pine kernels (nuts), toasted

salt and pepper

1 Cut the stalks and lower leaves off the artichokes. Snip off the leaf tips using scissors. Place 2 artichokes in a large bowl with half the water and half the lemon juice. Cover and cook on HIGH power for 10 minutes, turning the artichokes over halfway through, until a leaf pulls away easily from the base. Leave to stand, covered, for 3 minutes before draining. Turn the artichokes upside down and leave to cool. Repeat the process with the remaining artichokes.

2 Place the onion, garlic and oil in a bowl. Cover and cook on HIGH power for 2 minutes, stirring once. Add the mushrooms, olives and sun-dried tomatoes. Cover and cook on HIGH power for 2 minutes.

3 Stir in the basil, breadcrumbs and pine kernels (nuts). Season to taste.

4 Turn the artichokes the right way up and carefully pull the leaves apart. Remove the purple-tipped central leaves. Using a teaspoon, scrape out the hairy choke (heart) and discard.

5 Divide the stuffing into 4 and spoon into the centre of each artichoke. Push the leaves back around the stuffing.

6 Arrange in a shallow dish and drizzle over a little oil from the jar of sun-dried tomatoes. Cook on HIGH power for 7–8 minutes to reheat, turning the artichokes around halfway through. Serve.

Courgette (Zucchini) Fritters

These tasty little fritters are great with the sauce on page 69 as a relish for a drinks party.

NUTRITIONAL INFORMATION

Calories 162   Sugars 2g
Protein ....7g   Fat 6g
Carbohydrate ...20g   Saturates 2g

 5–10 MINS   20 MINS

MAKES 16–30

I N G R E D I E N T S

100 g/3 ½ oz self–raising flour

2 eggs, beaten

50 ml/2 fl oz milk

300 g/10 ½ oz courgettes (zucchini)

2 tbsp fresh thyme

1 tbsp oil

salt and pepper

1 Sift the self-raising flour into a large bowl and make a well in the centre. Add the eggs to the well, and using a wooden spoon, gradually draw in the flour.

2 Slowly add the milk to the mixture, stirring constantly to form a thick batter.

3 Meanwhile, wash the courgettes (zucchini). Grate the courgettes

zucchini) over a sheet of kitchen paper (paper towels) placed in a bowl to absorb some of the juices.

4 Add the courgettes (zucchini), thyme and salt and pepper to taste to the batter and mix thoroughly.

5 Heat the oil in a large, heavy-based frying pan (skillet). Taking a tablespoon of the batter for a medium-

sized fritter or half a tablespoon of batter for a smaller-sized fritter, spoon the mixture into the hot oil and cook, in batches, for 3–4 minutes on each side.

6 Remove the fritters with a perforated spoon and drain thoroughly on absorbent kitchen paper (paper towels). Keep each batch of fritters warm in the oven while making the rest. Transfer to serving plates and serve hot.

VARIATION

Try adding ½ teaspoon of dried, crushed chillies to the batter in step 4 for spicier tasting fritters.

Spinach & Ricotta Patties

Nudo or naked is the word used to describe this mixture, which can also be made into thin pancakes or used as a filling for tortelloni.

NUTRITIONAL INFORMATION

Calories 374	Sugars 4g	
Protein 16g	Fat 31g	
Carbohydrate 9g	Saturates 19g	

 5 MINS   30 MINS

SERVES 4

INGREDIENTS

450 g/1 lb fresh spinach

250 g/9 oz ricotta cheese

1 egg, beaten

2 tsp fennel seeds, lightly crushed

50 g/1¾ oz pecorino or Parmesan cheese, finely grated, plus extra to garnish

25 g/1 oz plain (all-purpose) flour, mixed with 1 tsp dried thyme

75 g/2 ¾ oz/5 tbsp butter

2 garlic cloves, crushed

salt and pepper

tomato wedges, to serve

1 Wash the spinach and trim off any long stalks. Place in a pan, cover and cook for 4–5 minutes until wilted. This will probably have to be done in batches as the volume of spinach is quite large. Place in a colander and leave to drain and cool.

2 Mash the ricotta and beat in the egg and the fennel seeds. Season with plenty of salt and pepper, then stir in the pecorino or Parmesan cheese.

3 Squeeze as much excess water as possible from the spinach and finely chop the leaves. Stir the spinach into the cheese mixture.

4 Taking about 1 tablespoon of the spinach and cheese mixture, shape it into a ball and flatten it slightly to form a patty. Gently roll in the seasoned flour. Continue this process until all of the mixture has been used up.

5 Half-fill a large frying pan (skillet) with water and bring to the boil.

Carefully add the patties and cook for 3–4 minutes or until they rise to the surface. Remove with a perforated spoon.

6 Melt the butter in a pan. Add the garlic and cook for 2–3 minutes. Pour the garlic butter over the patties, season with freshly ground black pepper and serve at once.

Avocado Margherita

The colours of the tomatoes, basil and Mozzarella cheese in this patriotic recipe represent the colours of the Italian flag.

NUTRITIONAL INFORMATION

Calories	249	Sugars	........2g
Protein	.........4g	Fat	..........24g
Carbohydrate	....4g	Saturates	.......6g

5-10 MINS   10-15 MINS

SERVES 4

INGREDIENTS

1 small red onion, sliced

1 garlic clove, crushed

1 tbsp olive oil

2 small tomatoes

2 avocados, halved and pitted

4 fresh basil leaves, torn into shreds

60 g/2 oz Mozzarella cheese, sliced thinly

salt and pepper

fresh basil leaves, to garnish

mixed salad leaves, to serve

1 Place the onion, garlic and the olive oil in a bowl. Cover and cook on HIGH power for 2 minutes.

2 Meanwhile, skin the tomatoes by cutting a cross in the base of the tomatoes and placing them in a small bowl. Pour on boiling water and leave for about 45 seconds. Drain and then plunge into cold water. The skins will slide off without too much difficulty.

3 Arrange the avocado halves on a plate with the narrow ends pointed towards the centre. Spoon the onions into the hollow of each half.

4 Cut and slice the tomatoes in half. Divide the tomatoes, basil and thin slices of Mozzarella between the avocado halves. Season with salt and pepper to taste.

5 Cook on MEDIUM power for 5 minutes or until the avocados are heated through and the cheese has melted. Transfer the avocados to serving plates, garnish with basil leaves and serve with mixed salad leaves.

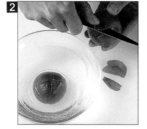  

VARIATION

If you are using a combination microwave oven with grill (broiler) – arrange the avocados on the low rack of the grill (broiler), or on the glass turntable. Cook on combination grill (broiler) 1 and LOW power for 8 minutes until browned and bubbling.

Deep-fried Risotto Balls

The Italian name for this dish translates as 'telephone wires' which refers to the strings of melted Mozzarella cheese contained within the risotto balls.

NUTRITIONAL INFORMATION

Calories	280	Sugars	.........2g
Protein	.........5g	Fat	..........13g
Carbohydrate	...35g	Saturates	.......3g

 5 MINS   35-40 MINS

SERVES 4

INGREDIENTS

2 tbsp olive oil

1 medium onion, finely chopped

1 garlic clove, chopped

½ red (bell) pepper, diced

150 g/5½ oz/¾ cup arborio (risotto) rice, washed

1 tsp dried oregano

400 ml/14 fl oz/1 ⅔ cup hot vegetable or chicken stock

100 ml/3 ½ fl oz/ ½ scant cup dry white wine

75 g/2 ¾ oz Mozzarella cheese

oil, for deep-frying

fresh basil sprig, to garnish

1 Heat the oil in a frying pan (skillet) and cook the onion and garlic for 3–4 minutes or until just softened.

2 Add the (bell) pepper, arborio (risotto) rice and oregano to the pan. Cook for 2–3 minutes, stirring to coat the rice in the oil.

3 Mix the stock together with the wine and add to the pan a ladleful at a time, waiting for the liquid to be absorbed by the rice before you add the next ladleful of liquid.

4 Once all of the liquid has been absorbed and the rice is tender (it should take about 15 minutes in total), remove the pan from the heat and leave until the mixture is cool enough to handle.

5 Cut the cheese into 12 pieces. Taking about 1 tablespoon of risotto, shape the mixture around the cheese pieces to make 12 balls.

6 Heat the oil until a cube of bread browns in 30 seconds. Cook the risotto balls, in batches of 4, for 2 minutes or until golden.

7 Remove the risotto balls with a perforated spoon and drain thoroughly on absorbent kitchen paper. Garnish with a sprig of basil and serve the risotto balls hot.

Olive & Anchovy Pâté

The flavour of olives is accentuated by the anchovies. Serve the pâté as an appetizer on thin pieces of toast with a very dry white wine.

NUTRITIONAL INFORMATION

Calories 214   Sugars 1g
Protein . . . . .2g   Fat 22g
Carbohydrate . . . .1g   Saturates 8g

5-10 MINS   35 MINS

SERVES 4

INGREDIENTS

175 g/6 oz black olives, pitted and chopped

finely grated rind and juice of 1 lemon

50 g/1½ oz unsalted butter

4 canned anchovy fillets, drained and rinsed

2 tbsp extra virgin olive oil

15 g/½ oz ground almonds

fresh herbs, to garnish

1 If you are making the pâté by hand, chop the olives very finely and then mash them along with the lemon rind, juice and butter, using a fork or potato masher. Alternatively, place the roughly chopped olives, lemon rind, juice and butter in a food processor and blend until all of the ingredients are finely chopped.

2 Chop the drained anchovies and add them to the olive and lemon mixture. Mash the pâté by hand or blend in a food processor for 20 seconds.

3 Gradually whisk in the olive oil and stir in the ground almonds. Place the black olive pâté in a serving bowl. Leave the pâté to chill in the refrigerator for about 30 minutes. Serve the pâté accompanied by thin pieces of toast, if wished.

COOK'S TIP

This pâté will keep for up to 5 days in a serving bowl in the refrigerator if you pour a thin layer of extra-virgin olive oil over the top of the pâté to seal it. Then use the oil to brush on the toast before spreading the pâté.

Tuna Stuffed Tomatoes

Deliciously sweet roasted tomatoes are filled with home-made lemon mayonnaise and tuna.

NUTRITIONAL INFORMATION

Calories . . . . . . .196 Sugars 2g
Protein . . . . .9g Fat 17g
Carbohydrate . . . .2g Saturates 3g

 5–10 MINS   25 MINS

SERVES 4

I N G R E D I E N T S

4 plum tomatoes

2 tbsp sun-dried tomato paste

2 egg yolks

2 tsp lemon juice

finely grated rind of 1 lemon

4 tbsp olive oil

115g/4 oz can tuna, drained

2 tbsp capers, rinsed

salt and pepper

TO GARNISH

2 sun-dried tomatoes, cut into strips

fresh basil leaves

1 Halve the tomatoes and scoop out the seeds. Divide the sun-dried tomato paste among the tomato halves and spread around the inside of the skin.

2 Place on a baking tray (cookie sheet) and roast in a preheated oven at 200°C/400°F/Gas Mark 6 for 12–15 minutes. Leave to cool slightly.

3 Meanwhile, make the mayonnaise. In a food processor, blend the egg yolks and lemon juice with the lemon rind until smooth. Once mixed and with the motor still running slowly, add the olive oil. Stop the processor as soon as the mayonnaise has thickened. Alternatively, use a hand whisk, beating the mixture continuously until it thickens.

4 Add the tuna and capers to the mayonnaise and season.

5 Spoon the tuna mayonnaise mixture into the tomato shells and garnish with sun-dried tomato strips and basil leaves. Return to the oven for a few minutes or serve chilled.

COOK'S TIP

For a picnic, do not roast the tomatoes, just scoop out the seeds, drain, cut-side down on absorbent kitchen paper for 1 hour, and fill with the mayonnaise mixture. They are firmer and easier to handle this way. If you prefer, shop-bought mayonnaise may be used instead – just stir in the lemon rind.

Mussels in White Wine

This soup of mussels, cooked in white wine with onions and cream, can be served as an appetizer or a main dish with plenty of crusty bread.

NUTRITIONAL INFORMATION

Calories	396	Sugars	.........2g
Protein	........23g	Fat	..........24g
Carbohydrate	....8g	Saturates	......15g

🥘 5-10 MINS   🕐 25 MINS

SERVES 4

I N G R E D I E N T S

about 3 litres/5¼ pints/12 cups fresh
   mussels

60 g/2 oz/¼ cup butter

1 large onion, chopped very finely

2–3 garlic cloves, crushed

350 ml/12 fl oz/1½ cups dry white wine

150 ml/¼ pint/⅔ cup water

2 tbsp lemon juice

good pinch of finely grated lemon rind

1 bouquet garni sachet

1 tbsp plain (all-purpose) flour

4 tbsp single (light) or double (thick) cream

2–3 tbsp chopped fresh parsley

salt and pepper

warm crusty bread, to serve

1 Scrub the mussels in several changes of cold water to remove all mud, sand, barnacles, etc. Pull off all the 'beards'. All of the mussels must be tightly closed; if they don't close when given a sharp tap, they must be discarded.

2 Melt half the butter in a large saucepan. Add the onion and garlic, and fry gently until soft but not coloured.

3 Add the wine, water, lemon juice and rind, bouquet garni and plenty of seasoning. Bring to the boil then cover and simmer for 4–5 minutes.

4 Add the mussels to the pan, cover tightly and simmer for 5 minutes, shaking the pan frequently, until all the mussels have opened. Discard any mussels which have not opened. Remove the bouquet garni.

5 Remove the empty half shell from each mussel. Blend the remaining butter with the flour and whisk into the soup, a little at a time. Simmer gently for 2–3 minutes until slightly thickened.

6 Add the cream and half the parsley to the soup and reheat gently. Adjust the seasoning. Ladle the mussels and soup into warmed large soup bowls, sprinkle with the remaining parsley and serve with plenty of warm crusty bread.

Deep-fried Seafood

Deep-fried seafood is popular all around the Mediterranean, where fish of all kinds is fresh and abundant.

NUTRITIONAL INFORMATION

Calories	393	Sugars	.......0.2g
Protein	........27g	Fat	..........26g
Carbohydrate	...12g	Saturates	.......3g

5 MINS   15 MINS

SERVES 4

I N G R E D I E N T S

200 g/7 oz prepared squid

200 g/7 oz blue (raw) tiger prawns
  (shrimp), peeled

150 g/5 ½ oz whitebait

oil, for deep-frying

50 g/1 ½ oz plain (all-purpose) flour

1 tsp dried basil

salt and pepper

TO SERVE

garlic mayonnaise (see page 30)

lemon wedges

1 Carefully rinse the squid, prawns (shrimp) and whitebait under cold running water, completely removing any dirt or grit.

2 Using a sharp knife, slice the squid into rings, leaving the tentacles whole.

3 Heat the oil in a large saucepan to 180°–190°C/350°–375°F or until a cube of bread browns in 30 seconds.

4 Place the flour in a bowl, add the basil and season with salt and pepper to taste. Mix together well.

5 Roll the squid, prawns (shrimp) and whitebait in the seasoned flour until coated all over. Carefully shake off any excess flour.

6 Cook the seafood in the heated oil, in batches, for 2–3 minutes or until crispy and golden all over. Remove all of the seafood with a perforated spoon and leave to drain thoroughly on kitchen paper.

7 Transfer the deep-fried seafood to serving plates and serve with garlic mayonnaise (see page 30) and a few lemon wedges.

Pasta & Cheese Pots

A layered pasta, cheese and Parma ham (prosciutto) delight, complemented by a tomato and basil sauce. This recipe is adapted for the microwave.

NUTRITIONAL INFORMATION

Calories ....286 Sugars 4g
Protein ....9g Fat 17g
Carbohydrate ...26g Saturates 7g

15 MINS   35 MINS

SERVES 4

INGREDIENTS

1 small onion, chopped

1 garlic clove, chopped

1 tbsp olive oil

4 tomatoes, skinned (see page 78)
   and chopped

1 tbsp tomato purée (paste)

4 fresh basil leaves, chopped

25 g/1 oz/2 tbsp butter

15 g/½ oz/2 tbsp dried brown breadcrumbs

15 g/½ oz/2 tbsp chopped hazelnuts,
   lightly toasted

90 g/3 oz dried cappellini pasta

15 g/½ oz/2 tbsp plain (all-purpose) flour

150 ml/¼ pint/⅔ cup milk

15 g/½ oz Roquefort (blue) cheese

about 75 g/2¾ oz Parma ham, chopped

4 pitted black olives, chopped

salt and pepper

sprigs of fresh basil, to garnish

1 Place the onion, garlic and oil in a bowl. Cover and cook on HIGH power for 3 minutes. Add the tomatoes and tomato purée (paste) and cook on HIGH power for 4 minutes, stirring halfway through. Add the basil and seasoning. Leave to stand, covered.

2 Place half of the butter in a small bowl and cook on HIGH power for 30 seconds until melted. Brush the insides of 4 ramekin dishes with the melted butter. Mix the breadcrumbs and hazelnuts together and coat the insides of the ramekins. Set aside.

3 Break the pasta into 3 short lengths and place in a large bowl. Pour over enough boiling water to cover the pasta by 2.5 cm/1 inch, and season lightly with salt. Cover and cook on HIGH power for 4 minutes, stirring halfway through. Leave to stand, covered, for 1 minute, then drain thoroughly.

4 Place the remaining butter, the flour and milk in a small bowl. Cook on HIGH power for 2–2½ minutes until thickened, stirring well every 30 seconds. Crumble the cheese into the sauce and stir until melted. Season to taste.

5 Add the pasta to the sauce and mix well. Divide half the pasta mixture between the ramekins and top with the ham and olives. Spoon the remaining pasta mixture on top. Cook on MEDIUM power for 6 minutes. Leave to stand, uncovered, for 2 minutes before carefully turning out on to serving plates with the tomato sauce. Garnish with sprigs of basil.

Crostini alla Fiorentina

Serve as a starter, or simply spread on small pieces of crusty fried bread (crostini) as an appetizer with drinks.

NUTRITIONAL INFORMATION

Calories	393	Sugars	.........2g
Protein	........17g	Fat	..........25g
Carbohydrate	...19g	Saturates	.......9g

 10 MINS   40–45 MINS

SERVES 4

I N G R E D I E N T S

3 tbsp olive oil

1 onion, chopped

1 celery stalk, chopped

1 carrot, chopped

1–2 garlic cloves, crushed

125 g/4½ oz chicken livers

125 g/4½ oz calf's, lamb's or pig's liver

150 ml/¼ pint/⅔ cup red wine

1 tbsp tomato purée (paste)

2 tbsp chopped fresh parsley

3–4 canned anchovy fillets, chopped finely

2 tbsp stock or water

25–40 g/1–1½ oz/2–3 tbsp butter

1 tbsp capers

salt and pepper

small pieces of fried crusty bread, to serve

chopped parsley, to garnish

1 Heat the oil in a pan, add the onion, celery, carrot and garlic, and cook gently for 4–5 minutes or until the onion is soft, but not coloured.

2 Meanwhile, rinse and dry the chicken livers. Dry the calf's or other liver, and slice into strips. Add the liver to the pan and fry gently for a few minutes until the strips are well sealed on all sides.

3 Add half of the wine and cook until it has mostly evaporated. Then add the rest of the wine, tomato purée (paste), half of the parsley, the anchovy fillets, stock or water, a little salt and plenty of black pepper.

4 Cover the pan and leave to simmer, stirring occasionally, for 15–20 minutes or until tender and most of the liquid has been absorbed.

5 Leave the mixture to cool a little, then either coarsely mince or put into a food processor and process to a chunky purée.

6 Return to the pan and add the butter, capers and remaining parsley. Heat through gently until the butter melts. Adjust the seasoning and turn out into a bowl. Serve warm or cold spread on the slices of crusty bread and sprinkled with chopped parsley.

Figs & Parma Ham (Prosciutto)

This colourful fresh salad is delicious at any time of the year. Prosciutto di Parma is thought to be the best ham in the world.

NUTRITIONAL INFORMATION

Calories . . . . .121 Sugars 6g
Protein . . . . .1g Fat 11g
Carbohydrate . . . .6g Saturates 2g

15 MINS   5 MINS

SERVES 4

INGREDIENTS

40 g/1½ oz rocket (arugula)

4 fresh figs

4 slices Parma ham (prosciutto)

4 tbsp olive oil

1 tbsp fresh orange juice

1 tbsp clear honey

1 small red chilli

1 Tear the rocket (arugula) into more manageable pieces and arrange on 4 serving plates.

2 Using a sharp knife, cut each of the figs into quarters and place them on top of the rocket (arugula) leaves.

3 Using a sharp knife, cut the Parma ham (prosciutto) into strips and scatter over the rocket (arugula) and figs.

4 Place the oil, orange juice and honey in a screw-top jar. Shake the jar until the mixture emulsifies and forms a thick dressing. Transfer to a bowl.

5 Using a sharp knife, dice the chilli, remembering not to touch your face before you have washed your hands (see Cook's Tip, below). Add the chopped chilli to the dressing and mix well.

6 Drizzle the dressing over the Parma ham (prosciutto), rocket (arugula) and figs, tossing to mix well. Serve at once.

COOK'S TIP

Chillies can burn the skin for several hours after chopping, so it is advisable to wear gloves when you are handling the very hot varieties.

Preserved Meats (Salumi)

Mix an attractive selection of these preserved meats (salumi) with olives and marinated vegetables for extra colour and variety.

NUTRITIONAL INFORMATION

Calories	227	Sugars	.........5g
Protein	........10g	Fat	..........19g
Carbohydrate	....5g	Saturates	.......1g

 10 MINS   5–10 MINS

SERVES 4

INGREDIENTS

3 ripe tomatoes

3 ripe figs

1 small melon

60 g/2 oz Italian salami, sliced thinly

4 thin slices mortadella

6 slices Parma ham (prosciutto)

6 slices bresaola

4 fresh basil leaves, chopped

olive oil

90 g/3 oz/½ cup marinated olives, pitted

freshly ground black pepper, to serve

1 Slice the tomatoes thinly and cut the figs into quarters.

2 Halve the melon, scoop out the seeds, and cut the flesh into wedges.

3 Arange the meats on one half of a serving platter. Arrange the tomato slices in the centre and sprinkle with the basil leaves and oil.

4 Cover the rest of the platter with the figs and melon and scatter the olives over the meats.

5 Serve with a little extra olive oil to drizzle over the bresaola, and sprinkle with coarsely ground black pepper.

Chick-peas & Parma Ham

Prosciutto is used in this recipe. It is a cured ham, which is air- and salt-dried for up to 1 year. There are many different varieties available.

NUTRITIONAL INFORMATION

Calories 180	Sugars 2g
Protein 12g	Fat 7g
Carbohydrate ...18g	Saturates 1g

  10 MINS   15 MINS

SERVES 4

INGREDIENTS

1 tbsp olive oil

1 medium onion, thinly sliced

1 garlic clove, chopped

1 small red (bell) pepper, deseeded and cut
    into thin strips

200 g/7 oz Parma ham (prosciutto),
    cut into cubes

400g/14 oz can chick-peas (garbanzo
    beans), drained and rinsed

1 tbsp chopped parsley, to garnish

crusty bread, to serve

COOK'S TIP

Whenever possible, use fresh herbs when cooking. They are becoming more readily available, especially since the introduction of 'growing' herbs, small pots of herbs which you can buy from the supermarket or greengrocer and grow at home. This ensures the herbs are fresh and also provides a continuous supply.

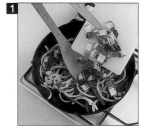

1 Heat the oil in a frying pan (skillet). Add the onion, garlic and (bell) pepper and cook for 3–4 minutes or until the vegetables have softened. Add the Parma ham (prosciutto) to the pan (skillet) and fry for 5 minutes or until the ham (prosciutto) is just beginning to brown.

2 Add the chick-peas (garbanzo beans) to the pan (skillet) and cook, stirring, for 2–3 minutes until warmed through.

3 Sprinkle with chopped parsley and transfer to warm serving plates. Serve with lots of fresh crusty bread.

Cured Meats, Olives & Tomatoes

This is a typical *antipasto* dish with the cold cured meats, stuffed olives and fresh tomatoes, basil and balsamic vinegar.

NUTRITIONAL INFORMATION

Calories . . . . .312 Sugars 1g
Protein . . . . .12g Fat 28g
Carbohydrate . . . .2g Saturates 1g

 10 MINS   5 MINS

SERVES 4

I N G R E D I E N T S

4 plum tomatoes

1 tbsp balsamic vinegar

6 canned anchovy fillets, drained and rinsed

2 tbsp capers, drained and rinsed

125 g/4½ oz green olives, pitted

175 g/6 oz mixed, cured meats, sliced

8 fresh basil leaves

1 tbsp extra virgin olive oil

salt and pepper

crusty bread, to serve

1 Using a sharp knife, cut the tomatoes into evenly-sized slices. Sprinkle the tomato slices with the balsamic vinegar and a little salt and pepper to taste, and set aside.

2 Chop the anchovy fillets into pieces measuring about the same length as the olives.

3 Push a piece of anchovy and a caper into each olive.

4 Arrange the sliced meat on 4 individual serving plates together with the tomatoes, filled olives and basil leaves.

5 Lightly drizzle the olive oil over the sliced meat, tomatoes and olives.

6 Serve the cured meats, olives and tomatoes with plenty of fresh crusty bread.

COOK'S TIP

The cured meats for this recipe are up to your individual taste. They can include a selection of Parma ham (prosciutto), pancetta, bresaola (dried salt beef) and salame di Milano (pork and beef sausage).

Snacks & Light Meals

Recipes for snacks and light meals offer something for every taste, including vegetables, meat and fish dishes. These recipes are suitable for when you are not too hungry, but still a bit peckish or if you are in a hurry and want to eat something quick, but still nutritious and tasty. Try the mouthwatering Italian flavours of Tomato & Mozzarella Bruschetta or an Italian-style omelette – they are sure to satisfy even the most discerning tastebuds. All of the recipes in this chapter are quick to prepare and easy to cook, and are sure to become staples in your Italian culinary repertoire.

Tomato & Mozzarella Bruschetta

These simple toasts are filled with colour and flavour. They are great as a speedy starter or delicious as a light meal or snack.

NUTRITIONAL INFORMATION

Calories 232	Sugars 4g	
Protein 4g	Fat 15g	
Carbohydrate . . .20g	Saturates 8g	

  5–10 MINS   10 MINS

SERVES 4

INGREDIENTS

4 muffins

4 garlic cloves, crushed

2 tbsp butter

1 tbsp chopped basil

4 large, ripe tomatoes

1 tbsp tomato purée (paste)

8 pitted black olives, halved

50 g/1¾ oz Mozzarella cheese, sliced

salt and pepper

fresh basil leaves, to garnish

DRESSING

1 tbsp olive oil

2 tsp lemon juice

1 tsp clear honey

VARIATION

Use balsamic vinegar instead of the lemon juice for an authentic Italian flavour.

1 Cut the muffins in half to give eight thick pieces. Toast the muffin halves under a hot grill (broiler) for 2–3 minutes until golden.

2 Mix the garlic, butter and basil together and spread on to each muffin half.

3 Cut a cross shape at the base of each tomato. Plunge the tomatoes in a bowl of boiling water – this will make the skin easier to peel. After a few minutes, pick each tomato up with a fork and peel away the skin. Chop the tomato flesh and mix with the tomato purée (paste) and olives. Divide the mixture between the muffins.

4 Mix the dressing ingredients and drizzle over each muffin. Arrange the Mozzarella cheese on top and season.

5 Return the muffins to the grill (broiler) for 1–2 minutes until the cheese melts.

6 Garnish with fresh basil leaves and serve at once.

Aubergine (Eggplant) Sandwiches

Serve these sandwiches as a vegetarian main course for two or as a side dish to accompany other barbecued (grilled) foods.

NUTRITIONAL INFORMATION

Calories 270	Sugars 4g
Protein 10g	Fat 15g
Carbohydrate . . .25g	Saturates 7g

  5 MINS   10–15 MINS

SERVES 2

I N G R E D I E N T S

1 large aubergine (eggplant)

1 tbsp lemon juice

3 tbsp olive oil

125 g/4 ½ oz grated Mozzarella cheese

2 sun-dried tomatoes, chopped

salt and pepper

T O   S E R V E

Italian bread, such as focaccia or ciabatta

mixed salad leaves

slices of tomato

1 Slice the aubergine (eggplant) into thin rounds.

2 Combine the lemon juice and olive oil in a small bowl and season the mixture with salt and pepper to taste.

3 Brush the aubergine (eggplant) slices with the oil and lemon juice mixture and barbecue (grill) over medium hot coals for 2–3 minutes, without turning, until they are golden on the under side.

4 Turn half of the aubergine (eggplant) slices over and sprinkle with cheese and chopped sun-dried tomatoes.

5 Place the remaining aubergine (eggplant) slices on top of the cheese and tomatoes, turning them so that the pale side is uppermost.

6 Barbecue (grill) for 1–2 minutes, then carefully turn the whole sandwich over and barbecue (grill) for 1–2 minutes. Baste with the oil mixture.

7 Serve the aubergine (eggplant) sandwiches with Italian bread, mixed salad leaves and a few slices of tomato.

VARIATION

Try Feta cheese instead of Mozzarella but omit the salt from the basting oil because Feta is quite salty. A creamy goat's cheese would be equally delicious.

Vegetable Kebabs (Kabobs)

Brighten up a barbecue (grill) meal with these colourful kebabs (kabobs). They are basted with a deliciously flavoured oil.

NUTRITIONAL INFORMATION

Calories 142   Sugars 4g
Protein ....1g   Fat 14g
Carbohydrate ....4g   Saturates 2g

15 MINS   15 MINS

SERVES 4

INGREDIENTS

1 red (bell) pepper, deseeded

1 yellow (bell) pepper, deseeded

1 green (bell) pepper, deseeded

1 small onion

8 cherry tomatoes

100 g/3 ½ oz wild mushrooms

SEASONED OIL

6 tbsp olive oil

1 clove garlic, crushed

½ tsp mixed dried herbs or
herbes de Provence

1 Cut the (bell) peppers into 2.5 cm/ 1 inch pieces.

2 Peel the onion and cut it into wedges, leaving the root end just intact to help keep the wedges together.

COOK'S TIP

To make walnut sauce, work 125 g/4½ oz walnuts in a food processor to form a paste. With the machine running, add 150 ml/5 fl oz/ ⅔ cup cream and 1 tbsp oil. Season. Or, chop the walnuts then pound them in a pestle and mortar to form a paste. Mix with the cream and oil, and season.

3 Thread the (bell) peppers, onion wedges, cherry tomatoes and mushrooms on to skewers, alternating the colours of the (bell) peppers.

4 To make the seasoned oil, mix together the olive oil, garlic and mixed dried herbs in a a small bowl. Brush the seasoned oil mixture liberally over the kebabs (kabobs).

5 Barbecue (grill) the kebabs (kabobs) over medium hot coals for 10–15 minutes, brushing with more of the seasoned oil and turning the skewers frequently.

6 Transfer the vegetable kebabs (kabobs) to warm serving plates. Serve the kebabs (kabobs) with walnut sauce (see Cook's Tip, left), if you wish.

Bruschetta with Tomatoes

Using ripe tomatoes and the best olive oil will make this Tuscan dish absolutely delicious.

NUTRITIONAL INFORMATION

Calories	330	Sugars	.........4g
Protein	.........8g	Fat	..........14g
Carbohydrate	...45g	Saturates	.......2g

15 MINS   5 MINS

SERVES 4

INGREDIENTS

300 g/10½ oz cherry tomatoes

4 sun-dried tomatoes

4 tbsp extra virgin olive oil

16 fresh basil leaves, shredded

2 garlic cloves, peeled

8 slices ciabatta

salt and pepper

1 Using a sharp knife, cut the cherry tomatoes in half.

2 Using a sharp knife, slice the sun-dried tomatoes into strips.

3 Place the cherry tomatoes and sun-dried tomatoes in a bowl. Add the olive oil and the shredded basil leaves and toss to mix well. Season to taste with a little salt and pepper.

4 Using a sharp knife, cut the garlic cloves in half. Lightly toast the ciabatta bread.

5 Rub the garlic, cut-side down, over both sides of the lightly toasted ciabatta bread.

6 Top the ciabatta bread with the tomato mixture and serve immediately.

Onion & Mozzarella Tarts

These individual tarts are delicious hot or cold and are great for lunchboxes or picnics.

NUTRITIONAL INFORMATION

Calories . . . . . . .327 Sugars 3g
Protein . . . . .5g Fat 23g
Carbohydrate . . .25g Saturates 9g

🍴 🍴 🍴

45 MINS   45 MINS

SERVES 4

INGREDIENTS

250g/9 oz packet puff pastry, defrosted
   if frozen

2 medium red onions

1 red (bell) pepper

8 cherry tomatoes, halved

100g/3½ oz Mozzarella cheese,
   cut into chunks

8 sprigs thyme

1 Roll out the pastry to make 4 x 7.5 cm/ 3 inch squares. Using a sharp knife, trim the edges of the pastry, reserving the trimmings. Leave the pastry to chill in the refrigerator for 30 minutes.

2 Place the pastry squares on a baking tray (cookie sheet). Brush a little water along each edge of the pastry squares and use the reserved pastry trimmings to make a rim around each tart.

3 Cut the red onions into thin wedges and halve and deseed the (bell) peppers.

4 Place the onions and (bell) pepper in a roasting tin (pan). Cook under a preheated grill (broiler) for 15 minutes or until charred.

5 Place the roasted (bell) pepper halves in a polythene bag and leave to sweat for 10 minutes. Peel off the skin from the (bell) peppers and cut the flesh into strips.

6 Line the pastry squares with squares of foil. Bake in a preheated oven at 200°C/400°F/Gas Mark 6 for 10 minutes. Remove the foil squares and bake for a further 5 minutes.

7 Place the onions, (bell) pepper strips, tomatoes and cheese in each tart and sprinkle with the fresh thyme.

8 Return to the oven for 15 minutes or until the pastry is golden. Serve hot.

Grilled Aubergines (Eggplants)

Serve plain as a simple vegetable dish, but for a tasty starter or vegetarian dish, serve it with pesto or minty cucumber sauce.

NUTRITIONAL INFORMATION

Calories 340	Sugars 3g
Protein 8g	Fat 33g
Carbohydrate 4g	Saturates 7g

 30 MINS 10 MINS

SERVES 4

INGREDIENTS

1 large aubergine (eggplant)

3 tbsp olive oil

1 tsp sesame oil

salt and pepper

PESTO

1 clove garlic

25 g/1 oz pine nuts

15 g/½ oz fresh basil leaves

2 tbsp Parmesan cheese

6 tbsp olive oil

CUCUMBER SAUCE

150 g/5 ½ oz natural yogurt

5 cm/2 inch cucumber

½ tsp mint sauce

1 Remove the stalk from the aubergine (eggplant), then cut it lengthwise into 8 thin slices.

2 Lay the slices on a plate or board and sprinkle them liberally with salt to remove the bitter juices. Leave to stand.

3 Meanwhile, prepare the baste. Combine the olive and sesame oils, season with pepper and set aside.

4 To make the pesto, put the garlic, pine nuts, basil and cheese in a food processor until finely chopped. With the machine running, gradually add the oil in a thin stream. Season to taste.

5 To make the minty cucumber sauce, place the yogurt in a mixing bowl. Remove the seeds from the cucumber and dice the flesh finely. Stir into the yogurt with the mint sauce.

6 Rinse the aubergine (eggplant) slices and pat them dry on absorbent kitchen paper. Baste with the oil mixture and barbecue (grill) over hot coals for about 10 minutes, turning once. The aubergine (eggplant) should be golden and just tender.

7 Transfer the aubergine (eggplant) slices to serving plates and serve with either the cucumber sauce or the pesto.

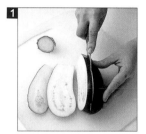

Italian Omelette

A baked omelette of substantial proportions with potatoes, onions, artichokes and sun-dried tomatoes.

NUTRITIONAL INFORMATION

Calories 481   Sugars 4g
Protein . . . . .22g   Fat 26g
Carbohydrate . . .42g   Saturates 10g

  10 MINS   45 MINS

SERVES 4

INGREDIENTS

900 g/2 lb potatoes

1 tbsp oil

1 large onion, sliced

2 garlic cloves, chopped

6 sun-dried tomatoes, cut into strips

400g/14 oz can artichoke hearts, drained
  and halved

250 g/9 oz ricotta cheese

4 large eggs, beaten

2 tbsp milk

50 g/1¾ oz Parmesan cheese, grated

3 tbsp chopped thyme

salt and pepper

1 Peel the potatoes and place them in a bowl of cold water (see Cook's Tip). Cut the potatoes into thin slices.

2 Bring a large pan of water to the boil and add the potato slices. Leave the potatoes to simmer for 5–6 minutes or until just tender.

3 Heat the oil in a large frying pan (skillet). Add the onions and garlic to the pan and cook, stirring occasionally, for about 3–4 minutes.

4 Add the sun-dried tomatoes and continue cooking for a further 2 minutes.

5 Place a layer of potatoes at the bottom of a deep, ovenproof dish. Top with a layer of the onion mixture, artichokes and ricotta cheese. Repeat the layers in the same order, finishing with a layer of potatoes on top.

6 Mix together the eggs, milk, half of the Parmesan, thyme and salt and pepper to taste and pour over the potatoes.

7 Top with the remaining Parmesan cheese and bake in a preheated oven, at 190°C/375°F/Gas Mark 5, for 20–25 minutes or until golden brown. Cut the omelette into slices and serve.

COOK'S TIP

Placing the potatoes in a bowl of cold water will prevent them from turning brown while you cut the rest into slices.

Bean & Tomato Casserole

This quick and easy casserole can be eaten as a healthy supper dish or as a side dish to accompany sausages or grilled fish.

NUTRITIONAL INFORMATION

Calories	273	Sugars	........8g
Protein	........15g	Fat	...........7g
Carbohydrate	...40g	Saturates	.......1g

10 MINS   15 MINS

SERVES 4

INGREDIENTS

400g/14 oz can cannellini beans

400g/14 oz can borlotti beans

2 tbsp olive oil

1 stick celery

2 garlic cloves, chopped

175 g/6 oz baby onions, halved

450 g/1 lb tomatoes

75 g/2¾ oz rocket (arugula)

1 Drain both cans of beans and reserve 6 tbsp of the liquid.

2 Heat the oil in a large pan. Add the celery, garlic and onions and sauté for 5 minutes or until the onions are golden.

3 Cut a cross in the base of each tomato and plunge them into a bowl of boiling water for 30 seconds until the skins split. Remove the tomatoes with a perforated spoon and leave until cool enough to handle. Peel off the skin and chop the flesh.

4 Add the tomato flesh and the reserved bean liquid to the pan and cook for 5 minutes.

5 Add the beans to the pan and cook for a further 3–4 minutes or until the beans are hot.

6 Stir in the rocket (arugula) and allow to wilt slightly before serving. Serve hot.

VARIATION

For a spicier tasting dish, add 1–2 teaspoons of hot pepper sauce with the cannellini and borlotti beans in step 5.

Omelette in Tomato Sauce

These omelette strips are delicious smothered in a tomato and rosemary flavoured sauce.

NUTRITIONAL INFORMATION

Calories 198   Sugars 6g
Protein ....10g   Fat 15g
Carbohydrate ....6g   Saturates 8g

 10 MINS   35 MINS

SERVES 4

INGREDIENTS

25 g/1 oz/2 tbsp butter

1 onion, finely chopped

2 garlic cloves, chopped

4 eggs, beaten

150 ml/¼ pint/⅔ cup milk

75 g/2¾ oz Gruyère cheese, diced

400g/14 oz can tomatoes, chopped

1 tbsp rosemary, stalks removed

150 ml/¼ pint/⅔ cup vegetable stock

freshly grated Parmesan cheese,
  for sprinkling

fresh, crusty bread, to serve

1 Melt the butter in a large frying pan (skillet). Add the onion and garlic and cook for 4–5 minutes, until softened.

2 Beat together the eggs and milk and add the mixture to the pan.

3 Using a spatula, raise the cooked edges of the omelette and tip any uncooked egg around the edge of the pan.

4 Scatter over the cheese. Cook for 5 minutes, turning once, until golden on both sides. Remove the omelette from the pan and roll up.

5 Add the tomatoes, rosemary and vegetable stock to the frying pan (skillet), stirring, and bring to the boil.

6 Leave the tomato sauce to simmer for about 10 minutes until reduced and thickened.

7 Slice the omelette into strips and add to the tomato sauce in the frying pan (skillet). Cook for 3–4 minutes or until piping hot.

8 Sprinkle the freshly grated Parmesan cheese over the omelette strips and serve with fresh, crusty bread.

VARIATION

Try adding 100 g/3½ oz diced pancetta or unsmoked bacon in step 1 and cooking the meat with the onions.

Baked Fennel

Fennel is used extensively in northern Italy. It is a very versatile vegetable, which is good cooked or used raw in salads.

NUTRITIONAL INFORMATION

Calories 111	Sugars 6g
Protein 7g	Fat 7g
Carbohydrate 7g	Saturates 3g

 10 MINS 35 MINS

SERVES 4

I N G R E D I E N T S

2 fennel bulbs

2 celery sticks, cut into 7.5 cm/3 inch sticks

6 sun-dried tomatoes, halved

200 g/7 oz passata (tomato paste)

2 tsp dried oregano

50 g/1¾ oz Parmesan cheese, grated

1 Using a sharp knife, trim the fennel, discarding any tough outer leaves, and cut the bulb into quarters.

2 Bring a large pan of water to the boil, add the fennel and celery and cook for 8–10 minutes or until just tender. Remove with a perforated spoon and drain.

3 Place the fennel pieces, celery and sun-dried tomatoes in a large ovenproof dish.

4 Mix the passata (tomato paste) and oregano and pour the mixture over the fennel.

5 Sprinkle with the Parmesan cheese and bake in a preheated oven at 190°C/375°F/Gas Mark 5 for 20 minutes or until hot. Serve as a starter with bread or as a vegetable side dish.

Garlic & Pine Nut Tarts

A crisp lining of bread is filled with garlic butter and pine nuts to make a delightful light meal.

NUTRITIONAL INFORMATION

Calories	435	Sugars	.........1g
Protein	.........6g	Fat	..........39g
Carbohydrate	...17g	Saturates	......20g

20 MINS   15 MINS

SERVES 4

INGREDIENTS

4 slices wholemeal or granary bread

50 g/1¾ oz pine nuts

150 g/5½ oz/10 tbsp butter

5 garlic cloves, peeled and halved

2 tbsp fresh oregano, chopped, plus extra
    for garnish

4 black olives, halved

oregano leaves, to garnish

1 Using a rolling pin, flatten the bread slightly. Using a pastry cutter, cut out 4 circles of bread to fit your individual tart tins (pans) – they should measure about 10 cm/4 inches across. Reserve the offcuts of bread and leave them in the refrigerator for 10 minutes or until required.

VARIATION

Puff pastry can be used for the tarts. Use 200 g/7oz puff pastry to line 4 tart tins (pans). Leave the pastry to chill for 20 minutes. Line the tins (pans) with the pastry and foil and bake blind for 10 minutes. Remove the foil and bake for 3–4 minutes or until the pastry is set. Cool, then continue from step 2, adding 2 tbsp breadcrumbs to the mixture.

2 Meanwhile, place the pine nuts on a baking tray (cookie sheet). Toast the pine nuts under a preheated grill (broiler) for 2–3 minutes or until golden.

3 Put the bread offcuts, pine nuts, butter, garlic and oregano into a food processor and blend for about 20 seconds. Alternatively, pound the ingredients by hand in a mortar and pestle. The mixture should have a rough texture.

4 Spoon the pine nut butter mixture into the lined tin (pan) and top with the olives. Bake in a preheated oven at 200°C/400°F/Gas Mark 6 for 10–15 minutes or until golden.

5 Transfer the tarts to serving plates and serve warm, garnished with the fresh oregano leaves.

Pasta Omelette

This is a superb way of using up any leftover pasta, such as penne, macaroni or conchiglie.

NUTRITIONAL INFORMATION

Calories ....460 Sugars 3g
Protein ....16g Fat 34g
Carbohydrate ...23g Saturates 6g

 10 MINS   30 MINS

SERVES 2

INGREDIENTS

4 tbsp olive oil

1 small onion, chopped

1 fennel bulb, thinly sliced

125 g/4½ oz potato, diced

1 garlic clove, chopped

4 eggs

1 tbsp chopped fresh flat leaf parsley

pinch of chilli powder

100 g/3½ oz cooked short pasta

2 tbsp stuffed green olives, halved

salt and pepper

fresh marjoram sprigs, to garnish

tomato salad, to serve

1 Heat half of the oil in a heavy-based frying pan (skillet) over a low heat. Add the onion, fennel and potato and fry, stirring occasionally, for 8–10 minutes, until the potato is just tender.

2 Stir in the garlic and cook for 1 minute. Remove the pan from the heat and transfer the vegetables to a plate and set aside.

3 Beat the eggs until they are frothy. Stir in the parsley and season with salt, pepper and a pinch of chilli powder.

4 Heat 1 tbsp of the remaining oil in a clean frying pan (skillet). Add half of the egg mixture to the pan, then add the cooked vegetables, pasta and half of the olives. Pour in the remaining egg mixture and cook until the sides begin to set.

5 Lift up the edges of the omelette with a palette knife (spatula) to allow the uncooked egg to spread underneath. Cook, shaking the pan occasionally, until the underside is a light golden brown colour.

6 Slide the omelette out of the pan on to a plate. Wipe the pan with kitchen paper (kitchen towels) and heat the remaining oil. Invert the omelette into the pan and cook until the other side is a golden brown colour.

7 Slide the omelette on to a warmed serving dish and garnish with the remaining olives and the sprigs of marjoram. Cut the omelette into wedges and serve with a tomato salad.

Spinach & Ricotta Shells

This is a classic combination in which the smooth, creamy cheese balances the sharper taste of the spinach.

NUTRITIONAL INFORMATION

Calories	672	Sugars	........10g
Protein	........23g	Fat	..........26g
Carbohydrate	...93g	Saturates	.......8g

 5 MINS 40 MINS

SERVES 4

INGREDIENTS

400 g/14 oz dried lumache rigate grande

5 tbsp olive oil

60 g/2 oz/1 cup fresh white breadcrumbs

125 ml/4 fl oz/½ cup milk

300 g/10½ oz frozen spinach, thawed
   and drained

225 g/8 oz/1 cup ricotta cheese

pinch of freshly grated nutmeg

400 g/14 oz can chopped tomatoes, drained

1 garlic clove, crushed

salt and pepper

1 Bring a large saucepan of lightly salted water to the boil. Add the lumache and 1 tbsp of the olive oil and cook for 8–10 minutes until just tender, but still firm to the bite. Drain the pasta, refresh under cold water and set aside until required.

2 Put the breadcrumbs, milk and 3 tbsp of the remaining olive oil in a food processor and work to combine.

3 Add the spinach and ricotta cheese to the food processor and work to a smooth mixture. Transfer to a bowl, stir in the nutmeg, and season with salt and pepper to taste.

4 Mix together the tomatoes, garlic and remaining oil and spoon the mixture into the base of a large ovenproof dish.

5 Using a teaspoon, fill the lumache with the spinach and ricotta mixture and arrange on top of the tomato mixture in the dish. Cover and bake in a preheated oven at 180°C/350°F/Gas 4 for 20 minutes. Serve hot.

COOK'S TIP

Ricotta is a creamy Italian cheese traditionally made from ewes' milk whey. It is soft and white, with a smooth texture and a slightly sweet flavour. It should be used within 2–3 days of purchase.

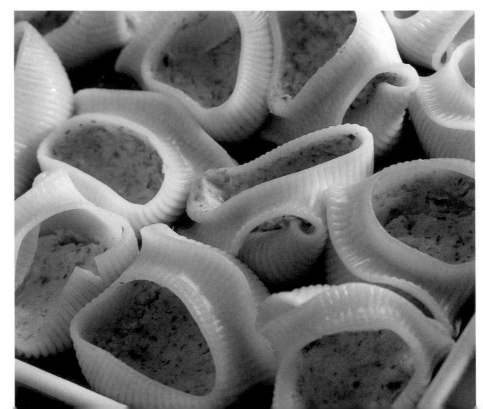

Rotelle with Spicy Sauce

Prepare the sauce well in advance – it is a good idea to freeze batches of the sauce so that you always have some to hand.

NUTRITIONAL INFORMATION

Calories	530	Sugars	.........4g
Protein	........13g	Fat	..........18g
Carbohydrate	...78g	Saturates	.......3g

8¼ HOURS   40 MINS

SERVES 4

INGREDIENTS

200 ml/7 fl oz/⅞ cup Italian Red Wine Sauce
   (see page 29)

5 tbsp olive oil

3 garlic cloves, crushed

2 fresh red chillies, chopped

1 green chilli, chopped

400 g/14 oz/3½ cups dried rotelle

salt and pepper

warm Italian bread, to serve

1 Make the Italian Red Wine Sauce (see page 29).

2 Heat 4 tbsp of the oil in a saucepan. Add the garlic and chillies and fry for 3 minutes.

3 Stir in the Italian Red Wine Sauce, season with salt and pepper to taste, and simmer gently over a low heat for 20 minutes.

4 Bring a large saucepan of lightly salted water to the boil. Add the rotelle and the remaining oil and cook for 8 minutes, until just tender, but still firm to the bite. Drain the pasta.

5 Pour the Italian Red Wine Sauce over the rotelle and toss to mix.

6 Transfer to a warm serving dish and serve with warm Italian bread.

COOK'S TIP

Remove chilli seeds before chopping the chillies, as they are the hottest part, and shouldn't be allowed to slip into the food.

Tagliarini with Gorgonzola

This simple, creamy pasta sauce is a classic Italian recipe. You could use Danish blue cheese instead of the Gorgonzola, if you prefer.

NUTRITIONAL INFORMATION

Calories 904	Sugars 4g	
Protein 27g	Fat 53g	
Carbohydrate ...83g	Saturates 36g	

 5 MINS   20 MINS

SERVES 4

INGREDIENTS

25 g/1 oz/2 tbsp butter

225 g/8 oz Gorgonzola cheese, roughly crumbled

150 ml/¼ pint/⅝ cup double (heavy) cream

30 ml/2 tbsp dry white wine

1 tsp cornflour (cornstarch)

4 fresh sage sprigs, finely chopped

400 g/14 oz dried tagliarini

2 tbsp olive oil

salt and white pepper

1 Melt the butter in a heavy-based pan. Stir in 175 g/6 oz of the cheese and melt, over a low heat, for about 2 minutes.

2 Add the cream, wine and cornflour (cornstarch) and beat with a whisk until fully incorporated.

COOK'S TIP

Gorgonzola is one of the world's oldest veined cheeses and, arguably, its finest. When buying, always check that it is creamy yellow with delicate green veining. Avoid hard or discoloured cheese. It should have a rich, piquant aroma, not a bitter smell.

3 Stir in the sage and season to taste with salt and white pepper. Bring to the boil over a low heat, whisking constantly, until the sauce thickens. Remove from the heat and set aside while you cook the pasta.

4 Bring a large saucepan of lightly salted water to the boil. Add the tagliarini and 1 tbsp of the olive oil. Cook the pasta for 8–10 minutes or until just tender, drain thoroughly and toss in the remaining olive oil. Transfer the pasta to a serving dish and keep warm.

5 Reheat the sauce over a low heat, whisking constantly. Spoon the Gorgonzola sauce over the tagliarini, generously sprinkle over the remaining cheese and serve immediately.

Spaghetti with Ricotta

This light pasta dish has a delicate flavour ideally suited for a summer lunch.

NUTRITIONAL INFORMATION

Calories 701	Sugars 12g
Protein 17g	Fat 40g
Carbohydrate ...73g	Saturates 15g

  5 MINS  25 MINS

SERVES 4

INGREDIENTS

350 g/12 oz dried spaghetti

3 tbsp olive oil

40 g/1 ½ oz/3 tbsp butter

2 tbsp chopped fresh flat leaf parsley

125 g/4 ½ oz/1 cup freshly ground almonds

125 g/4 ½ oz/ ½ cup ricotta cheese

pinch of grated nutmeg

pinch of ground cinnamon

150 ml/ ¼ pint/ ⅝ cup crème fraîche
    (unsweetened yogurt)

125 ml/4 fl oz hot chicken stock

1 tbsp pine nuts (kernels)

salt and pepper

fresh flat leaf parsley sprigs, to garnish

1 Bring a pan of lightly salted water to the boil. Add the spaghetti and 1 tbsp of the oil and cook for 8–10 minutes until tender, but still firm to the bite.

2 Drain the pasta, return to the pan and toss with the butter and chopped parsley. Set aside and keep warm.

3 To make the sauce, mix together the ground almonds, ricotta cheese, nutmeg, cinnamon and crème fraîche (unsweetened yogurt) over a low heat to form a thick paste. Gradually stir in the remaining oil. When the oil has been fully incorporated, gradually stir in the hot chicken stock, until smooth. Season to taste with black pepper.

4 Transfer the spaghetti to a warm serving dish, pour over the sauce and toss together well (see Cook's Tip, right). Sprinkle over the pine nuts (kernels), garnish with the sprigs of flat leaf parsley and serve warm.

COOK'S TIP

Use two large forks to toss spaghetti or other long pasta, so that it is thoroughly coated with the sauce. Special spaghetti forks are available from some cookware departments and kitchen shops.

Three Cheese Bake

Serve this dish while the cheese is still hot and melted, as cooked cheese turns very rubbery if it is allowed to cool down.

NUTRITIONAL INFORMATION

Calories 710   Sugars 6g
Protein . . . . .34g   Fat 30g
Carbohydrate . . .80g   Saturates 16g

5 MINS   1 HOUR

SERVES 4

I N G R E D I E N T S

butter, for greasing

400 g/14 oz dried penne

1 tbsp olive oil

2 eggs, beaten

350 g/12 oz/1½ cups ricotta cheese

4 fresh basil sprigs

100 g/3½ oz/1 cup grated Mozzarella or
    halloumi cheese

4 tbsp freshly grated Parmesan cheese

salt and pepper

fresh basil leaves (optional), to garnish

1 Lightly grease a large ovenproof dish
  with butter.

2 Bring a large pan of lightly salted
  water to the boil. Add the penne and
olive oil and cook for 8–10 minutes until just tender, but still firm to the bite. Drain the pasta, set aside and keep warm.

3 Beat the eggs into the ricotta cheese
  and season to taste.

4 Spoon half of the penne into the base
  of the dish and cover with half of the
basil leaves.

5 Spoon over half of the ricotta cheese
  mixture. Sprinkle over the Mozzarella
or halloumi cheese and top with the remaining basil leaves. Cover with the remaining penne and then spoon over the remaining ricotta cheese mixture. Lightly sprinkle over the freshly grated Parmesan cheese.

6 Bake in a preheated oven at
  190°C/375°F/Gas Mark 5 for 30–40
minutes, until golden brown and the cheese topping is hot and bubbling. Garnish with fresh basil leaves, if liked, and serve hot.

VARIATION

Try substituting smoked Bavarian cheese for the Mozzarella or halloumi and grated Cheddar cheese for the Parmesan, for a slightly different but just as delicious flavour.

Aubergine (Eggplant) & Pasta

Prepare the marinated aubergines well in advance so that all you have to do is cook the pasta.

12¼ HOURS   15 MINS

SERVES 4

I N G R E D I E N T S

150 ml/¼ pint/⅝ cup vegetable stock

150 ml/¼ pint/⅝ cup white wine vinegar

2 tsp balsamic vinegar

3 tbsp olive oil

fresh oregano sprig

450 g/1 lb aubergine (eggplant), peeled and
    thinly sliced

400 g/14 oz dried linguine

M A R I N A D E

2 tbsp extra virgin oil

2 garlic cloves, crushed

2 tbsp chopped fresh oregano

2 tbsp finely chopped roasted almonds

2 tbsp diced red (bell) pepper

2 tbsp lime juice

grated rind and juice of 1 orange

salt and pepper

1 Put the vegetable stock, wine vinegar and balsamic vinegar into a saucepan and bring to the boil over a low heat. Add 2 tsp of the olive oil and the sprig of oregano and simmer gently for about 1 minute.

2 Add the aubergine (eggplant) slices to the pan, remove from the heat and set aside for 10 minutes.

3 Meanwhile make the marinade. Combine the oil, garlic, fresh oregano, almonds, (bell) pepper, lime juice, orange rind and juice together in a large bowl and season to taste.

4 Carefully remove the aubergine (eggplant) from the saucepan with a slotted spoon, and drain well. Add the aubergine (eggplant) slices to the marinade, mixing well, and set aside in the refrigerator for about 12 hours.

5 Bring a large pan of lightly salted water to the boil. Add half of the remaining oil and the linguine and cook for 8–10 minutes until just tender. Drain the pasta thoroughly and toss with the remaining oil while still warm. Arrange the pasta on a serving plate with the aubergine (eggplant) slices and the marinade and serve.

Tricolour Timballini

An unusual way of serving pasta, these cheese moulds (molds) are excellent with a crunchy salad for a light lunch.

NUTRITIONAL INFORMATION

Calories 529   Sugars 7g
Protein . . . . .18g   Fat 29g
Carbohydrate . . .46g   Saturates 12g

🍴 🍴 🍴 🍴

30 MINS   1 HOUR

SERVES 4

I N G R E D I E N T S

15 g/½ oz/1 tbsp butter, softened

60 g/2 oz/1 cup dried white breadcrumbs

175 g/6 oz dried tricolour spaghetti, broken
   into 5 cm/2 inch lengths

3 tbsp olive oil

300 ml/½ pint/1¼ cups Béchamel Sauce
   (see page 28)

1 egg yolk

125 g/4½ oz/1 cup grated Gruyère (Swiss)
   cheese

1 onion, finely chopped

1 bay leaf

150 ml/¼ pint/⅔ cup dry white wine

150 ml/¼ pint/⅔ cup passata (sieved
   tomatoes)

1 tbsp tomato purée (paste)

salt and pepper

fresh basil leaves, to garnish

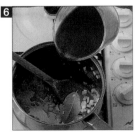

1 Grease four 180 ml/6 fl oz/¾ cup moulds (molds) or ramekins with the butter. Evenly coat the insides with half of the breadcrumbs.

2 Bring a pan of lightly salted water to the boil. Add the spaghetti and 1 tbsp oil and cook for 8–10 minutes or until just tender. Drain and transfer to a mixing bowl. Add the egg yolk and cheese to the pasta and season.

3 Pour the Béchamel Sauce into the bowl containing the pasta and mix. Spoon the mixture into the ramekins and sprinkle over the remaining breadcrumbs.

4 Stand the ramekins on a baking tray (cookie sheet) and bake in a preheated oven at 220°C/425°F/Gas Mark 7 for 20 minutes. Set aside for 10 minutes.

5 Meanwhile, make the sauce. Heat the remaining oil in a pan and gently fry the onion and bay leaf for 2-3 minutes.

6 Stir in the wine, passata (sieved tomatoes) and tomato purée (paste) and season with salt and pepper to taste. Simmer for 20 minutes, until thickened. Remove and discard the bay leaf.

7 Turn the timballini out on to serving plates, garnish with the basil leaves and serve with the tomato sauce.

Baked Tuna & Ricotta Rigatoni

Ribbed tubes of pasta are filled with tuna and ricotta cheese and then baked in a creamy sauce.

NUTRITIONAL INFORMATION

Calories	949	Sugars	.........5g
Protein	........51g	Fat	..........48g
Carbohydrate	...85g	Saturates	......26g

10 MINS   45 MINS

SERVES 4

INGREDIENTS

butter, for greasing

450 g/1 lb dried rigatoni

1 tbsp olive oil

200 g /7 oz can flaked tuna, drained

225 g/ 8 oz ricotta cheese

125 ml/4 fl oz/ ½ cup double (heavy) cream

225 g/8 oz/2 ⅔ cups grated
   Parmesan cheese

125 g/4 oz sun-dried tomatoes, drained
   and sliced

salt and pepper

1 Lightly grease a large ovenproof dish with butter.

2 Bring a large saucepan of lightly salted water to the boil. Add the rigatoni and olive oil and cook for 8–10 minutes until just tender, but still firm to the bite. Drain the pasta and set aside until cool enough to handle.

3 Meanwhile, in a bowl, mix together the tuna and ricotta cheese to form a soft paste. Spoon the mixture into a piping bag and use to fill the rigatoni. Arrange the filled pasta tubes side by side in the prepared ovenproof dish.

4 To make the sauce, mix the cream and Parmesan cheese and season with salt and pepper to taste. Spoon the sauce over the rigatoni and top with the sun-dried tomatoes, arranged in a criss-cross pattern. Bake in a preheated oven at 200°C/400°F/Gas Mark 6 for 20 minutes. Serve hot straight from the dish.

VARIATION

For a vegetarian alternative of this recipe, simply substitute a mixture of stoned (pitted) and chopped black olives and chopped walnuts for the tuna. Follow exactly the same cooking method.

Pancakes with Smoked Fish

These are delicious as a starter or light supper dish
and you can vary the filling with whichever fish you prefer.

NUTRITIONAL INFORMATION

Calories	399	Sugars	.........6g
Protein	........36g	Fat	........18g
Carbohydrate	...25g	Saturates	......10g

15 MINS   1 HR 20 MINS

Makes 12 pancakes

I N G R E D I E N T S

PANCAKES

100 g/3 ½ oz flour

½ tsp salt

1 egg, beaten

300 ml/ ½ pint/1 ¼ cups milk

1 tbsp oil, for frying

SAUCE

450 g/1 lb smoked haddock, skinned

300 ml/ ½ pint/1 ¼ cups milk

40 g/1 ½ oz/3 tbsp butter or margarine

40 g/1 ½ oz flour

300 ml/ ½ pint/1 ¼ cups fish stock

75 g/2 ¾ oz Parmesan cheese, grated

100 g/3 ½ oz frozen peas, defrosted

100 g/3 ½ oz prawns (shrimp), cooked
   and peeled

50 g/1 ¾ oz Gruyère cheese, grated

salt and pepper

1 To make the pancake batter, sift the flour and salt into a large bowl and make a well in the centre. Add the egg and, using a wooden spoon, begin to draw in the flour. Slowly add the milk and beat together to form a smooth batter. Set aside until required.

2 Place the fish in a large frying pan (skillet), add the milk and bring to the boil. Simmer for 10 minutes or until the fish begins to flake. Drain thoroughly, reserving the milk.

3 Melt the butter in a saucepan. Add the flour, mix to a paste and cook for 2–3 minutes. Remove the pan from the heat and add the reserved milk a little at a time, stirring to make a smooth sauce. Repeat with the fish stock. Return to the heat and bring to the boil, stirring. Stir in the Parmesan and season with salt and pepper to taste.

4 Grease a frying pan (skillet) with oil. Add 2 tablespoons of the pancake batter, swirling it around the pan and cook for 2–3 minutes. Loosen the sides with a palette knife (spatula) and flip over the pancake. Cook for 2–3 minutes until golden; repeat. Stack the pancakes with sheets of baking parchment between them and keep warm in the oven.

5 Stir the flaked fish, peas and prawns (shrimp) into half of the sauce and use to fill each pancake. Pour over the remaining sauce, top with the Gruyère and bake for 20 minutes until golden.

Pasta & Anchovy Sauce

This is an ideal dish for cooks in a hurry, as it is prepared in minutes from store-cupboard ingredients.

NUTRITIONAL INFORMATION

Calories 712   Sugars 4g
Protein ....25g   Fat 34g
Carbohydrate ...81g   Saturates 8g

 10 MINS   25 MINS

SERVES 4

INGREDIENTS

90 ml/3 fl oz olive oil

2 garlic cloves, crushed

60 g/2 oz can anchovy fillets, drained

450 g/1 lb dried spaghetti

60 g/2 oz Pesto Sauce (see page 39)

2 tbsp finely chopped fresh oregano

90 g/3 oz/1 cup grated Parmesan cheese,
   plus extra for serving (optional)

salt and pepper

2 fresh oregano sprigs, to garnish

1 Reserve 1 tbsp of the oil and heat the remainder in a small saucepan. Add the garlic and fry for 3 minutes.

2 Lower the heat, stir in the anchovies and cook, stirring occasionally, until the anchovies have disintegrated.

3 Bring a large saucepan of lightly salted water to the boil. Add the spaghetti and the remaining olive oil and cook for 8–10 minutes or until just tender, but still firm to the bite.

4 Add the Pesto Sauce (see page 39) and chopped fresh oregano to the anchovy mixture and then season with pepper to taste.

5 Drain the spaghetti, using a slotted spoon, and transfer to a warm serving dish. Pour the Pesto Sauce over the spaghetti and then sprinkle over the grated Parmesan cheese.

6 Garnish with oregano sprigs and serve with extra cheese, if using.

COOK'S TIP

If you find canned anchovies rather too salty, soak them in a saucer of cold milk for 5 minutes, drain and pat dry with kitchen paper (kitchen towels) before using. The milk absorbs the salt.

Roasted Seafood

Vegetables become deliciously sweet and juicy when they are roasted, and they go particularly well with fish and seafood.

NUTRITIONAL INFORMATION

Calories 280	Sugars 5g	
Protein 15g	Fat 12g	
Carbohydrate ...28g	Saturates 2g	

  15 MINS   50 MINS

SERVES 4

I N G R E D I E N T S

600 g/1 lb 5 oz new potatoes

3 red onions, cut into wedges

2 courgettes (zucchini), sliced into chunks

8 garlic cloves, peeled

2 lemons, cut into wedges

4 sprigs rosemary

4 tbsp olive oil

350 g/12 oz shell-on prawns (shrimp),
    preferably uncooked

2 small squid, chopped into rings

4 tomatoes, quartered

1 Scrub the potatoes to remove any excess dirt. Cut any large potatoes in half. Place the potatoes in a large roasting tin (pan), together with the onions, courgettes (zucchini), garlic, lemon and rosemary sprigs.

VARIATION

Most vegetables are suitable for roasting in the oven. Try adding 450 g/1 lb pumpkin, squash or aubergine (eggplant), if you prefer.

2 Pour over the oil and toss to coat all of the vegetables in the oil. Cook in a preheated oven, at 200°C/400°F/Gas Mark 6, for 40 minutes, turning occasionally, until the potatoes are tender.

3 Once the potatoes are tender, add the prawns (shrimp), squid and tomatoes, tossing to coat them in the oil, and roast

for 10 minutes. All of the vegetables should be cooked through and slightly charred for full flavour.

4 Transfer the roasted seafood and vegetables to warm serving plates and serve hot.

Penne with Fried Mussels

This is quick and simple, but one of the nicest of Italian fried fish dishes, served with penne.

NUTRITIONAL INFORMATION

Calories 537   Sugars 2g
Protein . . . . .22g   Fat 24g
Carbohydrate . . .62g   Saturates 3g

10 MINS   25 MINS

SERVES 6

I N G R E D I E N T S

400 g/14 oz/3 ½ cups dried penne

125 ml/4 fl oz/ ½ cup olive oil

450 g/1 lb mussels, cooked and shelled

1 tsp sea salt

90 g/3 oz/⅔ cup flour

100 g/3 ½ oz sun-dried tomatoes, sliced

2 tbsp chopped fresh basil leaves

salt and pepper

1 lemon, thinly sliced, to garnish

1 Bring a large saucepan of lightly salted water to the boil. Add the penne and 1 tbsp of the olive oil and cook for 8–10 minutes or until the pasta is just tender, but still firm to the bite.

2 Drain the pasta thoroughly and place in a large, warm serving dish. Set aside and keep warm while you cook the mussels.

3 Lightly sprinkle the mussels with the sea salt. Season the flour with salt and pepper to taste, sprinkle into a bowl and toss the mussels in the flour until well coated.

4 Heat the remaining oil in a large frying pan (skillet). Add the mussels and fry, stirring frequently, until a golden brown colour.

5 Toss the mussels with the penne and sprinkle with the sun-dried tomatoes and basil leaves. Garnish with slices of lemon and serve immediately.

COOK'S TIP

Sun-dried tomatoes, used in Italy for a long time, have become popular elsewhere only quite recently. They are dried and then preserved in oil. They have a concentrated, roasted flavour and a dense texture. They should be drained and chopped or sliced before using.

Potatoes, Olives & Anchovies

This side dish makes a delicious accompaniment for grilled (broiled) fish or for lamb chops. The fennel adds a subtle aniseed flavour.

NUTRITIONAL INFORMATION

Calories	202	Sugars	.........2g
Protein	.........7g	Fat	..........12g
Carbohydrate	...19g	Saturates	.......1g

 10 MINS   30 MINS

SERVES 4

INGREDIENTS

450 g/1 lb baby new potatoes, scrubbed

2 tbsp olive oil

2 fennel bulbs, trimmed and sliced

2 sprigs rosemary, stalks removed

75 g/2¾ oz mixed olives

8 canned anchovy fillets, drained and
  chopped

1 Bring a large saucepan of water to the boil and cook the potatoes for 8–10 minutes or until tender. Remove the potatoes from the saucepan using a perforated spoon and set aside to cool slightly.

2 Once the potatoes are just cool enough to handle, cut them into wedges, using a sharp knife.

3 Pit the mixed olives and cut them in half, using a sharp knife.

4 Using a sharp knife, chop the anchovy fillets into smaller strips.

5 Heat the oil in a large frying pan (skillet). Add the potato wedges, sliced fennel and rosemary. Cook for 7–8 minutes or until the potatoes are golden.

6 Stir in the olives and anchovies and cook for 1 minute or until completely warmed through.

7 Transfer to serving plates and serve immediately.

COOK'S TIP

Fresh rosemary is a particular favourite with Italians, but you can experiment with your favourite herbs in this recipe, if you prefer.

Mozzarella Snack

These deep-fried Mozzarella sandwiches are a tasty snack at any time of the day, or serve smaller triangles as an antipasto with drinks.

NUTRITIONAL INFORMATION

Calories 379	Sugars 4g
Protein 20g	Fat 22g
Carbohydrate . . .28g	Saturates 5g

20 MINS   5–10 MINS

SERVES 4

I N G R E D I E N T S

8 slices bread, preferably slightly stale, crusts removed

100 g/3 ½ oz Mozzarella cheese, sliced thickly

50 g/1 ¾ oz black olives, chopped

8 canned anchovy fillets, drained and chopped

16 fresh basil leaves

4 eggs, beaten

150 ml/5 floz/⅔ cup milk

oil, for deep-frying

salt and pepper

1 Cut each slice of bread into 2 triangles. Top 8 of the bread triangles with the Mozzarella slices, olives and chopped anchovies.

2 Place the basil leaves on top and season with salt and pepper to taste.

3 Lay the other 8 triangles of bread over the top and press down round the edges to seal.

4 Mix the eggs and milk and pour into an ovenproof dish. Add the sandwiches and leave to soak for about 5 minutes.

5 Heat the oil in a large saucepan to 180°–190°C/350°–375°F or until a cube of bread browns in 30 seconds.

6 Before cooking the sandwiches, squeeze the edges together again.

7 Carefully place the sandwiches in the oil and deep-fry for 2 minutes or until golden, turning once. Remove the sandwiches with a perforated spoon and drain on absorbent kitchen paper. Serve immediately while still hot.

Spinach & Anchovy Pasta

This colourful light meal can be made with a variety of different pasta, including spaghetti and linguine.

NUTRITIONAL INFORMATION

Calories	.619	Sugars	.5g
Protein	.21g	Fat	.31g
Carbohydrate	...67g	Saturates	.3g

 10 MINS   25 MINS

SERVES 4

I N G R E D I E N T S

900 g/2 lb fresh, young spinach leaves

400 g/14 oz dried fettuccine

6 tbsp olive oil

3 tbsp pine nuts (kernels)

3 garlic cloves, crushed

8 canned anchovy fillets, drained and
   chopped

salt

1 Trim off any tough spinach stalks. Rinse the spinach leaves and place them in a large saucepan with only the water that is clinging to them after washing. Cover and cook over a high heat, shaking the pan from time, until the spinach has wilted, but retains its colour. Drain well, set aside and keep warm.

COOK'S TIP

If you are in a hurry, you can use frozen spinach. Thaw and drain it thoroughly, pressing out as much moisture as possible. Cut the leaves into strips and add to the dish with the anchovies in step 4.

2 Bring a large saucepan of lightly salted water to the boil. Add the fettuccine and 1 tablespoon of the oil and cook for 8–10 minutes until it is just tender, but still firm to the bite.

3 Heat 4 tablespoons of the remaining oil in a saucepan. Add the pine kernels (nuts) and fry until golden. Remove the pine kernels (nuts) from the pan and set aside until required.

4 Add the garlic to the pan and fry until golden. Add the anchovies and stir in the spinach. Cook, stirring, for 2-3 minutes, until heated through. Return the pine nuts (kernels) to the pan.

5 Drain the fettuccine, toss in the remaining olive oil and transfer to a warm serving dish. Spoon the anchovy and spinach sauce over the fettuccine, toss lightly and serve immediately.

Ciabatta Rolls

Sandwiches are always a welcome snack, but can be mundane. These crisp rolls filled with roast (bell) peppers and cheese are irresistible.

NUTRITIONAL INFORMATION

Calories	328	Sugars	........6g
Protein	.........8g	Fat	..........19g
Carbohydrate	...34g	Saturates	.......9g

15 MINS   10 MINS

SERVES 4

I N G R E D I E N T S

4 ciabatta rolls

2 tbsp olive oil

1 garlic clove, crushed

F I L L I N G

1 red (bell) pepper

1 green (bell) pepper

1 yellow (bell) pepper

4 radishes, sliced

1 bunch watercress

100 g/3½ oz/8 tbsp cream cheese

1 Slice the ciabatta rolls in half. Heat the olive oil and crushed garlic in a saucepan. Pour the garlic and oil mixture over the cut surfaces of the rolls and leave to stand.

2 Halve the (bell) peppers and place, skin side uppermost, on a grill (broiler) rack. Cook under a hot grill (broiler) for 8–10 minutes, until just beginning to char. Remove the (bell) peppers from the grill (broiler), peel and slice thinly.

3 Arrange the radish slices on one half of each roll with a few watercress leaves. Spoon the cream cheese on top. Pile the (bell) peppers on top of the cream cheese and top with the other half of the roll. Serve immediately.

Baked Aubergines (Eggplants)

This delicious recipe is from Parma. Ensure that you simmer the tomato sauce gently to reduce it slightly before using.

NUTRITIONAL INFORMATION

Calories 578	Sugars 22g	
Protein 17g	Fat 43g	
Carbohydrate ...25g	Saturates 13g	

 15 MINS   1¼ HOURS

SERVES 4

INGREDIENTS

4 aubergines (eggplants), trimmed

3 tbsp olive oil

2 x 150g/5½ oz packets Mozzarella, thinly sliced

4 slices Parma ham (prosciutto), shredded

1 tbsp chopped fresh marjoram

1 tbsp chopped fresh basil

½ quantity Béchamel Sauce (see page 28)

25 g/1 oz/¼ cup Parmesan, grated

salt and pepper

TOMATO SAUCE

4 tbsp olive oil

1 large onion, sliced

4 garlic cloves, crushed

400 g/14 oz can chopped tomatoes

450 g/1 lb fresh tomatoes, peeled and chopped

4 tbsp chopped fresh parsley

600 ml/1 pint/2½ cups hot vegetable stock

1 tbsp sugar

2 tbsp lemon juice

150 ml/¼ pint/⅔ cup dry white wine

salt and pepper

1 To make the Tomato Sauce, heat the oil in a large pan. Fry the onion and garlic until just beginning to soften. Add the canned and fresh tomatoes, parsley, stock, sugar and lemon juice. Cover and simmer for 15 minutes. Stir in the wine and season.

2 Slice the aubergines (eggplant) thinly lengthways. Bring a large saucepan of water to the boil and cook the aubergine (eggplant) slices for 5 minutes. Drain the aubergine (eggplant) slices on paper towels and pat dry.

3 Pour half of the fresh tomato sauce into a large, greased ovenproof dish. Cover with half of the cooked aubergines (eggplants) and drizzle with a little oil. Cover with half of the Mozzarella, Parma ham (prosciutto) and herbs. Season with salt and pepper to taste.

4 Repeat the layers and cover with the Béchamel Sauce. Sprinkle with the Parmesan. Bake in a preheated oven, 190°C/375°F/Gas Mark 5, for 35–40 minutes until golden on top. Serve.

Chorizo & Mushroom Pasta

Simple and quick to make, this spicy dish is sure to set the taste buds tingling.

NUTRITIONAL INFORMATION

Calories	495	Sugars	.........1g
Protein	........15g	Fat	..........35g
Carbohydrate	...33g	Saturates	.......5g

 5 MINS   🕐 20 MINS

SERVES 6

I N G R E D I E N T S

680 g/1 ½ lb dried vermicelli

125 ml/4 fl oz/½ cup olive oil

2 garlic cloves

125 g/4 ½ oz chorizo, sliced

225 g/8 oz wild mushrooms

3 fresh red chillies, chopped

2 tbsp freshly grated Parmesan cheese

salt and pepper

10 anchovy fillets, to garnish

1 Bring a large saucepan of lightly salted water to the boil. Add the vermicelli and 1 tablespoon of the oil and cook for 8–10 minutes or until just tender, but still firm to the bite.

2 Drain the pasta thoroughly, place on a large, warm serving plate and keep warm.

3 Meanwhile, heat the remaining oil in a large frying pan (skillet). Add the garlic and fry for 1 minute.

4 Add the chorizo and wild mushrooms and cook for 4 minutes,

5 Add the chopped chillies and cook for 1 further minute.

6 Pour the chorizo and wild mushroom mixture over the vermicelli and season with a little salt and pepper.

7 Sprinkle with freshly grated Parmesan cheese, garnish with a lattice of anchovy fillets and serve immediately.

COOK'S TIP

Many varieties of mushrooms are now cultivated and most are indistinguishable from the wild varieties. Mixed colour oyster mushrooms have been used here, but you could also use chanterelles. Remember that chanterelles shrink during cooking, so you may need more.

Pan Bagna

This is a deliciously moist picnic dish, lunch dish or snack. It was originally designed for workers to take to the fields in a box.

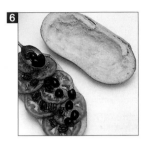

NUTRITIONAL INFORMATION

Calories	377	Sugars	.........3g
Protein	........20g	Fat	..........25g
Carbohydrate	...19g	Saturates	.......6g

 2½ HOURS   30 MINS

SERVES 4

INGREDIENTS

1 red (bell) pepper, halved, cored and
   deseeded

225 g/8 oz sirloin steak, 2.5 cm/1 inch thick

1 small white bloomer loaf or French stick

4 tbsp olive oil

2 extra-large tomatoes, sliced

10 black olives, halved

½ cucumber, peeled and sliced

6 anchovies, chopped

salt and pepper

1 Cook the (bell) pepper over a hot barbecue (grill) for 15 minutes, turning once. Put the (bell) pepper into a plastic bag and seal.

2 Meanwhile, sear both sides of the steak first and then grill for 8 minutes, turning once.

3 When the (bell) pepper is cool enough to handle, peel and slice it.

4 Using a sharp knife, cut the steak into thin strips.

5 Cut the loaf of bread lengthways and hollow out each half, leaving a 2.5 cm/1 inch crust. Brush both halves very liberally with olive oil.

6 Lay the tomatoes, olives, cucumber, steak strips, anchovies and red (bell) pepper strips on the bottom half. Season with salt and pepper to taste and cover with the top half.

7 Put the Pan Bagna on top of a piece of greaseproof paper (baking parchment). Squash the whole loaf and its filling down well and wrap tightly in cling film (plastic wrap). Secure with adhesive tape if necessary. Chill for at least 2 hours. If made in the morning, by lunchtime it will be ready to eat and all the flavours will have combined.

VARIATION

Different fillings, such as pâtés, sausages and other salad items, can be used according to appetite and taste. Mozzarella cheese is good, as it is so moist. Onions give a bit of a zing to the other ingredients.

Pasta with Bacon & Tomatoes

As this dish cooks, the mouth-watering aroma of bacon, sweet tomatoes and oregano is a feast in itself.

NUTRITIONAL INFORMATION

Calories . . . . .431 Sugars 8g
Protein . . . . .10g Fat 29g
Carbohydrate . . .34g Saturates 14g

10 MINS   35 MINS

SERVES 4

INGREDIENTS

900 g/2 lb small, sweet tomatoes

6 slices rindless smoked bacon

60 g/2 oz/4 tbsp butter

1 onion, chopped

1 garlic clove, crushed

4 fresh oregano sprigs, finely chopped

450 g/1 lb/4 cups dried orecchiette

1 tbsp olive oil

salt and pepper

freshly grated Pecorino cheese, to serve

1 Blanch the tomatoes in boiling water. Drain, skin and seed the tomatoes, then roughly chop the flesh.

2 Using a sharp knife, chop the bacon into small dice.

3 Melt the butter in a saucepan. Add the bacon and fry until it is golden.

4 Add the onion and garlic and fry over a medium heat for 5-7 minutes, until just softened.

5 Add the tomatoes and oregano to the pan and then season to taste with salt and pepper. Lower the heat and simmer for 10-12 minutes.

6 Bring a large pan of lightly salted water to the boil. Add the orecchiette and oil and cook for 12 minutes, until just tender, but still firm to the bite. Drain the pasta and transfer to a warm serving dish or bowl.

7 Spoon the bacon and tomato sauce over the pasta, toss to coat and serve with the cheese.

COOK'S TIP

For an authentic Italian flavour use pancetta, rather than ordinary bacon. This kind of bacon is streaked with fat and adds rich undertones of flavour to many traditional dishes. It is available both smoked and unsmoked from large supermarkets and Italian delicatessens.

Italian Platter

This popular hors d'oeuvre usually consists of vegetables soaked in olive oil and rich, creamy cheeses. Try this great low-fat version.

NUTRITIONAL INFORMATION

Calories ....198 Sugars 12g
Protein ....12g Fat 6g
Carbohydrate ...25g Saturates 3g

 10 MINS   0 MINS

SERVES 4

INGREDIENTS

125 g/4½ oz reduced-fat Mozzarella
   cheese, drained

60 g/2 oz lean Parma ham (prosciutto)

400 g/14 oz can artichoke hearts, drained

4 ripe figs

1 small mango

few plain Grissini (bread sticks), to serve

DRESSING

1 small orange

1 tbsp passata (sieved tomatoes)

1 tsp wholegrain mustard

4 tbsp low-fat natural (unsweetened) yogurt

fresh basil leaves

salt and pepper

1 Cut the cheese into 12 sticks, 6.5 cm/2½ inches long. Remove the fat from the ham and slice the meat into 12 strips. Carefully wrap a strip of ham around each stick of cheese and arrange neatly on a serving platter.

2 Halve the artichoke hearts and cut the figs into quarters. Arrange them on the serving platter in groups.

3 Peel the mango, then slice it down each side of the large, flat central stone. Slice the flesh into strips and arrange them so that they form a fan shape on the serving platter.

4 To make the dressing, pare the rind from half of the orange using a vegetable peeler. Cut the rind into small strips and place them in a bowl. Extract the juice from the orange and add it to the bowl containing the rind.

5 Add the passata (sieved tomatoes), mustard, yogurt and seasoning to the bowl and mix together. Shred the basil leaves and mix them into the dressing.

6 Spoon the dressing into a small dish and serve with the Italian Platter, accompanied with bread sticks.

VARIATION

For a change, serve with a French stick or an Italian bread, widely available from supermarkets, and use to mop up the delicious dressing.

Pancetta & Pecorino Cakes

This makes an excellent light meal when served with a topping of pesto or anchovy sauce.

NUTRITIONAL INFORMATION

Calories	.619	Sugars	.4g
Protein	.22g	Fat	.29g
Carbohydrate	.71g	Saturates	.8g

 20 MINS   25 MINS

SERVES 4

INGREDIENTS

25 g/1 oz/2 tbsp butter, plus extra for
　greasing

100 g/3 ½ oz pancetta, rind removed

225 g/8 oz/2 cups self-raising
　(self-rising) flour

75 g/2 ¾ oz/ ⅞ cup grated pecorino cheese

150 ml/ ¼ pint/ ⅝ cup milk, plus extra
　for glazing

1 tbsp tomato ketchup

1 tsp Worcestershire sauce

400 g/14 oz/3 ½ cups dried farfalle

1 tbsp olive oil

salt and pepper

3 tbsp Pesto (see page 39) or anchovy
　sauce (optional)

green salad, to serve

1 Grease a baking tray (cookie sheet) with butter. Grill (broil) the pancetta until it is cooked. Allow the pancetta to cool, then chop finely.

2 Sift together the flour and a pinch of salt into a mixing bowl. Add the butter and rub in with your fingertips. When the butter and flour have been thoroughly incorporated, add the pancetta and one-third of the grated cheese.

3 Mix together the milk, tomato ketchup and Worcestershire sauce and add to the dry ingredients, mixing to make a soft dough.

4 Roll out the dough on a lightly floured board to make an 18 cm/7 inch round. Brush with a little milk to glaze and cut into 8 wedges.

5 Arrange the dough wedges on the prepared baking tray (cookie sheet)

and sprinkle over the remaining cheese. Bake in a preheated oven at 200°C/ 400°F/Gas Mark 6 for 20 minutes.

6 Meanwhile, bring a saucepan of lightly salted water to the boil. Add the farfalle and the oil and cook for 8–10 minutes until just tender, but still firm to the bite. Drain and transfer to a large serving dish. Top with the pancetta and pecorino cakes. Serve with the sauce of your choice and a green salad.

Mozzarella & Ham Snack

A delicious way of serving Mozzarella – the cheese stretches out into melted strings as you cut into the bread.

 15 MINS   40 MINS

SERVES 4

INGREDIENTS

200 g/7 oz Mozzarella

4 slices, Parma ham (prosciutto),
  about 90 g/3 oz

8 two-day old slices white bread,
  crusts removed

butter, for spreading

2–3 eggs

3 tbsp milk

vegetable oil, for deep-frying

salt and pepper

TOMATO & (BELL) PEPPER SAUCE

1 onion, chopped

2 garlic cloves, crushed

3 tbsp olive oil

1 red (bell) pepper, cored, deseeded
  and chopped

400 g/14 oz can peeled tomatoes

2 tbsp tomato purée (paste)

3 tbsp water

1 tbsp lemon juice

salt and pepper

flat-leaf parsley, to garnish (optional)

1 To make the sauce, fry the onion and garlic in the oil until soft. Add the (bell) pepper and continue to cook for a few minutes. Add the tomatoes, tomato purée (paste), water, lemon juice and seasoning. Bring to the boil, cover and simmer for 10–15 minutes or until tender. Cool the sauce a little, then purée or liquidize until smooth and return to a clean pan.

2 Cut the Mozzarella into 4 slices as large as possible; if the cheese is a square piece cut into 8 slices. Trim the Parma ham (prosciutto) slices to the same size as the cheese.

3 Lightly butter the bread and use the cheese and ham to make 4 sandwiches, pressing the edges firmly together. If liked, they may be cut in half at this stage. Cover with cling film (plastic wrap) and chill.

4 Lightly beat the eggs with the milk and seasoning in a shallow dish. Dip the sandwiches in the egg mixture until well coated, and leave to soak for a few minutes.

5 Heat the oil to 180°–190°C/350°–375°F, or until a cube of bread browns in 30 seconds. Fry the sandwiches in batches until golden on both sides. Drain and keep warm. Serve with the reheated tomato and (bell) pepper sauce, and garnish with parsley.

Smoked Ham Linguini

Served with freshly-made Italian bread or tossed with pesto, this makes a mouth-watering light lunch.

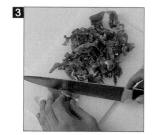

NUTRITIONAL INFORMATION

Calories 537	Sugars 4g
Protein 22g	Fat 29g
Carbohydrate 71g	Saturates 8g

 25 MINS   15 MINS

SERVES 4

I N G R E D I E N T S

450 g/1 lb dried linguini

450 g/1 lb green broccoli florets

225 g/8 oz Italian smoked ham

150 ml/¼ pint/⅝ cup Italian Cheese Sauce
  (see page 30)

salt and pepper

Italian bread, such as ciabatta or focaccia,
  to serve

1 Bring a large saucepan pan of lightly salted water to the boil. Add the linguini and broccoli florets and cook for about 10 minutes, or until the linguini is tender, but still firm to the bite.

2 Drain the linguini and broccoli thoroughly, set aside and keep warm until required.

3 Cut the Italian smoked ham into thin strips.

4 Toss the linguini, broccoli and ham into the Italian Cheese Sauce and gently warm through over a very low heat.

5 Transfer the pasta mixture to a warm serving dish. Sprinkle with pepper and serve with Italian bread.

COOK'S TIP

There are many types of Italian bread which would be suitable to serve with this dish. Ciabatta is made with olive oil and is available plain and with different ingredients, such as olives or sun-dried tomatoes.

Fish & Seafood

Italians eat everything that comes out of the sea, from the smallest whitebait to the massive tuna fish. Fish markets in Italy are fascinating, with a huge variety of fish on

display, but as most of the fish comes from the Mediterranean it is not always easy to find an equivalent elsewhere. However, fresh or frozen imported fish of all kinds is increasingly appearing in

fishmongers and supermarkets. After pasta, fish is probably the most important source of food in Italy, and in many recipes fish or seafood are served with one type of pasta or another – a winning combination!

Orange Mackerel

Mackerel can be quite rich, but when it is stuffed with oranges and toasted ground almonds it is tangy and light.

NUTRITIONAL INFORMATION

Calories 623	Sugars 7g	
Protein 42g	Fat 47g	
Carbohydrate 8g	Saturates 8g	

🍤 15 MINS   🕐 35 MINS

SERVES 4

INGREDIENTS

2 tbsp oil

4 spring onions (scallions), chopped

2 oranges

50 g/1¾ oz ground almonds

1 tbsp oats

50 g/1¾ oz mixed green and black olives,
   pitted and chopped

8 mackerel fillets

salt and pepper

crisp salad, to serve

1 Heat the oil in a frying pan (skillet). Add the spring onions (scallions) and cook for 2 minutes.

2 Finely grate the rind of the oranges, then, using a sharp knife, cut away the remaining skin and white pith.

3 Using a sharp knife, segment the oranges by cutting down either side of the lines of pith to loosen each segment. Do this over a plate so that you can reserve any juices. Cut each orange segment in half.

4 Lightly toast the almonds, under a preheated grill (broiler), for 2–3 minutes or until golden; watch them carefully as they brown very quickly.

5 Mix the spring onions (scallions), oranges, ground almonds, oats and olives together in a bowl and season to taste with salt and pepper.

6 Spoon the orange mixture along the centre of each fillet. Roll up each fillet, securing it in place with a cocktail stick (toothpick) or skewer.

7 Bake in a preheated oven at 190°C/375°F/Gas Mark 5 for 25 minutes until the fish is tender.

8 Transfer to serving plates and serve warm with a salad.

Marinated Fish

Marinating fish, for even a short period, adds a subtle flavour to the flesh and makes even simply grilled (broiled) or fried fish delicious.

NUTRITIONAL INFORMATION

Calories 361	Sugars 0g	
Protein 26g	Fat 29g	
Carbohydrate 0g	Saturates 5g	

 45 MINS   15 MINS

SERVES 4

I N G R E D I E N T S

4 whole mackerel, cleaned and gutted

4 tbsp chopped marjoram

2 tbsp extra virgin olive oil

finely grated rind and juice of 1 lime

2 garlic cloves, crushed

salt and pepper

1 Under gently running water, scrape the mackerel with the blunt side of a knife to remove any scales.

2 Using a sharp knife, make a slit in the stomach of the fish and cut horizontally along until the knife will go no further very easily. Gut the fish and rinse under water. You may prefer to remove the heads before cooking, but it is not necessary.

3 Using a sharp knife, cut 4–5 diagonal slashes on each side of the fish. Place the fish in a shallow, non-metallic dish.

4 To make the marinade, mix together the marjoram, olive oil, lime rind and juice, garlic and salt and pepper in a bowl.

5 Pour the mixture over the fish. Leave to marinate in the refrigerator for about 30 minutes.

6 Cook the mackerel, under a preheated grill (broiler), for 5–6 minutes on each side, brushing occasionally with the reserved marinade, until golden.

7 Transfer the fish to serving plates. Pour over any remaining marinade before serving.

COOK'S TIP

If the lime is too hard to squeeze, microwave on high power for 30 seconds to release the juice. This dish is also excellent cooked on the barbecue (grill).

Sea Bass with Olive Sauce

A favourite fish for chefs, the delicious sea bass is now becoming increasingly common in supermarkets and fish stores for family meals.

NUTRITIONAL INFORMATION

Calories 877   Sugars 3g
Protein ....50g   Fat 47g
Carbohydrate ...67g   Saturates 26g

 10 MINS   30 MINS

SERVES 4

INGREDIENTS

450 g/1 lb dried macaroni

1 tbsp olive oil

8 x 115 g/4 oz sea bass medallions

SAUCE

25 g/1 oz/2 tbsp butter

4 shallots, chopped

2 tbsp capers

175 g/6 oz/1½ cups stoned (pitted) green
   olives, chopped

4 tbsp balsamic vinegar

300 ml/½ pint/1¼ cups fish stock

300 ml/½ pint/1¼ cups double
   (heavy) cream

juice of 1 lemon

salt and pepper

TO GARNISH

lemon slices

shredded leek

shredded carrot

1 To make the sauce, melt the butter in a frying pan (skillet). Add the shallots and cook over a low heat for 4 minutes. Add the capers and olives and cook for a further 3 minutes.

2 Stir in the balsamic vinegar and fish stock, bring to the boil and reduce by half. Add the cream, stirring, and reduce again by half. Season to taste with salt and pepper and stir in the lemon juice. Remove the pan from the heat, set aside and keep warm.

3 Bring a large pan of lightly salted water to the boil. Add the pasta and olive oil and cook for about 12 minutes, until tender but still firm to the bite.

4 Meanwhile, lightly grill (broil) the sea bass medallions for 3–4 minutes on each side, until cooked through, but still moist and delicate.

5 Drain the pasta thoroughly and transfer to large individual serving dishes. Top the pasta with the fish medallions and pour over the olive sauce. Garnish with lemon slices, shredded leek and shredded carrot and serve immediately.

Baked Sea Bass

Sea bass is a delicious white-fleshed fish. If cooking two small fish, they can be grilled (broiled); if cooking one large fish, bake it in the oven.

NUTRITIONAL INFORMATION

Calories 378	Sugars 0g
Protein 62g	Fat 14g
Carbohydrate 0g	Saturates 2g

🕑 15-20 MINS   ⏲ 20-55 MINS

SERVES 4

INGREDIENTS

1.4 kg/3 lb fresh sea bass or

  2 x 750 g/1 lb 10 oz sea bass, gutted

2–4 sprigs fresh rosemary

½ lemon, sliced thinly

2 tbsp olive oil

bay leaves and lemon wedges, to garnish

GARLIC SAUCE

2 tsp coarse sea salt

2 tsp capers

2 garlic cloves, crushed

4 tbsp water

2 fresh bay leaves

1 tsp lemon juice or wine vinegar

2 tbsp olive oil

pepper

1 Scrape off the scales from the fish and cut off the sharp fins. Make diagonal cuts along both sides. Wash and dry thoroughly. Place a sprig of rosemary in the cavity of each of the smaller fish with half the lemon slices; or two sprigs and all the lemon in the large fish.

2 To grill (broil), place in a foil-lined pan, brush with 1–2 tbsp oil and grill (broil) under a moderate heat for 5 minutes each side or until cooked through.

3 To bake: place the fish in a foil-lined dish or roasting tin (pan) brushed with oil, and brush the fish with the rest of the oil. Cook in a preheated oven, 190°C/375°F/ Gas Mark 5, for 30 minutes for the small fish or 45–50 minutes for the large fish, until the thickest part of the fish is opaque.

4 For the sauce: crush the salt and capers with the garlic in a pestle and mortar and then work in the water. Or, work in a food processor or blender until smooth.

5 Bruise the bay leaves and remaining sprigs of rosemary and put in a bowl. Add the garlic mixture, lemon juice or vinegar and oil and pound together until the flavours are released. Season with pepper to taste.

6 Place the fish on a serving dish and, if liked, remove the skin. Spoon some of the sauce over the fish and serve the rest separately. Garnish with fresh bay leaves and lemon wedges.

Salt Cod Fritters

These tasty little fried fish cakes make an excellent snack or main course. Prepare in advance as the salt cod needs to be soaked overnight.

NUTRITIONAL INFORMATION

Calories	142	Sugars	.........2g
Protein	........10g	Fat	..........5g
Carbohydrate	...14g	Saturates	.......1g

30 MINS   45 MINS

SERVES 6

INGREDIENTS

100 g/3½ oz self-raising flour

1 egg, beaten

150 ml/¼ pint/⅔ cup milk

250 g/9 oz salt cod, soaked overnight

1 small red onion, finely chopped

1 small fennel bulb, finely chopped

1 red chilli, finely chopped

2 tbsp oil

TO SERVE

crisp salad and chilli relish, or cooked rice
   and fresh vegetables

1 Sift the flour into a large bowl. Make a well in the centre of the flour and add the egg.

2 Using a wooden spoon, gradually draw in the flour, slowly adding the milk, and mix to form a smooth batter. Leave to stand for 10 minutes.

3 Drain the salt cod and rinse it under cold running water. Drain again thoroughly.

4 Remove and discard the skin and any bones from the fish, then mash the flesh with a fork.

5 Place the fish in a large bowl and combine with the onion, fennel and chilli. Add the mixture to the batter and blend together.

6 Heat the oil in a large frying pan (skillet) and, taking about 1 tablespoon of the mixture at a time, spoon it into the hot oil. Cook the fritters, in batches, for 3–4 minutes on each side until golden and slightly puffed. Keep warm while cooking the remaining mixture.

7 Serve with salad and a chilli relish for a light meal or with vegetables and rice.

COOK'S TIP

If you prefer larger fritters, use 2 tablespoons per fritter and cook for slightly longer.

Celery & Salt Cod Casserole

Salt cod is dried and salted in order to preserve it. It has an unusual flavour, which goes particularly well with celery in this dish.

NUTRITIONAL INFORMATION

Calories 173	Sugars 3g
Protein 14g	Fat 12g
Carbohydrate 3g	Saturates 1g

🍳 25 MINS   🕐 25 MINS

SERVES 4

I N G R E D I E N T S

250 g/9 oz salt cod, soaked overnight

1 tbsp oil

4 shallots, finely chopped

2 garlic cloves, chopped

3 celery sticks, chopped

1 x 400g/14 oz can tomatoes, chopped

150 ml/¼ pint/⅔ cup fish stock

50 g/1¾ oz pine nuts

2 tbsp roughly chopped tarragon

2 tbsp capers

crusty bread or mashed potato, to serve

1 Drain the salt cod, rinse it under plenty of running water and drain again thoroughly. Remove and discard any skin and bones. Pat the fish dry with paper towels and cut it into chunks.

2 Heat the oil in a large frying pan (skillet). Add the shallots and garlic and cook for 2–3 minutes. Add the celery and cook for a further 2 minutes, then add the tomatoes and stock.

3 Bring the mixture to the boil, reduce the heat and leave to simmer for about 5 minutes.

4 Add the fish and cook for 10 minutes or until tender.

5 Meanwhile, place the pine nuts on a baking tray (cookie sheet). Place under a preheated grill (broiler) and toast for 2–3 minutes or until golden.

6 Stir the tarragon, capers and pine nuts into the fish casserole and heat gently to warm through.

7 Transfer to serving plates and serve with lots of fresh crusty bread or mashed potato.

COOK'S TIP

Salt cod is a useful ingredient to keep in the storecupboard and, once soaked, can be used in the same way as any other fish. It does, however, have a stronger, salty flavour than normal. It can be found in fishmongers, larger supermarkets and delicatessens.

Sole Fillets in Marsala

A rich wine and cream sauce makes this an excellent dinner party dish.
Make the stock the day before to cut down on the preparation time.

NUTRITIONAL INFORMATION

Calories 474   Sugars 3g
Protein ....47g   Fat 28g
Carbohydrate ....3g   Saturates 14g

1¼ HOURS   1½ HOURS

SERVES 4

I N G R E D I E N T S

1 tbsp peppercorns, lightly crushed

8 sole fillets

100 ml/3½ fl oz/⅓ cup Marsala

150 ml/¼ pint/⅔ cup double (heavy) cream

STOCK

600 ml/1 pint/2½ cups water

bones and skin from the sole fillets

1 onion, peeled and halved

1 carrot, peeled and halved

3 fresh bay leaves

SAUCE

1 tbsp olive oil

15 g/½ oz/1 tbsp butter

4 shallots, finely chopped

100 g/3½ oz baby button mushrooms,
wiped and halved

1 To make the stock, place the water, fish bones and skin, onion, carrot and bay leaves in a large saucepan and bring to the boil.

2 Reduce the heat and leave the mixture to simmer for 1 hour or until the stock has reduced to about 150 ml/¼ pint/⅔ cup. Drain the stock through a fine sieve (strainer), discarding the bones and vegetables, and set aside.

3 To make the sauce, heat the oil and butter in a frying pan (skillet). Add the shallots and cook, stirring, for 2–3 minutes or until just softened.

4 Add the mushrooms to the frying pan (skillet) and cook, stirring, for a further 2–3 minutes or until they are just beginning to brown.

5 Add the peppercorns and sole fillets to the frying pan (skillet) in batches. Fry the sole fillets for 3–4 minutes on each side or until golden brown. Remove the fish with a perforated spoon, set aside and keep warm while you cook the remainder.

6 When all the fillets have been cooked and removed from the pan, pour the wine and stock into the pan and leave to simmer for 3 minutes. Increase the heat and boil the mixture in the pan for about 5 minutes or until the sauce has reduced and thickened.

7 Pour in the cream and heat through. Pour the sauce over the fish and serve with the cooked vegetables of your choice.

Cannelloni Filetti di Sogliola

This is a lighter dish than the better-known cannelloni stuffed with minced beef.

NUTRITIONAL INFORMATION

Calories 555	Sugars 4g	
Protein 53g	Fat 21g	
Carbohydrate . . .36g	Saturates 12g	

20 MINS   45 MINS

SERVES 6

INGREDIENTS

12 small fillets of sole (115 g/4 oz each)

150 ml/¼ pint/⅝ cup red wine

90 g/3 oz/6 tbsp butter

115 g/4 oz/3⅞ cups sliced button
    mushrooms

4 shallots, finely chopped

115 g/4 oz tomatoes, chopped

2 tbsp tomato purée (paste)

60 g/2 oz/½ cup plain (all purpose)
    flour, sifted

150 ml/¼ pint/⅝ cup warm milk

2 tbsp double (heavy) cream

6 dried cannelloni tubes

175 g/6 oz cooked, peeled prawns (shrimp),
    preferably freshwater

salt and pepper

1 fresh fennel sprig, to garnish

1 Brush the fillets with a little wine, season with salt and pepper and roll them up, skin side inwards. Secure with a skewer or cocktail stick (toothpick).

2 Arrange the fish rolls in a single layer in a large frying pan (skillet), add the remaining red wine and poach for 4 minutes. Remove from the pan; reserve the liquid.

3 Melt the butter in another pan. Fry the mushrooms and shallots for 2 minutes, then add the tomatoes and tomato purée (paste). Season the flour and stir it into the pan. Stir in the reserved cooking liquid and half the milk. Cook over a low heat, stirring, for 4 minutes. Remove from the heat and stir in the cream.

4 Bring a large saucepan of lightly salted water to the boil. Add the cannelloni and cook for about 8 minutes, until tender but still firm to the bite. Drain and set aside to cool.

5 Remove the skewers or cocktail sticks (toothpicks) from the fish rolls. Put 2 sole fillets into each cannelloni tube with 2–3 prawns (shrimp) and a little red wine sauce. Arrange the cannelloni in an ovenproof dish, pour over the sauce and bake in a preheated oven at 200°C/400°F/Gas 6 for 20 minutes.

6 Serve the cannelloni with the red wine sauce, garnished with the remaining prawns (shrimp) and a fresh sprig of fennel.

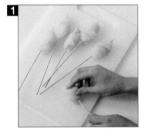

Spaghetti alla Bucaniera

Brill was once known as poor man's turbot, an unfair description as it is a delicately flavoured and delicious fish in its own right.

NUTRITIONAL INFORMATION

Calories	588	Sugars	.........5g
Protein	........36g	Fat	..........18g
Carbohydrate	...68g	Saturates	.......9g

 25 MINS 50 MINS

SERVES 4

I N G R E D I E N T S

90 g/3 oz/¾ cup plain (all-purpose) flour

450 g/1 lb brill or sole fillets,
   skinned and chopped

450 g/1 lb hake fillets,
   skinned and chopped

90 g/3 oz/6 tbsp butter

4 shallots, finely chopped

2 garlic cloves, crushed

1 carrot, diced

1 leek, finely chopped

300 ml/½ pint/1¼ cups
   dry (hard) cider

300 ml/½ pint/1¼ cups
   medium sweet cider

2 tsp anchovy essence (extract)

1 tbsp tarragon vinegar

450 g/1 lb dried spaghetti

1 tbsp olive oil

salt and pepper

chopped fresh parsley, to garnish

crusty brown bread, to serve

1 Season the flour with salt and pepper. Sprinkle 25 g/ 1 oz/¼ cup of the seasoned flour on to a shallow plate. Press the fish pieces into the seasoned flour to coat thoroughly.

2 Melt the butter in a flameproof casserole. Add the fish fillets, shallots, garlic, carrot and leek and cook over a low heat, stirring frequently, for about 10 minutes.

3 Sprinkle over the remaining seasoned flour and cook, stirring constantly, for 2 minutes. Gradually stir in the cider, anchovy essence (extract) and tarragon vinegar. Bring to the boil and simmer over a low heat for 35 minutes. Alternatively, bake in a preheated oven at 180°C/350°F/Gas 4 for 30 minutes.

4 About 15 minutes before the end of the cooking time, bring a large pan of lightly salted water to the boil. Add the spaghetti and olive oil and cook for about 12 minutes, until tender but still firm to the bite. Drain the pasta thoroughly and transfer to a large serving dish.

5 Arrange the fish on top of the spaghetti and pour over the sauce. Garnish with chopped parsley and serve immediately with warm, crusty brown bread.

Grilled (Broiled) Stuffed Sole

A delicious stuffing of sun-dried tomatoes and fresh lemon thyme are used to stuff whole sole.

NUTRITIONAL INFORMATION

Calories . . . . .207 Sugars 0.2g

Protein . . . . .24g Fat 10g

Carbohydrate . . . .8g Saturates 4g

 25 MINS 20 MINS

SERVES 4

I N G R E D I E N T S

1 tbsp olive oil

25 g/1 oz/2 tbsp butter

1 small onion, finely chopped

1 garlic clove, chopped

3 sun-dried tomatoes, chopped

2 tbsp lemon thyme

50 g/1¾ oz breadcrumbs

1 tbsp lemon juice

4 small whole sole, gutted and cleaned

salt and pepper

lemon wedges, to garnish

fresh green salad leaves, to serve

1 Heat the oil and butter in a frying pan (skillet) until it just begins to froth.

2 Add the onion and garlic to the frying pan (skillet) and cook, stirring, for 5 minutes until just softened.

3 To make the stuffing, mix the tomatoes, thyme, breadcrumbs and lemon juice in a bowl, and season.

4 Add the stuffing mixture to the pan, and stir to mix.

5 Using a sharp knife, pare the skin from the bone inside the gut hole of the fish to make a pocket. Spoon the tomato and herb stuffing into the pocket.

6 Cook the fish, under a preheated grill (broiler), for 6 minutes on each side or until golden brown.

7 Transfer the stuffed fish to serving plates and garnish with lemon wedges. Serve immediately with fresh green salad leaves.

COOK'S TIP

Lemon thyme (*Thymus* x *citriodorus*) has a delicate lemon scent and flavour. Ordinary thyme can be used instead, but mix it with 1 teaspoon of lemon rind to add extra flavour.

Lemon Sole & Haddock Ravioli

This delicate-tasting dish is surprisingly satisfying for even the hungriest appetites. Prepare the Italian Red Wine Sauce well in advance.

NUTRITIONAL INFORMATION

Calories 977	Sugars 7g	
Protein 67g	Fat 40g	
Carbohydrate . . .93g	Saturates 17g	

9³/₄ HOURS   25 MINS

SERVES 4

INGREDIENTS

450 g/1 lb lemon sole fillets, skinned

450 g/1 lb haddock fillets, skinned

3 eggs beaten

450 g/1 lb cooked potato gnocchi
  (see page 410)

175 g/6 oz/3 cups fresh breadcrumbs

50 ml/2 fl oz/¼ cup double
  (heavy) cream

450 g/1 lb Basic Pasta Dough
  (see page 24)

300 ml/½ pint/1¼ cups Italian Red Wine
  Sauce (see page 29)

60 g/2 oz/⅔ cup freshly grated
  Parmesan cheese

salt and pepper

COOK'S TIP

For square ravioli, divide the dough in two. Wrap half in cling film; thinly roll out the other half. Cover; roll out the remaining dough. Pipe the filling at regular intervals and brush the spaces in between with water or beaten egg. Lift the second sheet of dough into position with a rolling pin and press between the filling to seal. Cut with a ravioli cutter or a knife.

1 Flake the lemon sole and haddock fillets with a fork and transfer the flesh to a large mixing bowl.

2 Mix the eggs, cooked potato gnocchi, breadcrumbs and cream in a bowl until thoroughly combined. Add the fish to the bowl containing the gnocchi and season the mixture with salt and pepper to taste.

3 Roll out the pasta dough on to a lightly floured surface and cut out 7.5 cm/3 inch rounds using a plain cutter.

4 Place a spoonful of the fish stuffing on each round. Dampen the edges slightly and fold the pasta rounds over, pressing together to seal.

5 Bring a large saucepan of lightly salted water to the boil. Add the ravioli and cook for 15 minutes.

6 Drain the ravioli, using a slotted spoon, and transfer to a large serving dish. Pour over the Italian Red Wine Sauce, sprinkle over the Parmesan cheese and serve immediately.

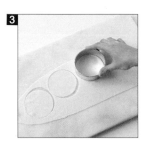

Trout in Red Wine

This recipe from Trentino is best when the fish are freshly caught, but it is a good way to cook any trout, giving it an interesting flavour.

NUTRITIONAL INFORMATION

Calories 489	Sugars 0.6g	
Protein 48g	Fat 27g	
Carbohydrate ...0.6g	Saturates 14g	

 20 MINS   45 MINS

SERVES 4

INGREDIENTS

4 fresh trout, about 300 g/10 oz each

250 ml/9 fl oz/1 cup red or
   white wine vinegar

300 ml/½ pint/1¼ cups red or
   dry white wine

150 ml/¼ pint/ ⅔ cup water

1 carrot, sliced

2–4 bay leaves

thinly pared rind of 1 lemon

1 small onion, sliced very thinly

4 sprigs fresh parsley

4 sprigs fresh thyme

1 tsp black peppercorns

6–8 whole cloves

90 g/3 oz/6 tbsp butter

1 tbsp chopped fresh mixed herbs

salt and pepper

TO GARNISH

sprigs of herbs

lemon slices

1 Gut the trout but leave their heads on. Dry on paper towels and lay the fish head to tail in a shallow container or baking tin (pan) large enough to hold them.

2 Bring the wine vinegar to the boil and pour slowly all over the fish. Leave the fish to marinate in the refrigerator for about 20 minutes.

3 Meanwhile, put the wine, water, carrot, bay leaves, lemon rind, onion, herbs, peppercorns and cloves into a pan with a good pinch of sea salt and heat gently.

4 Drain the fish thoroughly, discarding the vinegar. Place the fish in a fish kettle or large frying pan (skillet) so they touch. When the wine mixture boils, strain gently over the fish so they are about half covered. Cover the pan and simmer very gently for 15 minutes.

5 Carefully remove the fish from the pan, draining off as much of the liquid as possible, and arrange on a serving dish. Keep warm.

6 Boil the cooking liquid until reduced to about 4–6 tbsp. Melt the butter in a pan and strain in the cooking liquor. Season and spoon the sauce over the fish. Garnish and serve.

Trout with Smoked Bacon

Most trout available nowadays is farmed rainbow trout, however, if you can, buy wild brown trout for this recipe.

NUTRITIONAL INFORMATION

Calories	802	Sugars	.........8g
Protein	........68g	Fat	..........36g
Carbohydrate	...54g	Saturates	......10g

  35 MINS   25 MINS

SERVES 4

INGREDIENTS

butter, for greasing

4 x 275 g/9½ oz trout, gutted and cleaned

12 anchovies in oil, drained and chopped

2 apples, peeled, cored and sliced

4 fresh mint sprigs

juice of 1 lemon

12 slices rindless smoked fatty bacon

450 g/1 lb dried tagliatelle

1 tbsp olive oil

salt and pepper

TO GARNISH

2 apples, cored and sliced

4 fresh mint sprigs

1 Grease a deep baking tray (cookie sheet) with butter.

2 Open up the cavities of each trout and rinse with warm salt water.

3 Season each cavity with salt and pepper. Divide the anchovies, sliced apples and mint sprigs between each of the cavities. Sprinkle the lemon juice into each cavity.

4 Carefully cover the whole of each trout, except the head and tail, with three slices of smoked bacon in a spiral.

5 Arrange the trout on the baking tray (cookie sheet) with the loose ends of bacon tucked underneath. Season with pepper and bake in a preheated oven at 200°C/400°F/Gas Mark 6 for 20 minutes, turning the trout over after 10 minutes.

6 Meanwhile, bring a large pan of lightly salted water to the boil. Add the tagliatelle and olive oil and cook for about 12 minutes, until tender but still firm to the bite. Drain the pasta and transfer to a large, warm serving dish.

7 Remove the trout from the oven and arrange on the tagliatelle. Garnish with sliced apples and fresh mint sprigs and serve immediately.

Fillets of Red Mullet & Pasta

This simple recipe perfectly complements the sweet flavour and delicate texture of the fish.

NUTRITIONAL INFORMATION

Calories 457	Sugars 3g	
Protein 39g	Fat 12g	
Carbohydrate ...44g	Saturates 5g	

 15 MINS   1 HOUR

SERVES 4

INGREDIENTS

1 kg/2 lb 4 oz red mullet fillets

300 ml/½ pint/1¼ cups dry white wine

4 shallots, finely chopped

1 garlic clove, crushed

3 tbsp finely chopped mixed fresh herbs

finely grated rind and juice of 1 lemon

pinch of freshly grated nutmeg

3 anchovy fillets, roughly chopped

2 tbsp double (heavy) cream

1 tsp cornflour (cornstarch)

450 g/1 lb dried vermicelli

1 tbsp olive oil

salt and pepper

TO GARNISH

1 fresh mint sprig

lemon slices

lemon rind

1 Put the red mullet fillets in a large casserole. Pour over the wine and add the shallots, garlic, herbs, lemon rind and juice, nutmeg and anchovies. Season. Cover and bake in a preheated oven at 180°C/350°F/Gas Mark 4 for 35 minutes.

2 Transfer the mullet to a warm dish. Set aside and keep warm.

3 Pour the cooking liquid into a pan and bring to the boil. Simmer for 25 minutes, until reduced by half. Mix the cream and cornflour (cornstarch) and stir into the sauce to thicken.

4 Meanwhile, bring a pan of lightly salted water to the boil. Add the vermicelli and oil and cook for 8–10 minutes, until tender but still firm to the bite. Drain the pasta and transfer to a warm serving dish.

5 Arrange the red mullet fillets on top of the vermicelli and pour over the sauce. Garnish with a fresh mint sprig, slices of lemon and strips of lemon rind and serve immediately.

Sardinian Red Mullet

Red mullet has a beautiful pink skin, which is enhanced in this dish by being cooked in red wine and orange juice.

NUTRITIONAL INFORMATION

Calories	287	Sugars 15g
Protein	........31g	Fat 9g
Carbohydrate	...15g	Saturates 1g

  2¹/₂ HOURS   25 MINS

SERVES 4

INGREDIENTS

50 g/1¾ oz sultanas

150 ml/¼ pint/⅔ cup red wine

2 tbsp olive oil

2 medium onions, sliced

1 courgette (zucchini), cut into
   5 cm/2 inch sticks

2 oranges

2 tsp coriander seeds, lightly crushed

4 red mullet, boned and filleted

50 g/1¾ oz can anchovy fillets, drained

2 tbsp chopped, fresh oregano

1 Place the sultanas in a bowl. Pour over the red wine and leave to soak for about 10 minutes.

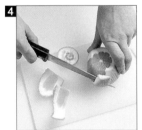

COOK'S TIP

Red mullet is usually available all year round – frozen, if not fresh – from your fishmonger or supermarket. If you cannot get hold of it try using telapia. This dish can also be served warm, if you prefer.

2 Heat the oil in a large frying pan (skillet). Add the onions and sauté for 2 minutes.

3 Add the courgettes (zucchini) to the pan and fry for a further 3 minutes or until tender.

4 Using a zester, pare long, thin strips from one of the oranges. Using a sharp knife, remove the skin from both of the oranges, then segment the oranges by slicing between the lines of pith.

5 Add the orange zest to the frying pan (skillet) with the coriander seeds, red wine, sultanas, red mullet and anchovies to the pan and leave to simmer for 10–15 minutes or until the fish is cooked through.

6 Stir in the oregano, set aside and leave to cool. Place the mixture in a large bowl and leave to chill, covered, in the refrigerator for at least 2 hours to allow the flavours to mingle. Transfer to serving plates and serve.

Red Mullet & Amaretto Sauce

This succulent fish and pasta dish is ideal for serving on a warm, summer's evening – preferably *al fresco*.

NUTRITIONAL INFORMATION

Calories	806	Sugars	.........6g
Protein	........64g	Fat	..........34g
Carbohydrate	...64g	Saturates	......16g

15 MINS   25 MINS

SERVES 4

INGREDIENTS

90 g/3 oz/3¾ cup plain (all-purpose) flour

8 red mullet fillets

25 g/1 oz/2 tbsp butter

150 ml/¼ pint/⅔ cup fish stock

1 tbsp crushed almonds

1 tsp pink peppercorns

1 orange, peeled and cut into segments

1 tbsp orange liqueur

grated rind of 1 orange

450 g/1 lb dried orecchiette

1 tbsp olive oil

150 ml/¼ pint/⅔ cup double
   (heavy) cream

4 tbsp amaretto

salt and pepper

TO GARNISH

2 tbsp snipped fresh chives

1 tbsp toasted almonds

1 Season the flour with salt and pepper and sprinkle into a shallow bowl. Press the fish fillets into the flour to coat. Melt the butter in a frying pan (skillet). Add the fish and fry over a low heat for 3 minutes, until browned.

2 Add the fish stock to the pan and cook for 4 minutes. Carefully remove the fish, cover with foil and keep warm.

3 Add the almonds, pink peppercorns, half the orange, the orange liqueur and orange rind to the pan. Simmer until the liquid has reduced by half.

4 Meanwhile, bring a large pan of lightly salted water to the boil. Add the orecchiette and oil and cook for 15 minutes, until tender but still firm to the bite.

5 Meanwhile, season the sauce with salt and pepper and stir in the cream and amaretto. Cook for 2 minutes. Return the fish to the pan to coat with the sauce.

6 Drain the pasta and transfer to a serving dish. Top with the fish fillets and their sauce. Garnish with the remaining orange segments, the chives and toasted almonds. Serve immediately.

Italian Cod

Cod roasted with herbs and topped with a lemon and rosemary crust is a delicious main course.

NUTRITIONAL INFORMATION

Calories 313   Sugars 0.4g
Protein . . . . .29g   Fat 20g
Carbohydrate . . . .6g   Saturates 5g

10 MINS   35 MINS

SERVES 4

INGREDIENTS

25 g/1 oz/2 tbsp butter

50 g/1¾ oz wholemeal breadcrumbs

25 g/1 oz chopped walnuts

grated rind and juice of 2 lemons

2 sprigs rosemary, stalks removed

2 tbsp chopped parsley

4 cod fillets, each about 150 g/5½ oz

1 garlic clove, crushed

3 tbsp walnut oil

1 small red chilli, diced

salad leaves, to serve

VARIATION

If preferred, the walnuts may be omitted from the crust. In addition, extra virgin olive oil can be used instead of walnut oil, if you prefer.

1 Melt the butter in a large saucepan, stirring.

2 Remove the pan from the heat and add the breadcrumbs, walnuts, the rind and juice of 1 lemon, half of the rosemary and half of the parsley.

3 Press the breadcrumb mixture over the top of the cod fillets. Place the cod fillets in a shallow, foil-lined roasting tin (pan).

4 Bake in a preheated oven at 200°C/400°F/Gas Mark 6 for 25–30 minutes.

5 Mix the garlic, the remaining lemon rind and juice, rosemary, parsley and chilli in a bowl. Beat in the walnut oil and mix to combine. Drizzle the dressing over the cod steaks as soon as they are cooked.

6 Transfer to serving plates and serve immediately.

Smoked Fish Lasagne

Use smoked cod or haddock in this delicious lasagne.
It's a great way to make a little go a long way.

NUTRITIONAL INFORMATION

Calories 483	Sugars 8g	
Protein 36g	Fat 24g	
Carbohydrate ...32g	Saturates 12g	

 20 MINS 1¼ HOURS

SERVES 4

INGREDIENTS

2 tsp olive or vegetable oil

1 garlic clove, crushed

1 small onion, chopped finely

125 g/4½ oz mushrooms, sliced

400 g/14 oz can chopped tomatoes

1 small courgette (zucchini), sliced

150 ml/¼ pint/⅔ cup vegetable stock
   or water

25 g/1 oz/2 tbsp butter or margarine

300 ml/½ pint/1¼ cups skimmed milk

25 g/1 oz/¼ cup plain (all-purpose) flour

125 g/4 oz/1 cup grated mature (sharp)
   Cheddar cheese

1 tbsp chopped fresh parsley

125 g/4½ oz (6 sheets) pre-cooked lasagne

350 g/12 oz skinned and boned smoked
   cod or haddock, cut into chunks

salt and pepper

fresh parsley sprigs to garnish

1 Heat the oil in a saucepan and fry the garlic and onion for about 5 minutes. Add the mushrooms and cook for 3 minutes, stirring.

2 Add the tomatoes, courgette (zucchini) and stock or water and simmer, uncovered, for 15–20 minutes until the vegetables are soft. Season.

3 Put the butter or margarine, milk and flour into a small saucepan and heat, whisking constantly, until the sauce boils and thickens. Remove from the heat and add half of the cheese and all of the parsley. Stir gently to melt the cheese and season to taste.

4 Spoon the tomato sauce mixture into a large, shallow ovenproof dish and top with half of the lasagne sheets. Scatter the chunks of fish evenly over the top, then pour over half of the cheese sauce. Top with the remaining lasagne sheets and then spread the rest of the cheese sauce on top. Sprinkle with the remaining cheese.

5 Bake in a preheated oven at 190°C/375°F/Gas Mark 5 for 40 minutes, until the top is golden brown and bubbling. Garnish with parsley sprigs and serve hot.

Pasta & Fish Pudding

A tasty mixture of creamy fish and pasta cooked in a bowl, unmoulded and drizzled with tomato sauce presents macaroni in a new guise.

NUTRITIONAL INFORMATION

Calories	454	Sugars	.........1g
Protein	........30g	Fat	..........30g
Carbohydrate	...17g	Saturates	......16g

 10 MINS 2 HOURS

SERVES 4

INGREDIENTS

115 g/4 oz/1 cup dried short-cut macaroni

  or other short pasta

1 tbsp olive oil

15 g/½ oz/1 tbsp butter,

  plus extra for greasing

450 g/1 lb white fish fillets,

  such as cod or haddock

2–3 fresh parsley sprigs

6 black peppercorns

125 ml/4 fl oz/½ cup double (heavy) cream

2 eggs, separated

2 tbsp chopped fresh dill or parsley

pinch of freshly grated nutmeg

60 g/2 oz/⅔ cup freshly grated Parmesan

  cheese

salt and pepper

fresh dill or parsley sprigs, to garnish

Tomato Sauce (see page 110), to serve

1 Bring a pan of salted water to the boil. Add the pasta and oil and cook for 8–10 minutes until tender, but still firm to the bite. Drain the pasta and return to the pan. Add the butter, cover and keep warm.

2 Place the fish in a frying pan (skillet). Add the parsley sprigs, peppercorns and enough water to cover. Bring to the boil, cover and simmer for 10 minutes. Lift out the fish and set aside to cool. Reserve the cooking liquid.

3 Skin the fish and cut into bite-size pieces. Put the pasta in a bowl. Mix the cream, egg yolks, chopped dill or parsley, nutmeg and cheese, pour into the pasta and mix. Spoon in the fish without breaking it. Add enough of the reserved cooking liquid to make a moist, but firm mixture. Whisk the egg whites until stiff, then fold them into the mixture.

4 Grease a heatproof bowl and spoon in the fish mixture to within 4 cm/ 1½ inches of the rim. Cover with greased greaseproof (baking) paper and foil and tie securely with string.

5 Stand the bowl on a trivet in a saucepan. Add boiling water to reach halfway up the sides. Cover and steam for 1½ hours.

6 Invert the pudding on to a serving plate. Pour over a little tomato sauce. Garnish and serve with the remaining tomato sauce.

Charred Tuna Steaks

Tuna has a firm flesh, which is ideal for barbecuing (grilling), but it can be a little dry unless it is marinated first.

NUTRITIONAL INFORMATION

Calories 153	Sugars 1g	
Protein 29g	Fat 3g	
Carbohydrate 1g	Saturates 1g	

 2 HOURS   🕐 15 MINS

SERVES 4

I N G R E D I E N T S

4 tuna steaks

3 tbsp soy sauce

1 tbsp Worcestershire sauce

1 tsp wholegrain mustard

1 tsp caster (superfine) sugar

1 tbsp sunflower oil

green salad, to serve

TO GARNISH

flat-leaf parsley

lemon wedges

1 Place the tuna steaks in a shallow dish.

2 Mix together the soy sauce, Worcestershire sauce, mustard, sugar and oil in a small bowl.

3 Pour the marinade over the tuna steaks.

4 Gently turn over the tuna steaks, using your fingers or a fork. Make sure that the fish steaks are well coated with the marinade.

5 Cover and place the tuna steaks in the refrigerator. Leave to chill for between 30 minutes and 2 hours.

6 Barbecue (grill) the marinated fish over hot coals for 10–15 minutes, turning once.

7 Baste frequently with any of the marinade that is left in the dish.

8 Garnish with flat-leaf parsley and lemon wedges. Serve with a fresh green salad.

COOK'S TIP

If a marinade contains soy sauce, the marinating time should be limited, usually to 2 hours. If allowed to marinate for too long, the fish will dry out and become tough.

Mediterranean Fish Stew

Popular in fishing ports around Europe, gentle stewing is an excellent way to maintain the flavour and succulent texture of fish and shellfish.

NUTRITIONAL INFORMATION

Calories	533	Sugars	........11g
Protein	........71g	Fat	..........10g
Carbohydrate	...30g	Saturates	......2g

   1¼ HOURS   25 MINS

SERVES 4

INGREDIENTS

2 tsp olive oil

2 red onions, sliced

2 garlic cloves, crushed

2 tbsp red wine vinegar

2 tsp caster (superfine) sugar

300 ml/½ pint/1¼ cups Fresh Fish Stock (see page 30)

300 ml/½ pint/1¼ cups dry red wine

2 × 400 g/14 oz cans chopped tomatoes

225 g/8 oz baby aubergines (eggplant), quartered

225 g/8 oz yellow courgettes (zucchini), quartered or sliced

1 green (bell) pepper, sliced

1 tbsp chopped fresh rosemary

500 g/1 lb 2 oz halibut fillet, skinned and cut into 2.5 cm/1 inch cubes

750 g/1 lb 10 oz fresh mussels, prepared

225 g/8 oz baby squid, cleaned, trimmed and sliced into rings

225 g/8 oz fresh tiger prawns (shrimp), peeled and deveined

salt and pepper

4 slices toasted French bread rubbed with a cut garlic clove

lemon wedges, to serve

1 Heat the oil in a large non-stick saucepan and fry the onions and garlic gently for 3 minutes.

2 Stir in the vinegar and sugar and cook for a further 2 minutes.

3 Stir in the stock, wine, canned tomatoes, aubergines (eggplant) courgettes (zucchini), (bell) pepper and rosemary. Bring to the boil and simmer, uncovered, for 10 minutes.

4 Add the halibut, mussels and squid. Mix well and simmer, covered, for 5 minutes until the fish is opaque.

5 Stir in the prawns (shrimp) and continue to simmer, covered, for a further 2–3 minutes until the prawns (shrimp) are pink and cooked through.

6 Discard any mussels which haven't opened and season to taste.

7 To serve, put a slice of the prepared garlic bread in the base of each warmed serving bowl and ladle the stew over the top. Serve with lemon wedges.

Seafood Pizza

Make a change from the standard pizza toppings – this dish is piled high with seafood baked with a red (bell) pepper and tomato sauce.

NUTRITIONAL INFORMATION

Calories 248	Sugars 7g	
Protein 27g	Fat 6g	
Carbohydrate ...22g	Saturates 2g	

25 MINS   55 MINS

SERVES 4

I N G R E D I E N T S

145 g/5 oz standard pizza base mix

4 tbsp chopped fresh dill or 2 tbsp dried dill

fresh dill, to garnish

S A U C E

1 large red (bell) pepper

400 g/14 oz can chopped tomatoes with onion and herbs

3 tbsp tomato purée (paste)

salt and pepper

T O P P I N G

350 g/12 oz assorted cooked seafood, thawed if frozen

1 tbsp capers in brine, drained

25 g/1 oz pitted black olives in brine, drained

25 g/1 oz low-fat Mozzarella cheese, grated

1 tbsp grated, fresh Parmesan cheese

1 Preheat the oven to 200°C/400°F/Gas Mark 6. Place the pizza base mix in a bowl and stir in the dill. Make the dough according to the instructions on the packet.

2 Press the dough into a round measuring 25.5 cm/10 inches across on a baking sheet lined with baking parchment. Set aside to prove (rise).

3 Preheat the grill (broiler) to hot. To make the sauce, halve and deseed the (bell) pepper and arrange on a grill (broiler) rack. Cook for 8–10 minutes until softened and charred. Leave to cool slightly, peel off the skin and chop the flesh.

4 Place the tomatoes and (bell) pepper in a saucepan. Bring to the boil and simmer for 10 minutes. Stir in the tomato purée (paste) and season to taste.

5 Spread the sauce over the pizza base and top with the seafood. Sprinkle over the capers and olives, top with the cheeses and bake for 25–30 minutes.

6 Garnish with sprigs of dill and serve hot.

Spaghetti al Tonno

The classic Italian combination of pasta and tuna is enhanced in this recipe with a delicious parsley sauce.

NUTRITIONAL INFORMATION

Calories 1065	Sugars 3g	
Protein 27g	Fat 85g	
Carbohydrate . . .52g	Saturates 18g	

10 MINS   15 MINS

SERVES 4

INGREDIENTS

200 g/7 oz can tuna, drained

60 g/2 oz can anchovies, drained

250 ml/9 fl oz/1⅛ cups olive oil

60 g/2 oz/1 cup roughly chopped
   flat leaf parsley

150 ml/¼ pint/⅔ cup crème fraîche

450 g/1 lb dried spaghetti

25 g/1 oz/2 tbsp butter

salt and pepper

black olives, to garnish

crusty bread, to serve

1 Remove any bones from the tuna. Put the tuna into a food processor or blender, together with the anchovies, 225 ml/ 8 fl oz/1 cup of the olive oil and the flat leaf parsley. Process until the sauce is very smooth.

VARIATION

If liked, you could add 1–2 garlic cloves to the sauce, substitute 25 g/1 oz/½ cup chopped fresh basil for half the parsley and garnish with capers instead of black olives.

2 Spoon the crème fraîche into the food processor or blender and process again for a few seconds to blend thoroughly. Season with salt and pepper to taste.

3 Bring a large pan of lightly salted water to the boil. Add the spaghetti and the remaining olive oil and cook for 8–10 minutes until tender, but still firm to the bite.

4 Drain the spaghetti, return to the pan and place over a medium heat. Add the butter and toss well to coat. Spoon in the sauce and quickly toss into the spaghetti, using 2 forks.

5 Remove the pan from the heat and divide the spaghetti between 4 warm individual serving plates. Garnish with the olives and serve immediately with warm, crusty bread.

Tuna with Roast (Bell) Peppers

Fresh tuna will be either a small bonito fish or steaks from a skipjack.
The more delicately flavoured fish have a paler flesh.

NUTRITIONAL INFORMATION

Calories	428	Sugars	.........5g
Protein	........60g	Fat	..........19g
Carbohydrate	....5g	Saturates	.......3g

   20 MINS   30 MINS

SERVES 4

INGREDIENTS

4 tuna steaks, about 250 g/9 oz each

3 tbsp lemon juice

1 litre/1¾ pints/4 cups water

6 tbsp olive oil

2 orange (bell) peppers

2 red (bell) peppers

12 black olives

1 tsp balsamic vinegar

salt and pepper

1 Put the tuna steaks into a bowl with the lemon juice and water. Leave for 15 minutes.

2 Drain and brush the steaks all over with olive oil and season well with salt and pepper.

3 Halve, core and deseed the (bell) peppers. Put them over a hot barbecue (grill) and cook for 12 minutes until they are charred all over. Put them into a plastic bag and seal it.

4 Meanwhile, cook the tuna over a hot barbecue (grill) for 12–15 minutes, turning once.

5 When the (bell) peppers are cool enough to handle, peel them and cut each piece into 4 strips. Toss them with the remaining olive oil, olives and balsamic vinegar.

6 Serve the tuna steaks piping hot, with the roasted (bell) pepper salad.

COOK'S TIP

Red, orange and yellow (bell) peppers can also be peeled by cooking them in a hot oven for 30 minutes, turning them frequently, or roasting them straight over a naked gas flame, again turning them frequently. In both methods, deseed the (bell) peppers after peeling.

Salmon with Caper Sauce

The richness of salmon is beautifully balanced by the tangy capers in this creamy herb sauce.

NUTRITIONAL INFORMATION

Calories	302	Sugars	.........0g
Protein	........21g	Fat	..........24g
Carbohydrate	....1g	Saturates	......9g

5 MINS   25 MINS

SERVES 4

INGREDIENTS

4 salmon fillets, skinned

1 fresh bay leaf

few black peppercorns

1 tsp white wine vinegar

150 ml/¼ pint/⅔ cup fish stock

3 tbsp double (heavy) cream

1 tbsp capers

1 tbsp chopped fresh dill

1 tbsp chopped fresh chives

1 tsp cornflour (cornstarch)

2 tbsp skimmed milk

salt and pepper

new potatoes, to serve

TO GARNISH

fresh dill sprigs

chive flowers

1 Lay the salmon fillets in a shallow ovenproof dish. Add the bay leaf, peppercorns, vinegar and stock.

2 Cover with foil and bake in a preheated oven at 180°C/350°F/Gas Mark 4 for 15–20 minutes until the flesh is opaque and flakes easily when tested with a fork.

3 Transfer the fish to warmed serving plates, cover and keep warm.

4 Strain the cooking liquid into a saucepan. Stir in the cream, capers, dill and chives and seasoning to taste.

5 Blend the cornflour (cornstarch) with the milk. Add to the saucepan and heat, stirring, until thickened slightly. Boil for 1 minute.

6 Spoon the sauce over the salmon, garnish with dill sprigs and chive flowers.

7 Serve with new potatoes.

COOK'S TIP

Ask the fishmonger to skin the fillets for you. The cooking time for the salmon will depend on the thickness of the fish: the thin tail end of the salmon takes the least time to cook.

Baked Red Snapper

You can substitute other whole fish for the snapper, or use cutlets of cod or halibut.

NUTRITIONAL INFORMATION

Calories 519	Sugars 12g	
Protein 61g	Fat 23g	
Carbohydrate . . .18g	Saturates 3g	

20 MINS   50 MINS

SERVES 4

INGREDIENTS

1 red snapper, about 1.25 kg/2 lb 12 oz, cleaned

juice of 2 limes, or 1 lemon

4-5 sprigs of thyme or parsley

3 tbsp olive oil

1 large onion, chopped

2 garlic cloves, finely chopped

1 x 425 g/15 oz can chopped tomatoes

2 tbsp tomato purée (paste)

2 tbsp red wine vinegar

5 tbsp low-fat yogurt

2 tbsp chopped parsley

2 tsp dried oregano

6 tbsp dry breadcrumbs

60 g/2 oz/¼ cup low-fat yogurt cheese, crumbled

salt and pepper

SALAD

1 small lettuce, thickly sliced

10-12 young spinach leaves, torn

½ small cucumber, sliced and quartered

4 spring onions (scallions), thickly sliced

3 tbsp chopped parsley

2 tbsp olive oil

2 tbsp plain low-fat yogurt

1 tbsp red wine vinegar

1 Sprinkle the lime or lemon juice inside and over the fish and season. Place the herbs inside the fish.

2 Heat the oil in a pan and fry the onion until translucent. Stir in the garlic and cook for 1 minute, then add the chopped tomatoes, tomato purée (paste) and vinegar. Simmer, uncovered, for 5 minutes. Allow the sauce to cool, then stir in the yogurt, parsley and oregano.

3 Pour half of the sauce into an ovenproof dish just large enough for the fish. Add the fish and then pour the remainder of the sauce over it, and sprinkle with breadcrumbs. Bake uncovered for 30–35 minutes. Sprinkle the cheese over the fish and serve with lime wedges and dill sprigs.

4 Arrange the salad ingredients in a bowl. Whisk the oil, yogurt and vinegar and pour over the salad.

Smoky Fish Pie

This flavoursome and colourful fish pie is perfect for a light supper. The addition of smoked salmon gives it a touch of luxury.

NUTRITIONAL INFORMATION

Calories ....523 Sugars 15g
Protein ....58g Fat 6g
Carbohydrate ...63g Saturates 2g

 15 MINS   1 HOUR

SERVES 4

INGREDIENTS

900 g/2 lb smoked haddock or cod fillets

600 ml/1 pint/2½ cups skimmed milk

2 bay leaves

115 g/4 oz button mushrooms, quartered

115 g/4 oz frozen peas

115 g/4 oz frozen sweetcorn kernels

675 g/1½ lb potatoes, diced

5 tbsp low-fat natural (unsweetened) yogurt

4 tbsp chopped fresh parsley

60 g/2 oz smoked salmon, sliced into thin strips

3 tbsp cornflour (cornstarch)

25 g/1 oz smoked cheese, grated

salt and pepper

COOK'S TIP

If possible, use smoked haddock or cod that has not been dyed bright yellow or artificially flavoured to give the illusion of having been smoked.

1 Preheat the oven to 200°C/400°F/Gas Mark 6. Place the fish in a pan and add the milk and bay leaves. Bring to the boil, cover and then simmer for 5 minutes.

2 Add the mushrooms, peas and sweetcorn, bring back to a simmer, cover and cook for 5–7 minutes. Leave to cool.

3 Place the potatoes in a saucepan, cover with water, boil and cook for 8 minutes. Drain well and mash with a fork or a potato masher. Stir in the yogurt, parsley and seasoning. Set aside.

4 Using a slotted spoon, remove the fish from the pan. Flake the cooked fish away from the skin and place in an ovenproof gratin dish. Reserve the cooking liquid.

5 Drain the vegetables, reserving the cooking liquid, and gently stir into the fish with the salmon strips.

6 Blend a little cooking liquid into the cornflour (cornstarch) to make a paste. Transfer the rest of the liquid to a saucepan and add the paste. Heat through, stirring, until thickened. Discard the bay leaves and season to taste. Pour the sauce over the fish and vegetables and mix. Spoon over the mashed potato so that the fish is covered, sprinkle with cheese and bake for 25–30 minutes.

Salmon Fillet with Herbs

This is a great party dish, as the salmon is cooked in one piece. The combination of the herbs and barbecue (grill) give a great flavour.

NUTRITIONAL INFORMATION

Calories 507   Sugars 0.4g
Protein . . . . .46g   Fat 35g
Carbohydrate . . .0.5g   Saturates 6g

 5 MINS   30 MINS

SERVES 4

I N G R E D I E N T S

½ large bunch dried thyme

5 fresh rosemary branches, 15–20 cm/
    6–8 inches long

8 bay leaves

1 kg/2 lb salmon fillet

1 bulb fennel, cut into 8 pieces

2 tbsp lemon juice

2 tbsp olive oil

TO SERVE

crusty bread

green salad

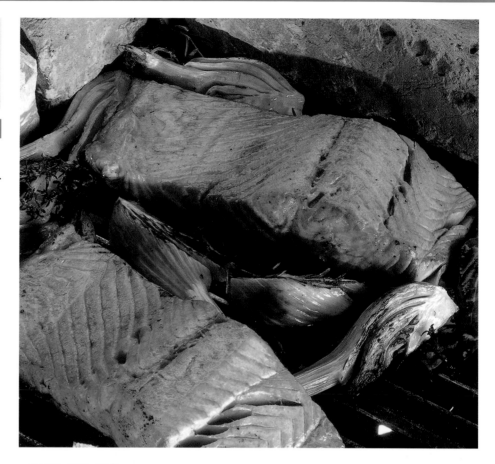

1 Make a base on a hot barbecue (grill) with the dried thyme, rosemary branches and bay leaves, overlapping them so that they cover a slightly bigger area than the salmon.

2 Carefully place the salmon on top of the herbs.

3 Arrange the fennel around the edge of the fish.

4 Combine the lemon juice and oil and brush the salmon with it.

5 Cover the salmon loosely with a piece of foil, to keep it moist.

6 Cook for about 20–30 minutes, basting frequently with the lemon juice mixture.

7 Remove the salmon from the barbecue, cut it into slices and serve with the fennel.

8 Serve with slices of crusty bread and a green salad.

VARIATION

Use whatever combination of herbs you may have to hand – but avoid the stronger tasting herbs, such as sage and marjoram, which are unsuitable for fish.

Smoked Haddock Casserole

This quick, easy and inexpensive dish would be ideal for a mid-week family supper.

  20 MINS   45 MINS

SERVES 4

INGREDIENTS

25 g/1 oz/2 tbsp butter, plus extra
   for greasing

450 g/1 lb smoked haddock fillets,
   cut into 4 slices

600 ml/1 pint/2½ cups milk

25 g/1 oz/¼ cup plain (all purpose) flour

pinch of freshly grated nutmeg

3 tbsp double (heavy) cream

1 tbsp chopped fresh parsley

2 eggs, hard boiled (hard cooked) and
   mashed to a pulp

450 g/1 lb/4 cups dried fusilli

1 tbsp lemon juice

salt and pepper

boiled new potatoes and beetroot (beet),
   to serve

1 Thoroughly grease a casserole with butter. Put the haddock in the casserole and pour over the milk. Bake in a preheated oven at 200°C/400°F/Gas Mark 6 for about 15 minutes. Carefully pour the cooking liquid into a jug (pitcher) without breaking up the fish.

2 Melt the butter in a saucepan and stir in the flour. Gradually whisk in the reserved cooking liquid. Season to taste with salt, pepper and nutmeg. Stir in the cream, parsley and mashed egg and cook, stirring constantly, for 2 minutes.

3 Meanwhile, bring a large saucepan of lightly salted water to the boil. Add the fusilli and lemon juice and cook for 8–10 minutes until tender, but still firm to the bite.

4 Drain the pasta and spoon or tip it over the fish. Top with the egg sauce and return the casserole to the oven for 10 minutes.

5 Serve the casserole with boiled new potatoes and beetroot (beet).

VARIATION

You can use any type of dried pasta for this casserole. Try penne, conchiglie or rigatoni.

Poached Salmon with Penne

Fresh salmon and pasta in a mouth-watering lemon and watercress sauce – a wonderful summer evening treat.

NUTRITIONAL INFORMATION

Calories 968	Sugars 3g	
Protein 59g	Fat 58g	
Carbohydrate . . .49g	Saturates 19g	

 10 MINS   30 MINS

SERVES 4

INGREDIENTS

4 x 275 g/9½ oz fresh salmon steaks

60 g/2 oz/4 tbsp butter

175 ml/6 fl oz/¾ cup dry white wine

sea salt

8 peppercorns

fresh dill sprig

fresh tarragon sprig

1 lemon, sliced

450 g/1 lb dried penne

2 tbsp olive oil

lemon slices and fresh watercress,
  to garnish

LEMON & WATERCRESS SAUCE

25 g/1 oz/2 tbsp butter

25 g/1 oz/¼ cup plain (all-purpose) flour

150 ml/¼ pint/⅝ cup warm milk

juice and finely grated rind of 2 lemons

60 g/2 oz watercress, chopped

salt and pepper

1 Put the salmon in a large, non-stick pan. Add the butter, wine, a pinch of sea salt, the peppercorns, dill, tarragon and lemon. Cover, bring to the boil, and simmer for 10 minutes.

2 Using a fish slice, carefully remove the salmon. Strain and reserve the cooking liquid. Remove and discard the salmon skin and centre bones. Place on a warm dish, cover and keep warm.

3 Meanwhile, bring a saucepan of salted water to the boil. Add the penne and 1 tbsp of the oil and cook for 8–10 minutes, until tender but still firm to the bite. Drain and sprinkle over the remaining olive oil. Place on a warm serving dish, top with the salmon steaks and keep warm.

4 To make the sauce, melt the butter and stir in the flour for 2 minutes. Stir in the milk and about 7 tbsp of the reserved cooking liquid. Add the lemon juice and rind and cook, stirring, for a further 10 minutes.

5 Add the watercress to the sauce, stir gently and season to taste with salt and pepper.

6 Pour the sauce over the salmon and penne, garnish with slices of lemon and fresh watercress and serve.

Salmon Lasagne Rolls

Sheets of green lasagne are filled with a mixture of fresh salmon and oyster mushrooms. This recipe has been adapted for the microwave.

NUTRITIONAL INFORMATION

Calories .... .352 Sugars 5g
Protein ....19g Fat 19g
Carbohydrate ...25g Saturates 9g

 20 MINS   35 MINS

SERVES 4

INGREDIENTS

8 sheets green lasagne

1 onion, sliced

15 g/½ oz/1 tbsp butter

½ red (bell) pepper, chopped

1 courgette (zucchini), diced

1 tsp chopped ginger root

125 g/4½ oz oyster mushrooms, preferably
   yellow, chopped coarsely

225 g/8 oz fresh salmon fillet, skinned, and
   cut into chunks

2 tbsp dry sherry

2 tsp cornflour (cornstarch)

20 g/¾ oz/3 tbsp plain (all-purpose) flour

20 g/¾ oz/1½ tbsp butter

300 ml/½ pint/1¼ cups milk

25 g/1 oz/¼ cup Cheddar cheese, grated

15 g/½ oz/¼ cup fresh white breadcrumbs

salt and pepper

salad leaves, to serve

1 Place the lasagne sheets in a large shallow dish. Cover with plenty of boiling water. Cook on HIGH power for 5 minutes. Leave to stand, covered, for a few minutes before draining. Rinse in cold water and lay the sheets out on a clean work surface.

2 Put the onion and butter into a bowl. Cover and cook on HIGH power for 2 minutes. Add the (bell) pepper, courgette (zucchini) and ginger root. Cover and cook on HIGH power for 3 minutes.

3 Add the mushrooms and salmon to the bowl. Mix the sherry into the cornflour (cornstarch) then stir into the bowl. Cover and cook on HIGH power for 4 minutes until the fish flakes when tested with a fork. Season to taste.

4 Whisk the flour, butter and milk in a bowl. Cook on HIGH power for 3–4 minutes, whisking every minute, to give a sauce of coating consistency. Stir in half the cheese and season with salt and pepper to taste.

5 Spoon the salmon filling in equal quantities along the shorter side of each lasagne sheet. Roll up to enclose the filling. Arrange in a lightly oiled large rectangular dish. Pour over the sauce and sprinkle over the remaining cheese and the breadcrumbs.

6 Cook on HIGH power for 3 minutes until heated through. If possible, lightly brown under a preheated grill (broiler) before serving. Serve with salad.

Spaghetti & Smoked Salmon

Made in moments, this is a luxurious dish to astonish and delight unexpected guests.

NUTRITIONAL INFORMATION

Calories 803	Sugars 3g	
Protein 21g	Fat 49g	
Carbohydrate ...52g	Saturates 27g	

🥣 10 MINS   🕐 20 MINS

SERVES 4

INGREDIENTS

450 g/1 lb dried buckwheat spaghetti

2 tbsp olive oil

90 g/3 oz/½ cup crumbled Feta cheese

salt

fresh coriander (cilantro) or parsley leaves,
   to garnish

SAUCE

300 ml/½ pint/1¼ cups double
   (heavy) cream

150 ml/¼ pint/⅝ cup whisky or brandy

125 g/4½ oz smoked salmon

pinch of cayenne pepper

pepper

2 tbsp chopped fresh coriander (cilantro)
   or parsley

1 Bring a large pan of lightly salted water to the boil. Add the spaghetti and 1 tbsp of the olive oil and cook for 8–10 minutes until tender, but still firm to the bite. Drain the spaghetti, return to the pan and sprinkle over the remaining olive oil. Cover, shake the pan, set aside and keep warm.

2 Pour the cream into a small saucepan and bring to simmering point, but do not let it boil. Pour the whisky or brandy into another small saucepan and bring to simmering point, but do not allow it to boil. Remove both saucepans from the heat and mix together the cream and whisky or brandy.

3 Cut the smoked salmon into thin strips and add to the cream mixture. Season to taste with cayenne and pepper. Just before serving, stir in the fresh coriander (cilantro) or parsley.

4 Transfer the spaghetti to a warm serving dish, pour over the sauce and toss thoroughly with 2 large forks. Scatter over the crumbled Feta cheese, garnish with the coriander (cilantro) or parsley leaves and serve immediately.

Squid & Macaroni Stew

This scrumptious seafood dish is quick and easy to make, yet deliciously satisfying to eat.

NUTRITIONAL INFORMATION

Calories	292	Sugars	.........3g
Protein	........13g	Fat	..........14g
Carbohydrate	...24g	Saturates	.......2g

 15 MINS   35 MINS

SERVES 6

I N G R E D I E N T S

225 g/8 oz/2 cups dried short-cut macaroni
 or other small pasta shapes

7 tbsp olive oil

2 onions, sliced

350 g/12 oz prepared squid, cut into
 4 cm/1½ inch strips

225 ml/8 fl oz/1 cup fish stock

150 ml/¼ pint/⅝ cup red wine

350 g/12 oz tomatoes, skinned and
 thinly sliced

2 tbsp tomato purée (paste)

1 tsp dried oregano

2 bay leaves

2 tbsp chopped fresh parsley

salt and pepper

crusty bread, to serve

COOK'S TIP

To prepare squid, peel off the skin, then cut off the head and tentacles. Discard the transparent flat oval bone from the body. Remove the sac of black ink, then turn the body sac inside out. Wash in cold water. Cut off the tentacles; discard the rest. Rinse.

1 Bring a large saucepan of lightly salted water to the boil. Add the pasta and 1 tablespoon of the olive oil and cook for 3 minutes. Drain, return to the pan, cover and keep warm.

2 Heat the remaining oil in a pan over a medium heat. Add the onions and fry until they are translucent. Add the squid and stock and simmer for 5 minutes. Pour in the wine and add the tomatoes, tomato purée (paste), oregano and bay leaves. Bring the sauce to the boil, season to taste and cook for 5 minutes.

3 Stir the pasta into the pan, cover and simmer for about 10 minutes, or until the squid and macaroni are tender and the sauce has thickened. If the sauce remains too liquid, uncover the pan and continue cooking for a few minutes longer.

4 Remove and discard the bay leaves. Reserve a little parsley and stir the remainder into the pan. Transfer to a warm serving dish and sprinkle over the remaining parsley. Serve with crusty bread to soak up the sauce.

Stuffed Squid

Whole squid are stuffed with a mixture of fresh herbs and sun-dried tomatoes and then cooked in a wine sauce.

NUTRITIONAL INFORMATION

Calories ....276 Sugars 1g
Protein ....23g Fat 8g
Carbohydrate ...20g Saturates 1g

 25 MINS   35 MINS

SERVES 4

INGREDIENTS

8 squid, cleaned and gutted but left whole
   (ask your fishmonger to do this)

6 canned anchovies, chopped

2 garlic cloves, chopped

2 tbsp rosemary, stalks removed and
   leaves chopped

2 sun-dried tomatoes, chopped

150 g/5½ oz breadcrumbs

1 tbsp olive oil

1 onion, finely chopped

200 ml/7 fl oz/¾ cup white wine

200 ml/7 fl oz/¾ cup fish stock

cooked rice, to serve

1 Remove the tentacles from the body of the squid and chop the flesh finely.

2 Grind the anchovies, garlic, rosemary and tomatoes to a paste in a mortar and pestle.

3 Add the breadcrumbs and the chopped squid tentacles and mix. If the mixture is too dry to form a thick paste at this point, add 1 teaspoon of water.

4 Spoon the paste into the body sacs of the squid then tie a length of cotton around the end of each sac to fasten them. Do not overfill the sacs, because they will expand during cooking.

5 Heat the oil in a frying pan (skillet). Add the onion and cook, stirring, for 3–4 minutes or until golden.

6 Add the stuffed squid to the pan and cook for 3–4 minutes or until brown all over.

7 Add the wine and stock and bring to the boil. Reduce the heat, cover and then leave to simmer for 15 minutes.

8 Remove the lid and cook for a further 5 minutes or until the squid is tender and the juices reduced. Serve with plenty of cooked rice.

Squid Casserole

Squid is often served fried in Italy, but here it is casseroled with tomatoes and (bell) peppers to give a rich sauce.

NUTRITIONAL INFORMATION

Calories . . . . .281 Sugars 8g

Protein . . . . .31g Fat 10g

Carbohydrate . . . .9g Saturates 1g

25 MINS   1¹/₂ HOURS

SERVES 4

INGREDIENTS

1 kg/2 lb 4 oz whole squid, cleaned or
    750 g/1 lb 10 oz squid rings, defrosted if
    frozen

3 tbsp olive oil

1 large onion, sliced thinly

2 garlic cloves, crushed

1 red (bell) pepper, cored,
    deseeded and sliced

1–2 sprigs fresh rosemary

150 ml/1/4 pint/²/₃ cup dry white wine and

250 ml/8 fl oz/1 cup water, or 350 ml/
    12 fl oz/1¹/₂ cups water or fish stock

400 g/14 oz can chopped tomatoes

2 tbsp tomato purée (paste)

1 tsp paprika

salt and pepper

fresh sprigs of rosemary or parsley,
to garnish

1 Cut the squid pouch into 1 cm/¹/₂ inch slices; cut the tentacles into lengths of about 5 cm/2 inches. If using frozen squid rings, make sure they are fully defrosted and well drained.

2 Heat the oil in a flameproof casserole and fry the onion and garlic gently until soft. Add the squid, increase the heat and continue to cook for about 10 minutes until sealed and beginning to colour lightly. Add the red (bell) pepper, rosemary, wine (if using) and water or stock and bring up to the boil. Cover and simmer gently for 45 minutes.

3 Discard the sprigs of rosemary (but don't take out any leaves that have come off). Add the tomatoes, tomato purée (paste), seasonings and paprika. Continue to simmer gently for 45–60 minutes, or cover the casserole tightly and cook in a moderate oven, 180°C/350°F/Gas Mark 4, for 45–60 minutes until tender.

4 Give the sauce a good stir, season and serve with fresh, crusty bread.

Pasta & Prawn (Shrimp) Parcels

This is the ideal dish when you have unexpected guests because the parcels can be prepared in advance, then put in the oven when you are ready to eat.

NUTRITIONAL INFORMATION

Calories	640	Sugars	.........1g
Protein	........50g	Fat	..........29g
Carbohydrate	...42g	Saturates	.......4g

 15 MINS   🕐 30 MINS

SERVES 4

INGREDIENTS

450 g/1 lb dried fettuccine

150 ml/¼ pint/⅝ cup Pesto Sauce
(see page 39)

4 tsp extra virgin olive oil

750 g/1 lb 10 oz large raw prawns (shrimp),
peeled and deveined

2 garlic cloves, crushed

125 ml/4 fl oz/½ cup dry white wine

salt and pepper

1 Cut out 4 x 30 cm/12 inch squares of greaseproof paper.

2 Bring a large saucepan of lightly salted water to the boil. Add the fettuccine and cook for 2–3 minutes, until just softened. Drain and set aside.

3 Mix together the fettuccine and half of the Pesto Sauce. Spread out the paper squares and put 1 tsp olive oil in the middle of each. Divide the fettuccine between the the squares, then divide the prawns (shrimp) and place on top of the fettuccine.

4 Mix together the remaining Pesto Sauce and the garlic and spoon it over the prawns (shrimp). Season each parcel with salt and black pepper and sprinkle with the white wine.

5 Dampen the edges of the greaseproof paper and wrap the parcels loosely, twisting the edges to seal.

6 Place the parcels on a baking tray (cookie sheet) and bake in a preheated oven at 200°C/400°F/Gas Mark 6 for 10–15 minutes. Transfer the parcels to 4 individual serving plates and serve.

COOK'S TIP

Traditionally, these parcels are designed to look like money bags. The resemblance is more effective with greaseproof paper than with foil.

Pan-Fried Prawns (Shrimp)

A luxurious dish which makes an impressive starter or light meal. Prawns (shrimp) and garlic are a winning combination.

NUTRITIONAL INFORMATION

Calories 455	Sugars 0g	
Protein 6g	Fat 37g	
Carbohydrate 0g	Saturates 18g	

 10 MINS   5 MINS

SERVES 4

I N G R E D I E N T S

4 garlic cloves

20–24 unshelled large raw prawns (shrimp)

125 g/4½ oz/8 tbsp butter

4 tbsp olive oil

6 tbsp brandy

salt and pepper

2 tbsp chopped fresh parsley

TO SERVE

lemon wedges

ciabatta bread

1 Using a sharp knife, peel and slice the garlic.

2 Wash the prawns (shrimp) and pat dry using paper towels.

3 Melt the butter with the oil in a large frying pan (skillet), add the garlic and prawns (shrimp), and fry over a high heat, stirring, for 3–4 minutes until the prawns (shrimp) are pink.

4 Sprinkle with brandy and season with salt and pepper to taste. Sprinkle with parsley and serve immediately with lemon wedges and ciabatta bread, if liked.

Macaroni & Seafood Bake

This adaptation of an eighteenth-century Italian dish is baked until it is golden brown and sizzling, then cut into wedges like a cake.

NUTRITIONAL INFORMATION

Calories	478	Sugars	.........6g
Protein	........27g	Fat	.........17g
Carbohydrate	...57g	Saturates	.......7g

30 MINS   50 MINS

SERVES 4

INGREDIENTS

350 g/12 oz/3 cups dried
   short-cut macaroni

1 tbsp olive oil, plus extra for brushing

90 g/3 oz/6 tbsp butter, plus extra
   for greasing

2 small fennel bulbs, thinly sliced and
   fronds reserved

175 g/6 oz mushrooms, thinly sliced

175 g/6 oz peeled, cooked prawns (shrimp)

pinch of cayenne pepper

300 ml/½ pint/1 ¼ cups Béchamel Sauce
   (see page 28)

60 g/2 oz/⅔ cup freshly grated
   Parmesan cheese

2 large tomatoes, sliced

1 tsp dried oregano

salt and pepper

1 Bring a saucepan of salted water to the boil. Add the pasta and oil and cook for 8–10 minutes until tender, but still firm to the bite. Drain the pasta and return to the pan.

2 Add 25 g/1 oz/2 tbsp of the butter to the pasta, cover, shake the pan and keep warm.

3 Melt the remaining butter in a saucepan. Fry the fennel for 3–4 minutes. Stir in the mushrooms and fry for a further 2 minutes.

4 Stir in the prawns (shrimp), then remove the pan from the heat.

5 Stir the cayenne pepper and prawn (shrimp) mixture into the Béchamel Sauce, stirring.

6 Pour into a greased ovenproof dish and spread evenly. Sprinkle over the Parmesan cheese and arrange the tomato slices in a ring around the edge. Brush the tomatoes with olive oil and then sprinkle over the oregano.

7 Bake in a preheated oven at 180°C/ 350°F/Gas Mark 4 for 25 minutes, until golden brown. Serve immediately.

Saffron Mussel Tagliatelle

Saffron is the most expensive spice in the world, but you only ever need a small quantity. Saffron threads or powdered saffron may be used.

NUTRITIONAL INFORMATION

Calories 854	Sugars 3g	
Protein 43g	Fat 49g	
Carbohydrate . . .57g	Saturates 28g	

 15 MINS 🕐 35 MINS

SERVES 4

INGREDIENTS

1 kg/2 lb 4 oz mussels

150 ml/¼ pint/⅔ cup white wine

1 medium onion, finely chopped

25 g/1 oz/2 tbsp butter

2 garlic cloves, crushed

2 tsp cornflour (cornstarch)

300 ml/½ pint/1¼ cups double (heavy) cream

pinch of saffron threads or saffron powder

juice of ½ lemon

1 egg yolk

450 g/1 lb dried tagliatelle

1 tbsp olive oil

salt and pepper

3 tbsp chopped fresh parsley, to garnish

1 Scrub and debeard the mussels under cold running water. Discard any that do not close when sharply tapped. Put the mussels in a pan with the wine and onion. Cover and cook over a high heat, shaking the pan, for 5–8 minutes, until the shells open.

2 Drain and reserve the cooking liquid. Discard any mussels that are still closed. Reserve a few mussels for the garnish and remove the remainder from their shells.

3 Strain the cooking liquid into a pan. Bring to the boil and reduce by about half. Remove the pan from the heat.

4 Melt the butter in a saucepan. Add the garlic and cook, stirring frequently, for 2 minutes, until golden brown. Stir in the cornflour (cornstarch) and cook, stirring, for 1 minute. Gradually stir in the cooking liquid and the cream. Crush the saffron threads and add to the pan. Season with salt and pepper to taste and simmer over a low heat for 2–3 minutes, until thickened.

5 Stir in the egg yolk, lemon juice and shelled mussels. Do not allow the mixture to boil.

6 Meanwhile, bring a pan of salted water to the boil. Add the pasta and oil and cook for 8–10 minutes until tender, but still firm to the bite. Drain and transfer to a serving dish. Add the mussel sauce and toss. Garnish with the parsley and reserved mussels and serve.

Mussel Casserole

Mussels are not difficult to cook, just a little messy to eat. Serve this dish with a finger bowl to help keep things clean!

NUTRITIONAL INFORMATION

Calories	299	Sugars	.........3g
Protein	........33g	Fat	...........7g
Carbohydrate	....3g	Saturates	.......1g

 25 MINS   25 MINS

SERVES 4

I N G R E D I E N T S

1 kg/2 lb 4 oz mussels

150 ml/¼ pint/⅔ cup white wine

1 tbsp oil

1 onion, finely chopped

3 garlic cloves, chopped

1 red chilli, finely chopped

100 g/3½ oz passata (sieved tomatoes)

1 tbsp chopped marjoram

toast or crusty bread, to serve

1 Scrub the mussels to remove any mud or sand.

2 Remove the beards from the mussels by pulling away the hairy bit between the two shells. Rinse the mussels in a bowl of clean water. Discard any mussels that do not close when they are tapped – they are dead and should not be eaten.

3 Place the mussels in a large saucepan. Pour in the wine and cook for 5 minutes, shaking the pan occasionally until the shells open. Remove and discard any mussels that do not open.

4 Remove the mussels from the saucepan with a perforated spoon. Strain the cooking liquid through a fine sieve set over a bowl, reserving the liquid.

5 Heat the oil in a large frying pan (skillet). Add the onion, garlic and chilli and cook for 4–5 minutes or until just softened.

6 Add the reserved cooking liquid to the pan and cook for 5 minutes or until reduced, stirring.

7 Stir in the passata (sieved tomatoes), marjoram and mussels and cook until hot, about 3 minutes.

8 Transfer to serving bowls and serve with toast or plenty of crusty bread to mop up the juices.

COOK'S TIP

Finger bowls are individual bowls of warm water with a slice of lemon floating in them. They are used to clean your fingers at the end of a meal.

Pasta Shells with Mussels

Serve this aromatic seafood dish to family and friends who admit to a love of garlic.

NUTRITIONAL INFORMATION

Calories ....686 Sugars 2g
Protein ....30g Fat 45g
Carbohydrate ...36g Saturates 27g

 15 MINS   25 MINS

SERVES 6

INGREDIENTS

1.25 kg/2 lb 12 oz mussels

225 ml/8 fl oz/1 cup dry white wine

2 large onions, chopped

115 g/4 oz/½ cup unsalted butter

6 large garlic cloves, finely chopped

5 tbsp chopped fresh parsley

300 ml/½ pint/1¼ cups double
   (heavy) cream

400 g/14 oz dried pasta shells

1 tbsp olive oil

salt and pepper

crusty bread, to serve

1 Scrub and debeard the mussels under cold running water. Discard any mussels that do not close immediately when sharply tapped. Put the mussels into a large saucepan, together with the wine and half of the onions. Cover and cook over a medium heat, shaking the pan frequently, for 2–3 minutes, or until the shells open.

2 Remove the pan from the heat. Drain the mussels and reserve the cooking liquid. Discard any mussels that have not opened. Strain the cooking liquid through a clean cloth into a glass jug (pitcher) or bowl and reserve.

3 Melt the butter in a pan over a medium heat. Add the remaining onion and fry until translucent. Stir in the garlic and cook for 1 minute. Gradually stir in the reserved cooking liquid. Stir in the parsley and cream and season to taste with salt and pepper. Bring to simmering point over a low heat.

4 Meanwhile, bring a large pan of lightly salted water to the boil. Add the pasta and oil and cook for 8–10 minutes until just tender, but still firm to the bite. Drain the pasta, return to the pan, cover and keep warm.

5 Reserve a few mussels for the garnish and remove the remainder from their shells. Stir the shelled mussels into the cream sauce and warm briefly.

6 Transfer the pasta to a serving dish. Pour over the sauce and toss to coat. Garnish with the reserved mussels.

Mussels with Tomato Sauce

This recipe for Mediterranean-style baked mussels, topped with a fresh tomato sauce and breadcrumbs, has been adapted for the microwave.

NUTRITIONAL INFORMATION

Calories	254	Sugars	.........1g
Protein	........37g	Fat	..........10g
Carbohydrate	....4g	Saturates	.......3g

    20 MINS   ⏱ 15 MINS

SERVES 4

I N G R E D I E N T S

½ small onion, chopped

1 garlic clove, crushed

1 tbsp olive oil

3 tomatoes

1 tbsp chopped fresh parsley

900 g/2 lb live mussels

1 tbsp freshly grated Parmesan cheese

1 tbsp fresh white breadcrumbs

salt and pepper

chopped fresh parsley, to garnish

1 Place the onion, garlic and oil in a bowl. Cover and cook on HIGH power for 3 minutes.

2 Cut a cross in the base of each tomato and place them in a small bowl. Pour on boiling water and leave for about 45 seconds. Drain and then plunge into cold water. The skins will slide off easily. Chop the tomatoes, removing any hard cores.

3 Add the tomatoes to the onion mixture, cover and cook on HIGH power for 3 minutes. Stir in the parsley and season to taste.

4 Scrub the mussels well in several changes of cold water. Remove the beards and discard any open mussels and those which do not close when tapped sharply with the back of a knife.

5 Place the mussels in a large bowl. Add enough boiling water to cover them. Cover and cook on HIGH power for 2 minutes, stirring halfway through, until the mussels open. Drain well and remove the empty half of each shell. Arrange the mussels in 1 layer on a plate.

6 Spoon the tomato sauce over each mussel. Mix the Parmesan cheese with the breadcrumbs and sprinkle on top.

Cook, uncovered, on HIGH power for 2 minutes. Garnish with parsley and serve.

COOK'S TIP

Dry out the breadcrumbs in the microwave for an extra crunchy topping. Spread them on a plate and cook on HIGH power for 2 minutes, stirring once. Leave to stand, uncovered.

Vermicelli with Clams

A quickly-cooked recipe that transforms store-cupboard ingredients into a dish with style.

NUTRITIONAL INFORMATION

Calories 520	Sugars 2g
Protein 26g	Fat 13g
Carbohydrate 71g	Saturates 4g

 10 MINS   25 MINS

SERVES 4

INGREDIENTS

400 g/14 oz dried vermicelli, spaghetti or
   other long pasta

2 tbsp olive oil

25 g/1 oz/2 tbsp butter

2 onions, chopped

2 garlic cloves, chopped

2 x 200 g/7 oz jars clams in brine

125 ml/4 fl oz/½ cup white wine

4 tbsp chopped fresh parsley

½ tsp dried oregano

pinch of freshly grated nutmeg

salt and pepper

TO GARNISH

2 tbsp Parmesan cheese shavings

fresh basil sprigs

1 Bring a large pan of lightly salted water to the boil. Add the pasta and half of the olive oil and cook for 8–10 minutes until tender, but still firm to the bite. Drain, return to the pan and add the butter. Cover the pan, shake well and keep warm.

2 Heat the remaining oil in a pan over a medium heat. Add the onions and fry until they are translucent. Stir in the garlic and cook for 1 minute.

3 Strain the liquid from 1 jar of clams and add the liquid to the pan, with the wine. Stir, bring to simmering point and simmer for 3 minutes. Drain the second jar of clams and discard the liquid.

4 Add the clams, parsley and oregano to the pan and season with pepper and nutmeg. Lower the heat and cook until the sauce is heated through.

5 Transfer the pasta to a warm serving dish and pour over the sauce. Sprinkle with the Parmesan cheese, garnish with the basil and serve immediately.

COOK'S TIP

There are many different types of clams found along almost every coast in the world. Those traditionally used in this dish are the tiny ones – only 2.5-5 cm/1-2 inches across – known in Italy as vongole.

Farfallini Buttered Lobster

This is one of those dishes that looks almost too lovely to eat – but you should!

NUTRITIONAL INFORMATION

Calories ....686 Sugars 1g
Protein ....45g Fat 36g
Carbohydrate ...44g Saturates 19g

 30 MINS   25 MINS

SERVES 4

INGREDIENTS

2 x 700 g/1 lb 9 oz lobsters, split into halves

juice and grated rind of 1 lemon

115 g/4 oz/½ cup butter

4 tbsp fresh white breadcrumbs

2 tbsp brandy

5 tbsp double (heavy) cream or crème fraîche

450 g/1 lb dried farfallini

1 tbsp olive oil

60 g/2 oz/⅔ cup freshly grated Parmesan cheese

salt and pepper

TO GARNISH

1 kiwi fruit, sliced

4 unpeeled, cooked king prawns (shrimp)

fresh dill sprigs

1 Carefully discard the stomach sac, vein and gills from each lobster. Remove all the meat from the tail and chop. Crack the claws and legs, remove the meat and chop. Transfer the meat to a bowl and add the lemon juice and grated lemon rind.

2 Clean the shells thoroughly and place in a warm oven at 170°C/325°/Gas Mark 3 to dry out.

3 Melt 25 g/1 oz/2 tbsp of the butter in a frying pan (skillet). Add the breadcrumbs and fry for about 3 minutes, until crisp and golden brown.

4 Melt the remaining butter in a saucepan. Add the lobster meat and heat through gently. Add the brandy and cook for a further 3 minutes, then add the cream or crème fraîche and season to taste with salt and pepper.

5 Meanwhile, bring a large pan of lightly salted water to the boil. Add the farfallini and olive oil and cook for 8–10 minutes, until tender but still firm to the bite. Drain and spoon the pasta into the clean lobster shells.

6 Top with the buttered lobster and sprinkle with a little grated Parmesan cheese and the breadcrumbs. Grill (broil) for 2–3 minutes, until golden brown.

7 Transfer the lobster shells to a warm serving dish, garnish with the lemon slices, kiwi fruit, king prawns (shrimp) and dill sprigs and serve immediately.

Baked Scallops & Pasta

This is another tempting seafood dish where the eye is delighted as much as the taste-buds.

NUTRITIONAL INFORMATION

Calories ....725 Sugars 2g
Protein ....38g Fat 48g
Carbohydrate ...38g Saturates 25g

20 MINS   30 MINS

SERVES 4

INGREDIENTS

12 scallops

3 tbsp olive oil

350 g/12 oz/3 cups small, dried wholemeal (whole wheat) pasta shells

150 ml/¼ pint/⅔ cup fish stock

1 onion, chopped

juice and finely grated rind of 2 lemons

150 ml/¼ pint/⅔ cup double (heavy) cream

225 g/8 oz/2 cups grated Cheddar cheese

salt and pepper

crusty brown bread, to serve

1 Remove the scallops from their shells. Scrape off the skirt and the black intestinal thread. Reserve the white part (the flesh) and the orange part (the coral or roe). Very carefully ease the flesh and coral from the shell with a short, but very strong knife.

2 Wash the shells thoroughly and dry them well. Put the shells on a baking tray (cookie sheet), sprinkle lightly with two thirds of the olive oil and set aside.

3 Meanwhile, bring a large saucepan of lightly salted water to the boil. Add the pasta shells and remaining olive oil and cook for 8–10 minutes or until tender, but still firm to the bite. Drain well and

spoon about 25 g/1 oz of pasta into each scallop shell.

4 Put the scallops, fish stock, lemon rind and onion in an ovenproof dish and season to taste with pepper. Cover with foil and bake in a preheated oven at 180°C/350°F/Gas Mark 4 for 8 minutes.

5 Remove the dish from the oven. Remove the foil and, using a slotted spoon, transfer the scallops to the shells.

Add 1 tablespoon of the cooking liquid to each shell, together with a drizzle of lemon juice and a little cream, and top with the grated cheese.

6 Increase the oven temperature to 230°C/450°F/Gas Mark 8 and return the scallops to the oven for a further 4 minutes.

7 Serve the scallops in their shells with crusty brown bread and butter.

Seafood Lasagne

You can use any fish and any sauce you like in this recipe: try smoked finnan haddock and whisky sauce or cod with cheese sauce.

NUTRITIONAL INFORMATION

Calories 790	Sugars 23g	
Protein 55g	Fat 32g	
Carbohydrate ...74g	Saturates 19g	

 30 MINS   45 MINS

SERVES 4

I N G R E D I E N T S

450 g/1 lb finnan haddock, filleted, skin
   removed and flesh flaked

115 g/ 4 oz prawns (shrimp)

115 g/4 oz sole fillet, skin removed and
   flesh sliced

juice of 1 lemon

60 g/2 oz/4 tbsp butter

3 leeks, very thinly sliced

60 g/2 oz/½ cup plain (all purpose) flour

about 600 ml/1 pint/2⅓ cups milk

2 tbsp clear honey

200g/7 oz /1¾ cups grated
   Mozzarella cheese

450g/1 lb pre-cooked lasagne

60 g/2 oz/⅔ cup freshly grated
   Parmesan cheese

pepper

Gradually stir in enough milk to make a thick, creamy sauce.

oven at 180°C/350°F/Gas Mark 4 for 30 minutes. Serve immediately.

1 Put the haddock fillet, prawns (shrimp) and sole fillet into a large bowl and season with pepper and lemon juice according to taste. Set aside while you make the sauce.

2 Melt the butter in a large saucepan. Add the leeks and cook, stirring occasionally, for 8 minutes. Add the flour and cook, stirring constantly, for 1 minute.

3 Blend in the honey and Mozzarella cheese and cook for a further 3 minutes. Remove the pan from the heat and mix in the fish and prawns (shrimp).

4 Make alternate layers of fish sauce and lasagne in an ovenproof dish, finishing with a layer of fish sauce on top. Generously sprinkle over the grated Parmesan cheese and bake in a preheated

VARIATION

For a cider sauce, substitute 1 finely chopped shallot for the leeks, 300 ml/½ pint/1½ cups cider and 300 ml/½ pint/1½ cups double (heavy) cream for the milk and 1 tsp mustard for the honey. For a Tuscan sauce, substitute 1 chopped fennel bulb for the leeks; omit the honey.

A Seafood Medley

You can use almost any kind of sea fish in this recipe. Red sea bream is an especially good choice.

NUTRITIONAL INFORMATION

Calories 699	Sugars 4g	
Protein 56g	Fat 35g	
Carbohydrate ...35g	Saturates 20g	

🍞 🍞 🍞

 20 MINS 　　🕐 30 MINS

SERVES 4

INGREDIENTS

12 raw tiger prawns (shrimp)

12 raw (small) shrimp

450 g/1 lb fillet of sea bream

60 g/2 oz/4 tbsp butter

12 scallops, shelled

125 g/4½ oz freshwater prawns (shrimp)

juice and finely grated rind of 1 lemon

pinch of saffron powder or threads

1 litre/1¾ pints/4 cups vegetable stock

150 ml/¼ pint/⅔ cup rose petal vinegar

450 g/1 lb dried farfalle

1 tbsp olive oil

150 ml/¼ pint/⅔ cup white wine

1 tbsp pink peppercorns

115 g/4 oz baby carrots

150 ml/¼ pint/⅔ cup double (heavy) cream
or fromage frais

salt and pepper

1 Peel and devein the prawns (shrimp) and (small) shrimp. Thinly slice the sea bream. Melt the butter in a frying pan (skillet), add the sea bream, scallops, prawns (shrimp) and (small) shrimp and cook for 1–2 minutes.

2 Season with pepper to taste. Add the lemon juice and grated rind. Very carefully add a pinch of saffron powder or a few strands of saffron to the cooking juices (not to the seafood).

3 Remove the seafood from the pan, set aside and keep warm.

4 Return the pan to the heat and add the stock. Bring to the boil and reduce by one third. Add the rose petal vinegar and cook for 4 minutes, until reduced.

5 Bring a pan of salted water to the boil. Add the farfalle and oil and cook for 8–10 minutes until tender, but still firm to the bite. Drain the pasta, transfer to a serving plate and top with the seafood.

6 Add the wine, peppercorns, and carrots to the pan and reduce the sauce for 6 minutes. Add the cream or fromage frais and simmer for 2 minutes.

7 Pour the sauce over the seafood and pasta and serve immediately.

Spaghetti & Seafood Sauce

Peeled prawns (shrimp) from the freezer can become the star ingredient in this colourful and tasty dish.

30 MINS   35 MINS

SERVES 4

INGREDIENTS

225 g/8 oz dried spaghetti, broken into
  15 cm/6 inch lengths

2 tbsp olive oil

300 ml/½ pint/1¼ cups chicken stock

1 tsp lemon juice

1 small cauliflower, cut into florets

2 carrots, thinly sliced

115 g/4 oz mangetout (snow peas)

60 g/2 oz/4 tbsp butter

1 onion, sliced

225 g/8 oz courgettes (zucchini), sliced

1 garlic clove, chopped

350 g/12 oz frozen, cooked, peeled prawns
  (shrimp), defrosted

2 tbsp chopped fresh parsley

25 g/1 oz/⅓ cup freshly grated
  Parmesan cheese

½ tsp paprika

salt and pepper

4 unpeeled, cooked prawns (shrimp),
  to garnish

1 Bring a pan of lightly salted water to the boil. Add the spaghetti and 1 tbsp of the olive oil and cook for 8–10 minutes until tender, but still firm to the bite. Drain the spaghetti and return to the pan. Toss with the remaining olive oil, cover and keep warm.

2 Bring the chicken stock and lemon juice to the boil. Add the cauliflower and carrots and cook for 3–4 minutes. Remove from the pan and set aside. Add the mangetout (snow peas) to the pan and cook for 1–2 minutes. Set aside with the other vegetables.

3 Melt half of the butter in a frying pan (skillet) over a medium heat. Add the onion and courgettes (zucchini) and fry for about 3 minutes. Add the garlic and prawns (shrimp) and cook for a further 2–3 minutes, until thoroughly heated through.

4 Stir in the reserved vegetables and heat through. Season to taste and stir in the remaining butter.

5 Transfer the spaghetti to a warm serving dish. Pour over the sauce and add the chopped parsley. Toss well with 2 forks until coated. Sprinkle over the Parmesan cheese and paprika, garnish with the unpeeled prawns (shrimp) and serve immediately.

Meat

Italians have their very own special way of butchering meat, producing very different cuts. Most meat is sold ready-boned and often cut straight across the grain. Veal is a great favourite and widely available. Pork is also popular, with roast pig being the traditional dish of Umbria. Suckling pig is roasted with lots of fresh herbs,

especially rosemary, until the skin is crisp and brown. Lamb is often served for special occasions, cooked on a spit or roasted in the oven with wine, garlic and herbs; and the very small cutlets from young lambs feature widely, especially in Rome. Offal plays an important role, too, with liver, brains, sweetbreads, tongue, heart, tripe and kidneys always available. Whatever your favourite Italian meat dish is, it's sure to be included in this chapter.

Beef & Spaghetti Surprise

This delicious Sicilian recipe originated as a handy way of using up leftover cooked pasta.

NUTRITIONAL INFORMATION

Calories 797   Sugars 7g
Protein ....31g   Fat 60g
Carbohydrate ...35g   Saturates 16g

30 MINS   1¹/₂ HOURS

SERVES 4

INGREDIENTS

150 ml/¼ pint/⅔ cup olive oil, plus extra
    for brushing

2 aubergines (eggplants)

350 g/12 oz/3 cups minced (ground) beef

1 onion, chopped

2 garlic cloves, crushed

2 tbsp tomato purée (paste)

400 g/14 oz can chopped tomatoes

1 tsp Worcestershire sauce

1 tsp chopped fresh marjoram or oregano
    or ½ tsp dried marjoram or oregano

60 g/2 oz/½ cup stoned (pitted) black
    olives, sliced

1 green, red or yellow (bell) pepper, cored,
    seeded and chopped

175 g/6 oz dried spaghetti

115 g/4 oz/1 cup freshly grated
    Parmesan cheese

salt and pepper

fresh oregano or parsley sprigs,
    to garnish

1 Brush a 20 cm/8 inch loose-based round cake tin (pan) with oil, line the base with baking parchment and brush with oil.

2 Slice the aubergines (eggplants). Heat a little oil in a pan and fry the aubergines (eggplant), in batches, for 3–4 minutes or until browned on both sides. Add more oil, as necessary. Drain on kitchen paper (paper towels).

3 Put the minced (ground) beef, onion and garlic in a saucepan and cook over a medium heat, stirring occasionally, until browned. Add the tomato purée (paste), tomatoes, Worcestershire sauce, marjoram or oregano and salt and pepper to taste. Leave to simmer, stirring occasionally, for 10 minutes. Add the olives and (bell) pepper and cook for a further 10 minutes.

4 Bring a pan of salted water to the boil. Add the spaghetti and 1 tbsp oil and cook for 8–10 minutes until tender, but still firm to the bite. Drain and turn the spaghetti into a bowl. Add the meat mixture and cheese and toss with 2 forks.

5 Arrange aubergine (eggplant) slices over the base and up the sides of the tin (pan). Add the spaghetti, pressing down firmly, and then cover with the rest of the aubergine (eggplant) slices. Bake in a preheated oven at 200°C/400°F/Gas Mark 6 for 40 minutes. Leave to stand for 5 minutes, then invert on to a serving dish. Discard the baking parchment. Garnish with the fresh herbs and serve.

Beef in Barolo

Barolo is a famous wine from the Piedmont area of Italy. Its mellow flavour is the key to this dish, so don't stint on the quality of the wine.

NUTRITIONAL INFORMATION

Calories	744	Sugars	.........1g
Protein	........66g	Fat	..........43g
Carbohydrate	....1g	Saturates	......16g

15 MINS   2¼ HOURS

SERVES 4

INGREDIENTS

4 tbsp oil

1 kg/2 lb 4 oz piece boned rolled rib of
   beef, or piece of silverside (round)

2 garlic cloves, crushed

4 shallots, sliced

1 tsp chopped fresh rosemary

1 tsp chopped fresh oregano

2 celery stalks, sliced

1 large carrot, diced

2 cloves

1 bottle Barolo wine

freshly grated nutmeg

salt and pepper

cooked vegetables, such as broccoli, carrots
   and new potatoes, to serve

1 Heat the oil in a flameproof casserole and brown the meat all over. Remove the meat from the casserole.

2 Add the garlic, shallots, herbs, celery, carrot and cloves and fry for 5 minutes.

3 Replace the meat on top of the vegetables. Pour in the wine. Cover the casserole and simmer gently for about 2 hours until tender. Remove the meat from the casserole, slice and keep warm.

4 Rub the contents of the pan through a sieve (strainer) or purée in a blender, adding a little hot beef stock if necessary. Season with nutmeg, salt and pepper.

5 Serve the meat with the sauce and accompanied by cooked vegetables, such as broccoli, carrots and new potatoes, if wished.

Layered Meat Loaf

The cheese-flavoured pasta layer comes as a pleasant surprise inside this lightly spiced meat loaf.

NUTRITIONAL INFORMATION

Calories 412   Sugars 3g
Protein . . . . .21g   Fat 30g
Carbohydrate . . .15g   Saturates 13g

🐚 🐚 🐚 🐚

🍲 35 MINS   🕐 1½ HOURS

SERVES 6

INGREDIENTS

25 g/1 oz/2 tbsp butter, plus extra
   for greasing

1 small onion, finely chopped

1 small red (bell) pepper, cored, seeded
   and chopped

1 garlic clove, chopped

450 g/1 lb/4 cups minced (ground) beef

25 g/1 oz/½ cup white breadcrumbs

½ tsp cayenne pepper

1 tbsp lemon juice

½ tsp grated lemon rind

2 tbsp chopped fresh parsley

90 g/3 oz/¾ cup dried short pasta,
   such as fusilli

1 tbsp olive oil

250 ml/9 fl oz/1 cup Italian Cheese Sauce
   (see page 30)

4 bay leaves

175 g/6 oz fatty bacon, rinds removed

salt and pepper

salad leaves (greens), to serve

1 Melt the butter in a pan over a medium heat and fry the onion and (bell) pepper for about 3 minutes. Stir in the garlic and cook for 1 minute.

2 Put the meat into a bowl and mash with a wooden spoon until sticky. Add the onion mixture, breadcrumbs, cayenne pepper, lemon juice, lemon rind and parsley. Season and set aside.

3 Bring a pan of salted water to the boil. Add the pasta and oil and cook for 8–10 minutes, until almost tender. Drain and stir into the Italian Cheese Sauce.

4 Grease a 1 kg/2 lb 4 oz loaf tin (pan) and arrange the bay leaves in the base. Stretch the bacon slices with the back of a knife and line the base and sides of the tin (pan) with them. Spoon in half the meat mixture and smooth the surface. Cover with the pasta mixed with Italian Cheese Sauce, then spoon in the remaining meat mixture. Level the top and cover with foil.

5 Bake the meat loaf in a preheated oven, at 180°C/350°F/Gas Mark 4, for 1 hour or until the juices run clear when a skewer is inserted into the centre and the loaf has shrunk away from the sides. Pour off any fat and turn out the loaf on to a serving dish. Serve with salad leaves (greens).

Rich Beef Stew

This slow-cooked beef stew is flavoured with oranges, red wine and porcini mushrooms.

NUTRITIONAL INFORMATION

Calories	388	Sugars	........15g
Protein	........30g	Fat	..........21g
Carbohydrate	...16g	Saturates	.......9g

 45 MINS   1³/₄ HOURS

SERVES 4

INGREDIENTS

1 tbsp oil

15 g/½ oz/1 tbsp butter

225 g/8 oz baby onions, peeled and halved

600 g/1 lb 5 oz stewing steak, diced into 4 cm/1½ inch chunks

300 ml/½ pint/1¼ cup beef stock

150 ml/¼ pint/⅔ cup red wine

4 tbsp chopped oregano

1 tbsp sugar

1 orange

25 g/1 oz porcini or other dried mushrooms

225 g/8 oz fresh plum tomatoes

cooked rice or potatoes, to serve

1 Heat the oil and butter in a large frying pan (skillet). Add the onions and sauté for 5 minutes or until golden. Remove the onions with a perforated spoon, set aside and keep warm.

2 Add the beef to the pan and cook, stirring, for 5 minutes or until browned all over.

3 Return the onions to the frying pan (skillet) and add the stock, wine, oregano and sugar, stirring to mix well. Transfer the mixture to an ovenproof casserole dish.

4 Pare the rind from the orange and cut it into strips. Slice the orange flesh into rings. Add the orange rings and the rind to the casserole. Cook in a preheated oven, at 180°C/350°F/Gas Mark 4, for 1¼ hours.

5 Soak the porcini mushrooms for 30 minutes in a small bowl containing 4 tablespoons of warm water.

6 Peel and halve the tomatoes. Add the tomatoes, porcini mushrooms and their soaking liquid to the casserole. Cook for a further 20 minutes until the beef is tender and the juices thickened. Serve with cooked rice or potatoes.

Creamed Strips of Sirloin

This quick and easy dish tastes superb and would make a delicious treat for a special occasion.

NUTRITIONAL INFORMATION

Calories	796	Sugars	.........2g
Protein	........29g	Fat	..........63g
Carbohydrate	...26g	Saturates	......39g

 15 MINS   30 MINS

SERVES 4

INGREDIENTS

75 g/2¾ oz/6 tbsp butter

450 g/1 lb sirloin steak, trimmed
and cut into thin strips

175 g/6 oz button mushrooms, sliced

1 tsp mustard

pinch of freshly grated root ginger

2 tbsp dry sherry

150 ml/¼ pint/⅔ cup double (heavy) cream

salt and pepper

4 slices hot toast, cut into triangles,
to serve

PASTA

450 g/1 lb dried rigatoni

2 tbsp olive oil

2 fresh basil sprigs

115 g/4 oz/8 tbsp butter

COOK'S TIP

Dried pasta will keep for up to 6 months. Keep it in the packet and reseal it once you have opened it, or transfer the pasta to an airtight jar.

1 Melt the butter in a large frying pan (skillet) and gently fry the steak over a low heat, stirring frequently, for 6 minutes. Using a slotted spoon, transfer the steak to an ovenproof dish and keep warm.

2 Add the sliced mushrooms to the frying pan (skillet) and cook for 2–3 minutes in the juices remaining in the pan. Add the mustard, ginger, salt and pepper. Cook for 2 minutes, then add the sherry and cream. Cook for a further 3 minutes, then pour the cream sauce over the steak.

3 Bake the steak and cream mixture in a preheated oven, at 190°C/375°F/Gas Mark 5, for 10 minutes.

4 Meanwhile, cook the pasta. Bring a large saucepan of lightly salted water to the boil. Add the rigatoni, olive oil and 1 of the basil sprigs and boil rapidly for 10 minutes, until tender but still firm to the bite. Drain the pasta and transfer to a warm serving plate. Toss the pasta with the butter and garnish with a sprig of basil.

5 Serve the creamed steak strips with the pasta and triangles of warm toast.

Pizzaiola Steak

This has a Neapolitan sauce, using the delicious red tomatoes so abundant in that area, but canned ones make an excellent alternative.

NUTRITIONAL INFORMATION

Calories	371	Sugars	.........7g
Protein	........43g	Fat	..........19g
Carbohydrate	....7g	Saturates	.......5g

🍲 25 MINS 🕐 30 MINS

SERVES 4

INGREDIENTS

2 x 400 g/14 oz cans peeled tomatoes or
750 g/1 lb 10 oz fresh tomatoes

4 tbsp olive oil

2–3 garlic cloves, crushed

1 onion, chopped finely

1 tbsp tomato purée (paste)

1½ tsp chopped fresh marjoram or oregano
or ¾ tsp dried marjoram or oregano

4 thin sirloin or rump steaks

2 tbsp chopped fresh parsley

1 tsp sugar

salt and pepper

fresh herbs, to garnish (optional)

sauté potatoes, to serve

1 If using canned tomatoes, purée them in a food processor, then sieve to remove the seeds. If using fresh tomatoes, peel, remove the seeds and chop finely.

2 Heat half of the oil in a pan and fry the garlic and onions very gently for about 5 minutes, or until softened.

3 Add the tomatoes, seasoning, tomato purée (paste) and chopped herbs to the pan. If using fresh tomatoes add 4 tablespoons water too, and then simmer very gently for 8–10 minutes, giving an occasional stir.

4 Meanwhile, trim the steaks if necessary and season. Heat the remaining oil in a frying pan (skillet) and fry the steaks quickly on both sides to seal, then continue until cooked to your liking – 2 minutes for rare, 3–4 minutes for medium, or 5 minutes for well done. Alternatively, cook the steaks under a hot grill (broiler) after brushing lightly with oil.

5 When the sauce has thickened a little, adjust the seasoning and stir in the chopped parsley and sugar.

6 Pour off the excess fat from the pan containing the steaks and add the tomato sauce. Reheat gently and serve at once, with the sauce spooned over and around the steaks. Garnish with sprigs of fresh herbs, if liked. Sauté potatoes and a green vegetable make very good accompaniments.

Fresh Spaghetti & Meatballs

This well-loved Italian dish is famous across the world. Make the most of it by using high-quality steak for the meatballs.

NUTRITIONAL INFORMATION

Calories 665   Sugars 9g
Protein . . . . .39g   Fat 24g
Carbohydrate . . .77g   Saturates 8g

 45 MINS   1¼ HOURS

SERVES 4

INGREDIENTS

150 g/5½ oz/2½ cups brown breadcrumbs

150 ml/¼ pint/⅔ cup milk

25 g/1 oz/2 tbsp butter

25 g/1 oz/¼ cup wholemeal
   (whole-wheat) flour

200 ml/7 fl oz/⅞ cup beef stock

400 g/14 oz can chopped tomatoes

2 tbsp tomato purée (paste)

1 tsp sugar

1 tbsp finely chopped fresh tarragon

1 large onion, chopped

450 g/1 lb/4 cups minced steak

1 tsp paprika

4 tbsp olive oil

450 g/1 lb fresh spaghetti

salt and pepper

fresh tarragon sprigs, to garnish

1 Place the breadcrumbs in a bowl, add the milk and set aside to soak for about 30 minutes.

2 Melt half of the butter in a pan. Add the flour and cook, stirring constantly, for 2 minutes. Gradually stir in the beef stock and cook, stirring constantly, for a further 5 minutes. Add the tomatoes, tomato purée (paste), sugar and tarragon. Season well and simmer for 25 minutes.

3 Mix the onion, steak and paprika into the breadcrumbs and season to taste. Shape the mixture into 14 meatballs.

4 Heat the oil and remaining butter in a frying pan (skillet) and fry the meatballs, turning, until brown all over. Place in a deep casserole, pour over the tomato sauce, cover and bake in a preheated oven, at 180°C/350°F/Gas Mark 4, for 25 minutes.

5 Bring a large saucepan of lightly salted water to the boil. Add the fresh spaghetti, bring back to the boil and cook for about 2–3 minutes or until tender, but still firm to the bite.

6 Meanwhile, remove the meatballs from the oven and allow them to cool for 3 minutes. Serve the meatballs and their sauce with the spaghetti, garnished with tarragon sprigs.

Beef & Potato Ravioli

In this recipe the 'pasta' dough is made with potatoes instead of flour. The small round ravioli are filled with a rich bolognese sauce.

NUTRITIONAL INFORMATION

Calories . . . . .618 Sugars 4g
Protein . . . . .16g Fat 31g
Carbohydrate . . .74g Saturates 12g

 30 MINS   50 MINS

SERVES 4

I N G R E D I E N T S

FILLING

1 tbsp vegetable oil

125 g/4½ oz ground beef

1 shallot, diced

1 garlic clove, crushed

1 tbsp plain (all-purpose) flour

1 tbsp tomato purée (paste)

150 ml/¼ pint/⅔ cup beef stock

1 celery stick, chopped

2 tomatoes, peeled and diced

2 tsp chopped fresh basil

salt and pepper

RAVIOLI

450 g/1 lb floury (mealy) potatoes, diced

3 small egg yolks

3 tbsp olive oil

175 g/6 oz/1½ cups plain (all-purpose) flour

60 g/2 oz/¼ cup butter, for frying

shredded basil leaves, to garnish

1 To make the filling, heat the vegetable oil in a pan and fry the beef for 3-4 minutes, breaking it up with a spoon.

2 Add the shallots and garlic to the pan and cook for 2-3 minutes, or until the shallots have softened.

3 Stir in the flour and tomato purée (paste) and cook for 1 minute. Stir in the beef stock, celery, tomatoes and chopped fresh basil. Season to taste with salt and pepper.

4 Cook the mixture over a low heat for 20 minutes. Remove from the heat and leave to cool.

5 To make the ravioli, cook the potatoes in a pan of boiling water for 10 minutes until cooked.

6 Mash the potatoes and place them in a mixing bowl. Blend in the egg yolks and oil. Season with salt and pepper, then stir in the flour and mix to form a dough.

7 On a lightly floured surface, divide the dough into 24 pieces and shape into flat rounds. Spoon the filling on to one half of each round and fold the dough over to encase the filling, pressing down to seal the edges.

8 Melt the butter in a frying pan (skillet) and cook the ravioli for 6-8 minutes, turning once, until golden. Serve hot, garnished with shredded basil leaves.

Beef & Pasta Bake

The combination of Italian and Indian ingredients makes a surprisingly delicious recipe. Marinate the steak in advance to save time.

NUTRITIONAL INFORMATION

Calories 1050	Sugars 4g	
Protein 47g	Fat 81g	
Carbohydrate . . .37g	Saturates 34g	

6¼ HOURS   1¼ HOURS

SERVES 4

INGREDIENTS

900g/2 lb steak, cut into cubes

150 ml/¼ pint/⅔ cup beef stock

450g/1 lb dried macaroni

300 ml/½ pint/1¼ cups double
(heavy) cream

½ tsp garam masala

salt

fresh coriander (cilantro) and flaked
(slivered) almonds, to garnish

KORMA PASTE

60 g/2 oz/½ cup blanched almonds

6 garlic cloves

2.5 cm/1 inch piece fresh root ginger,
coarsely chopped

6 tbsp beef stock

1 tsp ground cardamom

4 cloves, crushed

1 tsp cinnamon

2 large onions, chopped

1 tsp coriander seeds

2 tsp ground cumin seeds

pinch of cayenne pepper

6 tbsp of sunflower oil

1 To make the korma paste, grind the almonds finely using a pestle and mortar. Put the ground almonds and the rest of the korma paste ingredients into a food processor or blender and process to make a very smooth paste.

2 Put the steak in a shallow dish and spoon over the korma paste, turning to coat the steak well. Leave in the refrigerator to marinate for 6 hours.

3 Transfer the steak and korma paste to a large saucepan, and simmer over a low heat, adding a little beef stock if required, for 35 minutes.

4 Meanwhile, bring a large saucepan of lightly salted water to the boil. Add the macaroni and cook for 10 minutes until tender, but still firm to the bite. Drain the pasta thoroughly and transfer to a deep casserole. Add the steak, double (heavy) cream and garam masala.

5 Bake in a preheated oven at 200°C/ 400°F/Gas Mark 6 for 30 minutes. Remove the casserole from the oven and allow to stand for about 10 minutes. Garnish the bake with fresh coriander (cilantro) and serve.

Beef, Tomato & Olive Kebabs

These kebabs (kabobs) have a Mediterranean flavour. The sweetness of the tomatoes and the sharpness of the olives makes them rather more-ish.

  45 MINS 15 MINS

SERVES 8

INGREDIENTS

450 g/1 lb rump or sirloin steak

16 cherry tomatoes

16 large green olives, pitted

focaccia bread, to serve

BASTE

4 tbsp olive oil

1 tbsp sherry vinegar

1 clove garlic, crushed

salt and pepper

FRESH TOMATO RELISH

1 tbsp olive oil

½ red onion, chopped finely

1 clove garlic, chopped

6 plum tomatoes, deseeded, skinned
  and chopped

2 pitted green olives, sliced

1 tbsp chopped, fresh parsley

1 tbsp lemon juice

1 Using a sharp knife, trim any fat from the beef and cut the meat into about 24 evenly-sized pieces.

2 Thread the pieces of beef on to 8 wooden skewers, alternating the meat with the cherry tomatoes and the green olives.

3 To make the baste, combine the oil, vinegar, garlic and salt and pepper to taste in a bowl.

4 To make the relish, heat the oil in a small pan and fry the onion and garlic for 3–4 minutes until softened. Add the tomatoes and olives and cook for 2–3 minutes until the tomatoes have softened slightly. Stir in the parsley and lemon juice and season with salt and pepper to taste. Set aside and keep warm or leave to chill.

5 Barbecue (grill) the kebabs (kabobs) on an oiled rack over hot coals for 5–10 minutes, basting and turning frequently. Serve with the tomato relish and slices of focaccia.

COOK'S TIP

The kebabs (kabobs), baste and relish can be prepared several hours in advance, avoiding the need for any last minute rush. For a simple meal, serve with crusty fresh bread and a mixed salad.

Beef Olives in Rich Gravy

Wafer-thin slices of tender beef with a rich garlic and bacon stuffing, flavoured with the tang of orange.

NUTRITIONAL INFORMATION

Calories	379	Sugars 4g
Protein	........26g	Fat 24g
Carbohydrate	....4g	Saturates 8g

20 MINS | 20 MINS

SERVES 4

INGREDIENTS

8 ready prepared beef olives

4 tbsp chopped fresh parsley

4 garlic cloves, chopped finely

125 g/4½ oz smoked streaky bacon, rinded and chopped finely

grated rind of ½ small orange

2 tbsp olive oil

300 ml/½ pint/1¼ cups dry red wine

1 bay leaf

1 tsp sugar

60 g/2 oz pitted black olives, drained

salt and pepper

TO GARNISH

orange slices

chopped fresh parsley

1 Unroll the beef olives and flatten out as thinly as possible using a meat tenderizer or mallet. Trim the edges to neaten them.

2 Mix together the parsley, garlic, bacon, orange rind and salt and pepper to taste. Spread this mixture evenly over each beef olive.

3 Roll up each beef olive tightly, then secure with a cocktail stick (toothpick).

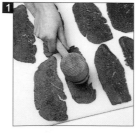

Heat the oil in a frying pan (skillet) and fry the beef on all sides for 10 minutes.

4 Drain the beef olives, reserving the pan juices, and keep warm. Pour the wine into the juices, add the bay leaf, sugar and seasoning. Bring to the boil and boil rapidly for 5 minutes to reduce slightly, stirring.

5 Return the cooked beef to the pan along with the black olives and heat through for a further 2 minutes. Discard the bay leaf and cocktail sticks (toothpicks).

6 Transfer the beef olives and gravy to a serving dish, and serve garnished with orange slices and parsley.

Meatballs in Red Wine Sauce

A different twist is given to this traditional pasta dish with a rich, but subtle sauce.

NUTRITIONAL INFORMATION

Calories 811   Sugars 7g
Protein . . . . .30g   Fat 43g
Carbohydrate . . .76g   Saturates 12g

   45 MINS   1½ HOURS

SERVES 4

I N G R E D I E N T S

150 ml/¼ pint/⅔ cup milk

150 g/5½ oz/2 cups white breadcrumbs

25 g/1 oz/2 tbsp butter

9 tbsp olive oil

225 g/8 oz/3 cups sliced
   oyster mushrooms

25 g/1 oz/¼ cup wholemeal
(whole-wheat) flour

200 ml/7 fl oz/⅞ cup beef stock

150 ml/¼ pint/⅔ cup red wine

4 tomatoes, skinned and chopped

1 tbsp tomato purée (paste)

1 tsp brown sugar

1 tbsp finely chopped fresh basil

12 shallots, chopped

450 g/1 lb/4 cups minced (ground) steak

1 tsp paprika

450 g/1 lb dried egg tagliarini

salt and pepper

fresh basil sprigs, to garnish

1 Pour the milk into a bowl and soak the breadcrumbs in the milk for 30 minutes.

2 Heat half of the butter and 4 tbsp of the oil in a pan. Fry the mushrooms for 4 minutes, then stir in the flour and cook for 2 minutes. Add the stock and wine and simmer for 15 minutes. Add the tomatoes, tomato purée (paste), sugar and basil. Season and simmer for 30 minutes.

3 Mix the shallots, steak and paprika with the breadcrumbs and season to taste. Shape the mixture into 14 meatballs.

4 Heat 4 tbsp of the remaining oil and the remaining butter in a large frying pan (skillet). Fry the meatballs, turning frequently, until brown all over. Transfer to a deep casserole, pour over the red wine and the mushroom sauce, cover and bake in a preheated oven, at 180°C/350°F/Gas Mark 4, for 30 minutes.

5 Bring a pan of salted water to the boil. Add the pasta and the remaining oil and cook for 8–10 minutes or until tender. Drain and transfer to a serving dish. Remove the casserole from the oven and cool for 3 minutes. Pour the meatballs and sauce on to the pasta, garnish and serve.

Neapolitan Pork Steaks

An Italian version of grilled pork steaks, this dish is easy to make and delicious to eat.

NUTRITIONAL INFORMATION

Calories 353	Sugars 3g	
Protein 39g	Fat 20g	
Carbohydrate 4g	Saturates 5g	

 10 MINS   25 MINS

SERVES 4

I N G R E D I E N T S

2 tbsp olive oil

1 garlic clove, chopped

1 large onion, sliced

400 g/14 oz can tomatoes

2 tsp yeast extract

4 pork loin steaks, each about 125 g/4½ oz

75 g/2¾ oz black olives, pitted

2 tbsp fresh basil, shredded

freshly grated Parmesan cheese, to serve

1 Heat the oil in a large frying pan (skillet). Add the onions and garlic and cook, stirring, for 3–4 minutes or until they just begin to soften.

2 Add the tomatoes and yeast extract to the frying pan (skillet) and leave to simmer for about 5 minutes or until the sauce starts to thicken.

COOK'S TIP

Parmesan is a mature and exceptionally hard cheese produced in Italy. You only need to add a little as it has a very strong flavour.

3 Cook the pork steaks, under a preheated grill (broiler), for 5 minutes on both sides, until the the meat is cooked through. Set the pork aside and keep warm.

4 Add the olives and fresh shredded basil to the sauce in the frying pan (skillet) and stir quickly to combine.

5 Transfer the steaks to warm serving plates. Top the steaks with the sauce, sprinkle with freshly grated Parmesan cheese and serve immediately.

Pork Chops with Sage

The fresh taste of sage is the perfect ingredient to counteract the richness of pork.

NUTRITIONAL INFORMATION

Calories 364	Sugars 5g
Protein 34g	Fat 19g
Carbohydrate ...14g	Saturates 7g

🍲 🍲

🧈 10 MINS 🕐 15 MINS

SERVES 4

INGREDIENTS

2 tbsp flour

1 tbsp chopped fresh sage or 1 tsp dried

4 lean boneless pork chops, trimmed of
    excess fat

2 tbsp olive oil

15 g/½ oz/1 tbsp butter

2 red onions, sliced into rings

1 tbsp lemon juice

2 tsp caster (superfine) sugar

4 plum tomatoes, quartered

salt and pepper

1 Mix the flour, sage and salt and pepper to taste on a plate. Lightly dust the pork chops on both sides with the seasoned flour.

2 Heat the oil and butter in a frying pan (skillet), add the chops and cook them for 6–7 minutes on each side until cooked through. Drain the chops, reserving the pan juices, and keep warm.

3 Toss the onion in the lemon juice and fry along with the sugar and tomatoes for 5 minutes until tender.

4 Serve the pork with the tomato and onion mixture and a green salad.

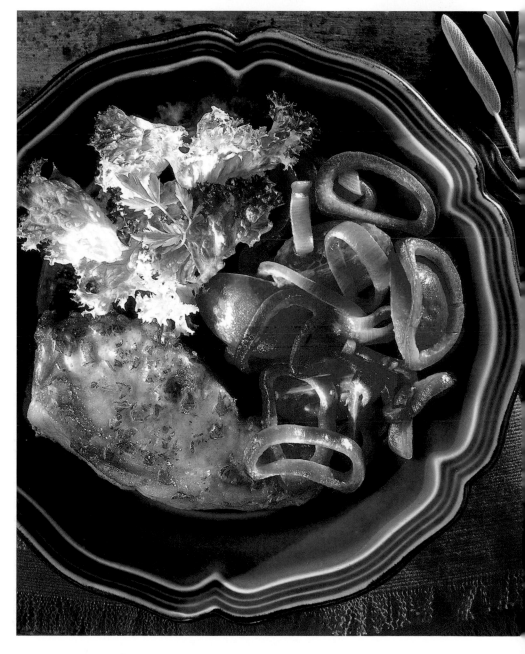

Pork with Fennel & Juniper

The addition of juniper and fennel to the pork chops gives an unusual and delicate flavour to this dish.

NUTRITIONAL INFORMATION

Calories 277   Sugars 0.4g
Protein . . . . .32g   Fat 16g
Carbohydrate . . .0.4g   Saturates 5g

2¹⁄₄ HOURS   15 MINS

SERVES 4

INGREDIENTS

½ fennel bulb

1 tbsp juniper berries

about 2 tbsp olive oil

finely grated rind and juice of 1 orange

4 pork chops, each about 150 g/5½ oz

fresh bread and a crisp salad, to serve

1 Finely chop the fennel bulb, discarding the green parts.

2 Grind the juniper berries in a pestle and mortar. Mix the crushed juniper berries with the fennel flesh, olive oil and orange rind.

3 Using a sharp knife, score a few cuts all over each chop.

4 Place the pork chops in a roasting tin (pan) or an ovenproof dish. Spoon the fennel and juniper mixture over the chops.

5 Pour the orange juice over the top of each chop, cover and marinate in the refrigerator for about 2 hours.

6 Cook the pork chops, under a preheated grill (broiler), for 10–15 minutes, depending on the thickness of the meat, or until the meat is tender and cooked through, turning occasionally.

7 Transfer the pork chops to serving plates and serve with a crisp, fresh salad and plenty of fresh bread to mop up the cooking juices.

COOK'S TIP

Juniper berries are most commonly associated with gin, but they are often added to meat dishes in Italy for a delicate citrus flavour. They can be bought dried from most health food shops and some larger supermarkets.

Pasta & Pork in Cream Sauce

This unusual and attractive dish is extremely delicious. Make the Italian Red Wine Sauce well in advance to reduce the preparation time.

NUTRITIONAL INFORMATION

Calories 735   Sugars 4g
Protein . . . . .31g   Fat 52g
Carbohydrate . . .37g   Saturates 19g

 8³/₄ HOURS   35 MINS

SERVES 4

I N G R E D I E N T S

450 g/1 lb pork fillet (tenderloin),
   thinly sliced

4 tbsp olive oil

225 g/8 oz button mushrooms, sliced

200 ml/7 fl oz/⅞ cup Italian Red Wine Sauce
   (see page 29)

1 tbsp lemon juice

pinch of saffron

350 g/12 oz/3 cups dried orecchioni

4 tbsp double (heavy) cream

12 quail eggs (see Cook's Tip)

salt

1 Pound the slices of pork between 2 sheets of cling film until wafer thin, then cut into strips.

2 Heat the olive oil in a large frying pan (skillet), add the pork and stir-fry for 5 minutes. Add the mushrooms to the pan and stir-fry for a further 2 minutes.

3 Pour over the Italian Red Wine Sauce, lower the heat and simmer gently for 20 minutes.

4 Meanwhile, bring a large saucepan of lightly salted water to the boil. Add the lemon juice, saffron and orecchioni

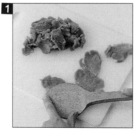

and cook for 8–10 minutes, until tender but still firm to the bite. Drain the pasta and keep warm.

5 Stir the cream into the pan with the pork and heat gently for a few minutes.

6 Boil the quail eggs for 3 minutes, cool them in cold water and remove the shells.

7 Transfer the pasta to a large, warm serving plate, top with the pork and

the sauce and garnish with the eggs. Serve immediately.

COOK'S TIP

In this recipe, the quail eggs are soft-boiled (soft-cooked). As they are extremely difficult to shell when warm, it is important that they are thoroughly cooled first. Otherwise, they will break up unattractively.

Pork Cooked in Milk

This traditional dish of boned pork cooked with garlic and milk can be served hot or cold.

NUTRITIONAL INFORMATION

Calories	498	Sugars	........15g
Protein	........50g	Fat	..........27g
Carbohydrate	...15g	Saturates	.......9g

 20 MINS   1³/₄ HOURS

SERVES 4

INGREDIENTS

800 g/1 lb 12 oz leg of pork, boned

1 tbsp oil

25 g/1 oz/2 tbsp butter

1 onion, chopped

2 garlic cloves, chopped

75 g/2¾ oz pancetta, diced

1.2 litres/2 pints/5 cups milk

1 tbsp green peppercorns, crushed

2 fresh bay leaves

2 tbsp marjoram

2 tbsp thyme

1 Using a sharp knife, remove the fat from the pork. Shape the meat into a neat form, tying it in place with a length of string.

2 Heat the oil and butter in a large pan. Add the onion, garlic and pancetta to the pan and cook for 2–3 minutes.

3 Add the pork to the pan and cook, turning occasionally, until it is browned all over.

4 Pour over the milk, add the peppercorns, bay leaves, marjoram and thyme and cook over a low heat for 1¼–1½ hours or until tender. Watch the

liquid carefully for the last 15 minutes of cooking time because it tends to reduce very quickly and will then burn. If the liquid reduces and the pork is still not tender, add another 100 ml/3½ fl oz milk and continue cooking. Reserve the cooking liquid (as the milk reduces naturally in this dish, it forms a thick and creamy sauce, which curdles slightly but tastes very delicious).

5 Remove the pork from the saucepan. Using a sharp knife, cut the meat into slices. Transfer the pork slices to serving plates and serve immediately with the reserved cooking liquid.

Pork with Lemon & Garlic

This is a simplified version of a traditional dish from the Marche region of Italy. Pork fillet pockets are stuffed with ham (prosciutto) and herbs.

NUTRITIONAL INFORMATION

Calories . . . . . . .428 Sugars 2g
Protein . . . . .31g Fat 32g
Carbohydrate . . . .4g Saturates 4g

 25 MINS   1 HOUR

SERVES 4

INGREDIENTS

450 g/1 lb pork fillet

50 g/1¾ oz chopped almonds

2 tbsp olive oil

100 g/3½ oz raw Parma ham (prosciutto),
   finely chopped

2 garlic cloves, chopped

1 tbsp fresh oregano, chopped

finely grated rind of 2 lemons

4 shallots, finely chopped

200 ml/7 fl oz/¾ cup ham or chicken stock

1 tsp sugar

1 Using a sharp knife, cut the pork fillet into 4 equal pieces. Place the pork between sheets of greaseproof paper and pound each piece with a meat mallet or the end of a rolling pin to flatten it.

2 Cut a horizontal slit in each piece of pork to make a pocket.

3 Place the almonds on a baking tray (cookie sheet). Lightly toast the almonds under a medium-hot grill (broiler) for 2–3 minutes or until golden.

4 Mix the almonds with 1 tbsp oil, ham (prosciutto), garlic, oregano and the finely grated rind from 1 lemon. Spoon the mixture into the pockets of the pork.

5 Heat the remaining oil in a large frying pan (skillet). Add the shallots and cook for 2 minutes.

6 Add the pork to the frying pan (skillet) and cook for 2 minutes on each side or until browned all over.

7 Add the ham or chicken stock to the pan, bring to the boil, cover and leave to simmer for 45 minutes or until the pork is tender. Remove the meat from the pan, set aside and keep warm.

8 Add the lemon rind and sugar to the pan, boil for 3–4 minutes or until reduced and syrupy. Pour the lemon sauce over the pork fillets and serve immediately.

Stuffed Cannelloni

Cannelloni, the thick, round pasta tubes, make perfect containers for close-textured sauces of all kinds.

NUTRITIONAL INFORMATION

Calories 520	Sugars 5g	
Protein 21g	Fat 39g	
Carbohydrate ...23g	Saturates 18g	

 30 MINS   1¼ HOURS

SERVES 4

INGREDIENTS

8 dried cannelloni tubes

1 tbsp olive oil

25 g/1 oz/¼ cup freshly grated
  Parmesan cheese

fresh herb sprigs, to garnish

FILLING

25 g/1 oz/2 tbsp butter

300 g/10½ oz frozen spinach, thawed
  and chopped

115 g/4 oz/½ cup ricotta cheese

25 g/1 oz/¼ cup freshly grated
  Parmesan cheese

60 g/2 oz/¼ cup chopped ham

pinch of freshly grated nutmeg

2 tbsp double (heavy) cream

2 eggs, lightly beaten

salt and pepper

SAUCE

25 g/1 oz/2 tbsp butter

25 g/1 oz/¼ cup plain
  (all-purpose) flour

300 ml/½ pint/1¼ cups milk

2 bay leaves

pinch of freshly grated nutmeg

1 To make the filling, melt the butter in a pan and stir-fry the spinach for 2–3 minutes. Remove from the heat and stir in the ricotta and Parmesan cheeses and the ham. Season to taste with nutmeg, salt and pepper. Beat in the cream and eggs to make a thick paste.

2 Bring a pan of lightly salted water to the boil. Add the pasta and the oil and cook for 10–12 minutes, or until almost tender. Drain and set aside to cool.

3 To make the sauce, melt the butter in a pan. Stir in the flour and cook, stirring, for 1 minute. Gradually stir in the milk. Add the bay leaves and simmer, stirring, for 5 minutes. Add the nutmeg and salt and pepper to taste. Remove from the heat and discard the bay leaves.

4 Spoon the filling into a piping bag and fill the cannelloni.

5 Spoon a little sauce into the base of an ovenproof dish. Arrange the cannelloni in the dish in a single layer and pour over the remaining sauce. Sprinkle over the Parmesan cheese and bake in a preheated oven at 190°C/375°F/Gas Mark 5 for 40–45 minutes. Garnish with fresh herb sprigs and serve.

Pork Stuffed with Prosciutto

This sophisticated roast with Mediterranean flavours is ideal served with a pungent olive paste.

NUTRITIONAL INFORMATION

Calories ....427 Sugars 0g

Protein ....31g Fat 34g

Carbohydrate ...0.2g Saturates 7g

 25 MINS   🕐 55 MINS

SERVES 4

INGREDIENTS

500 g/1 lb 2 oz piece of lean pork fillet

small bunch fresh of basil leaves, washed

2 tbsp freshly grated Parmesan

2 tbsp sun-dried tomato paste

6 thin slices Parma ham (prosciutto)

1 tbsp olive oil

salt and pepper

OLIVE PASTE

125 g/4 oz/⅔ cup pitted black olives

4 tbsp olive oil

2 garlic cloves, peeled

1 Trim away excess fat and membrane from the pork fillet. Slice the pork lengthways down the middle, taking care not to cut all the way through.

2 Open out the pork and season the inside. Lay the basil leaves down the centre. Mix the cheese and sun-dried tomato paste and spread over the basil.

3 Press the pork back together. Wrap the ham around the pork, overlapping, to cover. Place on a rack in a roasting tin (pan), seamside down, and brush with oil. Bake in a preheated oven, 190°C/375°F/Gas Mark 5, for 30–40 minutes depending on thickness until cooked through. Allow to stand for 10 minutes.

4 For the olive paste, place all the ingredients in a blender or food processor and blend until smooth. Alternatively, for a coarser paste, finely chop the olives and garlic and mix with the oil.

5 Drain the cooked pork and slice thinly. Serve with the olive paste and a salad.

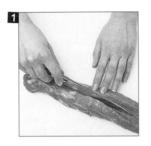

Pot Roasted Leg of Lamb

This dish from the Abruzzi uses a slow cooking method which ensures that the meat absorbs the flavourings and becomes very tender.

NUTRITIONAL INFORMATION

Calories 734	Sugars 6g	
Protein 71g	Fat 42g	
Carbohydrate 7g	Saturates 15g	

 35 MINS   🕐 3 HOURS

SERVES 4

I N G R E D I E N T S

1.75 kg/3½ lb leg of lamb

3–4 sprigs fresh rosemary

125 g/4½ oz streaky bacon rashers

4 tbsp olive oil

2–3 garlic cloves, crushed

2 onions, sliced

2 carrots, sliced

2 celery stalks, sliced

300 ml/½ pint/1¼ cups dry white wine

1 tbsp tomato purée (paste)

300 ml/½ pint/1¼ cups stock

350 g/12 oz tomatoes, peeled, quartered
  and deseeded

1 tbsp chopped fresh parsley

1 tbsp chopped fresh oregano or marjoram

salt and pepper

fresh rosemary sprigs, to garnish

1 Wipe the joint of lamb all over, trimming off any excess fat, then season well with salt and pepper, rubbing well in. Lay the sprigs of rosemary over the lamb, cover evenly with the bacon rashers and tie in place with string.

2 Heat the oil in a frying pan (skillet) and fry the lamb for about 10 minutes or until browned all over, turning several times. Remove from the pan.

3 Transfer the oil from the frying pan (skillet) to a large fireproof casserole and fry the garlic and onion together for 3–4 minutes until beginning to soften. Add the carrots and celery and continue to cook for a few minutes longer.

4 Lay the lamb on top of the vegetables and press down to partly submerge. Pour the wine over the lamb, add the tomato purée (paste) and simmer for 3–4 minutes. Add the stock, tomatoes and herbs and seasoning and bring back to the boil for a further 3–4 minutes.

5 Cover the casserole tightly and cook in a moderate oven, 180°C/350°F/Gas Mark 4, for 2–2½ hours until very tender.

6 Remove the lamb from the casserole and if preferred, take off the bacon and herbs along with the string. Keep warm. Strain the juices, skimming off any excess fat, and serve in a jug. The vegetables may be put around the joint or in a serving dish. Garnish with fresh sprigs of rosemary.

Roman Pan-fried Lamb

Chunks of tender lamb, pan-fried with garlic and stewed in red wine are a real Roman dish.

NUTRITIONAL INFORMATION

Calories 299	Sugars 1g	
Protein 31g	Fat 16g	
Carbohydrate 1g	Saturates 7g	

15 MINS   50 MINS

SERVES 4

I N G R E D I E N T S

1 tbsp oil

15 g/½ oz/1 tbsp butter

600 g/1 lb 5 oz lamb (shoulder or leg),
  cut into 2.5 cm/1 inch chunks

4 garlic cloves, peeled

3 sprigs thyme, stalks removed

6 canned anchovy fillets

150 ml/¼ pint/⅔ cup red wine

150 ml/¼ pint/⅔ cup lamb or
  vegetable stock

1 tsp sugar

50 g/1¾ oz black olives, pitted and halved

2 tbsp chopped parsley, to garnish

mashed potato, to serve

1 Heat the oil and butter in a large frying pan (skillet). Add the lamb and cook for 4–5 minutes, stirring, until the meat is browned all over.

2 Using a pestle and mortar, grind together the garlic, thyme and anchovies to make a smooth paste.

3 Add the wine and lamb or vegetable stock to the frying pan (skillet). Stir in the garlic and anchovy paste together with the sugar.

4 Bring the mixture to the boil, reduce the heat, cover and simmer for 30–40 minutes or until the lamb is tender. For the last 10 minutes of the cooking time, remove the lid to allow the sauce to reduce slightly.

5 Stir the olives into the sauce and mix to combine.

6 Transfer the lamb and the sauce to a serving bowl and garnish. Serve with creamy mashed potatoes.

COOK'S TIP

Rome is the capital of both the region of Lazio and Italy and thus has become a focal point for specialities from all over Italy. Food from this region tends to be fairly simple and quick to prepare, all with plenty of herbs and seasonings giving really robust flavours.

Pasta & Lamb Loaf

Any dried pasta shape can be used for this delicious recipe. It has been adapted for microwave cooking for convenience.

NUTRITIONAL INFORMATION

Calories	245	Sugars	.........2g
Protein	........15g	Fat	.........18g
Carbohydrate	....6g	Saturates	.......7g

 35 MINS   35 MINS

SERVES 4

INGREDIENTS

15 g/½ oz/1 tbsp butter

½ small aubergine (eggplant), diced

60 g/2 oz multi-coloured fusilli

2 tsp olive oil

225 g/8 oz/1 cup minced (ground) lamb

½ small onion, chopped

½ red (bell) pepper, chopped

1 garlic clove, crushed

1 tsp dried mixed herbs

2 eggs, beaten

2 tbsp single (light) cream

salt and pepper

TO SERVE

salad

pasta sauce of your choice

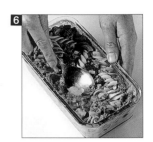

1 Place the butter in a 500 g/1 lb 2 oz loaf dish. Cook on HIGH power for 30 seconds until melted. Brush over the base and sides of the dish.

2 Sprinkle the aubergine (eggplant) with salt, put in a colander and leave for 20 minutes. Rinse the aubergine (eggplant) well and pat dry with paper towels.

3 Place the pasta in a bowl, add a little salt and enough boiling water to cover by 2.5 cm/1 inch. Cover and cook on HIGH power for 8 minutes, stirring halfway through. Leave to stand, covered, for a few minutes.

4 Place the oil, lamb and onion in a bowl. Cover and cook on HIGH power for 2 minutes.

5 Break up any lumps of meat using a fork. Add the (bell) pepper, garlic, herbs and aubergine (eggplant). Cover and cook on HIGH power for 5 minutes, stirring halfway through.

6 Drain the pasta and add to the lamb with the eggs and cream. Season well. Turn into the loaf dish and pat down using the back of a spoon.

7 Cook on MEDIUM power for 10 minutes until firm to the touch. Leave to stand for 5 minutes before turning out. Serve in slices with a salad and a pasta sauce.

Lamb Cutlets with Rosemary

A classic combination of flavours, this dish would make a perfect Sunday lunch. Serve with tomato and onion salad and jacket potatoes.

NUTRITIONAL INFORMATION

Calories 560   Sugars 1g
Protein ....48g   Fat 40g
Carbohydrate ....1g   Saturates 13g

🍗 1¼ HOURS   🕐 15 MINS

SERVES 4

I N G R E D I E N T S

8 lamb cutlets

5 tbsp olive oil

2 tbsp lemon juice

1 clove garlic, crushed

½ tsp lemon pepper

salt

8 sprigs rosemary

jacket potatoes, to serve

S A L A D

4 tomatoes, sliced

4 spring onions (scallion), sliced diagonally

D R E S S I N G

2 tbsp olive oil

1 tbsp lemon juice

1 clove garlic, chopped

¼ tsp fresh rosemary, chopped finely

1 Trim the lamb chops by cutting away the flesh with a sharp knife to expose the tips of the bones.

2 Place the oil, lemon juice, garlic, lemon pepper and salt in a shallow, non-metallic dish and whisk with a fork to combine.

3 Lay the sprigs of rosemary in the dish and place the lamb on top. Leave to marinate for at least 1 hour, turning the lamb cutlets once.

4 Remove the chops from the marinade and wrap a little kitchen foil around the bones to stop them from burning.

5 Place the rosemary sprigs on the rack and place the lamb on top. Barbecue (grill) for 10–15 minutes, turning once.

6 Meanwhile make the salad and dressing. Arrange the tomatoes on a serving dish and scatter the spring onions (scallions) on top. Place all the ingredients for the dressing in a screw-top jar, shake well and pour over the salad. Serve with the lamb cutlets and jacket potatoes.

COOK'S TIP

Choose medium to small baking potatoes if you want to cook jacket potatoes on the barbecue (grill). Scrub them well, prick with a fork and wrap in buttered kitchen foil. Bury them in the hot coals and barbecue (grill) for 50–60 minutes.

Lamb with Bay & Lemon

These lamb chops quickly become more elegant when the bone is removed to make noisettes.

NUTRITIONAL INFORMATION

Calories 268	Sugars 0.2g	
Protein 24g	Fat 16g	
Carbohydrate ...0.2g	Saturates 7g	

 10 MINS   35 MINS

SERVES 4

INGREDIENTS

4 lamb chops

1 tbsp oil

15 g/½ oz/1 tbsp butter

150 ml/¼ pint/⅔ cup white wine

150 ml/¼ pint/⅔ cup lamb or
   vegetable stock

2 bay leaves

pared rind of 1 lemon

salt and pepper

1 Using a sharp knife, carefully remove the bone from each lamb chop, keeping the meat intact. Alternatively, ask the butcher to prepare the lamb noisettes for you.

2 Shape the meat into rounds and secure with a length of string.

COOK'S TIP

Your local butcher will offer you good advice on how to prepare the lamb noisettes, if you are wary of preparing them yourself.

3 In a large frying pan (skillet), heat together the oil and butter until the mixture starts to froth.

4 Add the lamb noisettes to the frying pan (skillet) and cook for 2–3 minutes on each side or until browned all over.

5 Remove the frying pan (skillet) fom the heat, drain off all of the excess fat and discard.

6 Return the frying pan (skillet) to the heat. Add the wine, stock, bay leaves and lemon rind to the frying pan (skillet) and cook for 20–25 minutes or until the lamb is tender. Season the lamb noisettes and sauce to taste with a little salt and pepper.

7 Transfer to serving plates. Remove the string from each noisette and serve with the sauce.

Lamb with Olives

This is a very simple dish, and the chilli adds a bit of spiciness. It is quick to prepare and makes an ideal supper dish.

NUTRITIONAL INFORMATION

Calories	577	Sugars	.........1g
Protein	........62g	Fat	..........33g
Carbohydrate	....1g	Saturates	......10g

🥔 15 MINS   🕐 1½ HOURS

SERVES 4

INGREDIENTS

1.25 kg/2 lb 12 oz boned leg of lamb

90 ml/3 fl oz/⅓ cup olive oil

2 garlic cloves, crushed

1 onion, sliced

1 small red chilli, cored, deseeded and
chopped finely

175 ml/6 fl oz/¾ cup dry white wine

175 g/6 oz/1 cup pitted black olives

salt

chopped fresh parsley, to garnish

1 Using a sharp knife, cut the lamb into 2.5 cm/1 inch cubes.

2 Heat the oil in a frying pan (skillet) and fry the garlic, onion and chilli for 5 minutes.

3 Add the meat and wine and cook for a further 5 minutes.

4 Stir in the olives, then transfer the mixture to a casserole. Place in a preheated oven, 180°C/350°F/Gas Mark 4, and cook for 1 hour 20 minutes or until the meat is tender. Season with salt to taste, and serve garnished with chopped fresh parsley.

Aubergine (Eggplant) Cake

Layers of toasty-brown aubergine (eggplant), meat sauce and cheese-flavoured pasta make this a popular family supper dish.

NUTRITIONAL INFORMATION

Calories 859	Sugars 39g
Protein 36g	Fat 58g
Carbohydrate ...51g	Saturates 19g

 1¹/₂ HOURS   1¹/₂ HOURS

SERVES 4

INGREDIENTS

1 aubergine (eggplant), thinly sliced

5 tbsp olive oil

225 g/8 oz/2 cups dried fusilli

600 ml/1 pint/2½ cups Béchamel Sauce
   (see page 28)

90 g/3 oz/¾ cup grated Cheddar cheese

butter, for greasing

25 g/1 oz/⅓ cup freshly grated
   Parmesan cheese

salt and pepper

LAMB SAUCE

2 tbsp olive oil

1 large onion, sliced

2 celery sticks (stalks), thinly sliced

450 g/1 lb minced (ground) lamb

3 tbsp tomato purée (paste)

150 g/5½ oz bottled sun-dried tomatoes,
   drained and chopped

1 tsp dried oregano

1 tbsp red wine vinegar

150 ml/¼ pint/⅔ cup chicken stock

salt and pepper

1 Put the aubergine (eggplant) slices in a colander, sprinkle with salt and set aside for 45 minutes.

2 To make the lamb sauce, heat the oil in a pan. Fry the onion and celery for 3–4 minutes. Add the lamb and fry, stirring frequently, until browned. Stir in the remaining sauce ingredients, bring to the boil and cook for 20 minutes.

3 Rinse the aubergine (eggplant) slices, drain and pat dry. Heat 4 tablespoons of the oil in a frying pan (skillet). Fry the aubergine (eggplant) slices for about 4 minutes on each side. Remove from the pan and drain well.

4 Bring a large pan of lightly salted water to the boil. Add the fusilli and the remaining oil and cook for 8–10 minutes until almost tender, but still firm to the bite. Drain well.

5 Gently heat the Béchamel Sauce, stirring constantly. Stir in the Cheddar cheese. Stir half of the cheese sauce into the fusilli.

6 Make layers of fusilli, lamb sauce and aubergine (eggplant) slices in a greased dish. Spread the remaining cheese sauce over the top. Sprinkle over the Parmesan and bake in a preheated oven, at 190°C/375°F/Gas Mark 5, for 25 minutes. Serve hot or cold.

Barbecued Butterfly Lamb

The appearance of the lamb as it is opened out to cook on the barbecue gives this dish its name. Marinate the lamb in advance if possible.

NUTRITIONAL INFORMATION

Calories	733	Sugars	.........6g
Protein	........69g	Fat	.........48g
Carbohydrate	....6g	Saturates	......13g

6¼ HOURS   1 HOUR

SERVES 4

INGREDIENTS

boned leg of lamb, about 1.8 kg/4 lb

8 tbsp balsamic vinegar

grated rind and juice of 1 lemon

150 ml/¼ pint/⅔ cup sunflower oil

4 tbsp chopped, fresh mint

2 cloves garlic, crushed

2 tbsp light muscovado sugar

salt and pepper

TO SERVE

grilled (broiled) vegetables

green salad leaves

1 Open out the boned leg of lamb so that its shape resembles a butterfly. Thread 2–3 skewers through the meat in order to make it easier to turn on the barbecue (grill).

2 Combine the balsamic vinegar, lemon rind and juice, oil, mint, garlic, sugar and salt and pepper to taste in a non-metallic dish that is large enough to hold the lamb.

3 Place the lamb in the dish and turn it over a few times so that the meat is coated on both sides with the marinade. Leave to marinate for at least 6 hours or preferably overnight, turning occasionally.

  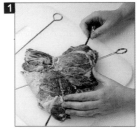

4 Remove the lamb from the marinade and reserve the liquid for basting.

5 Place the rack about 15 cm/6 inches above the coals and barbecue (grill) the lamb for about 30 minutes on each side, turning once and basting frequently with the marinade.

6 Transfer the lamb to a chopping board and remove the skewers. Cut the lamb into slices across the grain and serve.

COOK'S TIP

If you prefer, cook the lamb for half the cooking time in a preheated oven at 180°C/350°F/ Gas Mark 4, then finish off on the barbecue (grill).

Saltimbocca

The Italian name for this dish, *saltimbocca*, means 'jump into the mouth'. The stuffed rolls are quick and easy to make and taste delicious.

NUTRITIONAL INFORMATION

Calories	303	Sugars	.......0.3g
Protein	........29g	Fat	..........17g
Carbohydrate	....1g	Saturates	.......1g

15 MINS   20 MINS

SERVES 4

INGREDIENTS

4 turkey fillets or 4 veal escalopes, about
  450 g/1 lb in total

100 g/3½ oz Parma ham (prosciutto)

8 sage leaves

1 tbsp olive oil

1 onion, finely chopped

200 ml/7 fl oz/¾ cup white wine

200 ml/7 fl oz/¾ cup chicken stock

1 Place the turkey or veal between sheets of greaseproof paper. Pound the meat with a meat mallet or the end of a rolling pin to flatten it slightly. Cut each escalope in half.

2 Trim the Parma ham (prosciutto) to fit each piece of turkey or veal and place over the meat. Lay a sage leaf on top. Roll up the escalopes and secure with a cocktail stick (toothpick).

3 Heat the oil in a frying pan (skillet) and cook the onion for 3–4 minutes.

Add the turkey or veal rolls to the pan and cook for 5 minutes until browned all over.

4 Pour the white wine and chicken stock into the pan and leave to simmer for 15 minutes if using turkey, and 20 minutes if using veal, or until tender. Serve immediately.

VARIATION

Try a similar recipe called *bocconcini*, meaning 'little mouthfuls'. Follow the same method as given here, but replace the sage leaf with a piece of Gruyère cheese.

Veal in a Rose Petal Sauce

This truly spectacular dish is equally delicious whether you use veal or pork fillet. Make sure the roses are free of blemishes and pesticides.

NUTRITIONAL INFORMATION

Calories 810	Sugars 2g
Protein 31g	Fat 56g
Carbohydrate . . .49g	Saturates 28g

10 MINS   35 MINS

SERVES 4

I N G R E D I E N T S

450 g/1 lb dried fettuccine

7 tbsp olive oil

1 tsp chopped fresh oregano

1 tsp chopped fresh marjoram

175 g/6 oz/¾ cup butter

450 g/1 lb veal fillet, thinly sliced

150 ml/¼ pint/⅔ cup rose petal vinegar
  (see Cook's Tip)

150 ml/¼ pint/⅔ cup fish stock

50 ml/2 fl oz/¼ cup grapefruit juice

50 ml/2 fl oz/¼ cup double
  (heavy) cream

salt

TO GARNISH

12 pink grapefruit segments

12 pink peppercorns

rose petals

fresh herb leaves

1 Bring a large saucepan of lightly salted water to the boil. Add the fettuccine and 1 tablespoon of the oil and cook for 8–10 minutes or until tender, but still firm to the bite. Drain and transfer to a warm serving dish, sprinkle over 2 tablespoons of the olive oil, the oregano and marjoram.

2 Heat 50 g/2 oz/4 tbsp of the butter with the remaining oil in a large frying pan (skillet). Add the veal and cook over a low heat for 6 minutes. Remove the veal from the pan and place on top of the pasta.

3 Add the vinegar and fish stock to the pan and bring to the boil. Boil vigorously until reduced by two thirds. Add the grapefruit juice and cream and simmer over a low heat for 4 minutes. Dice the remaining butter and add to the pan, one piece at a time, whisking constantly until it has been completely incorporated.

4 Pour the sauce around the veal, garnish with grapefruit segments, pink peppercorns, the rose petals (washed) and your favourite herb leaves.

COOK'S TIP

To make rose petal vinegar, infuse the petals of 8 pesticide-free roses in 150 ml/¼ pint/⅔ cup white wine vinegar for 48 hours. Prepare well in advance to reduce the preparation time.

Vitello Tonnato

Veal dishes are the speciality of Lombardy, with this dish being one of the more sophisticated. Serve cold with seasonal salads.

NUTRITIONAL INFORMATION

Calories 654	Sugars 1g
Protein 49g	Fat 47g
Carbohydrate 1g	Saturates 8g

 30 MINS   1¼ HOURS

SERVES 4

INGREDIENTS

750 g/1 lb 10 oz boned leg of veal, rolled

2 bay leaves

10 black peppercorns

2–3 cloves

½ tsp salt

2 carrots, sliced

1 onion, sliced

2 celery stalks, sliced

about 700 ml/1¼ pints/3 cups stock
   or water

150 ml/¼ pint/⅔ cup dry white wine
   (optional)

90 g/3 oz canned tuna fish, well drained

50 g/1½ oz can anchovy fillets, drained

150 ml/¼ pint/⅔ cup olive oil

2 tsp bottled capers, drained

2 egg yolks

1 tbsp lemon juice

salt and pepper

TO GARNISH

capers

lemon wedges

fresh herbs

1 Put the veal in a saucepan with the bay leaves, peppercorns, cloves, salt and vegetables. Add sufficient stock or water and the wine (if using) to barely cover the veal. Bring to the boil, remove any scum from the surface, then cover the pan and simmer gently for about 1 hour or until tender. Leave in the water until cold, then drain thoroughly. If time allows, chill the veal to make it easier to carve.

2 For the tuna sauce: thoroughly mash the tuna with 4 anchovy fillets, 1 tablespoon of oil and the capers. Add the egg yolks and press through a sieve (strainer) or purée in a food processor or liquidizer until smooth.

3 Stir in the lemon juice then gradually whisk in the rest of the oil a few drops at a time until the sauce is smooth and has the consistency of thick cream. Season with salt and pepper to taste.

4 Slice the veal thinly and arrange on a platter in overlapping slices. Spoon the sauce over the veal to cover. Then cover the dish and chill overnight.

5 Before serving, uncover the veal carefully. Arrange the remaining anchovy fillets and the capers in a decorative pattern on top, and then garnish with lemon wedges and sprigs of fresh herbs.

Neapolitan Veal Cutlets

The delicious combination of apple, onion and mushroom perfectly complements the delicate flavour of veal.

NUTRITIONAL INFORMATION

Calories	1071	Sugars	........13g
Protein	........74g	Fat	..........59g
Carbohydrate	...66g	Saturates	......16g

   20 MINS   45 MINS

SERVES 4

INGREDIENTS

200 g/7 oz/⅞ cup butter

4 x 250 g/9 oz veal cutlets, trimmed

1 large onion, sliced

2 apples, peeled, cored and sliced

175 g/6 oz button mushrooms

1 tbsp chopped fresh tarragon

8 black peppercorns

1 tbsp sesame seeds

400 g/14 oz dried marille

100 ml/3½ fl oz/scant ½ cup extra virgin
   olive oil

175 g/6 oz/¾ cup mascarpone cheese,
   broken into small pieces

2 large beef tomatoes, cut in half

leaves of 1 fresh basil sprig

salt and pepper

fresh basil leaves, to garnish

1 Melt 60 g/2 oz/4 tbsp of the butter in a frying pan (skillet). Fry the veal over a low heat for 5 minutes on each side. Transfer to a dish and keep warm.

2 Fry the onion and apples in the pan until lightly browned. Transfer to a dish, place the veal on top and keep warm.

3 Melt the remaining butter in the frying pan (skillet). Gently fry the mushrooms, tarragon and peppercorns over a low heat for 3 minutes. Sprinkle over the sesame seeds.

4 Bring a pan of salted water to the boil. Add the pasta and 1 tbsp of oil. Cook for 8–10 minutes or until tender, but still firm to the bite. Drain; transfer to a plate.

5 Grill (broil) or fry the tomatoes and basil for 2–3 minutes.

6 Top the pasta with the mascarpone cheese and sprinkle over the remaining olive oil. Place the onions, apples and veal cutlets on top of the pasta. Spoon the mushrooms, peppercorns and pan juices on to the cutlets, place the tomatoes and basil leaves around the edge and place in a preheated oven at 150°C/300°F/Gas Mark 2 for 5 minutes.

7 Season to taste with salt and pepper, garnish with fresh basil leaves and serve immediately.

Veal Italienne

This dish is really superb if made with tender veal. However, if veal is unavailable, use pork or turkey escalopes instead.

NUTRITIONAL INFORMATION

Calories 592	Sugars 5g	
Protein 44g	Fat 23g	
Carbohydrate ...48g	Saturates 9g	

 25 MINS 1 HR 20 MINS

SERVES 4

I N G R E D I E N T S

60 g/2 oz/¼ cup butter

1 tbsp olive oil

675 g/1½ lb potatoes, cubed

4 veal escalopes, weighing 175 g/6 oz each

1 onion, cut into 8 wedges

2 garlic cloves, crushed

2 tbsp plain (all-purpose) flour

2 tbsp tomato purée (paste)

150 ml/¼ pint/⅔ cup red wine

300 ml/½ pint/1¼ cups chicken stock

8 ripe tomatoes, peeled, seeded and diced

25 g/1 oz stoned (pitted) black olives, halved

2 tbsp chopped fresh basil

salt and pepper

fresh basil leaves, to garnish

COOK'S TIP

For a quicker cooking time and really tender meat, pound the meat with a meat mallet to flatten it slightly before cooking.

1 Heat the butter and oil in a large frying pan (skillet). Add the potato cubes and cook for 5-7 minutes, stirring frequently, until they begin to brown.

2 Remove the potatoes from the pan (skillet) with a perforated spoon and set aside.

3 Place the veal in the frying pan (skillet) and cook for 2-3 minutes on each side until sealed. Remove from the pan and set aside.

4 Stir the onion and garlic into the pan (skillet) and cook for 2-3 minutes.

5 Add the flour and tomato purée (paste) and cook for 1 minute, stirring. Gradually blend in the red wine and chicken stock, stirring to make a smooth sauce.

6 Return the potatoes and veal to the pan (skillet). Stir in the tomatoes, olives and chopped basil and season with salt and pepper.

7 Transfer to a casserole dish and cook in a preheated oven, 180°C/350°F/Gas Mark 4, for 1 hour or until the potatoes and veal are cooked through. Garnish with basil leaves and serve.

Escalopes & Italian Sausage

Anchovies are often used to enhance flavour, particularly in meat dishes.
Either veal or turkey escalopes can be used for this pan-fried dish.

NUTRITIONAL INFORMATION

Calories	233	Sugars	.........1g
Protein	........28g	Fat	..........13g
Carbohydrate	....1g	Saturates	.......1g

10 MINS   20 MINS

SERVES 4

INGREDIENTS

1 tbsp olive oil

6 canned anchovy fillets, drained

1 tbsp capers, drained

1 tbsp fresh rosemary, stalks removed

finely grated rind and juice of 1 orange

75 g/2¾ oz Italian sausage, diced

3 tomatoes, skinned and chopped

4 turkey or veal escalopes, each about
   125 g/4½ oz

salt and pepper

crusty bread or cooked polenta, to serve

1 Heat the oil in a large frying pan (skillet). Add the anchovies, capers, fresh rosemary, orange rind and juice, Italian sausage and tomatoes to the pan and cook for 5–6 minutes, stirring occasionally.

2 Meanwhile, place the turkey or veal escalopes between sheets of greasproof paper. Pound the meat with a meat mallet or the end of a rolling pin to flatten it.

3 Add the meat to the mixture in the frying pan (skillet). Season to taste with salt and pepper, cover and cook for 3–5 minutes on each side, slightly longer if the meat is thicker.

4 Transfer to serving plates and serve with fresh crusty bread or cooked polenta, if you prefer.

VARIATION

Try using 4-minute steaks, slightly flattened, instead of the turkey or veal. Cook them for 4–5 minutes on top of the sauce in the pan.

Sausage & Bean Casserole

In this traditional Tuscan dish, Italian sausages are cooked with cannellini beans and tomatoes.

NUTRITIONAL INFORMATION

Calories 609   Sugars 7g
Protein . . . . .27g   Fat 47g
Carbohydrate . . .20g   Saturates 16g

15 MINS   35 MINS

SERVES 4

INGREDIENTS

8 Italian sausages

1 tbsp olive oil

1 large onion, chopped

2 garlic cloves, chopped

1 green (bell) pepper

225g/8 oz fresh tomatoes, skinned and
   chopped or 400 g/14 oz can tomatoes,
   chopped

2 tbsp sun-dried tomato paste

400 g/14 oz can cannellini beans

mashed potato or rice, to serve

COOK'S TIP

Italian sausages are coarse in texture and have quite a strong flavour. They can be bought in specialist sausage shops, Italian delicatessens and some larger supermarkets. They are replaceable in this recipe only by game sausages.

1 Using a sharp knife, deseed the (bell) pepper and cut it into thin strips.

2 Prick the Italian sausages all over with a fork. Cook the sausages, under a preheated grill (broiler), for 10–12 minutes, turning occasionally, until brown all over. Set aside and keep warm.

3 Heat the oil in a large frying pan (skillet). Add the onion, garlic and (bell) pepper to the frying pan (skillet) and cook for 5 minutes, stirring occasionally, or until softened.

4 Add the tomatoes to the frying pan (skillet) and leave the mixture to simmer for about 5 minutes, stirring occasionally, or until slightly reduced and thickened.

5 Stir the sun-dried tomato paste, cannellini beans and Italian sausages into the mixture in the frying pan (skillet). Cook for 4–5 minutes or until the mixture is piping hot. Add 4–5 tablespoons of water, if the mixture becomes too dry during cooking.

6 Transfer the Italian sausage and bean casserole to serving plates and serve with mashed potato or cooked rice.

Liver with Wine Sauce

Liver is popular in Italy and is served in many ways. Tender calf's liver is the best type to use for this recipe, but you could use lamb's liver.

NUTRITIONAL INFORMATION

Calories	435	Sugars	.........2g
Protein	........30g	Fat	.........31g
Carbohydrate	....4g	Saturates	......12g

🥄 25 MINS   🕐 20 MINS

SERVES 4

INGREDIENTS

4 slices calf's liver or 8 slices lamb's liver,
   about 500 g/1 lb 2 oz

flour, for coating

1 tbsp olive oil

25 g/1 oz/2 tbsp butter

125 g/4½ oz lean bacon rashers, rinded and
   cut into narrow strips

1 garlic clove, crushed

1 onion, chopped

1 celery stick, sliced thinly

150 ml/¼ pint/⅔ cup red wine

150 ml/¼ pint/⅔ cup beef stock

good pinch of ground allspice

1 tsp Worcestershire sauce

1 tsp chopped fresh sage or ½ tsp
   dried sage

3–4 tomatoes, peeled, quartered and
   deseeded

salt and pepper

fresh sage leaves, to garnish

new potatoes or sauté potatoes, to serve

1 Wipe the liver with kitchen paper (paper towels), season with salt and pepper to taste and then coat lightly in flour, shaking off any excess.

2 Heat the oil and butter in a pan and fry the liver until well sealed on both sides and just cooked through – take care not to overcook. Remove the liver from the pan, cover and keep warm, but do not allow to dry out.

3 Add the bacon to the fat left in the pan, with the garlic, onion and celery. Fry gently until soft.

4 Add the red wine, beef stock, allspice, Worcestershire sauce, sage and salt and pepper to taste. Bring to the boil and simmer for 3–4 minutes.

5 Cut each tomato segment in half. Add to the sauce and continue to cook for 2–3 minutes.

6 Serve the liver on a little of the sauce, with the remainder spooned over. Garnish with fresh sage leaves and serve with tiny new potatoes or sauté potatoes.

Poultry & Game

Poultry dishes provide some of Italy's finest food. Every part of the chicken is used, including the feet and innards for making soup. Spit-roasted chicken, flavoured strongly  with aromatic rosemary, has become almost a national dish. Turkey, capon, duck, goose and guinea fowl are also popular, as is game. Wild rabbit, hare, wild boar and deer are available, especially in Sardinia. This chapter contains a superb collection of mouthwatering recipes. You will be astonished at how quickly and easily you can prepare some of these gourmet dishes.

Italian Chicken Spirals

These little foil parcels retain all the natural juices of the chicken while cooking conveniently over the pasta while it boils.

NUTRITIONAL INFORMATION

Calories 367	Sugars 1g
Protein 33g	Fat 12g
Carbohydrate ...35g	Saturates 2g

 20 MINS   20 MINS

SERVES 4

I N G R E D I E N T S

4 skinless, boneless chicken breasts

25 g/1 oz/1 cup fresh basil leaves

15 g/½ oz/2 tbsp hazelnuts

1 garlic clove, crushed

250 g/9 oz/2 cups wholemeal (whole wheat) pasta spirals

2 sun-dried tomatoes or fresh tomatoes

1 tbsp lemon juice

1 tbsp olive oil

1 tbsp capers

60 g/2 oz/½ cup black olives

1 Beat the chicken breasts with a rolling pin to flatten evenly.

2 Place the basil and hazelnuts in a food processor and process until finely chopped. Mix with the garlic and salt and pepper to taste.

3 Spread the basil mixture over the chicken breasts and roll up from one short end to enclose the filling. Wrap the chicken roll tightly in foil so that they hold their shape, then seal the ends well.

4 Bring a pan of lightly salted water to the boil and cook the pasta for 8–10 minutes or until tender, but still firm to the bite. Meanwhile, place the chicken parcels in a steamer or colander set over the pan, cover tightly, and steam for 10 minutes.

5 Using a sharp knife, dice the tomatoes.

6 Drain the pasta and return to the pan with the lemon juice, olive oil, tomatoes, capers and olives. Heat through.

7 Pierce the chicken with a skewer to make sure that the juices run clear and not pink (this shows that the chicken is cooked through). Slice the chicken, arrange over the pasta and serve.

COOK'S TIP

Sun-dried tomatoes have a wonderful, rich flavour but if they're unavailable, use fresh tomatoes instead.

Chicken Marengo

Napoleon's chef was ordered to cook a sumptuous meal on the eve of the battle of Marengo – this feast of flavours was the result.

NUTRITIONAL INFORMATION

Calories	521	Sugars	.........6g
Protein	........47g	Fat	..........19g
Carbohydrate	...34g	Saturates	.......8g

🍲 20 MINS   🕐 50 MINS

SERVES 4

INGREDIENTS

8 chicken pieces

2 tbsp olive oil

300 g/10½ oz passata (sieved tomatoes)

200 ml/7 fl oz/¾ cup white wine

2 tsp dried mixed herbs

40 g/1½ oz butter, melted

2 garlic cloves, crushed

8 slices white bread

100 g/3½ oz mixed mushrooms
  (such as button, oyster and ceps)

40 g/1½ oz black olives, chopped

1 tsp sugar

fresh basil, to garnish

1 Using a sharp knife, remove the bone from each of the chicken pieces.

2 Heat 1 tbsp of oil in a large frying pan (skillet). Add the chicken pieces and cook for about 4–5 minutes, turning occassionally, or until browned all over.

3 Add the passata (sieved tomatoes), wine and mixed herbs to the frying pan (skillet). Bring to the boil and then leave to simmer for 30 minutes or until the chicken is tender and the juices run clear when a skewer is inserted into the thickest part of the meat.

4 Mix the melted butter and crushed garlic together. Lightly toast the slices of bread and brush with the garlic butter.

5 Add the remaining oil to a separate frying pan (skillet) and cook the mushrooms for 2–3 minutes or until just browned.

6 Add the olives and sugar to the chicken mixture and warm through.

7 Transfer the chicken and sauce to serving plates. Serve with the bruschetta (fried bread) and fried mushrooms.

Mustard Baked Chicken

Chicken pieces are cooked in a succulent, mild mustard sauce, then coated in poppy seeds and served on a bed of fresh pasta shells.

NUTRITIONAL INFORMATION

Calories 652	Sugars 5g	
Protein 51g	Fat 31g	
Carbohydrate ...46g	Saturates 12g	

10 MINS   35 MINS

SERVES 4

INGREDIENTS

8 chicken pieces (about 115 g/4 oz each)

60g/2 oz/4 tbsp butter, melted

4 tbsp mild mustard (see Cook's Tip)

2 tbsp lemon juice

1 tbsp brown sugar

1 tsp paprika

3 tbsp poppy seeds

400 g/14 oz fresh pasta shells

1 tbsp olive oil

salt and pepper

1 Arrange the chicken pieces in a single layer in a large ovenproof dish.

2 Mix together the butter, mustard, lemon juice, sugar and paprika in a bowl and season with salt and pepper to taste. Brush the mixture over the upper

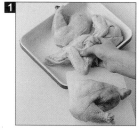

surfaces of the chicken pieces and bake in a preheated oven at 200°C/400°F/Gas Mark 6 for 15 minutes.

3 Remove the dish from the oven and carefully turn over the chicken pieces. Coat the upper surfaces of the chicken with the remaining mustard mixture, sprinkle the chicken pieces with poppy seeds and return to the oven for a further 15 minutes.

4 Meanwhile, bring a large saucepan of lightly salted water to the boil. Add the pasta shells and olive oil and cook for 8–10 minutes or until tender, but still firm to the bite.

5 Drain the pasta thoroughly and arrange on a warmed serving dish. Top the pasta with the chicken, pour over the sauce and serve immediately.

COOK'S TIP

Dijon is the type of mustard most often used in cooking, as it has a clean and only mildly spicy flavour. German mustard has a sweet-sour taste, with Bavarian mustard being slightly sweeter. American mustard is mild and sweet.

Pan-Cooked Chicken

Artichokes are a familiar ingredient in Italian cookery. In this dish, they are used to delicately flavour chicken.

NUTRITIONAL INFORMATION

Calories ....296 Sugars 2g
Protein ....27g Fat 15g
Carbohydrate ....7g Saturates 6g

 15 MINS   🕐 55 MINS

SERVES 4

I N G R E D I E N T S

4 chicken breasts, part boned

25 g/1 oz/2 tbsp butter

2 tbsp olive oil

2 red onions, cut into wedges

2 tbsp lemon juice

150 ml/¼ pt/⅔ cup dry white wine

150 ml/¼ pt/⅔ cup chicken stock

2 tsp plain (all-purpose) flour

400 g/14 oz can artichoke halves,
   drained and halved

salt and pepper

chopped fresh parsley, to garnish

1 Season the chicken with salt and pepper to taste. Heat the oil and 15 g/ ½ oz/1 tablespoon of the butter in a large frying pan (skillet). Add the chicken and fry for 4–5 minutes on each side until lightly golden. Remove from the pan using a slotted spoon.

2 Toss the onion in the lemon juice, and add to the frying pan (skillet). Gently fry, stirring, for 3–4 minutes until just beginning to soften.

3 Return the chicken to the pan. Pour in the wine and stock, bring to the boil, cover and simmer gently for 30 minutes.

4 Remove the chicken from the pan, reserving the cooking juices, and keep warm. Bring the juices to the boil, and boil rapidly for 5 minutes.

5 Blend the remaining butter with the flour to form a paste. Reduce the juices to a simmer and spoon the paste into the frying pan (skillet), stirring until thickened.

6 Adjust the seasoning according to taste, stir in the artichoke hearts and cook for a further 2 minutes. Pour the mixture over the chicken and garnish with chopped parsley.

Boned Chicken & Parmesan

It's really very easy to bone a whole chicken, but if you prefer, you can ask your butcher to do this for you.

NUTRITIONAL INFORMATION

Calories 578	Sugars 0.4g
Protein 42g	Fat 42g
Carbohydrate 9g	Saturates 15g

35 MINS · 1½ HOURS

SERVES 6

INGREDIENTS

1 chicken, weighing about 2.25 kg/5 lb

8 slices Mortadella or salami

125 g/4½ oz/2 cups fresh white or
    brown breadcrumbs

125 g/4½ oz/1 cup freshly grated
    Parmesan cheese

2 garlic cloves, crushed

6 tbsp chopped fresh basil or parsley

1 egg, beaten

pepper

fresh spring vegetables, to serve

1 Bone the chicken, keeping the skin intact. Dislocate each leg by breaking it at the thigh joint. Cut down each side of the backbone, taking care not to pierce the breast skin.

2 Pull the backbone clear of the flesh and discard. Remove the ribs, severing any attached flesh with a sharp knife.

3 Scrape the flesh from each leg and cut away the bone at the joint with a knife or shears.

4 Use the bones for stock. Lay out the boned chicken on a board, skin side down. Arrange the Mortadella slices over the chicken, overlapping slightly.

5 Put the breadcrumbs, Parmesan, garlic and basil or parsley in a bowl. Season with pepper to taste and mix together well. Stir in the beaten egg to bind the mixture together. Spoon the mixture down the middle of the boned chicken, roll the meat around it and then tie securely with string.

6 Place in a roasting dish and brush lightly with olive oil. Roast in a preheated oven, 200°C/400°F/Gas Mark 6, for 1½ hours or until the juices run clear when pierced.

7 Serve hot or cold, in slices, with fresh spring vegetables.

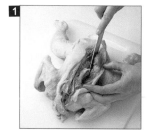

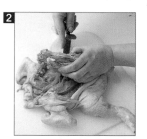

VARIATION

Replace the Mortadella with rashers of streaky bacon, if preferred.

Chicken Cacciatora

This is a popular Italian classic in which browned chicken quarters are cooked in a tomato and (bell) pepper sauce.

NUTRITIONAL INFORMATION

Calories	397	Sugars 4g
Protein	........37g	Fat 17g
Carbohydrate	...22g	Saturates 4g

🍳 20 MINS   🕐 1 HOUR

SERVES 4

INGREDIENTS

1 roasting chicken, about 1.5 kg/ 3 lb 5 oz,
    cut into 6 or 8 serving pieces

125 g/4½ oz/1 cup plain (all-purpose) flour

3 tbsp olive oil

150 ml/¼ pint/⅔ cup dry white wine

1 green (bell) pepper, deseeded and sliced

1 red (bell) pepper, deseeded and sliced

1 carrot, chopped finely

1 celery stalk, chopped finely

1 garlic clove, crushed

200 g/7 oz can of chopped tomatoes

salt and pepper

1 Rinse and pat dry the chicken pieces with paper towels. Lightly dust them with seasoned flour.

2 Heat the oil in a large frying pan (skillet). Add the chicken and fry over a medium heat until browned all over. Remove from the pan and set aside.

3 Drain off all but 2 tablespoons of the fat in the pan. Add the wine and stir for a few minutes. Then add the (bell) peppers, carrots, celery and garlic, season with salt and pepper to taste and simmer together for about 15 minutes.

4 Add the chopped tomatoes to the pan. Cover and simmer for 30 minutes, stirring often, until the chicken is completely cooked through.

5 Check the seasoning before serving piping hot.

Chicken Lasagne

You can use your favourite mushrooms, such as chanterelles or oyster mushrooms, for this delicately flavoured dish.

NUTRITIONAL INFORMATION

Calories	708	Sugars	........17g
Protein	........35g	Fat	..........35g
Carbohydrate	...57g	Saturates	......14g

  40 MINS   1³/₄ HOURS

SERVES 4

I N G R E D I E N T S

butter, for greasing

14 sheets pre-cooked lasagne

850 ml/1½ pints/3¾ cups Béchamel Sauce (see page 28)

75 g/3 oz/1 cup grated Parmesan cheese

WILD MUSHROOM SAUCE

2 tbsp olive oil

2 garlic cloves, crushed

1 large onion, finely chopped

225 g/8 oz wild mushrooms, sliced

300 g/10½ oz/2½ cups minced (ground) chicken

80 g/3 oz chicken livers, finely chopped

115 g/4 oz Parma ham (prosciutto), diced

150 ml/¼ pint/⅔ cup Marsala

285g/10 oz can chopped tomatoes

1 tbsp chopped fresh basil leaves

2 tbsp tomato purée (paste)

salt and pepper

1 To make the chicken and wild mushroom sauce, heat the olive oil in a large saucepan. Add the garlic, onion and mushrooms and cook, stirring frequently, for 6 minutes.

2 Add the minced (ground) chicken, chicken livers and Parma ham (prosciutto) and cook over a low heat for 12 minutes, or until the meat has browned.

3 Stir the Marsala, tomatoes, basil and tomato purée (paste) into the mixture in the pan and cook for 4 minutes. Season with salt and pepper to taste, cover and leave to simmer for 30 minutes. Uncover the pan, stir and leave to simmer for a further 15 minutes.

4 Lightly grease an ovenproof dish with butter. Arrange sheets of lasagne over the base of the dish, spoon over a layer of wild mushroom sauce, then spoon over a layer of Béchamel Sauce. Place another layer of lasagne on top and repeat the process twice, finishing with a layer of Béchamel Sauce. Sprinkle over the grated cheese and bake in a preheated oven at 190°C/375°F/Gas Mark 5 for 35 minutes until golden brown and bubbling. Serve immediately.

Barbecued (Grilled) Chicken

You need a bit of brute force to prepare the chicken, but once marinated it's an easy and tasty candidate for the barbecue (grill).

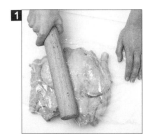
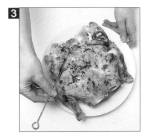

NUTRITIONAL INFORMATION

Calories	129	Sugars	.........0g
Protein	........22g	Fat	...........5g
Carbohydrate	....0g	Saturates	.......1g

2¹/₂ HOURS   30 MINS

SERVES 4

I N G R E D I E N T S

1.5 kg/3 lb 5 oz chicken

grated rind of 1 lemon

4 tbsp lemon juice

2 sprigs rosemary

1 small red chilli, chopped finely

150 ml/¼ pint/⅔ cup olive oil

1 Split the chicken down the breast bone and open it out. Trim off excess fat, and remove the parson's nose, wing and leg tips. Break the leg and wing joints to enable you to pound it flat. This ensures that it cooks evenly. Cover the split chicken with clingfilm (plastic wrap) and pound it as flat as possible with a rolling pin.

2 Mix the lemon rind and juice, rosemary sprigs, chilli and olive oil together in a small bowl. Place the chicken in a large dish and pour over the marinade, turning the chicken to coat it evenly. Cover the dish and leave the chicken to marinate for at least 2 hours.

3 Cook the chicken over a hot barbecue (the coals should be white, and red when fanned) for about 30 minutes, turning it regularly until the skin is golden and crisp. To test if it is cooked, pierce one of the chicken thighs; the juices will run clear, not pink, when it is ready. Serve.

Barbecued (Grilled) Chicken

Grilled (Broiled) Chicken

This Italian-style dish is richly flavoured with pesto, which is a mixture of basil, olive oil, pine nuts and Parmesan cheese.

NUTRITIONAL INFORMATION

Calories 787	Sugars 6g	
Protein 45g	Fat 38g	
Carbohydrate ...70g	Saturates 9g	

 10 MINS   25 MINS

SERVES 4

INGREDIENTS

8 part-boned chicken thighs

olive oil, for brushing

400 ml/14 fl oz/1⅔ cups passata
   (sieved tomatoes)

125 ml/4 fl oz/½ cup green or
   red pesto sauce

12 slices French bread

90 g/3 oz/1 cup freshly grated
   Parmesan cheese

60 g/2 oz/½ cup pine nuts or flaked
   (slivered) almonds

salad leaves, to serve

1 Arrange the chicken in a single layer in a wide flameproof dish and brush lightly with oil. Place under a preheated grill (broiler) for about 15 minutes, turning occasionally, until golden brown.

COOK'S TIP

Although leaving the skin on the chicken means that it will have a higher fat content, many people like the rich taste and crispy skin especially when it is blackened by the barbecue (grill). The skin also keeps in the cooking juices.

2 Pierce the chicken with a skewer to test if it is cooked through – the juices will run clear, not pink, when it is ready.

3 Pour off any excess fat. Warm the passata (sieved tomatoes) and half the pesto sauce in a small pan and pour over the chicken. Grill (broil) for a few more minutes, turning until coated.

4 Meanwhile, spread the remaining pesto on to the slices of bread. Arrange the bread over the chicken and sprinkle with the Parmesan cheese. Scatter the pine nuts over the cheese. Grill (broil) for 2–3 minutes, or until browned and bubbling. Serve with salad leaves.

Chicken with Green Olives

Olives are a popular flavouring for poultry and game in the Apulia region of Italy, where this recipe originates.

NUTRITIONAL INFORMATION

Calories 614   Sugars 6g
Protein . . . . .34g   Fat 30g
Carbohydrate . . .49g   Saturates 11g

 15 MINS   🕐 1½ HOURS

SERVES 4

INGREDIENTS

3 tbsp olive oil

25 g/1 oz/2 tbsp butter

4 chicken breasts, part boned

1 large onion, finely chopped

2 garlic cloves, crushed

2 red, yellow or green (bell) peppers, cored,
   seeded and cut into large pieces

250 g/9 oz button mushrooms, sliced
   or quartered

175 g/6 oz tomatoes, skinned and halved

150 ml/¼ pint/⅔ cup dry white wine

175 g/6 oz/1½ cups stoned (pitted)
   green olives

4–6 tbsp double (heavy) cream

400 g/14 oz dried pasta

salt and pepper

chopped flat leaf parsley, to garnish

1 Heat 2 tbsp of the oil and the butter in a frying pan (skillet). Add the chicken breasts and fry until golden brown all over. Remove the chicken from the pan.

2 Add the onion and garlic to the pan and fry over a medium heat until beginning to soften. Add the (bell) peppers and mushrooms and cook for 2–3 minutes.

3 Add the tomatoes and season to taste with salt and pepper. Transfer the vegetables to a casserole and arrange the chicken on top.

4 Add the wine to the pan and bring to the boil. Pour the wine over the chicken. Cover and cook in a preheated oven at 180°C/350°F/Gas Mark 4 for 50 minutes.

5 Add the olives to the casserole and mix in. Pour in the cream, cover and return to the oven for 10–20 minutes.

6 Meanwhile, bring a large pan of lightly salted water to the boil. Add the pasta and the remaining oil and cook for 8–10 minutes or until tender, but still firm to the bite. Drain the pasta well and transfer to a serving dish.

7 Arrange the chicken on top of the pasta, spoon over the sauce, garnish with the parsley and serve immediately. Alternatively, place the pasta in a large serving bowl and serve separately.

Chicken & Balsamic Vinegar

A rich caramelized sauce, flavoured with balsamic vinegar and wine, adds a piquant flavour. The chicken needs to be marinated overnight.

NUTRITIONAL INFORMATION

Calories	148	Sugars 0.2g
Protein	........11g	Fat 8g
Carbohydrate	...0.2g	Saturates 3g

 10 MINS   35 MINS

SERVES 4

INGREDIENTS

4 chicken thighs, boned

2 garlic cloves, crushed

200 ml/7 fl oz/¾ cup red wine

3 tbsp white wine vinegar

1 tbsp oil

15 g/½ oz/1 tbsp butter

6 shallots

3 tbsp balsamic vinegar

2 tbsp fresh thyme

salt and pepper

cooked polenta or rice, to serve

1 Using a sharp knife, make a few slashes in the skin of the chicken. Brush the chicken with the crushed garlic and place in a non-metallic dish.

2 Pour the wine and white wine vinegar over the chicken and season with salt and pepper to taste. Cover and leave to marinate in the refrigerator overnight.

3 Remove the chicken pieces with a perforated spoon, draining well, and reserve the marinade.

4 Heat the oil and butter in a frying pan (skillet). Add the shallots and cook for 2–3 minutes or until they begin to soften.

5 Add the chicken pieces to the pan and cook for 3-4 minutes, turning, until browned all over. Reduce the heat and add half of the reserved marinade. Cover and cook for 15–20 minutes, adding more marinade when necessary.

6 Once the chicken is tender, add the balsamic vinegar and thyme and cook for a further 4 minutes.

7 Transfer the chicken and marinade to serving plates and serve with polenta or rice.

COOK'S TIP

To make the chicken pieces look a little neater, use wooden skewers to hold them together or secure them with a length of string.

Chicken Scallops

Served in scallop shells, this makes a stylish presentation for a starter or a light lunch.

NUTRITIONAL INFORMATION

Calories	532	Sugars	.........3g
Protein	........25g	Fat	.........34g
Carbohydrate	...33g	Saturates	......14g

  20 MINS   25 MINS

SERVES 4

INGREDIENTS

175 g/6 oz short-cut macaroni, or other short pasta shapes

3 tbsp vegetable oil, plus extra for brushing

1 onion, chopped finely

3 rashers unsmoked collar or back bacon, rind removed, chopped

125 g/4½ oz button mushrooms, sliced thinly or chopped

175 g/6 oz/¾ cup cooked chicken, diced

175 ml/6 fl oz/¾ cup crème fraîche

4 tbsp dry breadcrumbs

60 g/2 oz/½ cup mature (sharp) Cheddar, grated

salt and pepper

flat-leaf parsley sprigs, to garnish

1 Cook the pasta in a large pan of boiling salted water, to which you have added 1 tablespoon of the oil, for 8–10 minutes or until tender. Drain the pasta, return to the pan and cover.

2 Heat the grill (broiler) to medium. Heat the remaining oil in a pan over medium heat and fry the onion until it is translucent. Add the chopped bacon and mushrooms and cook for 3–4 minutes, stirring once or twice.

3 Stir in the pasta, chicken and crème fraîche and season to taste with salt and pepper.

4 Brush four large scallop shells with oil. Spoon in the chicken mixture and smooth to make neat mounds.

5 Mix together the breadcrumbs and cheese, and sprinkle over the top of the shells. Press the topping lightly into the chicken mixture, and grill (broil) for 4–5 minutes, until golden brown and bubbling. Garnish with sprigs of flat-leaf parsley, and serve hot.

Chicken & Lobster on Penne

While this is certainly a treat to get the taste buds tingling, it is not as extravagant as it sounds.

NUTRITIONAL INFORMATION

Calories 696	Sugars 4g	
Protein 59g	Fat 32g	
Carbohydrate ...45g	Saturates 9g	

 20 MINS   30 MINS

SERVES 6

INGREDIENTS

butter, for greasing

6 chicken suprêmes

450 g/1 lb dried penne rigate

6 tbsp extra virgin olive oil

90 g/3 oz/1 cup freshly grated
   Parmesan cheese

salt

FILLING

115 g/4 oz lobster meat, chopped

2 shallots, very finely chopped

2 figs, chopped

1 tbsp Marsala

2 tbsp breadcrumbs

1 large egg, beaten

salt and pepper

COOK'S TIP

The cut of chicken known as suprême consists of the breast and wing. It is always skinned.

1 Grease 6 pieces of foil large enough to enclose each chicken suprême and lightly grease a baking tray (cookie sheet).

2 Place all of the filling ingredients into a mixing bowl and blend together thoroughly with a spoon.

3 Cut a pocket in each chicken suprême with a sharp knife and fill with the lobster mixture. Wrap each chicken suprême in foil, place the parcels on the greased baking tray (cookie sheet) and bake in a preheated oven at 200°C/ 400°F/Gas Mark 6 for 30 minutes.

4 Meanwhile, bring a large pan of lightly salted water to the boil. Add the pasta and 1 tablespoon of the olive oil and cook for about 10 minutes, or until tender but still firm to the bite. Drain the pasta thoroughly and transfer to a large serving plate. Sprinkle over the remaining olive oil and the grated Parmesan cheese, set aside and keep warm.

5 Carefully remove the foil from around the chicken suprêmes. Slice the suprêmes very thinly, arrange over the pasta and serve immediately.

Skewered Chicken Spirals

These unusual chicken kebabs (kabobs) have a wonderful Italian flavour, and the bacon helps keep them moist during cooking.

NUTRITIONAL INFORMATION

Calories	231	Sugars	.........1g
Protein	........29g	Fat	..........13g
Carbohydrate	....1g	Saturates	.......5g

  15 MINS   10 MINS

SERVES 4

INGREDIENTS

4 skinless, boneless chicken breasts

1 garlic clove, crushed

2 tbsp tomato purée (paste)

4 slices smoked back bacon

large handful of fresh basil leaves

oil for brushing

salt and pepper

 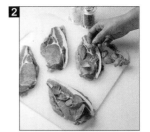 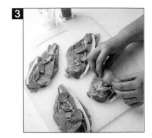

1 Spread out a piece of chicken between two sheets of cling film (plastic wrap) and beat firmly with a rolling pin to flatten the chicken to an even thickness. Repeat with the remaining chicken breasts.

2 Mix the garlic and tomato purée (paste) and spread over the chicken. Lay a bacon slice over each, then scatter with the basil. Season with salt and pepper.

3 Roll up each piece of chicken firmly, then cut into thick slices.

4 Thread the slices on to 4 skewers, making sure the skewer holds the chicken in a spiral shape.

5 Brush lightly with oil and cook on a preheated hot barbecue (grill) or grill (broiler) for about 10 minutes, turning once. Serve hot with a green salad.

Chicken with Orange Sauce

The refreshing combination of chicken and orange sauce makes this a perfect dish for a warm summer evening.

NUTRITIONAL INFORMATION

Calories	797	Sugars	........28g
Protein	........59g	Fat	.........25g
Carbohydrate	...77g	Saturates	.......6g

 15 MINS   25 MINS

SERVES 4

INGREDIENTS

30 ml/1 fl oz/⅛ cup rapeseed oil

3 tbsp olive oil

4 x 225 g/8 oz chicken suprêmes

150 ml/¼ pint/⅔ cup orange brandy

15 g/½ oz/2 tbsp plain (all-purpose) flour

150 ml/¼ pint/⅔ cup freshly squeezed orange juice

25 g/1 oz courgette (zucchini), cut into matchstick strips

25 g/1 oz red (bell) pepper, cut into matchstick strips

25 g/1 oz leek, finely shredded

400 g/14 oz dried wholemeal (whole-wheat) spaghetti

3 large oranges, peeled and cut into segments

rind of 1 orange, cut into very fine strips

2 tbsp chopped fresh tarragon

150 ml/¼ pint/⅔ cup fromage frais or ricotta cheese

salt and pepper

fresh tarragon leaves, to garnish

1 Heat the rapeseed oil and 1 tablespoon of the olive oil in a frying pan (skillet). Add the chicken and cook quickly until golden brown. Add the orange brandy and cook for 3 minutes. Sprinkle over the flour and cook for 2 minutes.

2 Lower the heat and add the orange juice, courgette (zucchini), (bell) pepper and leek and season. Simmer for 5 minutes until the sauce has thickened.

3 Meanwhile, bring a pan of salted water to the boil. Add the spaghetti and 1 tablespoon of the olive oil and cook for 10 minutes. Drain the spaghetti, transfer to a serving dish and drizzle over the remaining oil.

4 Add half of the orange segments, half of the orange rind, the tarragon and fromage frais or ricotta cheese to the sauce in the pan and cook for 3 minutes.

5 Place the chicken on top of the pasta, pour over a little sauce, garnish with orange segments, rind and tarragon. Serve immediately.

Chicken Pepperonata

All the sunshine colours and flavours of Italy are combined in this easy dish.

NUTRITIONAL INFORMATION

Calories	328	Sugars	.........7g
Protein	........35g	Fat	..........15g
Carbohydrate	...13g	Saturates	.......4g

15 MINS   40 MINS

SERVES 4

I N G R E D I E N T S

8 skinless chicken thighs

2 tbsp wholemeal (whole wheat) flour

2 tbsp olive oil

1 small onion, sliced thinly

1 garlic clove, crushed

1 each large red, yellow and green (bell)
  peppers, sliced thinly

400 g/14 oz can chopped tomatoes

1 tbsp chopped oregano

salt and pepper

fresh oregano, to garnish

crusty wholemeal (whole wheat) bread,
  to serve

1 Remove the skin from the chicken thighs and toss in the flour.

2 Heat the oil in a wide frying pan (skillet) and fry the chicken quickly until sealed and lightly browned, then remove from the pan.

3 Add the onion to the pan and gently fry until soft. Add the garlic, (bell) peppers, tomatoes and oregano, then bring to the boil, stirring.

4 Arrange the chicken over the vegetables, season well with salt and pepper, then cover the pan tightly and simmer for 20–25 minutes or until the chicken is completely cooked and tender.

5 Season with salt and pepper to taste, garnish with oregano and serve with crusty wholemeal (whole wheat) bread.

COOK'S TIP

For extra flavour, halve the (bell) peppers and grill (broil) under a preheated grill (broiler) until the skins are charred. Leave to cool then remove the skins and seeds. Slice the (bell) peppers thinly and use in the recipe.

Roman Chicken

This classic Roman dish makes an ideal light meal. It is equally good cold and could be taken on a picnic – serve with bread to mop up the juices.

NUTRITIONAL INFORMATION

Calories 317	Sugars 8g
Protein 22g	Fat 22g
Carbohydrate 9g	Saturates 4g

35 MINS   1 HOUR

SERVES 4

INGREDIENTS

4 tbsp olive oil

6 chicken pieces

2 garlic cloves, crushed with 1 tsp salt

1 large red onion, sliced

4 large mixed red, green and yellow
   (bell) peppers, cored, deseeded and
   cut into strips

125 g/4½ oz/⅔ cup pitted green olives

½ quantity Tomato Sauce (see page 120)

300 ml/½ pint/1¼ cups hot chicken stock

2 sprigs fresh marjoram

salt and pepper

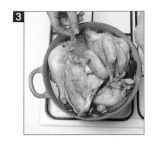

1 Heat half of the oil in a flameproof casserole and brown the chicken pieces on all sides. Remove the chicken and set aside.

2 Add the remaining oil to the casserole and fry the garlic and onion until softened. Stir in the (bell) peppers, olives and tomato sauce.

3 Return the chicken to the casserole with the stock and marjoram. Cover the casserole and simmer for about 45 minutes or until the chicken is tender. Season with salt and pepper to taste and serve with crusty bread.

Pasta with Chicken Sauce

Spinach ribbon noodles, topped with a rich tomato sauce and creamy chicken, make a very appetizing dish.

NUTRITIONAL INFORMATION

Calories	.995	Sugars	.8g
Protein	.36g	Fat	.74g
Carbohydrate	.50g	Saturates	.34g

 15 MINS   45 MINS

SERVES 4

INGREDIENTS

250 g/9 oz fresh green tagliatelle

1 tbsp olive oil

salt

fresh basil leaves, to garnish

TOMATO SAUCE

2 tbsp olive oil

1 small onion, chopped

1 garlic clove, chopped

400 g/14 oz can chopped tomatoes

2 tbsp chopped fresh parsley

1 tsp dried oregano

2 bay leaves

2 tbsp tomato purée (paste)

1 tsp sugar

salt and pepper

CHICKEN SAUCE

60 g/2 oz/4 tbsp unsalted butter

400 g/14 oz boned chicken breasts,
   skinned and cut into thin strips

90 g/3 oz/¾ cup blanched almonds

300 ml/½ pint/1¼ cups double
   (heavy) cream

salt and pepper

1 To make the tomato sauce, heat the oil in a pan over a medium heat. Add the onion and fry until translucent. Add the garlic and fry for 1 minute. Stir in the tomatoes, parsley, oregano, bay leaves, tomato purée (paste), sugar and salt and pepper to taste, bring to the boil and simmer, uncovered, for 15–20 minutes, until reduced by half. Remove the pan from the heat and discard the bay leaves.

2 To make the chicken sauce, melt the butter in a frying pan (skillet) over a medium heat. Add the chicken and almonds and stir-fry for 5–6 minutes, or until the chicken is cooked through.

3 Meanwhile, bring the cream to the boil in a small pan over a low heat and boil for about 10 minutes, until reduced by almost half. Pour the cream over the chicken and almonds, stir and season to taste with salt and pepper. Set aside and keep warm.

4 Bring a large pan of lightly salted water to the boil. Add the tagliatelle and olive oil and cook for 8–10 minutes until tender, but still firm to the bite. Drain and transfer to a warm serving dish. Spoon over the tomato sauce and arrange the chicken sauce down the centre. Garnish with the basil leaves and serve immediately.

Italian Chicken Parcels

This cooking method makes the chicken aromatic and succulent, and reduces the oil needed as the chicken and vegetables cook in their own juices.

NUTRITIONAL INFORMATION

Calories	234	Sugars	.........5g
Protein	........28g	Fat	..........12g
Carbohydrate	....5g	Saturates	.......5g

🧈 25 MINS   🕐 30 MINS

SERVES 6

I N G R E D I E N T S

1 tbsp olive oil

6 skinless chicken breast fillets

250 g/9 oz/2 cups Mozzarella cheese

500 g/1 lb 2 oz/3½ cups courgettes (zucchini), sliced

6 large tomatoes, sliced

1 small bunch fresh basil or oregano

pepper

rice or pasta, to serve

1 Cut 6 pieces of foil, each measuring about 25 cm/10 inches square. Brush the foil squares lightly with oil and set aside until required.

2 With a sharp knife, slash each chicken breast at regular intervals. Slice the Mozzarella cheese and place between the cuts in the chicken.

COOK'S TIP

To aid cooking, place the vegetables and chicken on the shiny side of the foil so that once the parcel is wrapped up the dull surface of the foil is facing outwards. This ensures that the heat is absorbed into the parcel and not reflected away from it.

3 Divide the courgettes (zucchini) and tomatoes between the pieces of foil and sprinkle with pepper to taste. Tear or roughly chop the basil or oregano and scatter over the vegetables in each parcel.

4 Place the chicken on top of each pile of vegetables then wrap in the foil to enclose the chicken and vegetables, tucking in the ends.

5 Place on a baking tray (cookie sheet) and bake in a preheated oven, 200°C/400°F/Gas Mark 6, for about 30 minutes.

6 To serve, unwrap each foil parcel and serve with rice or pasta.

Pasta & Chicken Medley

Strips of cooked chicken are tossed with coloured pasta, grapes and carrot sticks in a pesto-flavoured dressing.

NUTRITIONAL INFORMATION

Calories 609	Sugars 11g
Protein 26g	Fat 38g
Carbohydrate ...45g	Saturates 6g

 30 MINS   10 MINS

SERVES 2

I N G R E D I E N T S

125–150 g/4½–5½ oz dried pasta shapes,
   such as twists or bows

1 tbsp oil

2 tbsp mayonnaise

2 tsp bottled pesto sauce

1 tbsp soured cream or natural
   fromage frais

175 g/6 oz cooked skinless, boneless
   chicken meat

1–2 celery stalks

125 g/4½ oz/1 cup black grapes
   (preferably seedless)

1 large carrot, trimmed

salt and pepper

celery leaves, to garnish

F R E N C H   D R E S S I N G

1 tbsp wine vinegar

3 tbsp extra-virgin olive oil

salt and pepper

1 To make the French dressing, whisk all the ingredients together until smooth.

2 Cook the pasta with the oil for 8–10 minutes in plenty of boiling salted water until just tender. Drain thoroughly, rinse and drain again. Transfer to a bowl and mix in 1 tablespoon of the French dressing while hot; set aside until cold.

3 Combine the mayonnaise, pesto sauce and soured cream or fromage frais in a bowl, and season to taste.

4 Cut the chicken into narrow strips. Cut the celery diagonally into narrow slices. Reserve a few grapes for garnish, halve the rest and remove any pips (seeds). Cut the carrot into narrow julienne strips.

5 Add the chicken, the celery, the halved grapes, the carrot and the mayonnaise mixture to the pasta, and toss thoroughly. Check the seasoning, adding more salt and pepper if necessary.

6 Arrange the pasta mixture on two plates and garnish with the reserved black grapes and the celery leaves.

Parma-wrapped Chicken

Stuffed with ricotta, nutmeg and spinach, then wrapped with wafer thin slices of Parma ham (prosciutto) and gently cooked in white wine.

NUTRITIONAL INFORMATION

Calories	426	Sugars	........4g
Protein	.......44g	Fat	.........21g
Carbohydrate	....9g	Saturates	.......8g

 30 MINS   45 MINS

SERVES 4

I N G R E D I E N T S

125 g/4½ oz/½ cup frozen spinach, defrosted

125 g/4½ oz/½ cup ricotta cheese

pinch of grated nutmeg

4 skinless, boneless chicken breasts, each weighing 175 g/6 oz

4 Parma ham (prosciutto) slices

25 g/1 oz/2 tbsp butter

1 tbsp olive oil

12 small onions or shallots

125 g/4½ oz/1½ cups button mushrooms, sliced

1 tbsp plain (all-purpose) flour

150 ml/¼ pint/⅔ cup dry white or red wine

300 ml/½ pint/1¼ cups chicken stock

salt and pepper

1 Put the spinach into a sieve (strainer) and press out the water with a spoon. Mix with the ricotta and nutmeg and season with salt and pepper to taste.

2 Using a sharp knife, slit each chicken breast through the side and enlarge each cut to form a pocket. Fill with the spinach mixture, reshape the chicken breasts, wrap each breast tightly in a slice

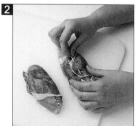

of ham and secure with cocktail sticks. Cover and chill in the refrigerator.

3 Heat the butter and oil in a frying pan (skillet) and brown the chicken breasts for 2 minutes on each side. Transfer the chicken to a large, shallow ovenproof dish and keep warm until required.

4 Fry the onions and mushrooms for 2–3 minutes until lightly browned. Stir in the plain (all-purpose) flour, then

gradually add the wine and stock. Bring to the boil, stirring constantly. Season with salt and pepper and spoon the mixture around the chicken.

5 Cook the chicken uncovered in a preheated oven, 200°C/400°F/Gas Mark 6, for 20 minutes. Turn the breasts over and cook for a further 10 minutes. Remove the cocktail sticks and serve with the sauce, together with carrot purée and green beans, if wished.

Chicken Tortellini

Tortellini were said to have been created in the image of the goddess Venus's navel. Whatever the story, they are a delicious blend of Italian flavours.

NUTRITIONAL INFORMATION

Calories	635	Sugars	.........4g
Protein	........31g	Fat	..........36g
Carbohydrate	...50g	Saturates	......16g

1 HOUR   35 MINS

SERVES 4

I N G R E D I E N T S

115 g/4 oz boned chicken breast, skinned

60 g/2 oz Parma ham (prosciutto)

40 g/1½ oz cooked spinach, well drained

1 tbsp finely chopped onion

2 tbsp freshly grated Parmesan cheese

pinch of ground allspice

1 egg, beaten

450 g/1 lb Basic Pasta Dough (see page 24)

salt and pepper

2 tbsp chopped fresh parsley, to garnish

S A U C E

300 ml/½ pint/1¼ cups single (light) cream

2 garlic cloves, crushed

115 g/4 oz button mushrooms, thinly sliced

4 tbsp freshly grated Parmesan cheese

1 Bring a saucepan of seasoned water to the boil. Add the chicken and poach for about 10 minutes. Leave to cool slightly, then put in a food processor with the Parma ham (prosciutto), spinach and onion and process until finely chopped. Stir in the Parmesan cheese, allspice and egg and season with salt and pepper to taste.

2 Thinly roll out the pasta dough and cut into 4–5 cm/1½–2 inch rounds.

3 Place ½ tsp of the filling in the centre of each round. Fold the pieces in half and press the edges to seal. Then wrap each piece around your index finger, cross over the ends and curl the rest of the dough backwards to make a navel shape. Re-roll the trimmings and repeat until all of the dough is used up.

4 Bring a saucepan of salted water to the boil. Add the tortellini, in batches, bring back to the boil and cook for

5 minutes. Drain well and transfer to a serving dish.

5 To make the sauce, bring the cream and garlic to the boil in a small pan, then simmer for 3 minutes. Add the mushrooms and half of the cheese, season with salt and pepper to taste and simmer for 2–3 minutes. Pour the sauce over the chicken tortellini. Sprinkle over the remaining Parmesan cheese, garnish with the parsley and serve.

Rich Chicken Casserole

This casserole is packed with the sunshine flavours of Italy. Sun-dried tomatoes add a wonderful richness.

NUTRITIONAL INFORMATION

Calories 320	Sugars 8g	
Protein 34g	Fat 17g	
Carbohydrate 8g	Saturates 4g	

 15 MINS 1¼ HOURS

SERVES 4

I N G R E D I E N T S

8 chicken thighs

2 tbsp olive oil

1 medium red onion, sliced

2 garlic cloves, crushed

1 large red (bell) pepper, sliced thickly

thinly pared rind and juice of 1 small orange

125 ml/4 fl oz/½ cup chicken stock

400 g/14 oz can chopped tomatoes

25 g/1 oz/½ cup sun-dried tomatoes, thinly sliced

1 tbsp chopped fresh thyme

50 g/1¾ oz/½ cup pitted black olives

salt and pepper

orange rind and thyme sprigs, to garnish

crusty fresh bread, to serve

COOK'S TIP

Sun-dried tomatoes have a dense texture and concentrated taste, and add intense flavour to slow-cooking casseroles.

1 In a heavy or non-stick large frying pan (skillet), fry the chicken without fat over a fairly high heat, turning occasionally until golden brown. Using a slotted spoon, drain off any excess fat from the chicken and transfer to a flameproof casserole.

2 Add the oil to the pan and fry the onion, garlic and (bell) pepper over a moderate heat for 3–4 minutes. Transfer the vegetables to the casserole.

3 Add the orange rind and juice, chicken stock, canned tomatoes and sun-dried tomatoes to the casserole and stir to combine.

4 Bring to the boil then cover the casserole with a lid and simmer very gently over a low heat for about 1 hour, stirring occasionally. Add the chopped fresh thyme and pitted black olives, then adjust the seasoning with salt and pepper to taste.

5 Scatter orange rind and thyme over the casserole to garnish, and serve with crusty bread.

Chicken with Vegetables

This dish combines succulent chicken with tasty vegetables, flavoured with wine and olives.

NUTRITIONAL INFORMATION

Calories 470	Sugars 7g	
Protein 29g	Fat 34g	
Carbohydrate 7g	Saturates 16g	

20 MINS   1 1/2 HOURS

SERVES 4

INGREDIENTS

4 chicken breasts, part boned

25 g/1 oz/2 tbsp butter

2 tbsp olive oil

1 large onion, chopped finely

2 garlic cloves, crushed

2 (bell) peppers, red, yellow or green, cored,
    deseeded and cut into large pieces

225 g/8 oz large closed cup mushrooms,
    sliced or quartered

175 g/6 oz tomatoes, peeled and halved

150 ml/1/4 pint/2/3 cup dry white wine

125–175 g/4–6 oz green olives, pitted

4–6 tbsp double (heavy) cream

salt and pepper

chopped flat-leaf parsley, to garnish

1 Season the chicken with salt and pepper to taste. Heat the oil and butter in a frying pan (skillet), add the chicken and fry until browned all over. Remove the chicken from the pan.

2 Add the onion and garlic to the frying pan (skillet) and fry gently until just beginning to soften. Add the (bell) peppers to the pan with the mushrooms and continue to cook for a few minutes longer, stirring occasionally.

3 Add the tomatoes and plenty of seasoning to the pan and then transfer the vegetable mixture to an ovenproof casserole. Place the chicken on the bed of vegetables.

4 Add the wine to the frying pan (skillet) and bring to the boil. Pour the wine over the chicken and cover the casserole tightly. Cook in a preheated oven, 180°C/350°F/Gas Mark 4, for 50 minutes.

5 Add the olives to the chicken, mix lightly then pour on the cream. Re-cover the casserole and return to the oven for 10–20 minutes or until the chicken is very tender.

6 Adjust the seasoning and serve the pieces of chicken, surrounded by the vegetables and sauce, with pasta or tiny new potatoes. Sprinkle with chopped parsley to garnish.

Chicken & Seafood Parcels

These mouth-watering mini-parcels of chicken and prawns (shrimp) on a bed of pasta will delight your guests.

NUTRITIONAL INFORMATION

Calories	799	Sugars	.........5g
Protein	........50g	Fat	..........45g
Carbohydrate	...51g	Saturates	......13g

45 MINS   25 MINS

SERVES 4

INGREDIENTS

60 g/2 oz/4 tbsp butter, plus extra
   for greasing

4 x 200 g/7 oz chicken suprêmes, trimmed

115 g/4 oz large spinach leaves, trimmed
   and blanched in hot salted water

4 slices of Parma ham (prosciutto)

12–16 raw tiger prawns (shrimp), shelled
   and deveined

450 g/1 lb dried tagliatelle

1 tbsp olive oil

3 leeks, shredded

1 large carrot, grated

150 ml/¼ pint/⅔ cup thick mayonnaise

2 large cooked beetroot (beet)

salt

1 Grease 4 large pieces of foil and set aside. Place each suprême between 2 pieces of baking parchment and pound with a rolling pin to flatten.

2 Divide half of the spinach between the suprêmes, add a slice of ham to each and top with more spinach. Place 3–4 prawns (shrimp) on top of the spinach. Fold the pointed end of the suprême over the prawns (shrimp), then fold over again to form a parcel. Wrap in foil, place on a baking tray (cookie sheet) and bake in a preheated oven at 200°C/400°F/Gas Mark 6 for 20 minutes.

3 Meanwhile, bring a saucepan of salted water to the boil. Add the pasta and oil and cook for 8–10 minutes or until tender. Drain and transfer to a serving dish.

4 Melt the butter in a frying pan (skillet). Fry the leeks and carrots for 3 minutes. Transfer the vegetables to the centre of the pasta.

5 Work the mayonnaise and 1 beetroot (beet) in a food processor or blender until smooth. Rub through a strainer and pour around the pasta and vegetables.

6 Cut the remaining beetroot (beet) into diamond shapes and place them neatly around the mayonnaise. Remove the foil from the chicken and, using a sharp knife, cut the suprêmes into thin slices. Arrange the chicken and prawn (shrimp) slices on top of the vegetables and pasta, and serve.

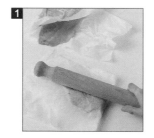
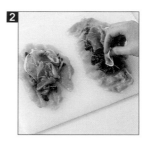

Garlic & Herb Chicken

There is a delicious surprise of creamy herb and garlic soft cheese hidden inside these chicken parcels!

NUTRITIONAL INFORMATION

Calories 272   Sugars 4g
Protein . . . . .29g   Fat 13g
Carbohydrate . . . .4g   Saturates 6g

🥘 20 MINS   🕐 25 MINS

SERVES 4

I N G R E D I E N T S

4 chicken breasts, skin removed

100 g/3½ oz full fat soft cheese, flavoured
   with herbs and garlic

8 slices Parma ham (prosciutto)

150 ml/¼ pint/⅔ cup red wine

150 ml/¼ pint/⅔ cup chicken stock

1 tbsp brown sugar

1 Using a sharp knife, make a horizontal slit along the length of each chicken breast to form a pocket.

2 Beat the cheese with a wooden spoon to soften it. Spoon the cheese into the pocket of the chicken breasts.

3 Wrap 2 slices of Parma ham (prosciutto) around each chicken breast and secure firmly in place with a length of string.

4 Pour the wine and chicken stock into a large frying pan (skillet) and bring to the boil. When the mixture is just starting to boil, add the sugar and stir well to dissolve.

5 Add the chicken breasts to the mixture in the frying pan (skillet). Leave to simmer for 12–15 minutes or until the chicken is tender and the juices run clear when a skewer is inserted into the thickest part of the meat.

6 Remove the chicken from the pan, set aside and keep warm.

7 Reheat the sauce and boil until reduced and thickened. Remove the string from the chicken and cut into slices. Pour the sauce over the chicken to serve.

VARIATION

Try adding 2 finely chopped sun-dried tomatoes to the soft cheese in step 2, if you prefer.

Italian-style Sunday Roast

A mixture of cheese, rosemary and sun-dried tomatoes is stuffed under the chicken skin, then roasted with garlic, potatoes and vegetables.

NUTRITIONAL INFORMATION

Calories 488	Sugars 6g	
Protein 37g	Fat 23g	
Carbohydrate ...34g	Saturates 11g	

 35 MINS   1½ HOURS

SERVES 6

INGREDIENTS

2.5 kg/5 lb 8 oz chicken

sprigs of fresh rosemary

175 g/6 oz/¾ cup feta cheese, coarsely grated

2 tbsp sun-dried tomato paste

60 g/2 oz/4 tbsp butter, softened

1 bulb garlic

1 kg/2 lb 4 oz new potatoes, halved if large

1 each red, green and yellow (bell) pepper, cut into chunks

3 courgettes (zucchini), sliced thinly

2 tbsp olive oil

2 tbsp plain (all-purpose) flour

600 ml/1 pint/2½ cups chicken stock

salt and pepper

1 Rinse the chicken inside and out with cold water and drain well. Carefully cut between the skin and the top of the breast meat using a small pointed knife. Slide a finger into the slit and carefully enlarge it to form a pocket. Continue until the skin is completely lifted away from both breasts and the top of the legs.

2 Chop the leaves from 3 rosemary stems. Mix with the feta cheese, sun-dried tomato paste, butter and pepper to taste, then spoon under the skin. Put the chicken in a large roasting tin (pan), cover with foil and cook in a preheated oven, 190°C/375°F/Gas Mark 5, for 20 minutes per 500 g/1 lb 2 oz, plus 20 minutes.

3 Break the garlic bulb into cloves but do not peel. Add the vegetables to the chicken after 40 minutes.

4 Drizzle with oil, tuck in a few stems of rosemary and season with salt and pepper. Cook for the remaining calculated time, removing the foil for the last 40 minutes to brown the chicken.

5 Transfer the chicken to a serving platter. Place some of the vegetables around the chicken and transfer the remainder to a warmed serving dish. Pour the fat out of the roasting tin (pan) and stir the flour into the remaining pan juices. Cook for 2 minutes then gradually stir in the stock. Bring to the boil, stirring until thickened. Strain into a sauce boat and serve with the chicken.

Slices of Duckling with Pasta

A raspberry and honey sauce superbly counterbalances the richness of the duckling.

NUTRITIONAL INFORMATION

Calories	686	Sugars	........15g
Protein	........62g	Fat	..........20g
Carbohydrate	...70g	Saturates	.......7g

15 MINS   25 MINS

SERVES 4

INGREDIENTS

4 x 275 g/9 oz boned breasts of duckling

25 g/1 oz/2 tbsp butter

50 g/1¾ oz/⅜ cup finely chopped carrots

50 g/1¾ oz/4 tbsp finely chopped shallots

1 tbsp lemon juice

150 ml/¼ pint/⅔ cup meat stock

4 tbsp clear honey

115 g/4 oz/¾ cup fresh or thawed frozen
   raspberries

25 g/1 oz/¼ cup plain (all-purpose) flour

1 tbsp Worcestershire sauce

400 g/14 oz fresh linguine

1 tbsp olive oil

salt and pepper

TO GARNISH

fresh raspberries

fresh sprig of flat-leaf parsley

1 Trim and score the duck breasts with a sharp knife and season well all over. Melt the butter in a frying pan (skillet), add the duck breasts and fry all over until lightly coloured.

2 Add the carrots, shallots, lemon juice and half the meat stock and simmer over a low heat for 1 minute. Stir in half of the honey and half of the raspberries.

Sprinkle over half of the flour and cook, stirring constantly for 3 minutes. Season with pepper to taste and add the Worcestershire sauce.

3 Stir in the remaining stock and cook for 1 minute. Stir in the remaining honey and remaining raspberries and sprinkle over the remaining flour. Cook for a further 3 minutes.

4 Remove the duck breasts from the pan, but leave the sauce to continue simmering over a very low heat.

5 Meanwhile, bring a large saucepan of lightly salted water to the boil. Add the linguine and olive oil and cook for 8–10 minutes or until tender, but still firm to the bite. Drain and divide between 4 individual plates.

6 Slice the duck breast lengthways into 5 mm/¼ inch thick pieces. Pour a little sauce over the pasta and arrange the sliced duck in a fan shape on top of it. Garnish with raspberries and flat-leaf parsley and serve immediately.

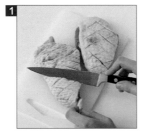

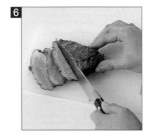

Pheasant Lasagne

This scrumptious and unusual baked lasagne is virtually a meal in itself. It is served with baby onions and green peas.

NUTRITIONAL INFORMATION

Calories . . . . . . .1038 Sugars 13g
Protein . . . . .65g Fat 64g
Carbohydrate . . .54g Saturates 27g

40 MINS   1¼ HOURS

SERVES 4

INGREDIENTS

butter, for greasing

14 sheets pre-cooked lasagne

850 ml/1½ pints/3¾ cups Béchamel Sauce
(see page 28)

75 g/2¾ oz/¾ cup grated Mozzarella
cheese

FILLING

225 g/8 oz pork fat, diced

60 g/2 oz/2 tbsp butter

16 small onions

8 large pheasant breasts, thinly sliced

25 g/1 oz/¼ cup plain (all-purpose) flour

600 ml/1 pint/2½ cups chicken stock

bouquet garni

450 g/1 lb fresh peas, shelled

salt and pepper

1 To make the filling, put the pork fat into a saucepan of boiling, salted water and simmer for 3 minutes, then drain and pat dry.

2 Melt the butter in a large frying pan (skillet). Add the pork fat and onions to the pan and cook for about 3 minutes, or until lightly browned.

3 Remove the pork fat and onions from the pan and set aside. Add the slices of pheasant and cook over a low heat for 12 minutes, until browned all over. Transfer to an ovenproof dish.

4 Stir the flour into the pan and cook until just brown, then blend in the stock. Pour the mixture over the pheasant, add the bouquet garni and cook in a preheated oven, at 200°C/400°F/Gas Mark 6, for 5 minutes. Remove the bouquet garni. Add the onions, pork fat and peas and return to the oven for 10 minutes.

5 Put the pheasant and pork fat in a food processor and mince (grind) finely.

6 Lower the oven temperature to 190°C/ 375°F/Gas Mark 5. Grease an ovenproof dish with butter. Make layers of lasagne, pheasant sauce and Béchamel Sauce in the dish, ending with Béchamel Sauce. Sprinkle over the cheese and bake for 30 minutes.

Pesto Baked Partridge

Partridge has a more delicate flavour than many game birds and this subtle sauce perfectly complements it.

NUTRITIONAL INFORMATION

Calories 895	Sugars 5g
Protein 79g	Fat 45g
Carbohydrate ...45g	Saturates 18g

15 MINS   40 MINS

SERVES 4

I N G R E D I E N T S

8 partridge pieces (about 115 g/4 oz each)

60 g/2 oz/4 tbsp butter, melted

4 tbsp Dijon mustard

2 tbsp lime juice

1 tbsp brown sugar

6 tbsp Pesto Sauce (see page 39)

450 g/1 lb dried rigatoni

1 tbsp olive oil

115 g/4 oz/1⅓ cups freshly grated
   Parmesan cheese

salt and pepper

1 Arrange the partridge pieces, smooth side down, in a single layer in a large, ovenproof dish.

2 Mix together the butter, Dijon mustard, lime juice and brown sugar in a bowl. Season to taste. Brush this mixture over the partridge pieces and bake in a preheated oven at 200°C/400°F/Gas Mark 6 for 15 minutes.

3 Remove the dish from the oven and coat the partridge pieces with 3 tbsp of the Pesto Sauce. Return to the oven and bake for a further 12 minutes.

4 Remove the dish from the oven and carefully turn over the partridge pieces. Coat the top of the partridges with the remaining mustard mixture and return to the oven for a further 10 minutes.

5 Meanwhile, bring a large pan of lightly salted water to the boil. Add the rigatoni and olive oil and cook for 8–10 minutes until tender, but still firm to the bite. Drain and transfer to a serving dish. Toss the pasta with the remaining Pesto Sauce and the Parmesan cheese.

6 Serve the partridge with the pasta, pouring over the cooking juices.

VARIATION

You could also prepare young pheasant in the same way.

Vegetables

Vegetables are a staple ingredient in Italian cooking. The different areas supply a prolific amount of fresh and succulent vegetables, including globe artichokes which grow wild on Sicily, sweet (bell) peppers which are sun-ripened in Italy, as are the universally popular sun-ripened tomatoes. Vegetables work well with a variety of different

ingredients, including pasta, rice, grains and pulses to make a selection of delicious dishes. However, vegetables can make a tasty meal in themselves. Try vegetables barbecued (grilled) on rosemary skewers – the aromatic flavour of this wonderful herb is imparted during the cooking process to make a very Italian dish. Vegetables have so much potential – experiment and enjoy!

Vegetable Ravioli

It is important not to overcook the vegetable filling or it will become sloppy and unexciting, instead of firm to the bite and delicious.

NUTRITIONAL INFORMATION

Calories	622	Sugars	........10g
Protein	........12g	Fat	..........40g
Carbohydrate	...58g	Saturates	.......6g

1½ HOURS   55 MINS

SERVES 4

INGREDIENTS

450 g/1 lb Basic Pasta Dough (see page 24)

1 tbsp olive oil

90 g/3 oz/6 tbsp butter

150 ml/5 fl oz/⅝ cup single (light) cream

75 g/3 oz/1 cup freshly grated
Parmesan cheese

fresh basil sprigs, to garnish

STUFFING

2 large aubergines (eggplant)

3 large courgettes (zucchini)

6 large tomatoes

1 large green (bell) pepper

1 large red (bell) pepper

3 garlic cloves

1 large onion

125 ml/4 fl oz/½ cup olive oil

60 g/2 oz tomato purée (paste)

½ tsp chopped fresh basil

salt and pepper

1 To make the stuffing, cut the aubergines (eggplant) and courgettes (zucchini) into 2.5 cm/1 inch chunks. Put the aubergine (eggplant) pieces in a colander, sprinkle with salt and set aside for 20 minutes. Rinse and drain.

2 Blanch the tomatoes in boiling water for 2 minutes. Drain, skin and chop the flesh. Core and seed the (bell) peppers and cut into 2.5 cm/1 inch dice. Chop the garlic and onion.

3 Heat the oil in a saucepan. Add the garlic and onion and fry for 3 minutes.

4 Stir in the aubergines (eggplant), courgettes (zucchini), tomatoes, (bell) peppers, tomato purée (paste) and basil. Season with salt and pepper to taste, cover and simmer for 20 minutes, stirring frequently.

5 Roll out the pasta dough and cut out 7.5 cm/3 inch rounds with a plain cutter. Put a spoonful of the vegetable stuffing on each round. Dampen the edges slightly and fold the pasta rounds over, pressing together to seal.

6 Bring a saucepan of salted water to the boil. Add the ravioli and the oil and cook for 3–4 minutes. Drain and transfer to a greased ovenproof dish, dotting each layer with butter. Pour over the cream and sprinkle over the Parmesan cheese. Bake in a preheated oven at 200°C/400°F/Gas Mark 6 for 20 minutes. Serve hot.

Braised Fennel & Linguine

This aniseed-flavoured vegetable gives that extra punch to this delicious creamy pasta dish.

NUTRITIONAL INFORMATION

Calories 650   Sugars 6g
Protein ....14g   Fat 39g
Carbohydrate ...62g   Saturates 22g

20 MINS   50 MINS

SERVES 4

INGREDIENTS

6 fennel bulbs

150 ml/ ¼ pint/ ⅔ cup vegetable stock

25 g/1 oz/2 tbsp butter

6 slices rindless smoked bacon, diced

6 shallots, quartered

25 g/1 oz/ ¼ cup plain (all-purpose) flour

7 tbsp double (heavy) cream

1 tbsp Madeira

450 g/1 lb dried linguine

1 tbsp olive oil

salt and pepper

1 Trim the fennel bulbs, then gently peel off and reserve the first layer of the bulbs. Cut the bulbs into quarters and put them in a large saucepan, together with the vegetable stock and the reserved outer layers. Bring to the boil, lower the heat and simmer for 5 minutes.

2 Using a slotted spoon, transfer the fennel to a large dish. Discard the outer layers of the fennel bulb. Bring the vegetable stock to the boil and allow to reduce by half. Set aside.

3 Melt the butter in a frying pan (skillet). Add the bacon and shallots and fry for 4 minutes. Add the flour, reduced stock, cream and Madeira and cook, stirring constantly, for 3 minutes, or until the sauce is smooth. Season to taste and pour over the fennel.

4 Bring a large saucepan of lightly salted water to the boil. Add the linguine and olive oil and cook for 8–10 minutes, or until tender but still firm to the bite. Drain and transfer to a deep ovenproof dish.

5 Add the fennel and sauce and braise in a preheated oven at 180°C/350°F/ Gas Mark 4 for 20 minutes. Serve immediately.

COOK'S TIP

Fennel will keep in the salad drawer of the refrigerator for 2–3 days, but it is best eaten as fresh as possible. Cut surfaces turn brown quickly, so do not prepare it too much in advance of cooking.

Stuffed Red (Bell) Peppers

Stuffed (bell) peppers are a well-known dish, but this is a new version adapted for the barbecue (grill).

NUTRITIONAL INFORMATION

Calories	144	Sugars	.........4g
Protein	.........1g	Fat	..........12g
Carbohydrate	....9g	Saturates	.......2g

 40 MINS   10 MINS

SERVES 4

I N G R E D I E N T S

2 red (bell) peppers, halved lengthways
    and deseeded

2 tomatoes, halved

2 courgettes (zucchini),
    sliced thinly lengthways

1 red onion, cut into 8 sections,
    each section held together by the root

4 tbsp olive oil

2 tbsp fresh thyme leaves

60 g/2 oz/⅓ cup mixed basmati and
    wild rice, cooked

salt and pepper

COOK'S TIP

When char-grilled, red, orange and yellow (bell) peppers all take on a remarkable sweet quality. They are often peeled in order to highlight this. Orange (bell) peppers are worth experimenting with as they do have a different flavour from red and green (bell) peppers.

1 Put the (bell) peppers, tomatoes, courgettes (zucchini) and onion sections on to a baking tray (cookie sheet).

2 Brush the vegetables with olive oil and sprinkle over the thyme leaves.

3 Cook the (bell) pepper, onion and courgette (zucchini) over a medium barbecue for 6 minutes, turning once.

4 When the (bell) peppers are cooked, put a spoonful of the cooked rice into each one.

5 Add the tomato halves to the barbecue (grill) and cook for 2–3 minutes only. Serve all the vegetables hot, seasoned with plenty of salt and pepper.

Italian Potato Wedges

These oven-cooked potato wedges use classic pizza ingredients and are delicious served with plain meats, such as pork or lamb.

NUTRITIONAL INFORMATION

Calories 115	Sugars 4g	
Protein 6g	Fat 5g	
Carbohydrate ...13g	Saturates 3g	

15 MINS   35 MINS

SERVES 4

INGREDIENTS

2 large waxy potatoes, unpeeled

4 large ripe tomatoes, peeled and seeded

150 ml/¼ pint/⅔ cup vegetable stock

2 tbsp tomato purée (paste)

1 small yellow (bell) pepper, cut into strips

125 g/4½ oz button mushrooms, quartered

1 tbsp chopped fresh basil

50 g/1¾ oz cheese, grated

salt and pepper

1 Cut each of the potatoes into 8 equal wedges. Parboil the potatoes in a pan of boiling water for 15 minutes. Drain well and place in a shallow ovenproof dish.

2 Chop the tomatoes and add to the dish. Mix together the vegetable stock and tomato purée (paste), then pour the mixture over the potatoes and tomatoes.

3 Add the yellow (bell) pepper strips, quartered mushrooms and chopped basil. Season well with salt and pepper.

4 Sprinkle the grated cheese over the top and cook in a preheated oven, 190°C/375°F/Gas Mark 5, for 15-20 minutes until the topping is golden brown. Serve at once.

Creamy Pasta & Broccoli

This colourful dish provides a mouth-watering contrast in the crisp *al dente* texture of the broccoli and the creamy cheese sauce.

NUTRITIONAL INFORMATION

Calories 472	Sugars 6g
Protein 15g	Fat 24g
Carbohydrate ...52g	Saturates 14g

 5 MINS   25 MINS

SERVES 4

I N G R E D I E N T S

60 g/2 oz/4 tbsp butter

1 large onion, finely chopped

450 g/1 lb dried ribbon pasta

450 g/1 lb broccoli,
  broken into florets

150 ml/¼ pint/⅔ cup boiling
  vegetable stock

1 tbsp plain (all-purpose) flour

150 ml/¼ pint/⅔ cup single (light) cream

60 g/2 oz/½ cup grated Mozzarella cheese

freshly grated nutmeg

salt and white pepper

fresh apple slices, to garnish

1 Melt half of the butter in a large saucepan over a medium heat. Add the onion and fry for 4 minutes.

VARIATION

This dish would also be delicious and look just as colourful made with Cape broccoli, which is actually a purple variety of cauliflower and not broccoli at all.

2 Add the broccoli and pasta to the pan and cook, stirring constantly, for 2 minutes. Add the vegetable stock, bring back to the boil and simmer for a further 12 minutes. Season well with salt and white pepper.

3 Meanwhile, melt the remaining butter in a saucepan over a medium heat. Sprinkle over the flour and cook, stirring constantly, for 2 minutes. Gradually stir in

the cream and bring to simmering point, but do not boil. Add the grated cheese and season with salt and a little freshly grated nutmeg.

4 Drain the pasta and broccoli mixture and pour over the cheese sauce. Cook, stirring occasionally, for about 2 minutes. Transfer the pasta and broccoli mixture to a warm, large, deep serving dish and serve garnished with slices of fresh apple.

Vegetable Frittata

A frittata is a type of Italian omelette – you can add almost anything to the eggs. It is also delicious eaten cold and makes an ideal picnic dish.

NUTRITIONAL INFORMATION

Calories	310	Sugars	. . . . .4g
Protein	. . . . .18g	Fat	. . . . .17g
Carbohydrate	. . .24g	Saturates	. . . . . . .4g

 15 MINS   20 MINS

SERVES 4

INGREDIENTS

3 tbsp olive oil

1 onion, chopped

2 garlic cloves, chopped

225 g/8 oz courgettes (zucchini),
   sliced thinly

4 eggs

400 g/14 oz can borlotti beans,
   drained and rinsed

3 tomatoes, skinned and chopped

2 tbsp chopped fresh parsley

1 tbsp chopped fresh basil

60 g/2 oz/½ cup grated Gruyère
   (Swiss) cheese

salt and pepper

1 Heat 2 tablespoons of the oil in a frying pan (skillet) and fry the onion and garlic, stirring occasionally, for 2–3 minutes or until soft. Add the courgettes (zucchini) and cook for 3–4 minutes, or until softened.

2 Break the eggs into a bowl and add salt and pepper to taste, the fried vegetables, beans, tomatoes and herbs.

3 Heat the remaining oil in a 24 cm/ 9½ inch omelette pan, add the egg mixture and fry gently for 5 minutes until the eggs have almost set and the underside is brown.

4 Sprinkle the cheese over the top and place the pan under a preheated moderate grill (broiler) for 3–4 minutes or until set on the top but still moist in the middle. Cut into wedges and serve warm or at room temperature.

COOK'S TIP

Gruyère (Swiss) cheese is made from unpasturised cow's milk and has a sweet, nutty flavour, which enhances the taste of this frittata. It is firm and close textured and has small holes interspersed throughout.

Spinach & Mushroom Lasagne

Always check the seasoning of vegetables – you can always add a little more to a recipe, but you cannot take it out once it has been added.

NUTRITIONAL INFORMATION

Calories 720	Sugars 9g	
Protein 31g	Fat 52g	
Carbohydrate ...36g	Saturates 32g	

 20 MINS 40 MINS

SERVES 4

INGREDIENTS

115 g/4 oz/8 tbsp butter, plus extra
  for greasing

2 garlic cloves, finely chopped

115 g/4 oz shallots

225 g/8 oz wild mushrooms,
  such as chanterelles

450 g/1 lb spinach, cooked, drained and
  finely chopped

225 g/8 oz/2 cups grated Cheddar cheese

¼ tsp freshly grated nutmeg

1 tsp chopped fresh basil

60 g/2 oz plain (all-purpose) flour

600 ml/1 pint/2½ cups hot milk

60 g/2 oz/ ⅔ cup grated Cheshire cheese

salt and pepper

8 sheets pre-cooked lasagne

VARIATION

You could substitute
4 (bell) peppers for the
spinach. Roast in a preheated
oven, at 200°C/400°F/Gas Mark 6,
for 20 minutes. Rub off the skins
under cold water, deseed and chop
before using.

1 Lightly grease a large ovenproof dish with a little butter.

2 Melt 60 g/2 oz/4 tbsp of the butter in a saucepan. Add the garlic, shallots and wild mushrooms and fry over a low heat for 3 minutes. Stir in the spinach, Cheddar cheese, nutmeg and basil. Season with salt and pepper to taste and set aside.

3 Melt the remaining butter in another saucepan over a low heat. Add the flour and cook, stirring constantly, for 1 minute. Gradually stir in the hot milk, whisking constantly until smooth. Stir in 25 g/1 oz/¼ cup of the Cheshire cheese and season to taste with salt and pepper.

4 Spread half of the mushroom and spinach mixture over the base of the prepared dish. Cover with a layer of lasagne and then with half of the cheese sauce. Repeat the process and sprinkle over the remaining Cheshire cheese.

5 Bake in a preheated oven, at 200°C/400°F/Gas Mark 6, for 30 minutes, or until golden brown. Serve hot.

Twice Baked Potatoes

The potatoes are baked until fluffy, then the flesh is scooped out and mixed with pesto before being returned to the potato shells and baked again.

NUTRITIONAL INFORMATION

Calories	424	Sugars 3g
Protein	.........9g	Fat 27g
Carbohydrate	...40g	Saturates 13g

 10 MINS   1¹/₂ HOURS

SERVES 4

INGREDIENTS

4 baking potatoes, about 225 g/8 oz each

150 ml/¼ pint/⅔ cup double (heavy) cream

85 ml/3 fl oz/⅓ cup vegetable stock

1 tbsp lemon juice

2 garlic cloves, crushed

3 tbsp chopped fresh basil

2 tbsp pine kernels (nuts)

2 tbsp grated Parmesan cheese

salt and pepper

1 Scrub the potatoes and prick the skins with a fork. Rub a little salt into the skins and place the potatoes on to a baking tray (cookie sheet).

2 Cook in a preheated oven, 190°C/ 375°F/Gas Mark 5, for 1 hour or until the potatoes are cooked through and the skins crisp.

3 Remove the potatoes from the oven and cut them in half lengthways. Using a spoon, scoop the potato flesh into a mixing bowl, leaving a thin shell of potato inside the skins. Mash the potato flesh with a fork.

4 Meanwhile, mix the cream and stock in a saucepan and simmer for 8-10 minutes or until reduced by half.

5 Stir in the lemon juice, garlic and chopped basil and season to taste with salt and pepper. Stir the mixture into the potato flesh with the pine kernels (nuts).

6 Spoon the mixture back into the potato shells and sprinkle the Parmesan cheese on top. Return the potatoes to the oven for 10 minutes or until the cheese has browned. Serve with salad.

VARIATION

Add full fat soft cheese or thinly sliced mushrooms to the mashed potato flesh in step 5, if you prefer.

Vermicelli & Vegetable Flan

Lightly cooked vermicelli is pressed into a flan ring and baked with a creamy mushroom filling.

NUTRITIONAL INFORMATION

Calories 528   Sugars 6g
Protein ....15g   Fat 32g
Carbohydrate ...47g   Saturates 17g

 15 MINS   1 HOUR

SERVES 4

INGREDIENTS

75 g/2¾ oz/6 tbsp butter, plus extra

   for greasing

225 g/8 oz dried vermicelli or spaghetti

1 tbsp olive oil

1 onion, chopped

140 g/5 oz button mushrooms

1 green (bell) pepper, cored, seeded and

   sliced into thin rings

150 ml/¼ pint/⅔ cup milk

3 eggs, lightly beaten

2 tbsp double (heavy) cream

1 tsp dried oregano

freshly grated nutmeg

1 tbsp freshly grated Parmesan cheese

salt and pepper

tomato and basil salad, to serve

1 Generously grease a 20 cm/8 inch loose-based flan tin (pan) with butter.

2 Bring a large pan of lightly salted water to the boil. Add the vermicelli and olive oil and cook for 8–10 minutes until tender, but still firm to the bite. Drain, return to the pan, add 25 g/1 oz/2 tbsp of the butter and shake the pan to coat the pasta.

3 Press the pasta on to the base and around the sides of the flan tin (pan) to make a flan case.

4 Melt the remaining butter in a frying pan (skillet) over a medium heat. Add the onion and fry until it is translucent.

5 Add the mushrooms and (bell) pepper rings to the frying pan (skillet) and cook, stirring, for 2–3 minutes. Spoon the onion, mushroom and (bell) pepper mixture into the flan case and press it evenly into the base.

6 Beat together the milk, eggs and cream, stir in the oregano and season to taste with nutmeg and pepper. Carefully pour this mixture over the vegetables and then sprinkle with the Parmesan cheese.

7 Bake the flan in a preheated oven at 180°C/350°F/Gas Mark 4 for 40–45 minutes, or until the filling has set.

8 Slide the flan out of the tin (pan) and serve warm with a tomato and basil salad, if wished.

Marinated Tofu (Bean Curd)

Tofu (bean curd) is full of protein, vitamins and minerals, and although it is bland on its own, it develops a fabulous flavour when it is marinated.

NUTRITIONAL INFORMATION

Calories 105	Sugars 3g	
Protein 8g	Fat 7g	
Carbohydrate 4g	Saturates 1g	

50 MINS   10 MINS

SERVES 4

INGREDIENTS

350 g/12 oz tofu (bean curd)

1 red (bell) pepper

1 yellow (bell) pepper

2 courgettes (zucchini)

8 button mushrooms

slices of lemon, to garnish

MARINADE

grated rind and juice of ½ lemon

1 clove garlic, crushed

½ tsp fresh rosemary, chopped

½ tsp chopped, fresh thyme

1 tbsp walnut oil

1 To make the marinade, combine the lemon rind and juice, garlic, rosemary, thyme and oil in a shallow dish.

2 Drain the tofu (bean curd), pat it dry on kitchen paper and cut it into squares. Add to the marinade and toss to coat. Leave to marinate for 20–30 minutes.

3 Meanwhile, deseed and cut the (bell) peppers into 2.5 cm/1 inch pieces. Blanch in boiling water for 4 minutes, refresh in cold water and drain.

4 Using a canelle knife (or potato peeler), remove strips of peel from the

courgettes (zucchini). Cut the courgette (zucchini) into 2.5 cm/1 inch chunks.

5 Remove the tofu (bean curd) from the marinade, reserving the liquid for basting. Thread the tofu (bean curd) on to 8 skewers, alternating with the (bell) peppers, courgette (zucchini) and button mushrooms.

6 Barbecue (grill) the skewers over medium hot coals for about 6 minutes, turning and basting with the marinade.

7 Transfer the skewers to warm serving plates, garnish with slices of lemon and serve.

VARIATION

For a spicy kebab (kabob), make a marinade from 1 tablespoon of curry paste, 2 tablespoons of oil and the juice of ½ lemon.

Pepperonata

A delicious mixture of (bell) peppers and onions, cooked with tomatoes and herbs for a rich side dish.

NUTRITIONAL INFORMATION

Calories ....180 Sugars 14g
Protein ....3g Fat 12g
Carbohydrate ...15g Saturates 2g

 15 MINS   40 MINS

SERVES 4

INGREDIENTS

4 tbsp olive oil

1 onion, halved and finely sliced

2 red (bell) peppers, cut into strips

2 green (bell) peppers, cut into strips

2 yellow (bell) peppers, cut into strips

2 garlic cloves, crushed

2 x 400 g/14 oz cans chopped
    tomatoes, drained

2 tbsp chopped coriander (cilantro)

2 tbsp chopped pitted black olives

salt and pepper

VARIATION

If you don't like the distinctive flavour of fresh coriander (cilantro), you can substitute it with 2 tbsp chopped fresh flat-leaf parsley. Use green olives instead of black ones, if you prefer.

1 Heat the oil in a large frying pan (skillet). Add the onion and sauté for 5 minutes, stirring until just beginning to colour.

2 Add the (bell) peppers and garlic to the pan and cook for a further 3–4 minutes.

3 Stir in the tomatoes and coriander (cilantro) and season with salt and pepper. Cover the pan and cook the vegetables gently for about 30 minutes or until the mixture is dry.

4 Stir in the pitted black olives and serve the pepperonata immediately.

Ricotta & Spinach Parcels

Ricotta and spinach make a great flavour combination, especially when encased in light puff-pastry parcels.

🥬 25 MINS   🕐 30 MINS

SERVES 4

I N G R E D I E N T S

350 g/12 oz/3 cups spinach,
   trimmed and washed thoroughly

25 g/1 oz/2 tbsp butter

1 small onion, chopped finely

1 tsp green peppercorns

500 g/1 lb 2 oz puff pastry

225 g/8 oz/1 cup Ricotta

1 egg, beaten

salt

sprigs of fresh herbs, to garnish

fresh vegetables, to serve

1 Pack the spinach into a large saucepan. Add a little salt and a very small amount of water and cook until wilted. Drain well, cool and then squeeze out any excess moisture with the back of a spoon. Chop roughly.

2 Melt the butter in a small saucepan and fry the onion gently for 2 minutes or until softened, but not browned. Add the green peppercorns and cook for 2 minutes. Remove from the heat, add the spinach and mix together.

3 Roll out the puff pastry thinly on a lightly floured work surface and cut into 4 squares, each 18 cm/7 inches across. Place a quarter of the spinach mixture in the centre of each square and top with a quarter of the cheese.

4 Brush a little beaten egg around the edges of the pastry squares and bring the corners together to form parcels. Press the edges together firmly to seal. Lift the parcels on to a greased baking tray (cookie sheet), brush with beaten egg and bake in a preheated oven, at 200°C/ 400°F/Gas Mark 6, for 20–25 minutes, or until risen and golden brown.

5 Serve hot, garnished with sprigs of fresh herbs and accompanied by fresh vegetables.

Garlic Potato Wedges

This is a great recipe for the barbecue (grill). Serve this tasty potato dish with grilled (broiled) meat or fish.

NUTRITIONAL INFORMATION

Calories 259	Sugars 1g
Protein 3g	Fat 17g
Carbohydrate ...26g	Saturates 5g

 10 MINS   35 MINS

SERVES 4

I N G R E D I E N T S

3 large baking potatoes, scrubbed

4 tbsp olive oil

25 g/1 oz butter

2 garlic cloves, chopped

1 tbsp chopped, fresh rosemary

1 tbsp chopped, fresh parsley

1 tbsp chopped, fresh thyme

salt and pepper

1 Bring a large saucepan of water to the boil, add the potatoes and par-boil them for 10 minutes. Drain the potatoes, refresh under cold water and drain them again thoroughly.

2 Transfer the potatoes to a chopping board. When the potatoes are cold enough to handle, cut them into thick wedges, but do not remove the skins.

COOK'S TIP

You may find it easier to barbecue (grill) these potatoes in a hinged rack or in a specially designed barbecue (grill) roasting tray.

3 Heat the oil and butter in a small pan together with the garlic. Cook gently until the garlic begins to brown, then remove the pan from the heat.

4 Stir the herbs and salt and pepper to taste into the mixture in the pan.

5 Brush the herb mixture all over the potatoes.

6 Barbecue (grill) the potatoes over hot coals for 10–15 minutes, brushing liberally with any of the remaining herb and butter mixture, or until the potatoes are just tender.

7 Transfer the barbecued (grilled) garlic potatoes to a warm serving plate and serve as a starter or as a side dish.

Spinach Frittata

This Italian dish may be made with many flavourings. Spinach is used as the main ingredient in this recipe for colour and flavour.

NUTRITIONAL INFORMATION

Calories 307   Sugars 4g
Protein . . . . .15g   Fat 25g
Carbohydrate . . . .6g   Saturates 8g

20 MINS   20 MINS

SERVES 4

INGREDIENTS

450 g/1 lb spinach

2 tsp water

4 eggs, beaten

2 tbsp single (light) cream

2 garlic cloves, crushed

50 g/1¾ oz/¾ cup canned
   sweetcorn, drained

1 celery stick, chopped

1 red chilli, chopped

2 tomatoes, seeded and diced

2 tbsp olive oil

2 tbsp butter

25 g/1 oz/¼ cup pecan nut halves

2 tbsp grated Pecorino cheese

25 g/1 oz/¼ cup Fontina cheese, cubed

a pinch of paprika

1 Cook the spinach in 2 teaspoons of water in a covered saucepan for 5 minutes. Drain thoroughly and pat dry on absorbent paper towels.

2 Beat the eggs in a bowl and stir in the spinach, single (light) cream, garlic, sweetcorn, celery, chilli and tomatoes until the ingredients are well mixed.

3 Heat the oil and butter in a 20 cm/ 8 inch heavy-based frying pan (skillet).

4 Spoon the egg mixture into the frying pan (skillet) and sprinkle with the pecan nut halves, Pecorino and Fontina cheeses and paprika. Cook, without stirring, over a medium heat for 5–7 minutes or until the underside of the frittata is brown.

5 Put a large plate over the pan and invert to turn out the frittata. Slide it back into the frying pan (skillet) and cook the other side for a further 2–3 minutes. Serve the frittata straight from the frying pan (skillet) or transfer to a serving plate.

COOK'S TIP

Be careful not to burn the underside of the frittata during the initial cooking stage – this is why it is important to use a heavy-based frying pan (skillet). Add a little extra oil to the pan when you turn the frittata over, if required.

(Bell) Peppers & Rosemary

The flavour of grilled (broiled) or roasted (bell) peppers is very different from when they are eaten raw, so do try them cooked in this way.

NUTRITIONAL INFORMATION

Calories	.201	Sugars	.6g
Protein	.2g	Fat	.19g
Carbohydrate	.6g	Saturates	.2g

 20 MINS   10 MINS

SERVES 4

I N G R E D I E N T S

4 tbsp olive oil

finely grated rind of 1 lemon

4 tbsp lemon juice

1 tbsp balsamic vinegar

1 tbsp crushed fresh rosemary, or 1 tsp
    dried rosemary

2 garlic cloves, crushed

2 red and 2 yellow (bell) peppers, halved,
    cored and deseeded

2 tbsp pine kernels (nuts)

salt and pepper

sprigs of fresh rosemary, to garnish

1 Mix together the olive oil, lemon rind, lemon juice, balsamic vinegar, rosemary and garlic. Season with salt and pepper to taste.

2 Place the (bell) peppers, skin-side uppermost, on the rack of a grill (broiler) pan, lined with foil. Brush the olive oil mixture over them.

3 Grill (broil) the (bell) peppers for 3–4 minutes or until the skin begins to char, basting frequently with the lemon juice mixture. Remove from the heat, cover with foil to trap the steam and leave for 5 minutes.

4 Meanwhile, scatter the pine kernels (nuts) on to the grill (broiler) rack and toast them lightly for 2–3 minutes. Keep a close eye on the pine kernels (nuts) as they tend to burn very quickly.

5 Peel the (bell) peppers, slice them into strips and place them in a warmed serving dish. Sprinkle with the pine kernels (nuts) and drizzle any remaining lemon juice mixture over them. Garnish with sprigs of fresh rosemary and serve at once.

Pasta-stuffed Tomatoes

This unusual and inexpensive dish would make a good starter for eight people or a delicious lunch for four.

 15 MINS   35 MINS

SERVES 4

INGREDIENTS

5 tbsp extra virgin olive oil, plus extra
   for greasing

8 beef tomatoes or large round tomatoes

115 g/4 oz/1 cup dried ditalini or other very
   small pasta shapes

8 black olives, stoned (pitted) and
   finely chopped

2 tbsp finely chopped fresh basil

1 tbsp finely chopped fresh parsley

60 g/2 oz/⅔ cup freshly grated
   Parmesan cheese

salt and pepper

fresh basil sprigs, to garnish

1 Brush a baking tray (cookie sheet) with olive oil.

2 Slice the tops off the tomatoes and reserve to make 'lids'. If the tomatoes will not stand up, cut a thin slice off the bottom of each tomato.

3 Using a teaspoon, scoop out the tomato pulp into a strainer, but do not pierce the tomato shells. Invert the tomato shells on to kitchen paper, pat dry and then set aside to drain.

4 Bring a large saucepan of lightly salted water to the boil. Add the ditalini or other pasta and 1 tablespoon of the remaining olive oil and cook for 8–10 minutes or until tender, but still firm to the bite. Drain the pasta and set aside.

5 Put the olives, basil, parsley and Parmesan cheese into a large mixing bowl and stir in the drained tomato pulp. Add the pasta to the bowl. Stir in the remaining olive oil, mix together well, and season to taste with salt and pepper.

6 Spoon the pasta mixture into the tomato shells and replace the lids. Arrange the tomatoes on the baking tray (cookie sheet) and bake in a preheated oven, at 190°C/375°F/Gas Mark 5, for 15–20 minutes.

7 Remove the tomatoes from the oven and allow to cool until just warm.

8 Arrange the pasta-stuffed tomatoes on a serving dish, garnish with the basil sprigs and serve.

Roasted Vegetables

Rosemary branches can be used as brushes for basting and as skewers. Soak the rosemary skewers well in advance to cut down preparation time.

NUTRITIONAL INFORMATION

Calories	16	Sugars	.........3g
Protein	.........1g	Fat	..........0.3g
Carbohydrate	....3g	Saturates	.......0g

 8¹/₂ HOURS 10 MINS

SERVES 6

INGREDIENTS

1 small red cabbage

1 head fennel

1 orange (bell) pepper, cut into
  3.5 cm/1½ inch dice

1 aubergine (eggplant), halved and sliced
  into 1 cm/½ inch pieces

2 courgettes (zucchini),
  sliced thickly diagonally

olive oil, for brushing

6 rosemary twigs, about 15 cm/6 inches
  long, soaked in water for 8 hours

salt and pepper

1 Put the red cabbage on its side on a chopping board and cut through the middle of its stem and heart. Divide each piece into four, each time including a bit of the stem in the slice to hold it together.

VARIATION

Fruit skewers are a deliciously quick and easy dessert. Thread pieces of banana, mango, peach, strawberry, apple and pear on to soaked wooden skewers and cook over the dying embers. Brush with sugar syrup towards the end of cooking.

2 Prepare the fennel in the same way as the red cabbage.

3 Blanch the red cabbage and fennel in boiling water for 3 minutes, then drain well.

4 With a wooden skewer, pierce a hole through the middle of each piece of vegetable.

5 On to each rosemary twig, thread a piece of orange (bell) pepper, fennel, red cabbage, aubergine (eggplant) and courgette (zucchini), pushing the rosemary through the holes.

6 Brush liberally with olive oil and season with plenty of salt and pepper.

7 Cook over a hot barbecue for 8–10 minutes, turning occasionally. Serve immediately.

Italian Stuffed (Bell) Peppers

Halved (bell) peppers are stuffed with the flavours of Italy in this sunshine-bright dish.

NUTRITIONAL INFORMATION

Calories 193	Sugars 8g
Protein 2g	Fat 17g
Carbohydrate 9g	Saturates 2g

20 MINS   25 MINS

SERVES 4

INGREDIENTS

1 red (bell) pepper

1 green (bell) pepper

1 yellow (bell) pepper

1 orange (bell) pepper

6 tbsp olive oil

1 small red onion, sliced

1 small aubergine (eggplant),
    chopped roughly

125 g/4½ oz button mushrooms, wiped

125 g/4½ oz/1 cup cherry tomatoes, halved

few drops of mushroom ketchup

handful of fresh basil leaves,
    torn into pieces

2 tbsp lemon juice

salt and pepper

sprigs of fresh basil, to garnish

lemon wedges, to serve

1 Halve the (bell) peppers, remove the cores and deseed them. Sprinkle over a few drops of olive oil and season.

2 Heat the remaining olive oil in a frying pan (skillet). Add the onion, aubergine (eggplant) and mushrooms, and fry for 3–4 minutes, stirring frequently. Remove from the heat and transfer to a mixing bowl.

3 Add the cherry tomatoes, mushroom ketchup, basil leaves and lemon juice to the aubergine (eggplant) mixture. Season well with salt and pepper.

4 Spoon the aubergine (eggplant) mixture into the (bell) pepper halves. Enclose in foil parcels (packages) and barbecue (grill) over the hot coals for about 15–20 minutes, turning once.

5 Unwrap carefully and serve garnished with sprigs of fresh basil. Serve with lemon wedges.

VARIATION

Dried herbs can be used instead of fresh ones if they are unavailable. Substitute 1 tsp dried basil or use mixed dried Italian herbs as an alternative. If you wish, top these stuffed (bell) peppers with grated Mozzarella or Cheddar cheese – 75 g/3 oz/¼ cup will be sufficient.

Vegetable Lasagne

This rich, baked pasta dish is packed full of vegetables, tomatoes and Italian Mozzarella cheese.

NUTRITIONAL INFORMATION

Calories 510   Sugars 14g
Protein . . . . .17g   Fat 38g
Carbohydrate . . .28g   Saturates 14g

50 MINS   50 MINS

SERVES 6

INGREDIENTS

1 kg/2 lb 4 oz aubergines (eggplant)

8 tbsp olive oil

25 g/1/ oz/2 tbsp garlic and herb butter

450 g/1 lb courgettes (zucchini), sliced

225 g/8 oz/2 cups grated
 Mozzarella cheese

600 ml/1 pint/2½ cups passata (sieved
 tomatoes)

6 sheets pre-cooked green lasagne

600 ml/1 pint/2½ cups Béchamel Sauce
 (see page 28)

60 g/2 oz/⅔ cup freshly grated
 Parmesan cheese

1 tsp dried oregano

salt and pepper

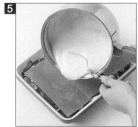

1 Thinly slice the aubergines (eggplant) and place in a colander. Sprinkle with salt and set aside for 20 minutes. Rinse and pat dry with kitchen paper.

2 Heat 4 tablespoons of the oil in a large frying pan (skillet). Fry half of the aubergine (eggplant) slices over a low heat for 6–7 minutes, or until golden. Drain thoroughly on kitchen paper. Repeat with the remaining oil and aubergine (eggplant) slices.

3 Melt the garlic and herb butter in the frying pan (skillet). Add the courgettes (zucchini) and fry for 5–6 minutes, until golden brown all over. Drain thoroughly on kitchen paper.

4 Place half of the aubergine (eggplant) and courgette (zucchini) slices in a large ovenproof dish. Season with pepper and sprinkle over half of the Mozzarella cheese. Spoon over half of the passata

(sieved tomatoes) and top with 3 sheets of lasagne. Repeat the process, ending with a layer of lasagne.

5 Spoon over the Béchamel Sauce and sprinkle over the Parmesan cheese and oregano. Put the dish on a baking tray (cookie sheet) and bake in a preheated oven, at 220°C/425°F/Gas Mark 7, for 30–35 minutes, or until golden brown. Serve immediately.

Macaroni Bake

This satisfying dish would make an excellent supper for a mid-week family meal.

NUTRITIONAL INFORMATION

Calories	728	Sugars	........11g
Protein	........17g	Fat	..........42g
Carbohydrate	...75g	Saturates	......23g

 15 MINS   45 MINS

SERVES 4

I N G R E D I E N T S

450 g/1 lb/4 cups dried short-cut macaroni

1 tbsp olive oil

60 g/2 oz/4 tbsp beef dripping (drippings)

450 g/1 lb potatoes, thinly sliced

450 g/1 lb onions, sliced

225 g/8 oz/2 cups grated
  Mozzarella cheese

150 ml/¼ pint/⅔ cup double (heavy) cream

salt and pepper

crusty brown bread and butter, to serve

1 Bring a large saucepan of lightly salted water to the boil. Add the macaroni and olive oil and cook for about 12 minutes, or until tender but still firm to the bite. Drain the macaroni thoroughly and set aside.

2 Melt the dripping (drippings) in a large flame-proof casserole, then remove from the heat.

3 Make alternate layers of potatoes, onions, macaroni and grated cheese in the dish, seasoning well with salt and pepper between each layer and finishing with a layer of cheese on top. Finally, pour the cream over the top layer of cheese.

4 Bake in a preheated oven at 200°C/400°F/Gas Mark 6 for 25 minutes. Remove the dish from the oven and carefully brown the top of the bake under a hot grill (broiler).

5 Serve the bake straight from the dish with crusty brown bread and butter as a main course. Alternatively, serve as a vegetable accompaniment with your favourite main course.

VARIATION

For a stronger flavour, use Mozzarella affumicata, a smoked version of this cheese, or Gruyère (Swiss) cheese instead of the Mozzarella.

Filled Aubergines (Eggplant)

Combined with tomatoes and Mozzarella cheese, pasta makes a tasty filling for baked aubergine (eggplant) shells.

NUTRITIONAL INFORMATION

Calories 342	Sugars 6g	
Protein 11g	Fat 16g	
Carbohydrate ...40g	Saturates 4g	

🍴 25 MINS 🕐 55 MINS

SERVES 4

INGREDIENTS

225 g/8 oz dried penne or other short
   pasta shapes

4 tbsp olive oil, plus extra for brushing

2 aubergines (eggplant)

1 large onion, chopped

2 garlic cloves, crushed

400 g/14 oz can chopped tomatoes

2 tsp dried oregano

60 g/2 oz Mozzarella cheese, thinly sliced

25 g/1 oz/⅓ cup freshly grated
   Parmesan cheese

2 tbsp dry breadcrumbs

salt and pepper

salad leaves (greens), to serve

1 Bring a saucepan of lightly salted water to the boil. Add the pasta and 1 tablespoon of the olive oil and cook for 8–10 minutes or until tender, but still firm to the bite. Drain, return to the pan, cover and keep warm.

2 Cut the aubergines (eggplant) in half lengthways and score around the inside with a sharp knife, being careful not to pierce the shells. Scoop out the flesh with a spoon. Brush the insides of the shells with olive oil. Chop the flesh and set aside.

3 Heat the remaining oil in a frying pan (skillet). Fry the onion until translucent. Add the garlic and fry for 1 minute. Add the chopped aubergine (eggplant) and fry, stirring frequently, for 5 minutes. Add the tomatoes and oregano and season to taste with salt and pepper. Bring to the boil and simmer for 10 minutes, or until thickened. Remove the pan from the heat and stir in the pasta.

4 Brush a baking tray (cookie sheet) with oil and arrange the aubergine (eggplant) shells in a single layer. Divide half of the tomato and pasta mixture between them. Sprinkle over the Mozzarella, then pile the remaining tomato and pasta mixture on top. Mix the Parmesan cheese and breadcrumbs and sprinkle over the top, patting it lightly into the mixture.

5 Bake in a preheated oven, at 200°C/ 400°C/Gas Mark 6 for about 25 minutes, or until the topping is golden brown. Serve hot with a selection of salad leaves (greens).

Spinach & Ricotta Tart

Frozen filo pastry is used to line a flan tin (pan), which is then filled with spinach, red (bell) peppers, cream, eggs and Ricotta cheese.

NUTRITIONAL INFORMATION

Calories	375	Sugars	.........3g
Protein	.........8g	Fat	..........32g
Carbohydrate	...14g	Saturates	......18g

 30 MINS   30 MINS

SERVES 8

I N G R E D I E N T S

225 g/8 oz frozen filo pastry, thawed

125 g/4½ oz butter, melted

350 g/12 oz frozen spinach, thawed

2 eggs

150 ml/¼ pint/⅔ cup single (thin) cream

250 g/8 oz Ricotta cheese

1 red (bell) pepper, deseeded and
    sliced into strips

60 g/2 oz pine kernels

salt and pepper

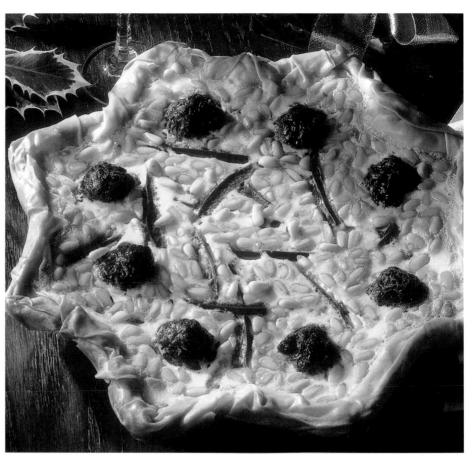

1 Use the sheets of filo pastry to line a 20 cm/8 inch flan tin (pan), brushing each layer with melted butter.

2 Put the spinach into a sieve or colander and squeeze out the excess moisture with the back of a spoon or your hand. Form into small balls and arrange in the prepared flan tin (pan).

3 Beat the eggs, cream and Ricotta cheese together until thoroughly blended. Season with salt and pepper to taste and pour over the spinach.

4 Put the remaining butter into a saucepan and sauté the red (bell) pepper strips until softened, about 4–5 minutes. Arrange the strips in the filling.

5 Scatter the pine kernels over the surface and bake in a preheated oven, at 190°C/375°F/Gas Mark 5, for 20–25 minutes, or until the filling has set and the pastry is golden brown. Serve.

VARIATION

If you're not fond of (bell) peppers, substitute mushrooms instead. Add a few sliced sundried tomatoes for extra colour and flavour. This recipe makes an ideal dish for vegetarians, although everyone else is sure to enjoy it too.

Patriotic Pasta

The ingredients of this dish have the same bright colours as the Italian flag – hence its name.

NUTRITIONAL INFORMATION

Calories 325	Sugars 5g
Protein 8g	Fat 13g
Carbohydrate . . .48g	Saturates 2g

 5 MINS   15 MINS

SERVES 4

INGREDIENTS

450 g/1 lb/4 cups dried farfalle

4 tbsp olive oil

450 g/1 lb cherry tomatoes

90 g/3 oz rocket (arugula)

salt and pepper

Pecorino cheese, to garnish

1 Bring a large saucepan of lightly salted water to the boil. Add the farfalle and 1 tablespoon of the olive oil and cook for 8–10 minutes or until tender, but still firm to the bite. Drain the farfalle thoroughly and return to the pan.

2 Cut the cherry tomatoes in half and trim the rocket (arugula).

COOK'S TIP

Pecorino cheese is a hard sheep's milk cheese which resembles Parmesan and is often used for grating over a variety of dishes. It has a sharp flavour and is only used in small quantities.

3 Heat the remaining olive oil in a large saucepan. Add the tomatoes to the pan and cook for 1 minute. Add the farfalle and the rocket (arugula) to the pan and stir gently to mix. Heat through and then season to taste with salt and pepper.

4 Meanwhile, using a vegetable peeler, shave thin slices of Pecorino cheese.

5 Transfer the farfalle and vegetables to a warm serving dish. Garnish with the Pecorino cheese shavings and serve immediately.

Potatoes in Italian Dressing

The warm potatoes quickly absorb the wonderful flavours of olives, tomatoes and olive oil. This salad is good warm, and cold.

NUTRITIONAL INFORMATION

Calories ....239 Sugars 2g
Protein ....4g   Fat 10g
Carbohydrate ...36g Saturates 1g

 15 MINS   15 MINS

SERVES 4

I N G R E D I E N T S

750 g/1 lb 10 oz waxy potatoes

1 shallot

2 tomatoes

1 tbsp chopped fresh basil

salt

I T A L I A N   D R E S S I N G

1 tomato, skinned and chopped finely

4 black olives, pitted and chopped finely

4 tbsp olive oil

1 tbsp wine vinegar

1 garlic clove, crushed

salt and pepper

1 Cook the potatoes in a saucepan of boiling salted water for 15 minutes or until they are tender.

2 Drain the potatoes well, chop roughly and put into a bowl.

3 Chop the shallot. Cut the tomatoes into wedges and add the shallot and tomatoes to the potatoes.

4 To make the dressing, put all the ingredients into a screw-top jar and mix together thoroughly.

5 Pour the dressing over the potato mixture and toss thoroughly.

6 Transfer the salad to a serving dish and sprinkle with the basil.

COOK'S TIP

This recipe works well with floury (mealy) potatoes. It doesn't look so attractive, as the potatoes break up when they are cooked, but they absorb the dressing wonderfully. Be sure to use an extra virgin olive oil for the dressing to give a really fruity flavour to the potatoes.

Green Tagliatelle with Garlic

A rich pasta dish for garlic lovers everywhere. It is quick and easy to prepare and full of flavour.

NUTRITIONAL INFORMATION

Calories	474	Sugars	........3g
Protein	........16g	Fat	..........24g
Carbohydrate	...52g	Saturates	.......9g

  20 MINS 15 MINS

SERVES 4

INGREDIENTS

2 tbsp walnut oil

1 bunch spring onions (scallions), sliced

2 garlic cloves, thinly sliced

225 g/8 oz/3¼ cups sliced mushrooms

450 g/1 lb fresh green and white tagliatelle

1 tbsp olive oil

225 g/8 oz frozen spinach, thawed
    and drained

115 g/4 oz/½ cup full-fat soft cheese with
    garlic and herbs

4 tbsp single (light) cream

60 g/2 oz/½ cup chopped, unsalted
    pistachio nuts

salt and pepper

Italian bread, to serve

TO GARNISH

2 tbsp shredded fresh basil

fresh basil sprigs

1 Heat the walnut oil in a large frying pan (skillet). Add the spring onions (scallions) and garlic and fry for 1 minute, until just softened.

2 Add the mushrooms to the pan, stir well, cover and cook over a low heat for about 5 minutes, until softened.

3 Meanwhile, bring a large saucepan of lightly salted water to the boil. Add the tagliatelle and olive oil and cook for 3–5 minutes, or until tender but still firm to the bite. Drain the tagliatelle thoroughly and return to the saucepan.

4 Add the spinach to the frying pan (skillet) and heat through for 1–2 minutes. Add the cheese to the pan and allow to melt slightly. Stir in the cream and cook, without allowing the mixture to come to the boil, until warmed through.

5 Pour the sauce over the pasta, season to taste with salt and pepper and mix well. Heat through gently, stirring constantly, for 2–3 minutes.

6 Transfer the pasta to a serving dish and sprinkle with the pistachio nuts and shredded basil. Garnish with the basil sprigs and serve immediately with the Italian bread of your choice.

Roasted (Bell) Pepper Terrine

This delicious terrine is ideal for Sunday lunch. It goes particularly well with Italian bread and a green salad.

NUTRITIONAL INFORMATION

Calories 196	Sugars 6g
Protein 6g	Fat 14g
Carbohydrate ...13g	Saturates 3g

30 MINS   30 MINS

SERVES 8

I N G R E D I E N T S

500 g/1 lb 2 oz/3 cups broad (fava) beans

6 red (bell) peppers, halved and deseeded

3 small courgettes (zucchini), sliced
    lengthways

1 aubergine (eggplant), sliced lengthways

3 leeks, halved lengthways

6 tbsp olive oil, plus extra for greasing

6 tbsp single (light) cream

2 tbsp chopped fresh basil

salt and pepper

1 Grease a 1.5 litre/2¾ pint/5 cup terrine. Blanch the broad (fava) beans in boiling water for 1–2 minutes and pop them out of their skins. It is not essential to do this, but the effort is worthwhile as the beans taste a lot sweeter.

2 Roast the red (bell) peppers over a hot barbecue (grill) until the skin is black – about 10–15 minutes. Remove and put into a plastic bag. Seal and set aside.

3 Brush the courgette (zucchini), aubergine (eggplant) and leeks with 5 tablespoons of the olive oil, and season with salt and pepper to taste. Cook over the hot barbecue (grill) until tender, about 8–10 minutes, turning once.

4 Meanwhile, purée the broad (fava) beans in a blender or food processor with 1 tablespoon of the olive oil, the cream and seasoning. Alternatively, chop and then press through a sieve (strainer).

5 Remove the red (bell) peppers from the bag and peel.

6 Put a layer of red (bell) pepper along the bottom and up the sides of the terrine.

7 Spread a third of the bean purée over the (bell) pepper. Cover with the aubergine (eggplant) slices and spread over half of the remaining bean purée.

8 Sprinkle over the basil. Top with courgettes (zucchini) and the remaining bean purée. Lay the leeks on top. Add any remaining pieces of red (bell) pepper. Put a piece of foil, folded 4 times, on the top and weigh down with cans.

9 Chill until required. Turn out on to a serving platter, slice and serve with Italian bread and a green salad.

Roast Leeks

Use a good-quality Italian olive oil for this deliciously simple yet sophisticated vegetable accompaniment.

NUTRITIONAL INFORMATION

Calories ....52 Sugars 0.4g
Protein ....0.3g Fat 5g
Carbohydrate ....1g Saturates 1g

 5 MINS   7 MINS

SERVES 6

INGREDIENTS

4 leeks

3 tbsp olive oil

2 tsp balsamic vinegar

sea salt and pepper

1 Halve the leeks lengthways, making sure that your knife goes straight, so that the leek is held together by the root.

2 Brush each leek liberally with the olive oil.

3 Cook over a hot barbecue (grill) for 6–7 minutes, turning once.

4 Remove the leeks from the barbecue (grill) and brush with balsamic vinegar.

5 Sprinkle with salt and pepper and serve hot or warm.

VARIATION

If in season, 8 baby leeks may be used instead of 4 standard-sized ones. Sherry vinegar makes a good substitute for the expensive balsamic vinegar and would work as well in this recipe.

Pesto Potatoes

Pesto sauce is more commonly used as a pasta sauce but is delicious served over potatoes as well.

NUTRITIONAL INFORMATION

Calories 531   Sugars 3g

Protein . . . . .13g   Fat 38g

Carbohydrate . . .36g   Saturates 8g

15 MINS   15 MINS

SERVES 4

I N G R E D I E N T S

900 g/2 lb small new potatoes

75 g/2¾ oz fresh basil

2 tbsp pine kernels (nuts)

3 garlic cloves, crushed

100 ml/3½ fl oz/½ cup olive oil

75 g/2¾ oz/¾ cup freshly grated Parmesan
    cheese and Pecorino cheese, mixed

salt and pepper

fresh basil sprigs, to garnish

1 Cook the potatoes in a saucepan of boiling salted water for 15 minutes or until tender. Drain well, transfer to a warm serving dish and keep warm until required.

2 Meanwhile, put the basil, pine kernels (nuts), garlic and a little salt and pepper to taste in a food processor. Blend for 30 seconds, adding the oil gradually, until smooth.

3 Remove the mixture from the food processor and place in a mixing bowl. Stir in the grated Parmesan and Pecorino cheeses.

4 Spoon the pesto sauce over the potatoes and mix well. Garnish with fresh basil sprigs and serve immediately.

Italian Vegetable Tart

A rich tomato pastry base topped with a mouthwatering selection of vegetables and cheese makes a tart that's tasty as well as attractive.

NUTRITIONAL INFORMATION

Calories	438	Sugars	.........8g
Protein	.........9g	Fat	.........28g
Carbohydrate	...40g	Saturates	......15g

1³/₄ HOURS   40 MINS

SERVES 6

INGREDIENTS

1 aubergine (eggplant), sliced

2 tbsp salt

4 tbsp olive oil

1 garlic clove, crushed

1 large yellow (bell) pepper, deseeded
  and sliced

300 ml/½ pint/1¼ cups ready-made
  tomato pasta sauce

125 g/4½ oz/⅔ cup sun-dried tomatoes in
  oil, drained and halved if necessary

175 g/6 oz Mozzarella,
  drained and sliced thinly

PASTRY

225 g/8 oz/2 cups plain (all-purpose) flour

pinch of celery salt

125 g/4½ oz/½ cup butter or margarine

2 tbsp tomato purée (paste)

2–3 tbsp milk

1 To make the pastry, sift the flour and celery salt into a bowl and rub in the butter or margarine until the mixture resembles fine breadcrumbs.

2 Mix together the tomato purée (paste) and milk and stir into the mixture to form a firm dough. Knead gently on a

lightly floured surface until smooth. Wrap and chill for 30 minutes.

3 Grease a 28 cm/11 inch loose-bottomed flan tin. Roll out the pastry on a lightly floured surface and use to line the tin. Trim and prick all over with a fork. Chill for 30 minutes.

4 Meanwhile, layer the aubergine (eggplant) in a dish, sprinkling with the salt. Leave for 30 minutes.

5 Bake the pastry case in a preheated oven, 200°C/400°F/Gas Mark 6, for

20–25 minutes until cooked and lightly golden. Set aside. Increase the oven temperature to 230°C/450°F/Gas Mark 8.

6 Rinse the aubergine (eggplant) and pat dry. Heat 3 tbsp of oil in a frying pan (skillet) and fry the garlic, aubergine (eggplant) and (bell) pepper for 5–6 minutes until just softened. Drain on paper towels.

7 Spread the pastry case with pasta sauce and arrange the cooked vegetables, sun-dried tomatoes and Mozzarella on top. Brush with the remaining oil and bake for 5 minutes until the cheese is just melting.

Spinach & Ricotta Pie

This puff pastry pie looks impressive and is actually fairly easy to make. Serve it hot or cold.

NUTRITIONAL INFORMATION

Calories 545	Sugars 3g
Protein 19g	Fat 42g
Carbohydrate ...25g	Saturates 13g

  25 MINS 50 MINS

SERVES 4

INGREDIENTS

225 g/8 oz spinach

25 g/1 oz pine nuts

100 g/3½ oz ricotta cheese

2 large eggs, beaten

50 g/1¾ oz ground almonds

40 g/1½ oz Parmesan cheese, grated

250 g/9 oz puff pastry, defrosted if frozen

1 small egg, beaten

1 Rinse the spinach, place in a large saucepan and cook for 4-5 minutes until wilted. Drain thoroughly. When the spinach is cool enough to handle, squeeze out the excess liquid.

2 Place the pine nuts on a baking tray (cookie sheet) and lightly toast under a preheated grill (broiler) for 2–3 minutes or until golden.

3 Place the ricotta, spinach and eggs in a bowl and mix together. Add the pine nuts, beat well, then stir in the ground almonds and Parmesan cheese.

4 Roll out the puff pastry and make 2 x 20 cm/8 inch squares. Trim the edges, reserving the pastry trimmings.

5 Place 1 pastry square on a baking tray (cookie sheet). Spoon over the spinach

 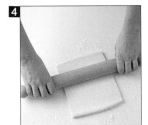 

mixture, keeping within 12 mm/½ inch of the edge of the pastry. Brush the edges with beaten egg and place the second square over the top.

6 Using a round-bladed knife, press the pastry edges together by tapping along the sealed edge. Use the pastry trimmings to make a few leaves to decorate the pie.

7 Brush the pie with the beaten egg and bake in a preheated oven, at 220°C/425°F/Gas Mark 8, for 10 minutes. Reduce the oven temperature to

190°C/375°F/Gas Mark 5 and bake for a further 25–30 minutes. Serve hot.

COOK'S TIP

Spinach is very nutritious as it is full of iron – this is particularly important for women and elderly people who may lack this in their diet.

Parmesan Potatoes

This is a very simple way to jazz up roast potatoes. Serve them in the same way as roast potatoes with roasted meats or fish.

NUTRITIONAL INFORMATION

Calories 307	Sugars 2g	
Protein 11g	Fat 14g	
Carbohydrate . . .37g	Saturates 6g	

 15 MINS   1 HR 5 MINS

SERVES 4

INGREDIENTS

6 potatoes

50 g/1¾ oz Parmesan cheese, grated

pinch of grated nutmeg

1 tbsp chopped fresh parsley

4 smoked bacon slices, cut into strips

oil, for roasting

salt

1 Cut the potatoes in half lengthways and cook them in a saucepan of boiling salted water for 10 minutes. Drain thoroughly.

2 Mix the grated Parmesan cheese, nutmeg and parsley together in a shallow bowl.

3 Roll the potato pieces in the cheese mixture to coat them completely. Shake off any excess.

4 Pour a little oil into a roasting tin (pan) and heat it in a preheated oven, 200°C/400°F/Gas Mark 6, for 10 minutes. Remove from the oven and place the potatoes into the tin (pan). Return the tin (pan) to the oven and cook for 30 minutes, turning once.

5 Remove from the oven and sprinkle the bacon on top of the potatoes. Return to the oven for 15 minutes or until the potatoes and bacon are cooked. Drain off any excess fat and serve.

VARIATION

If you prefer, use slices of salami or Parma ham (prosciutto) instead of the bacon, adding it to the dish 5 minutes before the end of the cooking time.

Spaghetti & Mushroom Sauce

This easy vegetarian dish is ideal for busy people with little time, but good taste!

NUTRITIONAL INFORMATION

Calories . . . . . . .604 Sugars 5g
Protein . . . . .11g Fat 39g
Carbohydrate . . .54g Saturates 21g

20 MINS   35 MINS

SERVES 4

I N G R E D I E N T S

60 g/2 oz/4 tbsp butter

2 tbsp olive oil

6 shallots, sliced

450 g/1 lb/6 cups sliced button mushrooms

1 tsp plain (all-purpose) flour

150 ml/¼ pint/⅔ cup double (heavy) cream

2 tbsp port

115 g/4 oz sun-dried tomatoes, chopped

freshly grated nutmeg

450g /1 lb dried spaghetti

1 tbsp freshly chopped parsley

salt and pepper

6 triangles of fried white bread, to serve

 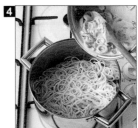

1 Heat the butter and 1 tbsp of the oil in a large pan. Add the shallots and cook over a medium heat for 3 minutes. Add the mushrooms and cook over a low heat for 2 minutes. Season with salt and pepper, sprinkle over the flour and cook, stirring constantly, for 1 minute.

2 Gradually stir in the cream and port, add the sun-dried tomatoes and a pinch of grated nutmeg and cook over a low heat for 8 minutes.

3 Meanwhile, bring a large saucepan of lightly salted water to the boil. Add the spaghetti and remaining olive oil and cook for 12–14 minutes, until tender but still firm to the bite.

4 Drain the spaghetti and return to the pan. Pour over the mushroom sauce and cook for 3 minutes. Transfer the spaghetti and mushroom sauce to a large serving plate and sprinkle over the chopped parsley. Serve with crispy triangles of fried bread.

VARIATION

Non-vegetarians could add 115 g/4 oz Parma ham (prosciutto), cut into thin strips and heated gently in 25 g/1 oz/ 2 tbsp butter, to the pasta along with the mushroom sauce.

Pasta & Bean Casserole

A satisfying winter dish, this is a slow-cooked, one-pot meal. The beans need to be soaked overnight so prepare well in advance.

NUTRITIONAL INFORMATION

Calories	377	Sugars	.........5g
Protein	........10g	Fat	..........18g
Carbohydrate	...43g	Saturates	.......5g

30 MINS   3¹/₂ HOURS

SERVES 6

I N G R E D I E N T S

225 g/8 oz/1¼ cups dried haricot (navy)
  beans, soaked overnight and drained

225 g/8 oz dried penne

6 tbsp olive oil

850 ml/1½ pints /3½ cups vegetable stock

2 large onions, sliced

2 garlic cloves, chopped

2 bay leaves

1 tsp dried oregano

1 tsp dried thyme

5 tbsp red wine

2 tbsp tomato purée (paste)

2 celery sticks (stalks), sliced

1 fennel bulb, sliced

115 g/4 oz/1⅝ cups sliced mushrooms

225 g/8 oz tomatoes, sliced

1 tsp dark muscovado sugar

4 tbsp dry white breadcrumbs

salt and pepper

salad leaves (greens) and crusty bread,
  to serve

1 Put the haricot (navy) beans in a large saucepan and add sufficient cold water to cover. Bring to the boil and continue to boil vigorously for 20 minutes. Drain, set aside and keep warm.

2 Bring a large saucepan of lightly salted water to the boil. Add the penne and 1 tbsp of the olive oil and cook for about 3 minutes. Drain the pasta thoroughly, set aside and keep warm.

3 Put the beans in a large, flameproof casserole. Add the vegetable stock and stir in the remaining olive oil, the onions, garlic, bay leaves, oregano, thyme, wine and tomato purée (paste). Bring to the boil, then cover and cook in a preheated oven at 180°C/350°°F/Gas Mark 4 for 2 hours.

4 Add the penne, celery, fennel, mushrooms and tomatoes to the casserole and season to taste with salt and pepper. Stir in the muscovado sugar and sprinkle over the breadcrumbs. Cover the dish and cook in the oven for 1 hour.

5 Serve the pasta and bean casserole hot with salad leaves (greens) and crusty bread.

Macaroni & Corn Pancakes

This vegetable pancake can be filled with your favourite vegetables – a favourite alternative is shredded parsnips with 1 tbsp mustard.

NUTRITIONAL INFORMATION

Calories 702   Sugars 4g
Protein . . . . .13g   Fat 50g
Carbohydrate . . .55g   Saturates 23g

  15 MINS   40 MINS

SERVES 4

I N G R E D I E N T S

2 corn cobs

60 g/2 oz/4 tbsp butter

115 g/4 oz red (bell) peppers, cored, seeded
   and finely diced

285 g/10 oz/2½ cups dried
   short-cut macaroni

150 ml/¼ pint/⅔ cup double (heavy) cream

25 g/1 oz/¼ cup plain (all-purpose) flour

4 egg yolks

4 tbsp olive oil

salt and pepper

TO SERVE

oyster mushrooms

fried leeks

1 Bring a saucepan of water to the boil, add the corn cobs and cook for about 8 minutes. Drain thoroughly and refresh under cold running water for 3 minutes. Carefully cut away the kernels on to kitchen paper (towels) and set aside to dry.

2 Melt 25 g/1 oz/2 tbsp of the butter in a frying pan (skillet). Add the (bell) peppers and cook over a low heat for 4 minutes. Drain and pat dry with kitchen paper (towels).

3 Bring a large saucepan of lightly salted water to the boil. Add the macaroni and cook for about 12 minutes, or until tender but still firm to the bite. Drain the macaroni thoroughly and leave to cool in cold water until required.

4 Beat together the cream, flour, a pinch of salt and the egg yolks in a bowl until smooth. Add the corn and (bell) peppers to the cream and egg mixture. Drain the macaroni and then toss into the

corn and cream mixture. Season with pepper to taste.

5 Heat the remaining butter with the oil in a large frying pan (skillet). Drop spoonfuls of the mixture into the pan and press down until the mixture forms a flat pancake. Fry until golden on both sides, and all the mixture is used up. Serve immediately with oyster mushrooms and fried leeks.

Fettuccine & Walnut Sauce

This mouthwatering dish would make an excellent light, vegetarian lunch for four or a good starter for six.

NUTRITIONAL INFORMATION

Calories	833	Sugars	.........5g
Protein	........20g	Fat	..........66g
Carbohydrate	...44g	Saturates	......15g

  15 MINS   10 MINS

SERVES 6

INGREDIENTS

2 thick slices wholemeal (whole-wheat)
   bread, crusts removed

300 ml/½ pint/1¼ cups milk

275 g/9½ oz/2½ cups shelled walnuts

2 garlic cloves, crushed

115 g/4 oz/1 cup stoned (pitted)
   black olives

60 g/2 oz/⅔ cup freshly grated
   Parmesan cheese

8 tbsp extra virgin olive oil

150 ml/¼ pint/⅔ cup double (heavy) cream

450 g/1 lb fresh fettuccine

salt and pepper

2–3 tbsp chopped fresh parsley

COOK'S TIP

Parmesan quickly loses its pungency and 'bite'. It is better to buy small quantities and grate it yourself. Wrapped in foil, it will keep in the refrigerator for several months.

1 Put the bread in a shallow dish, pour over the milk and set aside to soak until the liquid has been absorbed.

2 Spread the walnuts out on a baking tray (cookie sheet) and toast in a preheated oven, at 190°C/375°F/Gas Mark 5, for about 5 minutes, or until golden. Set aside to cool.

3 Put the soaked bread, walnuts, garlic, olives, Parmesan cheese and 6 tablespoons of the olive oil in a food processor and work to make a purée. Season to taste with salt and pepper and stir in the cream.

4 Bring a large pan of lightly salted water to the boil. Add the fettuccine and 1 tablespoon of the remaining oil and cook for 2–3 minutes, or until tender but still firm to the bite. Drain the fettuccine thoroughly and toss with the remaining olive oil.

5 Divide the fettuccine between individual serving plates and spoon the olive, garlic and walnut sauce on top. Sprinkle over the fresh parsley and serve.

Pasta with Garlic & Broccoli

Broccoli coated in a garlic-flavoured cream sauce, served on herb tagliatelle. Try sprinkling with toasted pine nuts to add extra crunch.

NUTRITIONAL INFORMATION

Calories 538	Sugars 4g	
Protein 23g	Fat 29g	
Carbohydrate ...50g	Saturates 17g	

 5 MINS   5 MINS

SERVES 4

INGREDIENTS

500 g/1 lb 2 oz broccoli

300 g/10½ oz/1¼ cups garlic & herb
 cream cheese

4 tbsp milk

350 g/12 oz fresh herb tagliatelle

25 g/1 oz/¼ cup grated Parmesan cheese

chopped fresh chives, to garnish

1 Cut the broccoli into even-sized florets. Cook the broccoli in a saucepan of boiling salted water for 3 minutes and drain thoroughly.

2 Put the soft cheese into a saucepan and heat gently, stirring, until melted. Add the milk and stir until well combined.

3 Add the broccoli to the cheese mixture and stir to coat.

4 Meanwhile, bring a large saucepan of salted water to the boil and add the tagliatelle. Stir and bring back to the boil. Reduce the heat slightly and cook the tagliatelle, uncovered, for 3–4 minutes until just tender.

5 Drain the tagliatelle thoroughly and divide among 4 warmed serving plates. Spoon the broccoli and cheese sauce on top. Sprinkle with grated Parmesan cheese, garnish with chopped chives and serve.

COOK'S TIP

A herb flavoured pasta goes particularly well with the broccoli sauce, but failing this, a tagliatelle verde or 'paglia e fieno' (literally 'straw and hay' – thin green and yellow noodles) will fit the bill.

Fettuccine all'Alfredo

This simple, traditional dish can be made with any long pasta, but is especially good with flat noodles, such as fettuccine or tagliatelle.

NUTRITIONAL INFORMATION

Calories 627	Sugars 2g
Protein 18g	Fat 41g
Carbohydrate ...51g	Saturates 23g

 5 MINS   10 MINS

SERVES 4

INGREDIENTS

25 g/1 oz/2 tbsp butter

200 ml/7 fl oz/⅞ cup double (heavy) cream

450 g/1 lb fresh fettuccine

1 tbsp olive oil

90 g/3 oz/1 cup freshly grated Parmesan cheese, plus extra to serve

pinch of freshly grated nutmeg

salt and pepper

fresh parsley sprigs, to garnish

1 Put the butter and 150 ml/ ¼ pint/⅔ cup of the cream in a large saucepan and bring the mixture to the boil over a medium heat. Reduce the heat and then simmer gently for about 1½ minutes, or until slightly thickened.

2 Meanwhile, bring a large pan of lightly salted water to the boil. Add

the fettuccine and olive oil and cook for 2–3 minutes, until tender but still firm to the bite. Drain the fettuccine thoroughly and then pour over the cream sauce.

3 Toss the fettuccine in the sauce over a low heat until thoroughly coated.

4 Add the remaining cream, the Parmesan cheese and nutmeg to the fettuccine mixture and season to taste

with salt and pepper. Toss thoroughly to coat while gently heating through.

5 Transfer the fettucine mixture to a warm serving plate and garnish with the fresh sprig of parsley. Serve immediately, handing extra grated Parmesan cheese separately.

VARIATION

This classic Roman dish is often served with the addition of strips of ham and fresh peas. Add 225 g/8 oz/2 cups shelled cooked peas and 175 g/6 oz ham strips with the Parmesan cheese in step 4.

Italian Spaghetti

Delicious vegetables, cooked in a rich tomato sauce, make an ideal topping for nutty wholemeal (whole-wheat) pasta.

NUTRITIONAL INFORMATION

Calories 381   Sugars 9g
Protein . . . . .11g   Fat 16g
Carbohydrate . . .53g   Saturates 5g

 20 MINS   ⏱ 35 MINS

SERVES 4

INGREDIENTS

2 tbsp olive oil

1 large red onion, chopped

2 garlic cloves, crushed

1 tbsp lemon juice

4 baby aubergines (eggplant), quartered

600 ml/1 pint/2½ cups passata
   (sieved tomatoes)

2 tsp caster (superfine) sugar

2 tbsp tomato purée (paste)

400 g/14 oz can artichoke hearts, drained
   and halved

115 g/4 oz/1 cup stoned (pitted)
   black olives

350 g/12 oz dried spaghetti

25 g/1 oz/2 tbsp butter

salt and pepper

fresh basil sprigs, to garnish

olive bread, to serve

1 Heat 1 tablespoon of the olive oil in a large frying pan (skillet). Add the onion, garlic, lemon juice and aubergines (eggplant) and cook over a low heat for 4–5 minutes, or until the onion and aubergines (eggplant) are lightly golden brown.

2 Pour in the passata (sieved tomatoes), season to taste with salt and pepper and stir in the caster (superfine) sugar and tomato purée (paste). Bring to the boil, lower the heat and then simmer, stirring occasionally, for 20 minutes.

3 Gently stir in the artichoke hearts and black olives and cook for 5 minutes.

4 Meanwhile, bring a large saucepan of lightly salted water to the boil. Add the spaghetti and the remaining oil and cook for 7–8 minutes, or until tender but still firm to the bite.

5 Drain the spaghetti thoroughly and toss with the butter. Transfer the spaghetti to a large serving dish.

6 Pour the vegetable sauce over the spaghetti, garnish with the sprigs of fresh basil and serve immediately with olive bread.

Pasta & Vegetable Sauce

The different shapes and textures of the vegetables make a mouthwatering presentation in this light and summery dish.

 10 MINS   30 MINS

SERVES 4

INGREDIENTS

225 g/8 oz/2 cups dried gemelli or other
pasta shapes

1 tbsp olive oil

1 head green broccoli, cut into florets

2 courgettes (zucchini), sliced

225 g/8 oz asparagus spears

115 g/4 oz mangetout (snow peas)

115 g/4 oz frozen peas

25 g/1 oz/2 tbsp butter

3 tbsp vegetable stock

4 tbsp double (heavy) cream

freshly grated nutmeg

2 tbsp chopped fresh parsley

2 tbsp freshly grated Parmesan cheese

salt and pepper

1 Bring a large saucepan of lightly salted water to the boil. Add the pasta and olive oil and cook for 8–10 minutes or until tender, but still firm to the bite. Drain the pasta, return to the pan, cover and keep warm.

2 Steam the broccoli, courgettes (zucchini), asparagus spears and mangetout (snow peas) over a pan of boiling salted water until they are just beginning to soften. Remove from the heat and refresh in cold water. Drain and set aside.

3 Bring a small pan of lightly salted water to the boil. Add the frozen peas and cook for 3 minutes. Drain the peas, refresh in cold water and then drain again. Set aside with the other vegetables.

4 Put the butter and vegetable stock in a pan over a medium heat. Add all of the vegetables, reserving a few of the asparagus spears, and toss carefully with a wooden spoon until they have heated through, taking care not to break them up.

5 Stir in the cream and heat through without bringing to the boil. Season to taste with salt, pepper and nutmeg.

6 Transfer the pasta to a warmed serving dish and stir in the chopped parsley. Spoon over the vegetable sauce and sprinkle over the Parmesan cheese. Arrange the reserved asparagus spears in a pattern on top and serve.

Paglia e Fieno

The name of this dish – 'straw and hay' – refers to the colours of the pasta when mixed together.

NUTRITIONAL INFORMATION

Calories	699	Sugars	.........7g
Protein	........26g	Fat	..........39g
Carbohydrate	...65g	Saturates	......23g

10 MINS   10 MINS

SERVES 4

INGREDIENTS

60 g/2 oz/4 tbsp butter

450 g/1 lb fresh peas, shelled

200 ml/7 fl oz/ 7⁄8 cup double (heavy) cream

450 g/1 lb mixed fresh green and white
spaghetti or tagliatelle

1 tbsp olive oil

60 g/2/ oz/2⁄3 cup freshly grated Parmesan
cheese, plus extra to serve

pinch of freshly grated nutmeg

salt and pepper

1 Melt the butter in a large saucepan. Add the peas and cook, over a low heat, for 2–3 minutes.

2 Using a measuring jug (pitcher), pour 150 ml/1⁄4 pint/2⁄3 cup of the cream into the pan, bring to the boil and simmer for 1–1½ minutes, or until slightly thickened. Remove the pan from the heat.

3 Meanwhile, bring a large pan of lightly salted water to the boil. Add the spaghetti or tagliatelle and olive oil and cook for 2–3 minutes, or until just tender but still firm to the bite. Remove the pan from the heat, drain the pasta thoroughly and return to the pan.

4 Add the peas and cream sauce to the pasta. Return the pan to the heat and add the remaining cream and the Parmesan cheese and season to taste with salt, pepper and grated nutmeg.

5 Using 2 forks, gently toss the pasta to coat with the peas and cream sauce, while heating through.

6 Transfer the pasta to a serving dish and serve immediately, with extra Parmesan cheese.

VARIATION

Fry 140 g/5 oz/2 cups sliced button or oyster mushrooms in 60 g/2 oz/4 tbsp butter over a low heat for 4–5 minutes. Stir into the peas and cream sauce just before adding to the pasta in step 4.

Spaghetti Olio e Aglio

This easy and satisfying Roman dish originated as a cheap meal for poor people, but has now become a favourite in restaurants and trattorias.

NUTRITIONAL INFORMATION

Calories 515	Sugars 1g	
Protein 8g	Fat 33g	
Carbohydrate . . .50g	Saturates 5g	

 5 MINS   5 MINS

SERVES 4

INGREDIENTS

125 ml/4 fl oz/½ cup olive oil

3 garlic cloves, crushed

450 g/1 lb fresh spaghetti

3 tbsp roughly chopped fresh parsley

salt and pepper

1 Reserve 1 tablespoon of the olive oil and heat the remainder in a medium saucepan. Add the garlic and a pinch of salt and cook over a low heat, stirring constantly, until golden brown, then remove the pan from the heat. Do not allow the garlic to burn as it will taint its flavour. (If it does burn, you will have to start all over again!)

2 Meanwhile, bring a large saucepan of lightly salted water to the boil. Add the spaghetti and remaining olive oil to the pan and cook for 2–3 minutes, or until tender, but still firm to the bite. Drain the spaghetti thoroughly and return to the pan.

3 Add the oil and garlic mixture to the spaghetti and toss to coat thoroughly. Season with pepper, add the chopped fresh parsley and toss to coat again.

4 Transfer the spaghetti to a warm serving dish and serve immediately.

COOK'S TIP

Oils produced by different countries, mainly Italy, Spain and Greece, have their own characteristic flavours. Some produce an oil which has a hot, peppery taste while others have a 'green' flavour.

Vegetables & Tofu (Bean Curd)

This is a simple, clean-tasting dish of green vegetables, tofu (bean curd) and pasta, lightly tossed in olive oil.

NUTRITIONAL INFORMATION

Calories	400	Sugars	.........5g
Protein	........19g	Fat	......17g
Carbohydrate	...46g	Saturates	.......5g

25 MINS   20 MINS

SERVES 4

I N G R E D I E N T S

225 g/8 oz asparagus

125 g/4½ oz mangetout (snow peas)

225 g/8 oz French (green) beans

1 leek

225 g/8 oz shelled small broad (fava) beans

300 g/10½ oz dried fusilli

2 tbsp olive oil

25 g/1 oz/2 tbsp butter or margarine

1 garlic clove, crushed

225 g/8 oz tofu (bean curd), cut into 2.5 cm/1 inch cubes

60 g/2 oz/⅓ cup pitted green olives in brine, drained

salt and pepper

freshly grated Parmesan, to serve

1 Cut the asparagus into 5 cm/2 inch lengths. Finely slice the mangetout (snow peas) diagonally and slice the French (green) beans into 2.5 cm/1 inch pieces. Finely slice the leek.

2 Bring a large saucepan of water to the boil and add the asparagus, green beans and broad (fava) beans. Bring back to the boil and cook for 4 minutes until just tender. Drain well and rinse in cold water. Set aside.

3 Bring a large saucepan of salted water to the boil and cook the fusilli for 8–9 minutes until just tender. Drain well. Toss in 1 tablespoon of the oil and season well.

4 Meanwhile, in a wok or large frying pan (skillet), heat the remaining oil and the butter or margarine and gently fry the leek, garlic and tofu (bean curd) for 1–2 minutes until the vegetables have just softened.

5 Stir in the mangetout (snow peas) and cook for 1 minute.

6 Add the boiled vegetables and olives to the pan and heat through for 1 minute. Carefully stir in the pasta and seasoning. Cook for 1 minute and pile into a warmed serving dish. Serve sprinkled with Parmesan.

Salads

If you need inspiration for salads to accompany your main courses, look no further than this chapter. All of the salads complement a wide variety of dishes, and many make ideal starters. You could even serve a proportion of these salads as main meals as they are often quite filling. Use plenty of colourful, fresh ingredients in your salad – choose from a

wide range of (bell) peppers, mangetout (snow peas) and baby corn cobs as they are all readily available. If possible, use Italian staple ingredients, such as extra-virgin olive oil and balsamic vinegar, for salad dressings, and sprinke over some Italian cheeses, such as Parmesan and Pecorino, for extra taste. All of the salads in this chapter are refreshing and full of flavour and are sure to get the tastebuds tingling.

Yellow (Bell) Pepper Salad

A colourful combination of yellow (bell) peppers, red radishes and celery combine to give a wonderfully crunchy texture and fresh taste.

NUTRITIONAL INFORMATION

Calories 176	Sugars 4g
Protein 4g	Fat 16g
Carbohydrate 4g	Saturates 4g

  25 MINS   5 MINS

SERVES 4

INGREDIENTS

4 rashers streaky bacon, chopped

2 yellow (bell) peppers

8 radishes, washed and trimmed

1 stick celery, finely chopped

3 plum tomatoes, cut into wedges

3 tbsp olive oil

1 tbsp fresh thyme

1 Dry fry the chopped bacon in a frying pan (skillet) for 4–5 minutes or until crispy. Remove the bacon from the frying pan (skillet), set aside and leave to cool until required.

2 Using a sharp knife, halve and deseed the (bell) peppers. Slice the (bell) peppers into long strips.

3 Using a sharp knife, halve the radishes and cut them into wedges.

4 Mix together the (bell) peppers, radishes, celery and tomatoes and toss the mixture in the olive oil and fresh thyme. Season to taste with a little salt and pepper.

5 Transfer the salad to serving plates and garnish with the reserved crispy bacon pieces.

COOK'S TIP

Tomatoes are actually berries and are related to potatoes. There are many different shapes and sizes of this versatile fruit. The one most used in Italian cooking is the plum tomato which is very flavoursome.

Pasta & Garlic Mayo Salad

This crisp salad would make an excellent accompaniment to grilled (broiled) meat and is ideal for summer barbecues (grills).

NUTRITIONAL INFORMATION

Calories ....858 Sugars 35g
Protein ....11g Fat 64g
Carbohydrate ...64g Saturates 8g

1½ HOURS   10 MINS

SERVES 4

INGREDIENTS

2 large lettuces

260 g/9 oz dried penne

1 tbsp olive oil

8 red eating apples

juice of 4 lemons

1 head of celery, sliced

115 g/4 oz/¾ cup shelled, halved walnuts

250 ml/9 fl oz/1⅛ cups fresh garlic
   mayonnaise (see Cook's Tip)

salt

1 Wash, drain and pat dry the lettuce leaves with kitchen paper. Transfer them to the refrigerator for 1 hour or until crisp.

2 Meanwhile, bring a large saucepan of lightly salted water to the boil. Add the pasta and olive oil and cook for 8–10 minutes or until tender, but still firm to the bite. Drain the pasta and refresh under cold running water. Drain thoroughly again and set aside.

3 Core and dice the apples, place them in a small bowl and sprinkle with the lemon juice.

4 Mix together the pasta, celery, apples and walnuts and toss the mixture in the garlic mayonnaise (see Cook's Tip, right). Add more mayonnaise, if liked.

5 Line a salad bowl with the lettuce leaves and spoon the pasta salad into the lined bowl. Serve when required.

COOK'S TIP

To make garlic mayo, beat 2 egg yolks with a pinch of salt and 6 crushed garlic cloves. Start beating in 350ml/12 fl oz/1½ cups oil, 1–2 tsp at a time. When ¼ of the oil has been incorporated, beat in 1–2 tbsp white wine vinegar. Continue beating in the oil. Stir in 1 tsp Dijon mustard and season.

Aubergine (Eggplant) Salad

A starter with a difference from Sicily. It has a real bite, both from the sweet-sour sauce, and from the texture of the celery.

NUTRITIONAL INFORMATION

Calories 390	Sugars 15g
Protein 8g	Fat 33g
Carbohydrate . . .16g	Saturates 5g

1½ HOURS   25 MINS

SERVES 4

I N G R E D I E N T S

2 large aubergines (eggplants),
   about 1 kg/2 lb 4 oz

6 tbsp olive oil

1 small onion, chopped finely

2 garlic cloves, crushed

6–8 celery sticks, cut into
   1 cm/½ inch slices

2 tbsp capers

12–16 green olives, pitted
   and sliced

2 tbsp pine kernels (nuts)

25 g/1 oz bitter or dark
   chocolate, grated

4 tbsp wine vinegar

1 tbsp brown sugar

salt and pepper

2 hard-boiled (hard-cooked) eggs,
   sliced, to serve

celery leaves or curly endive,
   to garnish

1 Cut the aubergines (eggplants) into 2.5 cm/1 inch cubes and sprinkle liberally with 2–3 tablespoons of salt. Leave to stand for 1 hour to extract the bitter juices, then rinse off the salt thoroughly under cold water, drain and dry on paper towels.

2 Heat most of the oil in a frying pan (skillet) and fry the aubergine (eggplant) cubes until golden brown all over. Drain on paper towels then put in a large bowl.

3 Add the onion and garlic to the pan with the remaining oil and fry very gently until just soft. Add the celery to the pan and fry for a few minutes, stirring frequently, until lightly coloured but still crisp.

4 Add the celery to the aubergines (eggplants) with the capers, olives and pine kernels (nuts) and mix lightly.

5 Add the chocolate, vinegar and sugar to the residue in the pan. Heat gently until melted, then bring to the boil. Season with salt and pepper to taste. Pour over the salad and mix lightly. Cover, leave until cold and then chill thoroughly.

6 Serve with sliced hard-boiled (hard-cooked) eggs and garnish with celery leaves or curly endive.

Green Salad

Herb-flavoured croûtons are topped with peppery rocket (arugula), red chard, green olives and pistachios to make an elegant combination.

NUTRITIONAL INFORMATION

Calories 256   Sugars 3g
Protein ....4g   Fat 17g
Carbohydrate ...23g   Saturates 3g

 25 MINS   10 MINS

SERVES 4

INGREDIENTS

25 g/1 oz pistachio nuts

5 tbsp extra virgin olive oil

1 tbsp rosemary, chopped

2 garlic cloves, chopped

4 slices rustic bread

1 tbsp red wine vinegar

1 tsp wholegrain mustard

1 tsp sugar

25 g/1 oz rocket (arugula)

25 g/1 oz red chard

50 g/1¾ oz green olives, pitted

2 tbsp fresh basil, shredded

1 Shell the pistachios and roughly chop them, using a sharp knife.

2 Place 2 tablespoons of the extra virgin olive oil in a frying pan (skillet). Add the rosemary and garlic and cook for 2 minutes.

3 Add the slices of bread to the pan and fry for 2–3 minutes on both sides until golden. Remove the bread from the pan and drain on absorbent kitchen paper.

4 To make the dressing, mix together the remaining olive oil with the red wine vinegar, mustard and sugar.

5 Place a slice of bread on to a serving plate and top with the rocket (arugula) and red chard. Sprinkle with the olives.

6 Drizzle the dressing over the top of the salad leaves. Sprinkle with the chopped pistachios and shredded basil leaves and serve the salad immediately.

COOK'S TIP

If you cannot find red chard, try slicing a tomato into very thin wedges to add a splash of vibrant red colour to the salad.

Niçoise with Pasta Shells

This is an Italian variation of the traditional Niçoise salad from southern France.

NUTRITIONAL INFORMATION

Calories	484	Sugars	.........5g
Protein	........28g	Fat	..........26g
Carbohydrate	...35g	Saturates	.......4g

45 MINS   30 MINS

SERVES 4

I N G R E D I E N T S

350 g/12 oz dried small pasta shells

1 tbsp olive oil

115 g/4 oz green (French) beans

50 g/1¾ oz can anchovies, drained

25 ml/1 fl oz/⅛ cup milk

2 small crisp lettuces

450 g/1 lb or 3 large beef tomatoes

4 hard-boiled (hard-cooked) eggs

225 g/8 oz can tuna, drained

115 g/4 oz/1 cup stoned (pitted) black olives

salt and pepper

V I N A I G R E T T E   D R E S S I N G

50 ml/2 fl oz extra virgin olive oil

25 ml/1 fl oz white wine vinegar

1 tsp wholegrain mustard

salt and pepper

COOK'S TIP

It is very convenient to make salad dressings in a screw top jar. Put all the ingredients in the jar, cover securely and shake well to mix and emulsify the oil.

1 Bring a large saucepan of lightly salted water to the boil. Add the pasta and the olive oil and cook for 8–10 minutes or until tender, but still firm to the bite. Drain and refresh in cold water.

2 Bring a small saucepan of lightly salted water to the boil. Add the beans and cook for 10–12 minutes, until tender but still firm to the bite. Drain, refresh in cold water, drain thoroughly once more and then set aside.

3 Put the anchovies in a shallow bowl, pour over the milk and set aside for 10 minutes. Meanwhile, tear the lettuces into large pieces. Blanch the tomatoes in boiling water for 1–2 minutes, then drain, skin and roughly chop the flesh. Shell the eggs and cut into quarters. Cut the tuna into large chunks.

4 Drain the anchovies and the pasta. Put all of the salad ingredients, the beans and the olives into a large bowl and gently mix together.

5 To make the vinaigrette dressing, beat together all of the dressing ingredients and keep in the refrigerator until required. Just before serving, pour the vinaigrette dressing over the salad.

Tuscan Bean & Tuna Salad

The combination of beans and tuna is a favourite in Tuscany. The hint of honey and lemon in the dressing makes this salad very refreshing.

NUTRITIONAL INFORMATION

Calories . . . . . . .224 Sugars 4g
Protein . . . . .19g Fat 10g
Carbohydrate . . .16g Saturates 2g

30 MINS   0 MINS

SERVES 4

INGREDIENTS

1 small white onion or 2 spring onions (scallions), finely chopped

2 x 400 g/14 oz cans butter beans, drained

2 medium tomatoes

185 g/6½ oz can tuna, drained

2 tbsp flat leaf parsley, chopped

2 tbsp olive oil

1 tbsp lemon juice

2 tsp clear honey

1 garlic clove, crushed

1 Place the chopped onions or spring onions (scallions) and butter beans in a bowl and mix well to combine.

2 Using a sharp knife, cut the tomatoes into wedges.

3 Add the tomatoes to the onion and bean mixture.

4 Flake the tuna with a fork and add it to the onion and bean mixture together with the parsley.

5 In a screw-top jar, mix together the olive oil, lemon juice, honey and garlic. Shake the jar until the dressing emulsifies and thickens.

6 Pour the dressing over the bean salad. Toss the ingredients together using 2 spoons and serve.

VARIATION

Substitute fresh salmon for the tuna if you wish to create a luxurious version of this recipe for a special occasion.

Chargrilled Chicken Salad

This is a quick starter to serve at a barbecue – if the bread is bent in half, the chicken salad can be put in the middleand eaten as finger food.

NUTRITIONAL INFORMATION

Calories	225	Sugars	.........5g
Protein	........16g	Fat	..........12g
Carbohydrate	...15g	Saturates	......2g

🍲 10 MINS   🕐 15 MINS

SERVES 4

I N G R E D I E N T S

2 skinless, boneless chicken breasts

1 red onion

oil for brushing

1 avocado, peeled and pitted

1 tbsp lemon juice

125 ml/4 fl oz/½ cup low-fat mayonnaise

¼ tsp chilli powder

½ tsp pepper

¼ tsp salt

4 tomatoes, quartered

½ loaf sun-dried tomato-flavoured focaccia bread

green salad, to serve

1 Using a sharp knife, cut the chicken breasts into 1 cm/½ inch strips.

VARIATION

Instead of focaccia, serve the salad in pitta bread which have been warmed through on the bar-becue (grill).

2 Cut the onion into eight pieces, held together at the root. Rinse under cold running water and then brush with oil.

3 Purée or mash the avocado and lemon juice together. Whisk in the mayonnaise. Add the chilli powder, pepper and salt.

4 Put the chicken and onion over a hot barbecue and grill for 3–4 minutes

on each side. Combine the chicken, onion, tomatoes and avocado mixture together.

5 Cut the bread in half twice, so that you have quarter-circle-shaped pieces, then in half horizontally. Toast on the hot barbecue (grill) for about 2 minutes on each side.

6 Spoon the chicken mixture on to the toasts and serve with a green salad.

Roast (Bell) Pepper Salad

Serve chilled as an antipasto with cold meats, or warm as a side dish. Garlic bread makes a delicious accompaniment.

NUTRITIONAL INFORMATION

Calories 141	Sugars 8g
Protein 1g	Fat 11g
Carbohydrate 9g	Saturates 2g

 20 MINS   20 MINS

SERVES

INGREDIENTS

4 large mixed red, green and yellow (bell) peppers

4 tbsp olive oil

1 large red onion, sliced

2 garlic cloves, crushed

4 tomatoes, peeled and chopped

pinch of sugar

1 tsp lemon juice

salt and pepper

1 Trim and halve the (bell) peppers and remove the seeds.

2 Place the (bell) peppers, skin-side up, under a preheated hot grill (broiler). Cook until the skins char. Rinse under cold water and remove the skins.

3 Trim off any thick membranes and slice thinly.

4 Heat the oil and fry the onion and garlic until softened. Then add the (bell) peppers and tomatoes and fry over a low heat for 10 minutes.

5 Remove from the heat, add the sugar and lemon juice, and season to taste. Serve immediately or leave to cool (the flavours will develop as the salad cools).

Spinach Salad

Fresh baby spinach is tasty and light, and it makes an excellent salad to go with the chicken and creamy dressing.

NUTRITIONAL INFORMATION

Calories 145	Sugars 3g
Protein 10g	Fat 10g
Carbohydrate 4g	Saturates 1g

 30 MINS   0 MINS

SERVES 4

INGREDIENTS

100 g/3½ oz baby spinach, washed

75 g/2¾ oz radicchio leaves, shredded

50 g/1¾ oz mushrooms

100 g/3½ oz cooked chicken,
  preferably breast

50 g/1¾ oz Parma ham (prosciutto)

2 tbsp olive oil

finely grated rind of ½ orange and juice
  of 1 orange

1 tbsp natural yogurt

1 Wipe the mushrooms with a damp cloth to remove any excess dirt.

2 Gently mix together the spinach and radicchio in a large salad bowl.

3 Using a sharp knife, thinly slice the wiped mushrooms and add them to the bowl containing the spinach and radicchio.

4 Tear the cooked chicken breast and Parma ham (prosciutto) into strips and mix them into the spinach salad.

5 To make the dressing, place the olive oil, orange rind, juice and yogurt into a screw-top jar. Shake the jar until the mixture is well combined. Season to taste with salt and pepper.

6 Drizzle the dressing over the spinach salad and toss to mix well. Serve.

VARIATION

Spinach is delicious when served raw. Try raw spinach in a salad garnished with bacon or garlicky croûtons. The young leaves have a wonderfully sharp flavour.

Goat's Cheese & Penne Salad

This superb salad is delicious when served with strongly flavoured meat dishes, such as venison.

NUTRITIONAL INFORMATION

Calories	634	Sugars 13g
Protein	........18g	Fat 51g
Carbohydrate	...27g	Saturates 13g

  1½ HOURS   15 MINS

SERVES 4

I N G R E D I E N T S

250 g/9 oz dried penne

5 tbsp olive oil

1 head radicchio, torn into pieces

1 Webbs lettuce, torn into pieces

7 tbsp chopped walnuts

2 ripe pears, cored and diced

1 fresh basil sprig

1 bunch of watercress, trimmed

2 tbsp lemon juice

3 tbsp garlic vinegar

4 tomatoes, quartered

1 small onion, sliced

1 large carrot, grated

250 g/9 oz goat's cheese, diced

salt and pepper

1 Bring a large saucepan of lightly salted water to the boil. Add the penne and 1 tablespoon of the olive oil and cook for 8–10 minutes or until tender, but still firm to the bite. Drain the pasta, refresh under cold running water, drain thoroughly again and set aside to cool.

2 Place the radicchio and Webbs lettuce in a large salad bowl and mix together well. Top with the pasta, walnuts, pears, basil and watercress.

3 Mix together the lemon juice, the remaining olive oil and the vinegar in a measuring jug (pitcher). Pour the mixture over the salad ingredients and toss to coat the salad leaves well.

4 Add the tomato quarters, onion slices, grated carrot and diced goat's cheese and toss together, using 2 forks, until well mixed. Leave the salad to chill in the refrigerator for about 1 hour before serving.

COOK'S TIP

Radiccio is a variety of chicory (endive) originating in Italy. It has a slightly bitter flavour.

Potato & Sausage Salad

Sliced Italian sausage blends well with the other Mediterranean flavours of sun-dried tomato and basil in this salad.

NUTRITIONAL INFORMATION

Calories 450	Sugars 6g	
Protein 13g	Fat 28g	
Carbohydrate . . .38g	Saturates 1g	

 25 MINS 25 MINS

SERVES 4

INGREDIENTS

450 g/1 lb waxy potatoes

1 raddichio or lollo rosso lettuce

1 green (bell) pepper, sliced

175 g/6 oz Italian sausage, sliced

1 red onion, halved and sliced

125 g/4½ oz sun-dried tomatoes, sliced

2 tbsp shredded fresh basil

DRESSING

1 tbsp balsamic vinegar

1 tsp tomato purée (paste)

2 tbsp olive oil

salt and pepper

COOK'S TIP

Any sliced Italian sausage or salami can be used in this salad. Italy is home of the salami and there are numerous varieties to choose from – those from the south tend to be more highly spiced than those from the north of the country.

1 Cook the potatoes in a saucepan of boiling water for 20 minutes or until cooked through. Drain and leave to cool.

2 Line a large serving platter with the radicchio or lollo rosso lettuce leaves.

3 Slice the cooled potatoes and arrange them in layers on the lettuce-lined serving platter together with the sliced green (bell) pepper, sliced Italian sausage, red onion, sun-dried tomatoes and shredded fresh basil.

4 In a small bowl, whisk the balsamic vinegar, tomato purée (paste) and olive oil together and season to taste with salt and pepper. Pour the dressing over the potato salad and serve immediately.

Minted Fennel Salad

This is a very refreshing salad. The subtle liquorice flavour of fennel combines well with the cucumber and mint.

NUTRITIONAL INFORMATION

Calories	90	Sugars	........7g
Protein	........4g	Fat	..........5g
Carbohydrate	....7g	Saturates	.......1g

 25 MINS   0 MINS

SERVES 4

I N G R E D I E N T S

1 bulb fennel

2 small oranges

1 small or ½ a large cucumber

1 tbsp chopped mint

1 tbsp virgin olive oil

2 eggs, hard boiled (cooked)

1 Using a sharp knife, trim the outer leaves from the fennel. Slice the fennel bulb thinly into a bowl of water and sprinkle with lemon juice (see Cook's Tip).

2 Grate the rind of the oranges over a bowl. Using a sharp knife, pare away the orange peel, then segment the orange by carefully slicing between each line of pith. Do this over the bowl in order to retain the juice.

3 Using a sharp knife, cut the cucumber into 12 mm/½ inch rounds and then cut each round into quarters.

4 Add the cucumber to the fennel and orange mixture together with the mint.

5 Pour the olive oil over the fennel and cucumber salad and toss well.

6 Peel and quarter the eggs and use these to decorate the top of the salad. Serve at once.

COOK'S TIP

Fennel will discolour if it is left for any length of time without a dressing. To prevent any discoloration, place it in a bowl of water and sprinkle with lemon juice.

Pasta Salad & Basil Vinaigrette

All the ingredients of pesto sauce are included in this salad, which has a fabulous summery taste, perfect for *al fresco* eating.

NUTRITIONAL INFORMATION

Calories 432	Sugars 3g
Protein 14g	Fat 29g
Carbohydrate ...30g	Saturates 6g

25 MINS   15 MINS

SERVES 4

INGREDIENTS

225 g/8 oz fusilli

4 tomatoes

50 g/1 ¾ oz black olives

25 g/1 oz sun-dried tomatoes in oil

2 tbsp pine nuts

2 tbsp grated Parmesan cheese

fresh basil, to garnish

VINAIGRETTE

15 g/½ oz basil leaves

1 clove garlic

2 tbsp grated Parmesan cheese

4 tbsp extra virgin olive oil

2 tbsp lemon juice

salt and pepper

COOK'S TIP

Sun-dried tomatoes have a strong, intense flavour. They are most frequently found packed in oil with herbs and garlic. Do not waste the oil, which has an excellent flavour, instead use it in salad dressings.

1 Cook the pasta in a saucepan of lightly salted boiling water for 8–10 minutes or until just tender. Drain the pasta, rinse under cold water, then drain again thoroughly. Place the pasta in a large bowl.

2 To make the vinaigrette, place the basil leaves, garlic, cheese, oil and lemon juice in a food processor. Season with salt and pepper to taste. Process until the leaves are well chopped and the ingredients are combined. Alternatively, finely chop the basil leaves by hand and combine with the other vinaigrette ingredients. Pour the vinaigrette over the pasta and toss to coat.

3 Cut the tomatoes into wedges. Pit and halve the olives. Slice the sun-dried tomatoes. Place the pine nuts on a baking tray (cookie sheet) and toast under the grill (broiler) until golden.

4 Add the tomatoes (fresh and sun-dried) and the olives to the pasta and mix.

5 Transfer the pasta to a serving dish, scatter over the Parmesan and pine nuts and garnish with a few basil leaves.

Seafood Salad

Seafood is plentiful in Italy and each region has its own seafood salad. The dressing needs to be chilled for several hours so prepare in advance.

45-55 MINS   40 MINS

SERVES 4

INGREDIENTS

175 g/6 oz squid rings, defrosted if frozen

600 ml/1 pint/2½ cups water

150 ml/¼ pint/⅔ cup dry white wine

225 g/8 oz hake or monkfish, cut into cubes

16–20 mussels, scrubbed and debearded

20 clams in shells, scrubbed, if available
(otherwise use extra mussels)

125–175 g/4½–6 oz peeled prawns
(shrimp)

3–4 spring onions (scallions), trimmed and
sliced (optional)

radicchio and curly endive leaves, to serve

lemon wedges, to garnish

DRESSING

6 tbsp olive oil

1 tbsp wine vinegar

2 tbsp chopped fresh parsley

1–2 garlic cloves, crushed

salt and pepper

GARLIC MAYONNAISE

5 tbsp thick mayonnaise

2–3 tbsp fromage frais or natural yogurt

2 garlic cloves, crushed

1 tbsp capers

2 tbsp chopped fresh parsley or mixed herbs

1 Poach the squid in the water and wine for 20 minutes or until nearly tender. Add the fish and continue to cook gently for 7–8 minutes or until tender. Strain, reserving the fish. Pour the stock into a clean pan.

2 Bring the fish stock to the boil and add the mussels and clams. Cover the pan and simmer gently for about 5 minutes or until the shells open. Discard any that remain closed.

3 Drain the shellfish and remove from their shells. Put into a bowl with the cooked fish and add the prawns (shrimp) and spring onions (scallions), if using.

4 For the dressing, whisk together the oil, vinegar, parsley, garlic, salt and pepper to taste. Pour over the fish, mixing well. Cover and chill for several hours.

5 Arrange small leaves of radicchio and curly endive on 4 plates and spoon the fish salad into the centre. Garnish with lemon wedges. Combine all the ingredients for the garlic mayonnaise and serve with the salad.

Rare Beef Pasta Salad

This salad is a meal in itself and would be perfect for an *al fresco* lunch, perhaps with a bottle of red wine.

NUTRITIONAL INFORMATION

Calories	575	Sugars	.........4g
Protein	........31g	Fat	.......33g
Carbohydrate	...44g	Saturates	.......9g

 15 MINS   30 MINS

SERVES 4

INGREDIENTS

450 g/1 lb rump or sirloin steak in
   one piece

450 g/1 lb dried fusilli

5 tbsp olive oil

2 tbsp lime juice

2 tbsp Thai fish sauce
   (see Cook's Tip)

2 tsp clear honey

4 spring onions (scallions), sliced

1 cucumber, peeled and cut into
   2.5 cm/1 inch chunks

3 tomatoes, cut into wedges

3 tsp finely chopped fresh mint

salt and pepper

1 Season the steak with salt and pepper. Grill (broil) or pan-fry the steak for 4 minutes on each side. Allow to rest for 5 minutes, then slice thinly across the grain.

2 Meanwhile, bring a large saucepan of lightly salted water to the boil. Add the fusilli and 1 tbsp of the olive oil and cook for 8–10 minutes or until tender, but still firm to the bite. Drain the fusilli, refresh in cold water and drain again thoroughly. Toss the fusilli in the remaining olive oil.

3 Combine the lime juice, fish sauce and honey in a small saucepan and cook over a medium heat for 2 minutes.

4 Add the spring onions (scallions), cucumber, tomatoes and mint to the pan, then add the steak and mix well. Season to taste with salt.

5 Transfer the fusilli to a large, warm serving dish and top with the steak and salad mixture. Serve just warm or allow to cool completely.

COOK'S TIP

Thai fish sauce, also known as nam pla, is made from salted anchovies and has quite a strong flavour, so it should be used with discretion. It is available from some supermarkets and from Oriental food stores.

Mushroom Salad

Raw mushrooms are a great favourite in Italian dishes – they have a fresh, almost creamy flavour.

NUTRITIONAL INFORMATION

Calories 121   Sugars 0.1g
Protein . . . . .2g   Fat 13g
Carbohydrate . . .0.1g   Saturates 2g

 20 MINS   0 MINS

SERVES 4

I N G R E D I E N T S

150 g/5½ oz firm white mushrooms

4 tbsp virgin olive oil

1 tbsp lemon juice

5 anchovy fillets, drained and chopped

1 tbsp fresh marjoram

salt and pepper

1 Gently wipe each mushroom with a damp cloth in order to remove any excess dirt.

2 Slice the mushrooms thinly, using a sharp knife.

3 To make the dressing, mix together the olive oil and lemon juice.

4 Pour the dressing mixture over the mushrooms. Toss together so that the mushrooms are completely coated with the lemon juice and oil.

5 Stir the chopped anchovy fillets into the mushrooms.

6 Season the mushroom mixture with pepper to taste and garnish with the fresh marjoram.

7 Leave the mushroom salad to stand for about 5 minutes before serving in order for all the flavours to be absorbed.

8 Season the mushroom salad with a little salt (see Cook's Tip) and then serve.

COOK'S TIP

Do not season the mushroom salad with salt until the very last minute as it will cause the mushrooms to blacken and the juices to leak. The result will not be as tasty as it should be as the full flavours won't be absorbed and it will also look very unattractive.

Pasta Salad & Mixed Cabbage

This crunchy, colourful salad would be a good accompaniment for grilled (broiled) meat or fish.

NUTRITIONAL INFORMATION

Calories	388	Sugars	........17g
Protein	........18g	Fat	..........18g
Carbohydrate	...41g	Saturates	.......3g

  25 MINS   30 MINS

SERVES 4

INGREDIENTS

250 g/9 oz/2¼ cups dried
   short-cut macaroni

5 tbsp olive oil

1 large red cabbage, shredded

1 large white cabbage, shredded

2 large apples, diced

250 g/9 oz cooked smoked bacon or
   ham, diced

8 tbsp wine vinegar

1 tbsp sugar

salt and pepper

1 Bring a pan of lightly salted water to the boil. Add the macaroni and 1 tablespoon of the oil and cook for 8–10 minutes or until tender, but still firm to the bite. Drain the pasta, then refresh in cold water. Drain again and set aside.

VARIATION

Alternative dressings for this salad can be made with 4 tbsp olive oil, 4 tbsp red wine, 4 tbsp red wine vinegar and 1 tbsp sugar. Or substitute 3 tbsp olive oil and 1 tbsp walnut or hazelnut oil for the olive oil.

2 Bring a large saucepan of lightly salted water to the boil. Add the shredded red cabbage and cook for 5 minutes. Drain the cabbage thoroughly and set aside to cool.

3 Bring a large saucepan of lightly salted water to the boil. Add the white cabbage and cook for 5 minutes. Drain the cabbage thoroughly and set aside to cool.

4 In a large bowl, mix together the pasta, red cabbage and apple. In a separate bowl, mix together the white cabbage and bacon or ham.

5 In a small bowl, mix together the remaining oil, the vinegar and sugar and season to taste with salt and pepper. Pour the dressing over each of the 2 cabbage mixtures and, finally, mix them all together. Serve immediately.

Italian Potato Salad

Potato salad is always a favourite, but it is even more delicious with the addition of sun-dried tomatoes and fresh parsley.

NUTRITIONAL INFORMATION

Calories ....425 Sugars 6g
Protein ....6g Fat 27g
Carbohydrate ...43g Saturates 5g

  40 MINS   15 MINS

SERVES 4

I N G R E D I E N T S

450 g/1 lb baby potatoes, unpeeled, or
   larger potatoes, halved

4 tbsp natural yogurt

4 tbsp mayonnaise

8 sun-dried tomatoes

2 tbsp flat leaf parsley, chopped

salt and pepper

1 Rinse and clean the potatoes and place them in a large pan of water. Bring to the boil and cook for 8–12 minutes or until just tender. (The cooking time will vary according to the size of the potatoes.)

2 Using a sharp knife, cut the sun-dried tomatoes into thin slices.

3 To make the dressing, mix together the yogurt and mayonnaise in a bowl and season to taste with a little salt and pepper. Stir in the sun-dried tomato slices and the chopped flat leaf parsley.

4 Remove the potatoes with a perforated spoon, drain them thoroughly and then set them aside to cool. If you are using larger potatoes, cut them into 5 cm/2 inch chunks.

5 Pour the dressing over the potatoes and toss to mix.

6 Leave the potato salad to chill in the refrigerator for about 20 minutes, then serve as a starter or as an accompaniment.

COOK'S TIP

It is easier to cut the larger potatoes once they are cooked. Although smaller pieces of potato will cook more quickly, they tend to disintegrate and become mushy.

Italian (Bell) Pepper Salad

This salad goes well with all barbecued (grilled) foods, especially meats. Alternatively, serve it with a selection of Italian bread for a simple starter.

NUTRITIONAL INFORMATION

Calories 150	Sugars 6g	
Protein 4g	Fat 12g	
Carbohydrate 7g	Saturates 1g	

🍽 30 MINS   🕐 30 MINS

SERVES 4

I N G R E D I E N T S

2 red (bell) peppers, halved and
    deseeded

2 yellow (bell) peppers, halved and
    deseeded

3 tbsp extra virgin olive oil

1 onion, cut into wedges

2 large courgettes (zucchini), sliced

2 garlic cloves, sliced

1 tbsp balsamic vinegar

50 g/1¾ oz anchovy fillets, chopped

25 g/1 oz pitted black olives, quartered

fresh basil leaves

1 Place the (bell) pepper halves, cut side down, on a grill (broiler) pan and cook until the skin blackens and chars. Leave to cool slightly then pop them into a plastic bag for about 10 minutes.

2 Peel away the skin from the (bell) peppers and discard. Cut the flesh into thick strips.

3 Heat the oil in a large frying pan (skillet), add the onion and cook gently for 10 minutes or until softened. Add the courgette (zucchini) slices, garlic and (bell) pepper strips to the pan and cook, stirring occasionally, for a further 10 minutes.

4 Add the vinegar, anchovies and olives to the pan. Season with salt and pepper to taste. Mix well and leave to cool.

5 Reserve a few basil leaves for garnishing, then tear the remainder into small pieces. Stir them into the salad.

6 Transfer the salad to a serving dish and garnish with a few whole basil leaves.

COOK'S TIP

Balsamic vinegar is made in and around Modena in Italy. Its rich, mellow flavour is perfect for Mediterranean-style salads, but if it is unavailable, use sherry vinegar or white wine vinegar instead.

Lentil & Tuna Salad

In this recipe, lentils, combined with spices, lemon juice and tuna, make a wonderfully tasty and filling salad.

NUTRITIONAL INFORMATION

Calories ....227 Sugars 2g
Protein ....19g Fat 9g
Carbohydrate ...19g Saturates 1g

 25 MINS   0 MINS

SERVES 4

INGREDIENTS

3 tbsp virgin olive oil

1 tbsp lemon juice

1 tsp wholegrain mustard

1 garlic clove, crushed

½ tsp cumin powder

½ tsp ground coriander

1 small red onion

2 ripe tomatoes

400 g/14 oz can lentils, drained

185 g/6½ can tuna, drained

2 tbsp fresh coriander (cilantro), chopped

pepper

1 Using a sharp knife, deseed the tomatoes and then chop them into fine dice.

2 Using a sharp knife, finely chop the red onion.

3 To make the dressing, whisk together the virgin olive oil, lemon juice, mustard, garlic, cumin powder and ground coriander in a small bowl. Set aside until required.

4 Mix together the chopped onion, diced tomatoes and drained lentils in a large bowl.

5 Flake the tuna and stir it into the onion, tomato and lentil mixture.

6 Stir in the chopped fresh coriander (cilantro).

7 Pour the dressing over the lentil and tuna salad and season with pepper to taste. Serve at once.

COOK'S TIP

Lentils are a good source of protein and contain important vitamins and minerals. Buy them dried for soaking and cooking yourself, or buy canned varieties for speed and convenience.

Spicy Sausage Salad

A warm sausage and pasta dressing spooned over chilled salad leaves makes a refreshing combination to start a meal.

NUTRITIONAL INFORMATION

Calories	383	Sugars	.........2g
Protein	........11g	Fat	..........28g
Carbohydrate	...20g	Saturates	.......1g

15 MINS   25 MINS

SERVES 4

I N G R E D I E N T S

125g/4½ oz small pasta shapes, such as
    elbow tubetti

3 tbsp olive oil

1 medium onion, chopped

2 cloves garlic, crushed

1 small yellow (bell) pepper, cored, seeded
    and cut into matchstick strips

175 g/6 oz spicy pork sausage such as
    chorizo, skinned and sliced

2 tbsp red wine

1 tbsp red wine vinegar

mixed salad leaves, chilled

salt

VARIATION

Other sausages to use are the Italian pepperoni, flavoured with chilli peppers, fennel and spices, and one of the many varieties of salami, usually flavoured with garlic and pepper.

1 Cook the pasta in a pan of boiling salted water, adding 1 tablespoon of the oil, for 8–10 minutes or until tender. Drain in a colander and set aside.

2 Heat the remaining oil in a saucepan over a medium heat. Fry the onion until it is translucent, stir in the garlic, (bell) pepper and sliced sausage and cook for 3-4 minutes, stirring once or twice.

3 Add the wine, wine vinegar and reserved pasta to the pan, stir to blend well and bring the mixture just to the boil.

4 Arrange the chilled salad leaves on 4 individual serving plates and spoon on the warm sausage and pasta mixture. Serve at once.

Capri Salad

This tomato, olive and Mozzarella salad, dressed with balsamic vinegar and olive oil, makes a delicious starter on its own.

NUTRITIONAL INFORMATION

Calories 95	Sugars 3g	
Protein 3g	Fat 8g	
Carbohydrate 3g	Saturates 3g	

20 MINS   3–5 MINS

SERVES 4

INGREDIENTS

2 beef tomatoes

125 g/4½ oz Mozzarella cheese

12 black olives

8 basil leaves

1 tbsp balsamic vinegar

1 tbsp olive oil

salt and pepper

basil leaves, to garnish

1 Using a sharp knife, cut the tomatoes into thin slices.

2 Using a sharp knife, cut the Mozzarella into slices.

3 Pit the olives and slice them into rings.

4 Layer the tomato, Mozzarella cheese and olives in a stack, finishing with a layer of cheese on top.

5 Place each stack under a preheated hot grill (broiler) for 2–3 minutes or just long enough to melt the Mozzarella.

6 Drizzle over the vinegar and olive oil, and season to taste with a little salt and pepper.

7 Transfer to serving plates and garnish with basil leaves. Serve immediately.

COOK'S TIP

Buffalo Mozzarella cheese, although it is usually more expensive because of the comparative rarity of buffalo, does have a better flavour than the cow's milk variety. It is popular in salads, but also provides a tangy layer in baked dishes.

Neapolitan Seafood Salad

This delicious mix of seafood, salad leaves (greens) and ripe tomatoes conjures up all the warmth and sunshine of Naples.

NUTRITIONAL INFORMATION

Calories 1152	Sugars 3g	
Protein 67g	Fat 81g	
Carbohydrate . . .35g	Saturates 12g	

6¹/₂ HOURS   25 MINS

SERVES 4

INGREDIENTS

450 g/1 lb prepared squid,
  cut into strips

750 g/1 lb 10 oz cooked mussels

450 g/1 lb cooked cockles in brine

150 ml/¼ pint/²⁄₃ cup white wine

300 ml/½ pint/1¼ cups olive oil

225 g/8 oz/2 cups dried campanelle or
  other small pasta shapes

juice of 1 lemon

1 bunch chives, snipped

1 bunch fresh parsley,
finely chopped

4 large tomatoes

mixed salad leaves (greens)

salt and pepper

sprig of fresh basil, to garnish

VARIATION

You can substitute cooked scallops for the mussels and clams in brine for the cockles, if you prefer. The seafood needs to be marinated for 6 hours, so prepare well in advance.

1 Put all of the seafood into a large bowl, pour over the wine and half of the olive oil, and set aside for 6 hours.

2 Put the seafood mixture into a saucepan and simmer over a low heat for 10 minutes. Set aside to cool.

3 Bring a large saucepan of lightly salted water to the boil. Add the pasta and 1 tbsp of the remaining olive oil and cook for 8–10 minutes or until tender, but still firm to the bite. Drain thoroughly and refresh in cold water.

4 Strain off about half of the cooking liquid from the seafood and discard the rest. Mix in the lemon juice, chives, parsley and the remaining olive oil. Season to taste with salt and pepper. Drain the pasta and add to the seafood.

5 Cut the tomatoes into quarters. Shred the salad leaves (greens) and arrange them at the base of a salad bowl. Spoon in the seafood salad and garnish with the tomatoes and a sprig of basil. Serve.

Sweet & Sour Salad

This delicious sweet and sour aubergine (eggplant) salad from Sicily was first brought to Italy by the Moors.

NUTRITIONAL INFORMATION

Calories . . . . .217 Sugars 12g

Protein . . . . .2g Fat 18g

Carbohydrate . . .13g Saturates 3g

25 MINS   30 MINS

SERVES 4

INGREDIENTS

6 tbsp olive oil

1 onion, chopped

2 garlic cloves, chopped

2 sticks celery, chopped

450 g/1 lb aubergines (eggplant)

400 g/14 oz can tomatoes, chopped

50 g/1¾ oz green olives, stoned
  and chopped

25 g/1 oz granulated sugar

100 ml/3½ fl oz/2⅓ cup red wine vinegar

25 g/1 oz capers, drained

salt and pepper

1 tbsp flat leaf parsley, roughly chopped,
  to garnish

1 Heat 2 tablespoons of the oil in a large frying pan (skillet). Add the prepared onions, garlic and celery to the frying pan (skillet) and cook, stirring, for 3–4 minutes.

2 Using a sharp knife, slice the aubergines (eggplants) into thick rounds, then cut each round into 4 pieces.

3 Add the aubergine (eggplant) pieces to the frying pan (skillet) with the remaining olive oil and fry for 5 minutes or until golden.

4 Add the tomatoes, olives and sugar to the pan, stirring until the sugar has completely dissolved.

5 Add the red wine vinegar, reduce the heat and leave to simmer for 10–15 minutes or until the sauce is thick and the aubergines (eggplants) are tender.

6 While the pan is still on the heat, stir in the capers. Season to taste with salt and pepper.

7 Transfer to serving plates and garnish with the chopped fresh parsley.

COOK'S TIP

This salad is best served cold the day after it is made, which allows the flavours to mingle and be fully absorbed.

Goat's Cheese Salad

The black olive vinaigrette and bitter salad leaves give a real tang to this quick snack.

NUTRITIONAL INFORMATION

Calories 362	Sugars 3g
Protein 14g	Fat 22g
Carbohydrate ...29g	Saturates 10g

 30 MINS   5–6 MINS

SERVES 4

INGREDIENTS

3 tbsp olive oil

1 tbsp white wine vinegar

1 tsp black olive paste

1 garlic clove, crushed

1 tsp chopped fresh thyme

1 ciabatta loaf

4 small tomatoes, sliced

12 fresh basil leaves

2 x 125 g/4½ oz logs goat's cheese

fresh basil sprigs, to garnish

salad leaves, to serve

1 Put the oil, vinegar, olive paste, garlic and thyme in a small bowl and whisk together.

2 Cut the ciabatta in half horizontally then in half vertically to make 4 pieces.

COOK'S TIP

Goat's cheeses range in flavour from fresh and creamy to strong and tangy, developing flavour as they mature. Fresh goat's cheese must be eaten within 2 days but the mature cheeses, which have a firmer, drier texture, will keep for longer.

3 Drizzle some of the dressing over the bread then arrange the tomatoes and basil leaves on top.

4 Cut each log of goat's cheese into 6 slices and lay 3 slices on each piece of ciabatta.

5 Brush the cheese with some of the dressing and place in a preheated

oven, at 230°C/450°F/Gas Mark 8, for 5-6 minutes or until just turning brown at the edges.

6 Cut each piece of bread in half. Arrange the salad leaves on to serving plates and top with the baked bread. Pour over the remaining dressing, garnish with the fresh basil sprigs and serve with salad leaves.

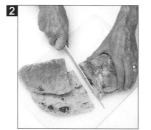

Cheese, Nut & Pasta Salad

Use colourful salad leaves (greens) to provide visual contrast to match the contrasts of taste and texture.

NUTRITIONAL INFORMATION

Calories 694	Sugars 1g
Protein 22g	Fat 57g
Carbohydrate ...24g	Saturates 15g

   15 MINS 15–20 MINS

SERVES 4

INGREDIENTS

225 g/8 oz/2 cups dried pasta shells

1 tbsp olive oil

115 g/4 oz/1 cup shelled and
   halved walnuts

mixed salad leaves (greens), such as
   radicchio, escarole, rocket (arugula),
   lamb's lettuce (corn salad) and frisée

225 g/8 oz dolcelatte cheese, crumbled

salt

DRESSING

2 tbsp walnut oil

4 tbsp extra virgin olive oil

2 tbsp red wine vinegar

salt and pepper

1 Bring a large saucepan of lightly salted water to the boil. Add the pasta shells and olive oil and cook for 8–10 minutes or until just tender, but still firm to the bite. Drain the pasta, refresh under cold running water, drain thoroughly again and set aside.

2 Spread out the shelled walnut halves on to a baking tray (cookie sheet) and toast under a preheated grill (broiler) for 2–3 minutes. Set aside to cool while you make the dressing.

3 To make the dressing, whisk together the walnut oil, olive oil and vinegar in a small bowl, and season to taste.

4 Arrange the salad leaves (greens) in a large serving bowl. Pile the cooled pasta in the middle of the salad leaves (greens) and sprinkle over the dolcelatte cheese. Pour the dressing over the pasta salad, scatter over the walnut halves and toss together to mix. Serve immediately.

COOK'S TIP

Dolcelatte is a semi-soft, blue-veined cheese from Italy. Its texture is creamy and smooth and the flavour is delicate, but piquant. You could use Roquefort instead. It is essential that whatever cheese you choose, it is of the best quality and in peak condition.

Artichoke & Ham Salad

This elegant starter would make a good first course. Serve it with a little fresh bread for mopping up the juices.

NUTRITIONAL INFORMATION

Calories 124	Sugars 2g	
Protein 2g	Fat 11g	
Carbohydrate 4g	Saturates 1g	

 25 MINS 0 MINS

SERVES 4

INGREDIENTS

275 g/9 ½ oz can artichoke hearts
  in oil, drained

4 small tomatoes

25 g/1 oz sun-dried tomatoes in oil

40 g/1 ½ oz Parma ham (prosciutto)

25 g/1 oz pitted black olives, halved

a few basil leaves

DRESSING

3 tbsp olive oil

1 tbsp white wine vinegar

1 clove garlic, crushed

½ tsp mild mustard

1 tsp clear honey

salt and pepper

COOK'S TIP

Use bottled artichokes in oil if you can find them as they have a better flavour. If only canned artichokes are available, rinse them carefully to remove the salty liquid.

1 Make sure the artichokes hearts are thoroughly drained, then cut them into quarters and place in a bowl.

2 Cut each fresh tomato into wedges. Slice the sun-dried tomatoes into thin strips. Cut the Parma ham (prosciutto) into thin strips and add to the bowl with the tomatoes and olive halves.

3 Keeping a few basil leaves whole for garnishing, tear the remainder of the leaves into small pieces and add to the bowl containing the other salad ingredients.

4 To make the dressing, put the oil, wine vinegar, garlic, mustard, honey and salt and pepper to taste in a screw-top jar and shake vigorously until the ingredients are well blended.

5 Pour the dressing over the salad and toss together.

6 Serve the salad garnished with a few whole basil leaves.

Tuna, Bean & Anchovy Salad

Serve as part of a selection of *antipasti*, or for a summer lunch with hot garlic bread.

NUTRITIONAL INFORMATION

Calories	397	Sugars	.........8g
Protein	........23g	Fat	..........30g
Carbohydrate	...10g	Saturates	.......4g

 35 MINS   0 MINS

SERVES 4

INGREDIENTS

500 g/1 lb 2 oz tomatoes

200 g/7 oz can tuna fish, drained

2 tbsp chopped fresh parsley

½ cucumber

1 small red onion, sliced

225 g/8 oz cooked green beans

1 small red (bell) pepper, cored and
    deseeded

1 small crisp lettuce

6 tbsp Italian-style dressing

3 hard-boiled (hard-cooked) eggs

60 g/2 oz can anchovies, drained

12 black olives, pitted

1 Cut the tomatoes into wedges, flake the tuna and put both into the bowl with the parsley.

2 Cut the cucumber in half lengthways, then cut into slices. Slice the onion. Add the cucumber and onion to the bowl.

3 Cut the beans in half, chop the (bell) pepper and add both to the bowl with the lettuce leaves. Pour over the dressing and toss to mix, then spoon into a salad bowl. Cut the eggs into quarters, arrange over the top with the anchovies and scatter with the olives.

Italian Pasta Salad

Tomatoes and Mozzarella cheese are a classic Italian combination. Here they are joined with pasta and avocado for an extra touch of luxury.

NUTRITIONAL INFORMATION

Calories 541	Sugars 5g
Protein 12g	Fat 43g
Carbohydrate . . .29g	Saturates 10g

15 MINS   15 MINS

SERVES 4

INGREDIENTS

2 tbsp pine nuts (kernels)

175 g/6 oz/1½ cups dried fusilli

1 tbsp olive oil

6 tomatoes

225 g/8 oz Mozzarella cheese

1 large avocado pear

2 tbsp lemon juice

3 tbsp chopped fresh basil

salt and pepper

fresh basil sprigs, to garnish

DRESSING

6 tbsp extra virgin olive oil

2 tbsp white wine vinegar

1 tsp wholegrain mustard

pinch of sugar

 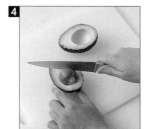 

1 Spread the pine nuts (kernels) out on a baking tray (cookie sheet) and toast them under a preheated grill (broiler) for 1–2 minutes. Remove and set aside to cool.

2 Bring a large saucepan of lightly salted water to the boil. Add the fusilli and olive oil and cook for 8–10 minutes or until tender, but still firm to the bite. Drain the pasta and refresh in cold water. Drain again and set aside to cool.

3 Thinly slice the tomatoes and the Mozzarella cheese.

4 Cut the avocado pear in half, then carefully remove the stone (pit) and skin. Cut into thin slices lengthways and sprinkle with lemon juice to prevent discoloration.

5 To make the dressing, whisk together the oil, vinegar, mustard and sugar in a small bowl, and season to taste with salt and pepper.

6 Arrange the tomatoes, Mozzarella cheese and avocado pear alternately in overlapping slices on to a large serving platter.

7 Toss the pasta with half of the dressing and the chopped basil and season to taste with salt and pepper. Spoon the pasta into the centre of the platter and pour over the remaining dressing. Sprinkle over the pine nuts (kernels), garnish with fresh basil sprigs and serve immediately.

Pasta with Pesto Vinaigrette

Sun-dried tomatoes and olives enhance this delicious pesto-inspired salad, which is just as tasty served cold.

NUTRITIONAL INFORMATION

Calories .... .275	Sugars 2g
Protein 9g	Fat .... .19g
Carbohydrate ...17g	Saturates 4g

35–40 MINS   15 MINS

SERVES 6

I N G R E D I E N T S

225 g/8 oz pasta spirals

4 tomatoes, skinned

60 g/2 oz/½ cup black olives

25 g/1 oz/¼ cup sun-dried tomatoes

2 tbsp pine kernels (nuts), toasted

2 tbsp Parmesan shavings

sprig of fresh basil, to garnish

P E S T O   V I N A I G R E T T E

4 tbsp chopped fresh basil

1 garlic clove, crushed

2 tbsp freshly grated Parmesan

4 tbsp olive oil

2 tbsp lemon juice

pepper

1 Cook the pasta in a saucepan of boiling salted water for 8–10 minutes or until 'al dente'. Drain the pasta and rinse well in hot water, then drain again thoroughly.

2 To make the vinaigrette, whisk the basil, garlic, Parmesan, olive oil, lemon juice and pepper until well blended.

3 Put the pasta into a bowl, pour over the basil vinaigrette and toss thoroughly.

4 Cut the tomatoes into wedges. Halve and pit the olives and slice the sun-dried tomatoes.

5 Add the tomatoes, olives and sun-dried tomatoes to the pasta and mix.

6 Transfer to a salad bowl and scatter the nuts and Parmesan shavings over the top. Serve warm, garnished with a sprig of basil.

Vegetable & Pasta Salad

Roasted vegetables and pasta make a delicious, colourful salad, ideal as a starter or to serve with a platter of cold meats.

NUTRITIONAL INFORMATION

Calories	462	Sugars	.........9g
Protein	........11g	Fat	..........32g
Carbohydrate	...33g	Saturates	.......7g

 1½ HOURS   1 HOUR

SERVES 4

I N G R E D I E N T S

2 small aubergines (eggplant), thinly sliced

1 large onion, sliced

2 large beef-steak tomatoes, skinned and cut into wedges

1 red (bell) pepper, cored, seeded and sliced

1 fennel bulb, thinly sliced

2 garlic cloves, sliced

4 tbsp olive oil

175 g/6 oz small pasta shapes

90 g/3 oz/½ cup Feta cheese, crumbled

a few basil leaves, torn

salt and pepper

salad leaves, to serve

D R E S S I N G

5 tbsp olive oil

juice of 1 orange

1 tsp grated orange zest

¼ tsp paprika

4 canned anchovies, finely chopped

1 Place the sliced aubergines (eggplant) in a colander, sprinkle with salt and set them aside for about 1 hour to draw out some of the bitter juices. Rinse under cold, running water to remove the salt, then drain. Toss on paper towels to dry.

2 Arrange the aubergines (eggplant), onion, tomatoes, (bell) pepper, fennel and garlic in a single layer in an ovenproof dish, sprinkle on 3 tablespoons of the oil and season. Bake uncovered in a preheated oven, at 220°C/450°F/Gas Mark 7, for 45 minutes, or until the vegetables begin to turn brown. Remove from the oven and set aside to cool.

3 Cook the pasta in a large pan of boiling salted water, to which you have added the remaining olive oil, for 8–10 minutes or until tender. Drain the pasta, then transfer to a bowl.

4 To make the dressing, mix together the olive oil, orange juice, orange zest and paprika. Stir in the finely chopped anchovies and season with pepper to taste. Pour the dressing over the pasta while it is still hot, and toss well. Set the pasta aside to cool.

5 To assemble the salad, line a shallow serving dish with the salad leaves and arrange the cold roasted vegetables in the centre. Spoon the pasta in a ring around the vegetables and scatter over the Feta cheese and basil leaves. Serve the salad at once.

Tomato & Basil Salad

These extra-large tomatoes make an excellent salad, especially when combined with basil, garlic, kiwi fruit, onion rings and new potatoes.

NUTRITIONAL INFORMATION

Calories 167	Sugars 4g
Protein 2g	Fat 11g
Carbohydrate ...16g	Saturates 2g

35 MINS   15 MINS

SERVES 8

INGREDIENTS

500 g/1 lb 2 oz tiny new or salad potatoes, scrubbed

4–5 extra-large tomatoes

2 kiwi fruit

1 onion, sliced very thinly

2 tbsp roughly chopped fresh basil leaves

fresh basil leaves, to garnish

DRESSING

4 tbsp virgin olive oil

2 tbsp balsamic vinegar

1 garlic clove, crushed

2 tbsp mayonnaise or soured cream

salt and pepper

1 Cook the potatoes in their skins in a saucepan of salted water for about 10–15 minutes or until just tender. Drain the potatoes thoroughly.

2 To make the dressing, whisk together the oil, vinegar, garlic and salt and pepper to taste until completely emulsified. Transfer half of the dressing to another bowl and whisk in the mayonnaise or soured cream.

3 Add the creamy dressing to the warm potatoes and toss thoroughly, then leave until cold.

4 Wipe the tomatoes and slice thinly. Peel the kiwi fruit and cut into thin slices. Layer the tomatoes with the kiwi fruit, slices of onion and chopped basil in a fairly shallow dish, leaving a space in the centre for the potatoes.

5 Spoon the potatoes in their dressing into the centre of the tomato salad.

6 Drizzle a little of the dressing over the tomatoes, or serve separately in a bowl or jug. Garnish the salad with fresh basil leaves. Cover the dish with cling film (plastic wrap) and chill until ready to serve.

COOK'S TIP

Ordinary tomatoes can be used for this salad, but make sure they are firm and bright red. You will need 8–10 ordinary-sized tomatoes.

Artichoke Salad

Use bottled artichokes rather than canned ones if possible, as they have a better flavour.

NUTRITIONAL INFORMATION

Calories	139	Sugars	.........4g
Protein	.........2g	Fat	..........12g
Carbohydrate	....6g	Saturates	.......1g

 30 MINS   0 MINS

SERVES 4

INGREDIENTS

250 ml/9 fl oz bottle of artichokes
  in oil, drained

4 small tomatoes

25 g/1 oz/¼ cup sun-dried tomatoes,
cut into strips

25 g/1 oz/¼ cup black olives,
  halved and pitted

25 g/1 oz/¼ cup Parma ham (prosciutto),
  cut into strips

1 tbsp chopped fresh basil

DRESSING

3 tbsp olive oil

1 tbsp wine vinegar

1 small garlic clove, crushed

½ tsp mustard

1 tsp clear honey

salt and pepper

1 Drain the artichokes thoroughly, then cut them into quarters and place in a bowl.

2 Cut each tomato into 6 wedges and place in the bowl with the sun-dried tomatoes, olives and Parma ham (prosciutto).

3 To make the dressing, put all the ingredients into a screw-top jar and shake vigorously until the ingredients are thoroughly blended.

4 Pour the dressing over the salad and toss well together. Transfer the salad to individual plates and sprinkle with the chopped basil.

Italian Mozzarella Salad

This colourful salad is packed full of delicious flavours but is easy to make.

NUTRITIONAL INFORMATION

Calories	79	Sugars	.........2g
Protein	.........4g	Fat	...........6g
Carbohydrate	....2g	Saturates	.......2g

 20 MINS   0 MINS

SERVES 6

I N G R E D I E N T S

200 g/7 oz baby spinach

125 g/4 ½ oz watercress

125 g/4 ½ oz Mozzarella cheese

225 g/8 oz cherry tomatoes

2 tsp balsamic vinegar

1 ½ tbsp extra virgin olive oil

salt and pepper

1 Wash the spinach and watercress and drain thoroughly on absorbent kitchen paper. Remove any tough stalks. Place the spinach and watercress leaves in a large serving dish.

2 Cut the Mozzarella into small pieces and scatter them over the spinach and watercress leaves.

3 Cut the cherry tomatoes in half and scatter them over the salad.

4 Sprinkle over the balsamic vinegar and oil, and season with salt and pepper to taste. Toss the mixture together to coat the leaves. Serve at once or leave to chill in the refrigerator until required.

Cherry Tomato & Pasta Salad

Pasta tastes perfect in this lively salad, dressed with red wine vinegar, lemon juice, basil and olive oil.

NUTRITIONAL INFORMATION

Calories	228	Sugars	.........4g
Protein	.........5g	Fat	..........12g
Carbohydrate	...27g	Saturates	.......2g

50 MINS   20 MINS

SERVES 4

I N G R E D I E N T S

175 g/6 oz/1½ cups pasta shapes

1 yellow (bell) pepper, halved, cored and deseeded

2 small courgettes (zucchini), sliced

1 red onion, sliced thinly

125 g/4½ oz cherry tomatoes, halved

a handful of fresh basil leaves, torn into small pieces

salt

sprigs of fresh basil, to garnish

D R E S S I N G

4 tbsp olive oil

2 tbsp red wine vinegar

2 tsp lemon juice

1 tsp mustard

½ tsp caster (superfine) sugar

salt and pepper

1 Cook the pasta in a pan of boiling, lightly salted water for 8–10 minutes, or until just tender.

2 Meanwhile, place the (bell) pepper halves, skin-side uppermost, under a preheated grill (broiler) until they just begin to char. Leave them to cool, then peel and slice them into strips.

3 Cook the courgettes (zucchini) in a small amount of boiling, lightly salted water for 3–4 minutes, until cooked, yet still crunchy. Drain and refresh under cold running water to cool quickly.

4 To make the dressing, mix together the olive oil, red wine vinegar, lemon juice, mustard and sugar. Season well with salt and pepper. Add the basil leaves.

5 Drain the pasta well and tip it into a large serving bowl. Add the dressing and toss well. Add the pepper, courgettes (zucchini), onion and cherry tomatoes, stirring to combine. Cover and leave at room temperature for about 30 minutes to allow the flavours to develop.

6 Serve, garnished with a few sprigs of fresh basil.

Mozzarella with Radicchio

Sliced Mozzarella is served with tomatoes and radicchio, which is singed over hot coals and drizzled with pesto dressing.

NUTRITIONAL INFORMATION

Calories 413	Sugars 6g	
Protcin 12g	Fat 38g	
Carbohydrate 6g	Saturates 14g	

   15 MINS   2–3 MINS

SERVES 4

INGREDIENTS

500 g/1 lb 2 oz Mozzarella

4 large tomatoes, sliced

2 radicchio

DRESSING

fresh basil leaves, to garnish

1 tbsp red or green pesto

6 tbsp virgin olive oil

3 tbsp red wine vinegar

handful of fresh basil leaves

salt and pepper

1 To make the dressing, mix the pesto, oil and red wine vinegar together.

2 Tear the basil leaves into tiny pieces and add them to the dressing. Season.

3 Slice the Mozzarella thinly and arrange on 4 serving plates with the tomatoes.

4 Leaving the root end on the radicchio, slice each one into quarters. Barbecue (grill) them quickly, so that the leaves singe on the outside. Place two quarters on each serving plate.

5 Drizzle the dressing over the radicchio, cheese and tomatoes. Garnish with extra basil leaves and serve.

Sesame Seed Salad

This salad uses tahini paste (sesame seed paste) as a flavouring for the dressing, which complements the aubergine (eggplant).

NUTRITIONAL INFORMATION

Calories 89	Sugars 1g
Protein 3g	Fat 8g
Carbohydrate 1g	Saturates 1g

45 MINS   15 MINS

SERVES 4

INGREDIENTS

1 large aubergine (eggplant)

3 tbsp tahini paste
   (sesame seed paste)

juice and rind of 1 lemon

1 garlic clove, crushed

pinch of paprika

1 tbsp chopped coriander (cilantro)

salt and pepper

Little Gem lettuce leaves

GARNISH

strips of pimiento

lemon wedges

toasted sesame seeds

1 Cut the aubergine (eggplant) in half, place in a colander and sprinkle with salt. Leave to stand for 30 minutes, rinse under cold running water and drain well. Pat dry with paper towels.

2 Place the aubergine (eggplant) halves, skin-side uppermost, on an oiled baking tray (cookie sheet). Cook in a preheated oven, 230°C/450°F/Gas Mark 8, for 10–15 minutes. Remove from the oven and allow to cool.

3 Cut the aubergine (eggplant) into cubes and set aside until required. Mix the tahini paste (sesame seed paste), lemon juice and rind, garlic, paprika and coriander (cilantro) together. Season with salt and pepper to taste and stir in the aubergine (eggplant).

4 Line a serving dish with lettuce leaves and spoon the aubergine (eggplant) into the centre. Garnish the salad with pimiento slices, lemon wedges and toasted sesame seeds and serve.

COOK'S TIP

Tahini paste (sesame seed paste) is a nutty-flavoured sauce available from most health food shops.

Pink Grapefruit & Cheese Salad

Fresh pink grapefruit segments, ripe avocados and sliced Italian Dolcelatte cheese make a deliciously different salad combination.

NUTRITIONAL INFORMATION

Calories 390	Sugars 3g	
Protein 13g	Fat 36g	
Carbohydrate 4g	Saturates 13g	

 25 MINS   0 MINS

SERVES 4

INGREDIENTS

½ cos (romaine) lettuce

½ oak leaf lettuce

2 pink grapefruit

2 ripe avocados

175 g/6 oz Dolcelatte cheese, sliced thinly

sprigs of fresh basil, to garnish

DRESSING

4 tbsp olive oil

1 tbsp white wine vinegar

salt and pepper

1 Arrange the lettuce leaves on 4 serving plates or in a salad bowl.

2 Remove the peel and pith from the grapefruit with a sharp serrated knife, catching the grapefruit juice in a bowl.

3 Segment the grapefruit by cutting down each side of the membrane. Remove all the membrane. Arrange the segments on the serving plates.

4 Peel, stone (pit) and slice the avocados, dipping them in the grapefruit juice to prevent them from going brown. Arrange the slices on the salad with the Dolcelatte cheese.

5 To make the dressing, combine any remaining grapefruit juice with the olive oil and wine vinegar. Season with salt and pepper to taste, mixing well to combine.

6 Drizzle the dressing over the salads. Garnish with fresh basil leaves and serve at once.

COOK'S TIP

Pink grapefruit segments make a very attractive colour combination with the avocados, but ordinary grapefruit will work just as well. To help avocados to ripen, keep them at room temperature in a brown paper bag.

Pasta

The simplicity and satisfying nature of pasta in all its varieties makes it a universal favourite. Easy to cook and economical, pasta is wonderfully versatile. It can be served with sauces made from meat, fish or vegetables, or baked in the oven. The classic Spaghetti Bolognese needs no introduction, and yet it is said that there are almost as

many versions of this delicious regional dish as there are lovers of Italian food! Fish and seafood are irresistible combined with pasta and need only the briefest of cooking times. Pasta combined with vegetables provides inspiration for countless dishes which will please vegetarians and meat-eaters alike. The delicious pasta dishes in this chapter range from easy, economic mid-week suppers to sophisticated and elegant meals for special occasions.

Pasta Carbonara

Lightly cooked eggs and pancetta are combined with cheese to make this rich, classic sauce.

NUTRITIONAL INFORMATION

Calories . . . . . . .547 Sugars 1g
Protein . . . . .21g Fat 31g
Carbohydrate . . .49g Saturates 14g

 15 MINS   🕐 20 MINS

SERVES 4

I N G R E D I E N T S

1 tbsp olive oil

40 g/1½ oz/3 tbsp butter

100 g/3½ oz pancetta or
   unsmoked bacon, diced

3 eggs, beaten

2 tbsp milk

1 tbsp thyme, stalks removed

675 g/1½ lb fresh or 350 g/12 oz dried
   conchigoni rigati

50 g/1¾ oz Parmesan cheese, grated

salt and pepper

1 Heat the oil and butter in a frying pan (skillet) until the mixture is just beginning to froth.

2 Add the pancetta or bacon to the pan and cook for 5 minutes or until browned all over.

3 Mix together the eggs and milk in a small bowl. Stir in the thyme and season to taste with salt and pepper.

4 Cook the pasta in a saucepan of boiling water for 8–10 minutes until tender, but still has 'bite'. Drain thoroughly.

5 Add the cooked, drained pasta to the frying pan (skillet) with the eggs and cook over a high heat for about 30 seconds or until the eggs just begin to cook and set. Do not overcook the eggs or they will become rubbery.

6 Add half of the grated Parmesan cheese, stirring to combine.

7 Transfer the pasta to a serving plate, pour over the sauce and toss to mix well.

8 Sprinkle the rest of the grated Parmesan over the top and serve immediately.

VARIATION

For an extra rich Carbonara sauce, stir in 4 tablespoons of double (heavy) cream with the eggs and milk in step 3. Follow exactly the same cooking method.

Spaghetti Bolognese

The original recipe takes about 4 hours to cook and should be left over night to allow the flavours to mingle. This version is much quicker.

NUTRITIONAL INFORMATION

Calories 591	Sugars 7g
Protein 29g	Fat 24g
Carbohydrate . . .64g	Saturates 9g

 20 MINS   1 HR 5 MINS

SERVES 4

I N G R E D I E N T S

1 tbsp olive oil

1 onion, finely chopped

2 garlic cloves, chopped

1 carrot, scraped and chopped

1 stick celery, chopped

50 g/1¾ oz pancetta or streaky bacon, diced

350 g/12 oz lean minced beef

400 g/14 oz can chopped tomatoes

2 tsp dried oregano

125 ml/4 fl oz/scant ½ cup red wine

2 tbsp tomato purée (paste)

salt and pepper

675 g/1½ lb fresh spaghetti or 350 g/12 oz
   dried spaghetti

1 Heat the oil in a large frying pan (skillet). Add the onions and cook for 3 minutes.

2 Add the garlic, carrot, celery and pancetta or bacon and sauté for 3–4 minutes or until just beginning to brown.

3 Add the beef and cook over a high heat for another 3 minutes or until all of the meat is brown.

4 Stir in the tomatoes, oregano and red wine and bring to the boil. Reduce the heat and leave to simmer for about 45 minutes.

5 Stir in the tomato purée (paste) and season with salt and pepper.

6 Cook the spaghetti in a pan of boiling water for 8–10 minutes until tender, but still has 'bite'. Drain thoroughly.

7 Transfer the spaghetti to a serving plate and pour over the bolognese sauce. Toss to mix well and serve hot.

VARIATION

Try adding 25 g/1 oz dried porcini, soaked for 10 minutes in 2 tablespoons of warm water, to the bolognese sauce in step 4, if you wish.

Chicken & Tomato Lasagne

This variation of the traditional beef dish has layers of pasta and chicken or turkey baked in red wine, tomatoes and a delicious cheese sauce.

NUTRITIONAL INFORMATION

Calories	550	Sugars	........11g
Protein	........35g	Fat	..........29g
Carbohydrate	...34g	Saturates	......12g

 20 MINS 1¼ HOURS

SERVES 4

INGREDIENTS

350 g/12 oz fresh lasagne (about 9 sheets)

　or 150 g/5½ oz dried lasagne

　(about 9 sheets)

1 tbsp olive oil

1 red onion, finely chopped

1 garlic clove, crushed

100 g/3½ oz mushrooms, wiped and sliced

350 g/12 oz chicken or turkey breast, cut

　into chunks

150 ml/¼ pint/⅔ cup red wine, diluted with

　100 ml/3½ fl oz/scant ⅓ cup water

250 g/9 oz passata (sieved tomatoes)

1 tsp sugar

BECHAMEL SAUCE

75 g/2¾ oz/5 tbsp butter

50 g/1¾ oz plain (all-purpose) flour

600 ml/1 pint/2½ cups milk

1 egg, beaten

75 g/2¾ oz Parmesan cheese, grated

salt and pepper

1 Cook the lasagne in a pan of boiling water according to the instructions on the packet. Lightly grease a deep ovenproof dish.

2 Heat the oil in a pan. Add the onion and garlic and cook for 3–4 minutes. Add the mushrooms and chicken and stir-fry for 4 minutes or until the meat browns.

3 Add the wine, bring to the boil, then simmer for 5 minutes. Stir in the passata (sieved tomatoes) and sugar and cook for 3–5 minutes until the meat is tender and cooked through. The sauce should have thickened, but still be quite runny.

4 To make the Béchamel Sauce, melt the butter in a pan, stir in the flour and cook for 2 minutes. Remove the pan from the heat and gradually add the milk, mixing to form a smooth sauce. Return the pan to the heat and bring to the boil, stirring until thickened. Leave to cool slightly, then beat in the egg and half of the cheese. Season to taste.

5 Place 3 sheets of lasagne in the base of the dish and spread with half of the chicken mixture. Repeat the layers. Top with the last 3 sheets of lasagne, pour over the Béchamel Sauce and sprinkle with the Parmesan. Bake in a preheated oven, at 190°C/375°F/Gas Mark 5, for 30 minutes until golden and the pasta is cooked.

Traditional Cannelloni

You can buy ready made dried pasta tubes. However, if using fresh pasta (see page 24), you must cut out squares and roll them yourself.

NUTRITIONAL INFORMATION

Calories	342	Sugars	.........6g
Protein	........15g	Fat	..........15g
Carbohydrate	...38g	Saturates	.......8g

 50 MINS   30 MINS

SERVES 4

INGREDIENTS

20 tubes dried cannelloni (about 200 g/
  7 oz) or 20 square sheets of fresh pasta
  (about 350 g/12 oz)

250 g/9 oz ricotta cheese

150 g/5½ oz frozen spinach, defrosted

½ small red (bell) pepper, diced

2 spring onions (scallions), chopped

150 ml/¼ pint/⅔ cup hot vegetable or
  chicken stock

1 portion of Basil & Tomato Sauce
  (see page 364)

25 g/1 oz Parmesan or pecorino cheese,
  grated

salt and pepper

1 If you are using dried cannelloni, check the packet instructions; many varieties do not need pre-cooking. If necessary, pre-cook your pasta: bring a large saucepan of water to the boil, add 1 tablespoon of oil and cook the pasta for 3–4 minutes – it is far easier to do this in batches.

2 In a bowl, mix together the ricotta, spinach, (bell) pepper, and spring onions (scallions) and season to taste with salt and pepper.

3 Lightly butter an ovenproof dish, large enough to contain all of the pasta tubes in a single layer. Spoon the ricotta mixture into the pasta tubes and place them into the prepared dish. If you are using fresh sheets of pasta, spread the ricotta mixture along one side of each fresh pasta square and roll up to form a tube.

4 Mix together the stock and Basil and Tomato Sauce and pour over the pasta tubes.

5 Sprinkle the Parmesan or pecorino cheese over the cannelloni and bake

in a preheated oven, 190°C/375°F/Gas Mark 5, for 20–25 minutes or until the pasta is cooked through. Serve.

VARIATION

If you would prefer a creamier version, omit the stock and the Basil and Tomato sauce and replace with Béchamel Sauce (see page 336).

Tagliatelle & Chicken Sauce

Spinach ribbon noodles covered with a rich tomato sauce and topped with creamy chicken makes a very appetizing dish.

NUTRITIONAL INFORMATION

Calories 853	Sugars 6g	
Protein 32g	Fat 71g	
Carbohydrate . . .23g	Saturates 34g	

  30 MINS   25 MINS

SERVES 4

I N G R E D I E N T S

Basic Tomato Sauce (see page 28)

225 g/8 oz fresh green ribbon noodles

1 tbsp olive oil

salt

basil leaves, to garnish

CHICKEN SAUCE

60 g/2 oz/¼ cup unsalted butter

400 g/14 oz boned, skinned chicken
    breast, thinly sliced

90 g/3 oz/¾ cup blanched almonds

300 ml/½ pint/1¼ cups double
    (heavy) cream

salt and pepper

basil leaves, to garnish

1 Make the tomato sauce, and keep warm.

2 To make the chicken sauce, melt the butter in a pan over a medium heat and fry the chicken strips and almonds for 5–6 minutes, stirring frequently, until the chicken is cooked through.

3 Meanwhile, pour the cream into a small pan over a low heat, bring it to the boil and boil for about 10 minutes, until reduced by almost half. Pour the cream over the chicken and almonds, stir well, and season with salt and pepper to taste. Set aside and keep warm.

4 Cook the pasta in a pan of boiling salted water, to which you have added the oil, for 8–10 minutes or until tender. Drain, then return to the pan, cover and keep warm.

5 Turn the pasta into a warmed serving dish and spoon the tomato sauce over it. Spoon the chicken and cream over the centre, scatter over the basil leaves and serve at once.

Meat & Pasta Loaf

The cheesy pasta layer comes as a pleasant surprise inside this lightly spiced meat loaf.

NUTRITIONAL INFORMATION

Calories 497	Sugars 4g
Protein 26g	Fat 37g
Carbohydrate ...16g	Saturates 16g

45 MINS   1¼ HOURS

SERVES 6

INGREDIENTS

25 g/1 oz/2 tbsp butter, plus extra
  for greasing

1 onion, chopped finely

1 small red (bell) pepper, cored, deseeded
  and chopped

1 garlic clove, chopped

500 g/1 lb 2 oz minced (ground) lean beef

25 g/1 oz/½ cup soft white breadcrumbs

½ tsp cayenne pepper

1 tbsp lemon juice

½ tsp grated lemon rind

2 tbsp chopped fresh parsley

90 g/3 oz short pasta, such as fusilli

4 bay leaves

1 tbsp olive oil

Cheese Sauce (see page 29)

175 g/6 oz streaky bacon rashers, rind
  removed

salt and pepper

salad leaves, to garnish

1 Melt the butter in a pan over a medium heat and fry the onion and pepper for about 3 minutes, until the onion is translucent. Stir in the garlic and cook for 1 minute.

2 Put the meat into a large bowl and mash it with a wooden spoon until it becomes a sticky paste. Tip in the fried vegetables and stir in the breadcrumbs, cayenne, lemon juice, lemon rind and parsley. Season the mixture with salt and pepper and set aside.

3 Cook the pasta in a large pan of boiling water, to which you have added salt and the olive oil, for 8–10 minutes or until tender. Drain the pasta, then stir it into the cheese sauce.

4 Grease a 1 kg/2 lb 4 oz loaf tin (pan) and arrange the bay leaves in the base. Stretch the bacon rashers with the back of a knife blade and arrange them to line the base and the sides of the tin (pan).

5 Spoon in half of the meat mixture, level the surface and cover it with the pasta. Spoon in the remaining meat mixture, level the top and cover the tin (pan) with foil.

6 Cook the meat loaf in the preheated oven, 180°C/350°F/Gas Mark 4, for 1 hour, or until the juices run clear and the loaf has shrunk away from the sides of the tin (pan). Pour off any excess fat from the tin (pan) and turn the loaf out on a warmed serving dish. Garnish with the salad leaves and serve hot.

Tortelloni

These tasty little squares of pasta stuffed with mushrooms and cheese are surprisingly filling. This recipe makes 36 tortelloni.

NUTRITIONAL INFORMATION

Calories . . . . . . .360 Sugars 1g
Protein . . . . .9g Fat 21g
Carbohydrate . . .36g Saturates 12g

 1¼ HOURS   25 MINS

SERVES 4

INGREDIENTS

about 300 g/10½ oz fresh pasta (see page 24), rolled out to thin sheets

75 g/2¾ oz/5 tbsp butter

50 g/1¾ oz shallots, finely chopped

3 garlic clove, crushed

50 g/1¾ oz mushrooms, wiped and finely chopped

½ stick celery, finely chopped

25 g/1 oz pecorino cheese, finely grated, plus extra to garnish

1 tbsp oil

salt and pepper

1 Using a serrated pasta cutter, cut 5 cm/2 inch squares from the sheets of fresh pasta. To make 36 tortelloni you will need 72 squares. Once the pasta is cut, cover the squares with cling film (plastic wrap) to stop them drying out.

2 Heat 25 g/1 oz/3 tbsp of the butter in a frying pan (skillet). Add the shallots, 1 crushed garlic clove, the mushrooms and celery and cook for 4–5 minutes.

3 Remove the pan from the heat, stir in the cheese and season with salt and pepper to taste.

4 Spoon ½ teaspoon of the mixture on to the middle of 36 pasta squares. Brush the edges of the squares with water and top with the remaining 36 squares. Press the edges together to seal. Leave to rest for 5 minutes.

5 Bring a large pan of water to the boil, add the oil and cook the tortelloni, in batches, for 2–3 minutes. The tortelloni will rise to the surface when cooked and the pasta should be tender with a slight 'bite'. Remove from the pan with a perforated spoon and drain thoroughly.

6 Meanwhile, melt the remaining butter in a pan. Add the remaining garlic and plenty of pepper and cook for 1–2 minutes. Transfer the tortelloni to serving plates and pour over the garlic butter. Garnish with grated pecorino cheese and serve immediately.

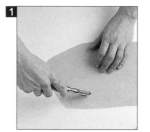

Tagliatelle with Meatballs

There is an appetizing contrast of textures and flavours in this satisfying family dish.

NUTRITIONAL INFORMATION

Calories	910	Sugars	. . . . .13g
Protein	. . . . .40g	Fat	. . . . .54g
Carbohydrate	. . .65g	Saturates	. . . . . .19g

45 MINS   1 HR 5 MINS

SERVES 4

I N G R E D I E N T S

500 g/1 lb 2 oz minced (ground) lean beef

60 g/2 oz/1 cup soft white breadcrumbs

1 garlic clove, crushed

2 tbsp chopped fresh parsley

1 tsp dried oregano

large pinch of freshly grated nutmeg

¼ tsp ground coriander

60 g/2 oz/½ cup Parmesan, grated

2–3 tbsp milk

flour, for dusting

4 tbsp olive oil

400 g/14 oz tagliatelle

25 g/1 oz/2 tbsp butter, diced

salt and pepper

S A U C E

3 tbsp olive oil

2 large onions, sliced

2 celery sticks, sliced thinly

2 garlic cloves, chopped

400 g/14 oz can chopped tomatoes

125 g/4½ oz bottled sun-dried tomatoes, drained and chopped

2 tbsp tomato purée (paste)

1 tbsp dark muscovado sugar

150 ml/¼ pint/⅔ cup white wine, or water

1 To make the sauce, heat the oil in a frying pan (skillet) and fry the onions and celery until translucent. Add the garlic and cook for 1 minute. Stir in the tomatoes, tomato purée (paste), sugar and wine, and season. Bring to the boil and simmer for 10 minutes.

2 Meanwhile, break up the meat in a bowl with a wooden spoon until it becomes a sticky paste. Stir in the breadcrumbs, garlic, herbs and spices. Stir in the cheese and enough milk to make a firm paste. Flour your hands, take large spoonfuls of the mixture and shape it into 12 balls. Heat 3 tbsp of the oil in a frying pan (skillet) and fry the meatballs for 5–6 minutes until browned.

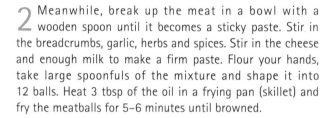

3 Pour the tomato sauce over the meatballs. Lower the heat, cover the pan and simmer for 30 minutes, turning once or twice. Add a little extra water if the sauce begins to dry.

4 Cook the pasta in a large saucepan of boiling salted water, adding the remaining oil, for 8–10 minutes or until tender. Drain the pasta, then turn into a warmed serving dish, dot with the butter and toss with two forks. Spoon the meatballs and sauce over the pasta and serve.

Stuffed Cannelloni

Cannelloni, the thick round pasta tubes, make perfect containers for close-textured sauces of all kinds.

NUTRITIONAL INFORMATION

Calories 575   Sugars 6g
Protein . . . . .22g   Fat 42g
Carbohydrate . . .28g   Saturates 21g

30 MINS   1¼ HOURS

SERVES 4

I N G R E D I E N T S

8 cannelloni tubes

1 tbsp olive oil

fresh herb sprigs, to garnish

F I L L I N G

25 g/1 oz/2 tbsp butter

300 g/10½ oz frozen spinach, defrosted and
   chopped

125 g/4½ oz /½ cup Ricotta

25 g/1 oz/¼ cup Parmesan, grated

60 g/2 oz/¼ cup chopped ham

¼ tsp freshly grated nutmeg

2 tbsp double (heavy) cream

2 eggs, lightly beaten

salt and pepper

S A U C E

25 g/1 oz/2 tbsp butter

25 g/1 oz/¼ cup plain (all-purpose) flour

300 ml/½ pint/1¼ cups milk

2 bay leaves

large pinch of grated nutmeg

25 g/1 oz /¼ cup Parmesan, grated

1 To prepare the filling, melt the butter in a pan and stir in the spinach. Cook for 2–3 minutes, stirring, to allow the moisture to evaporate, then remove the pan from the heat. Stir in the cheeses and the ham. Season with nutmeg, and salt and pepper. Beat in the cream and eggs to make a thick paste. Set aside to cool.

2 Cook the cannelloni in a large pan of boiling salted water, adding the olive oil, for 8–10 minutes, or until tender. Drain the cannelloni in a colander and set aside to cool.

3 To make the sauce, melt the butter in a pan, stir in the flour and, when it has formed a roux, gradually pour on the milk, stirring all the time. Add the bay leaves, bring to simmering point, and cook for 5 minutes. Season with nutmeg, salt and pepper. Remove the pan from the heat and discard the bay leaves.

4 To assemble the dish, spoon the filling into a piping bag and pipe it into each of the cannelloni tubes.

5 Spoon a little of the sauce into a shallow baking dish. Arrange the cannelloni in a single layer, then pour over the remaining sauce. Sprinkle on the remaining Parmesan cheese and bake in a preheated oven, 190°C/375°F/Gas Mark 5, for 40–45 minutes or until the sauce is golden brown and bubbling. Serve garnished with fresh herb sprigs.

Pasticciο

A recipe that has both Italian and Greek origins, this dish may be served hot or cold, cut into thick, satisfying squares.

NUTRITIONAL INFORMATION

Calories ....590 Sugars 8g
Protein ....34g Fat 39g
Carbohydrate ...23g Saturates 16g

35 MINS   1¼ HOURS

SERVES 6

INGREDIENTS

225 g/8 oz fusilli, or other short
   pasta shapes

1 tbsp olive oil

4 tbsp double (heavy) cream

salt

rosemary sprigs, to garnish

SAUCE

2 tbsp olive oil, plus extra for brushing

1 onion, sliced thinly

1 red (bell) pepper, cored, deseeded
   and chopped

2 cloves garlic, chopped

625 g/1 lb 6 oz minced (ground) lean beef

400 g/14 oz can chopped tomatoes

125 ml/4 fl oz/½ cup dry white wine

2 tbsp chopped fresh parsley

50 g/1¾ oz can anchovies, drained
   and chopped

salt and pepper

TOPPING

300 ml/½ pint/1¼ cups natural
   (unsweetened) yogurt

3 eggs

pinch of freshly grated nutmeg

40 g/1½ oz/⅓ cup Parmesan, grated

1 To make the sauce, heat the oil in a large frying pan (skillet) and fry the onion and red (bell) pepper for 3 minutes. Stir in the garlic and cook for 1 minute more. Stir in the beef and cook, stirring frequently, until no longer pink.

2 Add the tomatoes and wine, stir well and bring to the boil. Simmer, uncovered, for 20 minutes, or until the sauce is fairly thick. Stir in the parsley and anchovies, and season to taste.

3 Cook the pasta in a large pan of boiling salted water, adding the oil, for 8–10 minutes or until tender. Drain the pasta in a colander, then transfer to a bowl. Stir in the cream and set aside.

4 To make the topping, beat together the yogurt and eggs and season with nutmeg, and salt and pepper to taste.

5 Brush a shallow baking dish with oil. Spoon in half of the pasta and cover with half of the meat sauce. Repeat these layers, then spread the topping evenly over the final layer. Sprinkle the cheese on top.

6 Bake in a preheated oven, 190°C/ 375°F/Gas Mark 5, for 25 minutes, or until the topping is golden brown and bubbling. Garnish with sprigs of rosemary and serve with a selection of raw vegetable crudités.

Lasagne Verde

The sauce in this delicious baked pasta dish can be used as an alternative sauce for Spaghetti Bolognese (see page 335).

NUTRITIONAL INFORMATION

Calories 619	Sugars 7g
Protein 29g	Fat 45g
Carbohydrate . . .21g	Saturates 19g

  1³/₄ HOURS 🕐 55 MINS

SERVES 6

I N G R E D I E N T S

Ragù Sauce (see page 12)

1 tbsp olive oil

225 g/8 oz lasagne verde

Béchamel Sauce (see page 28)

60 g/2 oz/½ cup Parmesan, grated

salt and pepper

green salad, tomato salad or black olives,
to serve

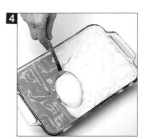

1 Begin by making the Ragù Sauce as described on page 12, but cook for 10–12 minutes longer than the time given, in an uncovered pan, to allow the excess liquid to evaporate. To layer the sauce with lasagne, it needs to be reduced to the consistency of a thick paste.

2 Have ready a large saucepan of boiling, salted water and add the olive oil. Drop the pasta sheets into the boiling water a few at a time, and return the water to the boil before adding further pasta sheets. If you are using fresh lasagne, cook the sheets for a total of 8 minutes. If you are using dried or partly precooked pasta, cook it according to the directions given on the packet.

3 Remove the pasta sheets from the saucepan with a slotted spoon. Spread them in a single layer on damp tea towels (dish cloths).

4 Grease a rectangular ovenproof dish, about 25–28 cm/10–11 inches long. To assemble the dish, spoon a little of the meat sauce into the prepared dish, cover with a layer of lasagne, then spoon over a little Béchamel Sauce and sprinkle with some of the cheese. Continue making layers in this way, covering the final layer of lasagne with the remaining Béchamel Sauce.

5 Sprinkle on the remaining cheese and bake in a preheated oven, 190°C/375°F/Gas Mark 5, for 40 minutes or until the sauce is golden brown and bubbling. Serve with a green salad, a tomato salad, or a bowl of black olives.

Vegetable Pasta Nests

These large pasta nests look impressive when presented filled with grilled (broiled) mixed vegetables, and taste delicious.

NUTRITIONAL INFORMATION

Calories	392	Sugars	.........1g
Protein	.........6g	Fat	.........28g
Carbohydrate	...32g	Saturates	.......9g

 25 MINS 40 MINS

SERVES 4

INGREDIENTS

175 g/6 oz spaghetti

1 aubergine (eggplant), halved and sliced

1 courgette (zucchini), diced

1 red (bell) pepper, seeded and chopped
   diagonally

6 tbsp olive oil

2 garlic cloves, crushed

50 g/1¾ oz/4 tbsp butter or margarine,
   melted

15 g/½ oz/1 tbsp dry white breadcrumbs

salt and pepper

fresh parsley sprigs, to garnish

1 Bring a large saucepan of water to the boil and cook the spaghetti for 8–10 minutes or until 'al dente'. Drain the spaghetti in a colander and set aside until required.

2 Place the aubergine (eggplant), courgette (zucchini) and (bell) pepper on a baking tray (cookie sheet).

3 Mix the oil and garlic together and pour over the vegetables, tossing to coat all over.

4 Cook under a preheated hot grill (broiler) for about 10 minutes, turning, until tender and lightly charred. Set aside and keep warm.

5 Divide the spaghetti among 4 lightly greased Yorkshire pudding tins (pans). Using 2 forks, curl the spaghetti to form nests.

6 Brush the pasta nests with melted butter or margarine and sprinkle with the breadcrumbs. Bake in a preheated oven, at 200°C/400°F/ Gas Mark 6, for 15 minutes or until lightly golden. Remove the pasta nests from the tins (pans) and transfer to serving plates. Divide the grilled (broiled) vegetables between the pasta nests, season and garnish.

COOK'S TIP

'Al dente' means 'to the bite' and describes cooked pasta that is not too soft, but still has a 'bite' to it.

Aubergine (Eggplant) Layers

Layers of toasty-brown aubergine (eggplant), meat sauce and cheese-flavoured pasta make this a popular family supper dish.

NUTRITIONAL INFORMATION

Calories 900	Sugars 10g	
Protein 43g	Fat 62g	
Carbohydrate . . .44g	Saturates 27g	

1½ HOURS   50 MINS

SERVES 4

INGREDIENTS

1 aubergine (eggplant), sliced thinly

5 tbsp olive oil

225 g/8 oz short pasta shapes, such as
   fusilli

60 g/2 oz/¼ cup butter, plus extra
   for greasing

45 g/1½ oz/6 tbsp plain (all-purpose) flour

300 ml/½ pint/1¼ cups milk

150 ml/¼ pint/⅔ cup single (light) cream

150 ml/¼ pint/⅔ cup chicken stock

large pinch of freshly grated nutmeg

90 g/3 oz/¾ cup mature (sharp)
   Cheddar, grated

25 g/1 oz/¼ cup Parmesan, grated

Lamb Sauce (see page 28)

salt and pepper

artichoke heart and tomato salad, to serve

1 Put the aubergine (eggplant) slices in a colander, sprinkle with salt and leave for about 45 minutes. Rinse under cold, running water and drain. Pat dry with paper towels.

2 Heat 4 tablespoons of the oil in a frying pan (skillet) over a medium heat. Fry the aubergine (eggplant) slices for about 4 minutes on each side, until golden. Remove with a slotted spoon and drain on paper towels.

3 Meanwhile, cook the pasta in a large pan of boiling salted water, adding 1 tablespoon of olive oil, for 8–10 minutes or until tender. Drain the pasta in a colander and return to the pan. Cover and keep warm.

4 Melt the butter in a small pan, stir in the flour and cook for 1 minute. Gradually pour in the milk, stirring all the time, then stir in the cream and chicken stock. Season with nutmeg and salt and pepper to taste, bring to the boil and simmer for 5 minutes. Stir in the Cheddar and remove from the heat. Pour half of the sauce over the pasta and mix well. Reserve the remaining sauce.

5 Grease a shallow ovenproof dish. Spoon in half of the pasta, cover with half of the Lamb Sauce and then with the aubergines (eggplant) in a single layer. Repeat the layers of pasta and Lamb Sauce and spread the remaining cheese sauce over the top. Sprinkle with Parmesan. Bake in the preheated oven, 190°C/375°F/Gas Mark 5, for 25 minutes, until golden brown. Serve hot or cold, with an artichoke heart and tomato salad.

Sicilian Spaghetti Cake

Any variety of long pasta could be used for this very tasty dish from Sicily.

NUTRITIONAL INFORMATION

Calories 876	Sugars 10g
Protein 37g	Fat 65g
Carbohydrate ...39g	Saturates 18g

 30 MINS 50 MINS

SERVES 4

INGREDIENTS

2 aubergines (eggplant), about 650 g/
   1 lb 7 oz

150 ml/¼ pint/⅔ cup olive oil

350 g/12 oz finely minced (ground)
   lean beef

1 onion, chopped

2 garlic cloves, crushed

2 tbsp tomato purée (paste)

400 g/14 oz can chopped tomatoes

1 tsp Worcestershire sauce

1 tsp chopped fresh oregano or marjoram
   or ½ tsp dried oregano or marjoram

45 g/1½ oz stoned black olives, sliced

1 green, red or yellow (bell) pepper, cored,
   deseeded and chopped

175 g/6 oz spaghetti

125 g/4½ oz/1 cup Parmesan, grated

1 Brush a 20 cm/8 inch loose-based round cake tin (pan) with olive oil, place a disc of baking parchment in the base and brush with oil. Trim the aubergines (eggplants) and cut into slanting slices, 5 mm/¼ inch thick. Heat some of the oil in a frying pan (skillet). Fry a few slices of aubergine (eggplant) at a time until lightly browned, turning once, and adding more oil as necessary. Drain on kitchen paper.

2 Put the minced (ground) beef, onion and garlic into a saucepan and cook, stirring frequently, until browned all over. Add the tomato purée (paste), tomatoes, Worcestershire sauce, herbs and seasoning. Simmer for 10 minutes, stirring occasionally, then add the olives and (bell) pepper and cook for 10 minutes.

3 Bring a large saucepan of salted water to the boil. Cook the spaghetti for 8–10 minutes or until just tender. Drain the spaghetti thoroughly. Turn the spaghetti into a bowl and mix in the meat mixture and Parmesan, tossing together with 2 forks.

4 Lay overlapping slices of aubergine (eggplant) over the base of the cake tin (pan) and up the sides. Add the meat mixture, pressing it down, and cover with the remaining aubergine (eggplant) slices.

5 Stand the cake tin (pan) in a baking tin (pan) and cook in a preheated oven, 200°C/400°F/Gas Mark 6, for 40 minutes. Leave to stand for 5 minutes then loosen around the edges and invert on to a warmed serving dish, releasing the tin (pan) clip. Remove the baking parchment. Serve immediately.

Penne & Butternut Squash

The creamy, nutty flavour of squash complements the 'al dente' texture of the pasta perfectly. This recipe has been adapted for the microwave.

NUTRITIONAL INFORMATION

Calories 499	Sugars 4g	
Protein 20g	Fat 26g	
Carbohydrate . . .49g	Saturates 13g	

15 MINS   30 MINS

SERVES 4

INGREDIENTS

2 tbsp olive oil

1 garlic clove, crushed

60 g/2 oz/1 cup fresh white breadcrumbs

500 g/1 lb 2 oz peeled and deseeded
   butternut squash

8 tbsp water

500 g/1 lb 2 oz fresh penne,
   or other pasta shape

15 g/½ oz/1 tbsp butter

1 onion, sliced

125 g/4½ oz/½ cup ham, cut into strips

200 ml/7 fl oz/scant cup single (light) cream

60 g/2 oz/½ cup Cheddar cheese, grated

2 tbsp chopped fresh parsley

salt and pepper

COOK'S TIP

If the squash weighs more than is needed for this recipe, blanch the excess for 3–4 minutes on HIGH power in a covered bowl with a little water. Drain, cool and place in a freezer bag. Store in the freezer for up to 3 months.

1 Mix together the oil, garlic and breadcrumbs and spread out on a large plate. Cook on HIGH power for 4–5 minutes, stirring every minute, until crisp and beginning to brown. Set aside.

2 Dice the squash. Place in a large bowl with half of the water. Cover and cook on HIGH power for 8–9 minutes, stirring occasionally. Leave to stand for 2 minutes.

3 Place the pasta in a large bowl, add a little salt and pour over boiling water to cover by 2.5 cm/1 inch. Cover and cook on HIGH power for 5 minutes, stirring once, until the pasta is just tender but still firm to the bite. Leave to stand, covered, for 1 minute before draining.

4 Place the butter and onion in a large bowl. Cover and cook on HIGH power for 3 minutes.

5 Coarsely mash the squash, using a fork. Add to the onion with the pasta, ham, cream, cheese, parsley and remaining water. Season generously and mix well. Cover and cook on HIGH power for 4 minutes until heated through.

6 Serve the pasta sprinkled with the crisp garlic crumbs.

Spaghetti, Tuna & Parsley

This is a recipe to look forward to when parsley is at its most prolific, in the growing season.

NUTRITIONAL INFORMATION

Calories	970	Sugars	.........2g
Protein	........23g	Fat	..........80g
Carbohydrate	...42g	Saturates	......18g

 10 MINS   15 MINS

SERVES 4

I N G R E D I E N T S

500 g/1 lb 2 oz spaghetti

1 tbsp olive oil

25 g/1 oz/2 tbsp butter

black olives, to serve (optional)

S A U C E

200 g/7 oz can tuna, drained

60 g/2 oz can anchovies, drained

250 ml/9 fl oz/1 cup olive oil

250 ml/9 fl oz/1 cup roughly chopped fresh, flat-leaf parsley

150 ml/¼ pint/⅔ cup crème fraîche

salt and pepper

1 Cook the spaghetti in a large saucepan of salted boiling water, adding the olive oil, for 8–10 minutes or until tender. Drain the spaghetti in a colander and return to the pan. Add the butter, toss thoroughly to coat and keep warm until required.

2 Remove any bones from the tuna and flake into smaller pieces, using 2 forks. Put the tuna in a blender or food processor with the anchovies, olive oil and parsley and process until the sauce is smooth. Pour in the crème fraîche and process for a few seconds to blend. Taste the sauce and season with salt and pepper.

3 Warm 4 plates. Shake the saucepan of spaghetti over a medium heat for a few minutes or until it is thoroughly warmed through.

4 Pour the sauce over the spaghetti and toss quickly, using 2 forks. Serve immediately with a small dish of black olives, if liked.

Pasta Vongole

Fresh clams are available from most good fishmongers. If you prefer, used canned clams, which are less messy to eat but not as attractive.

NUTRITIONAL INFORMATION

Calories 410	Sugars 1g
Protein 39g	Fat 9g
Carbohydrate . . .39g	Saturates 1g

 20 MINS 20 MINS

SERVES 4

INGREDIENTS

675 g/1½ lb fresh clams or 1 x 290 g/10 oz
  can clams, drained

400 g/14 oz mixed seafood, such as
  prawns (shrimps), squid and mussels,
  defrosted if frozen

2 tbsp olive oil

2 cloves garlic, finely chopped

150 ml/¼ pint/⅔ cup white wine

150 ml/¼ pint/⅔ cup fish stock

2 tbsp chopped tarragon

salt and pepper

675 g/1½ lb fresh pasta or
  350 g/12 oz dried pasta

VARIATION

Red clam sauce can be made by adding 8 tablespoons of passata (sieved tomatoes) to the sauce along with the stock in step 4. Follow the same cooking method.

1 If you are using fresh clams, scrub them clean and discard any that are already open.

2 Heat the oil in a large frying pan (skillet). Add the garlic and the clams to the pan and cook for 2 minutes, shaking the pan to ensure that all of the clams are coated in the oil.

3 Add the remaining seafood mixture to the pan and cook for a further 2 minutes.

4 Pour the wine and stock over the mixed seafood and garlic and bring to the boil. Cover the pan, reduce the heat and leave to simmer for 8–10 minutes or until the shells open. Discard any clams or mussels that do not open.

5 Meanwhile, cook the pasta in a saucepan of boiling water for 8–10 minutes or until it is cooked through, but still has 'bite'. Drain the pasta thoroughly.

6 Stir the tarragon into the sauce and season with salt and pepper to taste.

7 Transfer the pasta to a serving plate and pour over the sauce. Serve immediately.

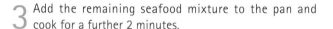

Spaghetti & Shellfish

Frozen shelled prawns (shrimp) from the freezer can become the star ingredient in this colourful and tasty dish.

NUTRITIONAL INFORMATION

Calories	.510	Sugars	.38g
Protein	.33g	Fat	.24g
Carbohydrate	.44g	Saturates	.11g

 35 MINS   30 MINS

SERVES 4

INGREDIENTS

225 g/8 oz short-cut spaghetti, or long
   spaghetti broken into 15 cm/6 inch
   lengths

2 tbsp olive oil

300 ml/½ pint/1¼ cups chicken stock

1 tsp lemon juice

1 small cauliflower, cut into florets

2 carrots, sliced thinly

125 g/4½ oz mangetout (snow peas),
   trimmed

60 g/2 oz/¼ cup butter

1 onion, sliced

225 g/8 oz courgettes (zucchini),
   sliced thinly

1 garlic clove, chopped

350 g/12 oz frozen shelled prawns
   (shrimp), defrosted

2 tbsp chopped fresh parsley

25 g/1 oz/¼ cup Parmesan, grated

salt and pepper

½ tsp paprika, to sprinkle

4 unshelled prawns (shrimp),
   to garnish (optional)

1   Cook the spaghetti in a large pan of boiling salted water, adding 1 tbsp of the oil, for 8–10 minutes or until tender. Drain, then return to the pan and stir in the remaining oil. Cover and keep warm.

2   Bring the chicken stock and lemon juice to the boil. Add the cauliflower and carrots and cook for 3–4 minutes until they are barely tender. Remove with a slotted spoon and set aside. Add the mangetout (snow peas) and cook for 1–2 minutes, until they begin to soften. Remove with a slotted spoon and add to the other vegetables. Reserve the stock for future use.

3   Melt half of the butter in a frying pan (skillet) over a medium heat and fry the onion and courgettes (zucchini) for about 3 minutes. Add the garlic and prawns (shrimp) and cook for a further 2–3 minutes until thoroughly heated through.

4   Stir in the reserved vegetables and heat through. Season with salt and pepper, then stir in the remaining butter.

5   Transfer the spaghetti to a warmed serving dish. Pour on the sauce and parsley. Toss well using 2 forks, until thoroughly coated. Sprinkle on the grated cheese and paprika, and garnish with unshelled prawns (shrimp), if using. Serve immediately.

Pasta Pudding

A tasty mixture of creamy fish and pasta cooked in a bowl, unmoulded and drizzled with tomato sauce presents macaroni in a new guise.

NUTRITIONAL INFORMATION

Calories 536   Sugars 4g
Protein ....35g   Fat 35g
Carbohydrate ...21g   Saturates 17g

 35 MINS   2 HOURS

SERVES 4

INGREDIENTS

125 g/4½ oz short-cut macaroni, or other
   short pasta shapes

1 tbsp olive oil

15 g/½ oz/1 tbsp butter, plus extra for
   greasing

500 g/1 lb 2 oz white fish fillets, such as
   cod, haddock or coley

a few parsley stalks

6 black peppercorns

125 ml/4 fl oz/½ cup double (heavy) cream

2 eggs, separated

2 tbsp chopped dill, or parsley

pinch of grated nutmeg

60 g/2 oz/½ cup Parmesan, grated

Basic Tomato Sauce (see page 28), to serve

pepper

dill or parsley sprigs, to garnish

1 Cook the pasta in a pan of salted boiling water, adding the oil, for 8–10 minutes. Drain, return to the pan, add the butter and cover. Keep warm.

2 Place the fish in a frying pan (skillet) with the parsley stalks and peppercorns and pour on just enough water to cover. Bring to the boil, cover, and simmer for 10 minutes. Lift out the fish with a fish slice, reserving the liquor. When the fish is cool enough to handle, skin and remove any bones. Cut into bite-sized pieces.

3 Transfer the pasta to a large bowl and stir in the cream, egg yolks and dill. Stir in the fish, taking care not to break it up, and enough liquor to make a moist but firm mixture. It should fall easily from a spoon, but not be too runny. Whisk the egg whites until stiff but not dry, then fold into the mixture.

4 Grease a heatproof bowl or pudding basin and spoon in the mixture to within 4 cm/1½ inch of the rim. Cover the top with greased greaseproof paper and a cloth, or with foil, and tie firmly around the rim. Do not use foil if you cook the pudding in a microwave.

5 Stand the pudding on a trivet in a large pan of boiling water to come halfway up the sides. Cover and steam for 1½ hours, topping up the boiling water as needed, or cook in a microwave on maximum power for 7 minutes.

6 Run a knife around the inside of the bowl and invert on to a warm serving dish. Pour some tomato sauce over the top; serve the rest separately. Garnish and serve.

Macaroni & Prawn Bake

This adaptation of an 18th-century Italian dish is baked until it is golden brown and sizzling, then cut into wedges, like a cake.

NUTRITIONAL INFORMATION

Calories	576	Sugars	........6g
Protein	........25g	Fat	..........35g
Carbohydrate	...42g	Saturates	......19g

 20 MINS   🕐 1 HR 5 MINS

SERVES 4

INGREDIENTS

350 g/12 oz short pasta, such as
  short-cut macaroni

1 tbsp olive oil, plus extra for brushing

90 g/3 oz/6 tbsp butter, plus extra
  for greasing

2 small fennel bulbs, sliced thinly,
  leaves reserved

175 g/6 oz mushrooms, sliced thinly

175 g/6 oz shelled prawns (shrimp)

60 g/2 oz/½ cup Parmesan, grated

2 large tomatoes, sliced

1 tsp dried oregano

salt and pepper

pinch of cayenne

Béchamel Sauce (see page 28)

1 Cook the pasta in a large saucepan of boiling, salted water, with 1 tablespoon of olive oil, for 8–10 minutes or until tender. Drain the pasta in a colander, return to the pan and dot with 25 g/1 oz/2 tablespoons of the butter. Shake the pan well, cover and keep warm.

2 Melt the remaining butter in a pan over medium heat and fry the fennel for 3–4 minutes, until it begins to soften. Stir in the mushrooms and fry for 2 minutes. Stir in the prawns (shrimp), remove the pan from the heat and set aside until required.

3 Make the Béchamel Sauce and add the cayenne. Remove the pan from the heat and stir in the reserved vegetables, prawns (shrimp) and the pasta.

4 Grease a round, shallow baking dish. Pour in the pasta mixture and spread evenly. Sprinkle with the Parmesan and arrange the tomato slices in a ring around the edge of the dish. Brush the tomato with olive oil and sprinkle with the dried oregano.

5 Bake in a preheated oven, 180°C/ 350°F/Gas Mark 4, for 25 minutes, or until golden brown. Serve hot.

Pasta & Sicilian Sauce

This Sicilian recipe of anchovies mixed with pine nuts and sultanas in a tomato sauce is delicious with all types of pasta.

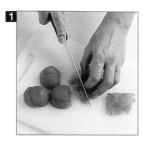

NUTRITIONAL INFORMATION

Calories	286	Sugars	........14g
Protein	........11g	Fat	...........8g
Carbohydrate	...46g	Saturates	.......1g

 25 MINS   🕐 30 MINS

SERVES 4

INGREDIENTS

450 g/1 lb tomatoes, halved

25 g/1 oz pine nuts

50 g/1¾ oz sultanas

50 g/1¾ oz can anchovies, drained and
   halved lengthways

2 tbsp concentrated tomato purée (paste)

675 g/1½ lb fresh or
   350 g/12 oz dried penne

1 Cook the tomatoes under a preheated grill (broiler) for about 10 minutes. Leave to cool slightly, then once cool enough to handle, peel off the skin and dice the flesh.

2 Place the pine nuts on a baking tray (cookie sheet) and lightly toast under the grill (broiler) for 2–3 minutes or until golden brown.

VARIATION

Add 100 g/3½ oz bacon, grilled (broiled) for 5 minutes until crispy, then chopped, instead of the anchovies, if you prefer.

3 Soak the sultanas in a bowl of warm water for about 20 minutes. Drain the sultanas thoroughly.

4 Place the tomatoes, pine nuts and sultanas in a small saucepan and gently heat.

5 Add the anchovies and tomato purée, heating the sauce for a further 2–3 minutes or until hot.

6 Cook the pasta in a saucepan of boiling water for 8–10 minutes or until it is cooked through, but still has 'bite'. Drain thoroughly.

7 Transfer the pasta to a serving plate and serve with the hot Sicilian sauce.

Pasta & Mussel Sauce

Serve this aromatic seafood dish with plenty of fresh, crusty bread to soak up the delicious sauce.

NUTRITIONAL INFORMATION

Calories	735	Sugars	.........3g
Protein	........37g	Fat	..........46g
Carbohydrate	...41g	Saturates	......26g

🍞 🍞

🧈 25 MINS 🕐 25 MINS

SERVES 6

INGREDIENTS

400 g/14 oz pasta shells

1 tbsp olive oil

SAUCE

3.5 litres/6 pints mussels, scrubbed

250 ml/9 fl oz/1 cup dry white wine

2 large onions, chopped

125 g/4½ oz/½ cup unsalted butter

6 large garlic cloves, chopped finely

5 tbsp chopped fresh parsley

300 ml/½ pint/1¼ cups double
   (heavy) cream

salt and pepper

crusty bread, to serve

1 Pull off the 'beards' from the mussels and rinse well in several changes of water. Discard any mussels that refuse to close when tapped. Put the mussels in a large pan with the white wine and half of the onions. Cover the pan, shake and cook over a medium heat for 2–3 minutes until the mussels open.

2 Remove the pan from the heat, lift out the mussels with a slotted spoon, reserving the liquor, and set aside until they are cool enough to handle. Discard any mussels that have not opened.

3 Melt the butter in a pan over medium heat and fry the remaining onion for 3–4 minutes or until translucent. Stir in the garlic and cook for 1 minute. Gradually pour on the reserved cooking liquor, stirring to blend thoroughly. Stir in the parsley and cream. Season to taste and bring to simmering point. Taste and adjust the seasoning if necessary.

4 Cook the pasta in a large pan of salted boiling water, adding the oil,

for 8–10 minutes or until tender. Drain the pasta in a colander, return to the pan, cover and keep warm.

5 Remove the mussels from their shells, reserving a few shells for garnish. Stir the mussels into the cream sauce. Tip the pasta into a warmed serving dish, pour on the sauce and, using 2 large spoons, toss it together well. Garnish with a few of the reserved mussel shells. Serve hot, with warm, crusty bread.

Spaghetti & Salmon Sauce

The smoked salmon ideally complements the spaghetti to give a very luxurious dish.

NUTRITIONAL INFORMATION

Calories 782	Sugars 3g	
Protein 20g	Fat 48g	
Carbohydrate ...48g	Saturates 27g	

10 MINS   15 MINS

SERVES 4

INGREDIENTS

500 g/1 lb 2 oz buckwheat spaghetti

2 tbsp olive oil

90 g/3 oz/½ cup feta cheese, crumbled

coriander (cilantro) or parsley, to garnish

SAUCE

300 ml/½ pint/1¼ cups double (heavy) cream

150 ml/¼ pint/⅔ cup whisky or brandy

125 g/4½ oz smoked salmon

large pinch of cayenne pepper

2 tbsp chopped coriander (cilantro) or parsley

salt and pepper

1 Cook the spaghetti in a large saucepan of salted boiling water, adding 1 tablespoon of the olive oil, for 8–10 minutes or until tender. Drain the pasta in a colander. Return the pasta to the pan, sprinkle over the remaining oil, cover and shake the pan. Set aside and keep warm until required.

2 In separate small saucepans, heat the cream and the whisky or brandy to simmering point. Do not let them boil.

3 Combine the cream with the whisky or brandy.

4 Cut the smoked salmon into thin strips and add to the cream mixture. Season with a little black pepper and cayenne pepper to taste, and then stir in the chopped coriander (cilantro) or parsley.

5 Transfer the spaghetti to a warmed serving dish, pour on the sauce and toss thoroughly using two large forks. Scatter the crumbled cheese over the pasta and garnish with the coriander (cilantro) or parsley. Serve at once.

Seafood Pasta

This attractive seafood salad platter is full of different flavours, textures and colours.

NUTRITIONAL INFORMATION

Calories 188   Sugars 2g
Protein . . . . .16g   Fat 7g
Carbohydrate . . .13g   Saturates 1g

🧊 30 MINS   🕐 30 MINS

SERVES 8

I N G R E D I E N T S

175 g/6 oz/1½ cups dried pasta shapes

1 tbsp oil

4 tbsp Italian dressing

2 garlic cloves, crushed

6 tbsp white wine

125 g/4½ oz baby button
    mushrooms, trimmed

3 carrots

600 ml/1 pint/2½ cups fresh mussels in
    shells

125–175 g/4½–6 oz frozen squid or
    octopus rings, thawed

175 g/6 oz/1 cup peeled tiger prawns
    (shrimp), thawed if frozen

6 sun-dried tomatoes, drained and sliced

3 tbsp chives, cut into 2.5 cm/1 inch pieces

salt and pepper

TO GARNISH

24 mangetout (snow peas), trimmed

12 baby corn

12 prawns (shrimp) in shells

1 Cook the pasta in a pan of boiling salted water, with the oil added, for 8–10 minutes or until just tender. Drain the pasta thoroughly.

2 Combine the dressing, garlic and 2 tablespoons of wine. Mix in the mushrooms and leave to marinate.

3 Slice the carrots about 1 cm/½ inch thick and using a cocktail cutter, cut each slice into shapes. Blanch for 3–4 minutes, drain and add to the mushrooms.

4 Scrub the mussels, discarding any that are open or do not close when sharply tapped. Put into a saucepan with 150 ml/ ¼ pint/⅔ cup water and the remaining wine. Bring to the boil, cover and simmer for 3–4 minutes or until they open. Drain, discarding any that are still closed. Reserve 12 mussels for garnish, leaving them on the half shell; remove the other mussels from the shells and add to the mushroom mixture with the squid or octopus rings and prawns (shrimp).

5 Add the sun-dried tomatoes, pasta and chives to the salad. Toss to mix and turn on to a large platter.

6 Blanch the mangetout (snow peas) for 1 minute and baby corn for 3 minutes, rinse under cold water and drain. Arrange around the edge of the salad, alternating with the mussels on shells and whole prawns (shrimp). Cover with cling film (plastic wrap) and leave to chill until ready to serve.

Macaroni & Squid Casserole

This pasta dish is easy to make and is a very hearty meal for a large number of guests.

NUTRITIONAL INFORMATION

Calories 237   Sugars 4g
Protein ....12g   Fat 11g
Carbohydrate ...19g   Saturates 2g

15 MINS   35 MINS

SERVES 6

INGREDIENTS

225 g/8 oz short-cut macaroni, or other
  short pasta shapes

1 tbsp olive oil

2 tbsp chopped fresh parsley

salt and pepper

SAUCE

350 g/12 oz cleaned squid,
  cut into 4 cm/½ in strips

6 tbsp olive oil

2 onions, sliced

250 ml/9 fl oz/1 cup fish stock

150 ml/¼ pint/⅔ cup red wine

350 g/12 oz tomatoes, peeled
  and thinly sliced

2 tbsp tomato purée (paste)

1 tsp dried oregano

2 bay leaves

1 Cook the pasta for only 3 minutes in a large pan of boiling salted water, adding the oil. Drain in a colander, return to the pan, cover and keep warm.

2 To make the sauce, heat the oil in a pan over medium heat and fry the onion until translucent. Add the squid and stock and simmer for 5 minutes. Pour on the wine and add the tomatoes, tomato purée (paste), oregano and bay leaves. Bring the sauce to the boil, season with salt and pepper to taste and cook, uncovered, for 5 minutes.

3 Add the pasta, stir well, cover the pan and continue simmering for 10 minutes, or until the macaroni and squid are almost tender. By this time the sauce should be thick and syrupy. If it is too liquid, uncover the pan and continue cooking for a few minutes. Taste the sauce and adjust the seasoning if necessary.

4 Remove the bay leaves and stir in most of the parsley, reserving a little to garnish. Transfer to a warmed serving dish. Sprinkle on the remaining parsley and serve hot. Serve with warm, crusty bread, such as ciabatta.

Vermicelli & Clam Sauce

This recipe is quick to prepare and cook – it's so delicious that it will be devoured even faster!

NUTRITIONAL INFORMATION

Calories ....502 Sugars 2g
Protein ....27g Fat 17g
Carbohydrate ...58g Saturates 7g

 15 MINS   25 MINS

SERVES 4

I N G R E D I E N T S

400 g/14 oz vermicelli, spaghetti, or other
    long pasta

1 tbsp olive oil

25 g/1 oz/2 tbsp butter

2 tbsp Parmesan shavings, to garnish

sprig of basil, to garnish

S A U C E

1 tbsp olive oil

2 onions, chopped

2 garlic cloves, chopped

2 x 200 g/7 oz jars clams in brine

125 ml/4 fl oz/½ cup white wine

4 tbsp chopped fresh parsley

½ tsp dried oregano

pinch of freshly grated nutmeg

salt and pepper

1 Cook the pasta in a large pan of boiling salted water, adding the olive oil, for 8–10 minutes or until tender. Drain the pasta in a colander and return to the pan. Add the butter, cover and shake the pan. Keep warm until required.

2 To make the clam sauce, heat the oil in a pan over a medium heat and fry the onion until it is translucent. Stir in the garlic and cook for 1 minute.

3 Strain the liquid from one jar of clams, pour into the pan and add the wine. Stir well, bring to simmering point and simmer for 3 minutes. Drain the brine from the second jar of clams and discard.

4 Add the shellfish and herbs to the pan, and season with pepper to taste

and the nutmeg. Lower the heat and cook until the sauce is heated through.

5 Transfer the pasta to a warmed serving dish and pour on the sauce.

6 Sprinkle with the Parmesan and garnish with the basil sprig. Serve hot.

Pasta & Chilli Tomatoes

The pappardelle and vegetables are tossed in a delicious chilli and tomato sauce for a quick and economical meal.

NUTRITIONAL INFORMATION

Calories ....353 Sugars 7g
Protein ....10g Fat 24g
Carbohydrate ...26g Saturates 4g

 15 MINS   20 MINS

SERVES 4

INGREDIENTS

275 g/9½ oz pappardelle

3 tbsp groundnut oil

2 cloves garlic, crushed

2 shallots, sliced

225 g/8 oz green beans, sliced

100 g/3½ oz cherry tomatoes, halved

1 tsp chilli flakes

4 tbsp crunchy peanut butter

150 ml/¼ pint/⅔ cup coconut milk

1 tbsp tomato purée (paste)

sliced spring onions (scallions), to garnish

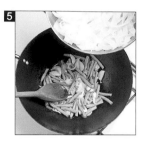

1 Cook the pappardelle in a large saucepan of boiling, lightly salted water for 5-6 minutes.

VARIATION

Add slices of chicken or beef to the recipe and stir-fry with the beans and pasta in step 5 for a more substantial main meal.

2 Heat the groundnut oil in a large pan or preheated wok.

3 Add the garlic and shallots and stir-fry for 1 minute.

4 Drain the pappardelle thoroughly and set aside.

5 Add the green beans and drained pasta to the wok and stir-fry for 5 minutes.

6 Add the cherry tomatoes to the wok and mix well.

7 Mix together the chilli flakes, peanut butter, coconut milk and tomato purée (paste).

8 Pour the chilli mixture over the noodles, toss well to combine and heat through.

9 Transfer to warm serving dishes and garnish. Serve immediately.

Fish & Vegetable Lasagne

Layers of cheese sauce, smoked cod and wholewheat lasagne can be assembled overnight and left ready to cook on the following day.

NUTRITIONAL INFORMATION

Calories	456	Sugars	........8g
Protein	........33g	Fat	.........24g
Carbohydrate	...24g	Saturates	......15g

 25 MINS   50 MINS

SERVES 6

INGREDIENTS

8 sheets wholewheat lasagne

500 g/1 lb 2 oz smoked cod

600 ml/1 pint/2½ cups milk

1 tbsp lemon juice

8 peppercorns

2 bay leaves

a few parsley stalks

60 g/2 oz/½ cup mature (sharp)
   Cheddar, grated

25 g/1 oz/¼ cup Parmesan, grated

salt and pepper

a few whole prawns (shrimp), to garnish

SAUCE

60 g/2 oz/¼ cup butter, plus extra for
   greasing

1 large onion, sliced

1 green (bell) pepper, cored, deseeded and
   chopped

1 small courgette (zucchini), sliced

60 g/2 oz/½ cup plain (all-purpose) flour

150 ml/¼ pint/⅔ cup white wine

150 ml/¼ pint/⅔ cup single (light) cream

125 g/4½ oz shelled prawns (shrimp)

60 g/2 oz/½ cup mature (sharp)
   Cheddar, grated

1 Cook the lasagne in a pan of boiling, salted water until almost tender, as described on page 344. Drain and reserve.

2 Place the smoked cod, milk, lemon juice, peppercorns, bay leaves and parsley stalks in a frying pan (skillet). Bring to the boil, cover and simmer for 10 minutes.

3 Lift the fish from the pan with a slotted spoon. Remove the skin and any bones. Flake the fish. Strain and reserve the liquor.

4 To make the sauce, melt the butter in a pan and fry the onion, (bell) pepper and courgette (zucchini) for 2–3 minutes. Stir in the flour and cook for 1 minute. Gradually add the fish liquor, then stir in the wine, cream and prawns (shrimp). Simmer for 2 minutes. Remove from the heat, add the cheese, and season.

5 Grease a shallow baking dish. Pour in a quarter of the sauce and spread evenly over the base. Cover the sauce with three sheets of lasagne, then with another quarter of the sauce.

6 Arrange the fish on top, then cover with half of the remaining sauce. Finish with the remaining lasagne, then the rest of the sauce. Sprinkle the Cheddar and Parmesan over the sauce.

7 Bake in a preheated oven, 190°C/ 375°F/Gas Mark 5, for 25 minutes, or until the top is golden brown and bubbling. Garnish and serve.

Macaroni & Tuna Fish Layer

A layer of tuna fish with garlic, mushroom and red (bell) pepper is sandwiched between two layers of macaroni with a crunchy topping.

NUTRITIONAL INFORMATION

Calories	.691	Sugars	.10g
Protein	.41g	Fat	.33g
Carbohydrate	.62g	Saturates	.15g

20 MINS   50 MINS

SERVES 2

INGREDIENTS

125–150 g/4½–5½ oz/1¼ cup dried
   macaroni

2 tbsp oil

1 garlic clove, crushed

60 g/2 oz/¾ cup button mushrooms, sliced

½ red (bell) pepper, thinly sliced

200 g/7 oz can of tuna fish in brine,
   drained and flaked

½ tsp dried oregano

salt and pepper

SAUCE

25 g/1 oz/2 tbsp butter or margarine

1 tbsp plain (all-purpose) flour

250 ml/9 fl oz/1 cup milk

2 tomatoes, sliced

2 tbsp dried breadcrumbs

25 g/1 oz/¼ cup mature (sharp) Cheddar or
   Parmesan cheese, grated

VARIATION

Replace the tuna fish with chopped cooked chicken, beef, pork or ham or with 3–4 sliced hard-boiled (hard-cooked) eggs.

1 Cook the macaroni in boiling salted water, with 1 tablespoon of the oil added, for 10–12 minutes or until tender. Drain, rinse and drain thoroughly.

2 Heat the remaining oil in a saucepan or frying pan (skillet) and fry the garlic, mushrooms and (bell) pepper until soft. Add the tuna fish, oregano and seasoning, and heat through.

3 Grease an ovenproof dish (about 1 litre/1¾ pint/4 cup capacity), and add half of the cooked macaroni. Cover with the tuna mixture and then add the remaining macaroni.

4 To make the sauce, melt the butter or margarine in a saucepan, stir in the flour and cook for 1 minute. Add the milk gradually and bring to the boil. Simmer for 1–2 minutes, stirring continuously, until thickened. Season to taste. Pour the sauce over the macaroni.

5 Lay the sliced tomatoes over the sauce and sprinkle with the breadcrumbs and cheese.

6 Place in a preheated oven, at 200°C/400°F/Gas Mark 6, for about 25 minutes, or until piping hot and the top is well browned.

Pasta with Nuts & Cheese

Simple and inexpensive, this tasty pasta dish can be prepared fairly quickly.

NUTRITIONAL INFORMATION

Calories	531	Sugars	.........4g
Protein	........20g	Fat	..........35g
Carbohydrate	...35g	Saturates	......16g

 10 MINS   30 MINS

SERVES 4

I N G R E D I E N T S

60 g/2 oz/1 cup pine kernels (nuts)

350 g/12 oz dried pasta shapes

2 courgettes (zucchini), sliced

125 g/4½ oz/1¼ cups broccoli,
   broken into florets

200 g/7 oz/1 cup full-fat soft cheese

150 ml/¼ pint/⅔ cup milk

1 tbsp chopped fresh basil

125 g/4½ oz button mushrooms, sliced

90 g/3 oz blue cheese, crumbled

salt and pepper

sprigs of fresh basil, to garnish

green salad, to serve

1 Scatter the pine kernels (nuts) on to a baking tray (cookie sheet) and grill (broil), turning occasionally, until lightly browned all over. Set aside.

2 Cook the pasta in plenty of boiling salted water for 8–10 minutes or until just tender.

3 Meanwhile, cook the courgettes (zucchini) and broccoli in a small amount of boiling, lightly salted water for about 5 minutes or until just tender.

4 Put the soft cheese into a pan and heat gently, stirring constantly. Add the milk and stir to mix. Add the basil and mushrooms and cook gently for 2–3 minutes. Stir in the blue cheese and season to taste.

5 Drain the pasta and the vegetables and mix together. Pour over the cheese and mushroom sauce and add the pine kernels (nuts). Toss gently to mix. Garnish with basil sprigs and serve with a green salad.

Basil & Tomato Pasta

Roasting the tomatoes gives a sweeter flavour to this sauce. Buy Italian tomatoes, such as plum or flavia, as these have a better flavour and colour.

NUTRITIONAL INFORMATION

Calories 177	Sugars 4g	
Protein 5g	Fat 4g	
Carbohydrate ...31g	Saturates 1g	

 15 MINS   35 MINS

SERVES 4

I N G R E D I E N T S

1 tbsp olive oil

2 sprigs rosemary

2 cloves garlic

450 g/1 lb tomatoes, halved

1 tbsp sun-dried tomato paste

12 fresh basil leaves, plus extra to garnish

salt and pepper

675 g/1½ lb fresh farfalle or 350 g/12 oz
   dried farfalle

1 Place the oil, rosemary, garlic and tomatoes, skin side up, in a shallow roasting tin (pan).

2 Drizzle with a little oil and cook under a preheated grill (broiler) for 20 minutes or until the tomato skins are slightly charred.

COOK'S TIP

This sauce tastes just as good when served cold in a pasta salad.

3 Peel the skin from the tomatoes. Roughly chop the tomato flesh and place in a pan.

4 Squeeze the pulp from the garlic cloves and mix with the tomato flesh and sun-dried tomato paste.

5 Roughly tear the fresh basil leaves into smaller pieces and then stir them into the sauce. Season with a little salt and pepper to taste. Set aside.

6 Cook the farfalle in a saucepan of boiling water for 8–10 minutes or until it is cooked through, but still has 'bite'. Drain well.

7 Gently re-heat the tomato and basil sauce, stirring.

8 Transfer the farfalle to serving plates and pour over the basil and tomato sauce. Serve at once.

Tagliatelle & Garlic Sauce

This pasta dish can be prepared in a moment – the intense flavours are sure to make this a popular recipe.

NUTRITIONAL INFORMATION

Calories 501	Sugars 3g
Protein 15g	Fat 31g
Carbohydrate . . .43g	Saturates 11g

 15 MINS   20 MINS

SERVES 4

INGREDIENTS

2 tbsp walnut oil

1 bunch spring onions (scallions), sliced

2 garlic cloves, sliced thinly

225 g/8 oz mushrooms, sliced

500 g/1 lb 2 oz fresh green and white tagliatelle

225 g/8 oz frozen chopped leaf spinach, thawed and drained

125 g/4½ oz/½ cup full-fat soft cheese with garlic and herbs

4 tbsp single (light) cream

60 g/2 oz/½ cup chopped, unsalted pistachio nuts

2 tbsp shredded fresh basil

salt and pepper

sprigs of fresh basil, to garnish

Italian bread, to serve

1 Gently heat the oil in a wok or frying pan (skillet) and fry the spring onions (scallions) and garlic for 1 minute or until just softened. Add the mushrooms, stir well, cover and cook gently for 5 minutes or until softened.

2 Meanwhile, bring a large saucepan of lightly salted water to the boil and cook the pasta for 3–5 minutes or until just tender. Drain the pasta thoroughly and return to the saucepan.

3 Add the spinach to the mushrooms and heat through for 1–2 minutes. Add the cheese and allow to melt slightly. Stir in the cream and continue to heat without allowing to boil.

4 Pour the mixture over the pasta, season to taste and mix well. Heat gently, stirring, for 2–3 minutes.

5 Pile into a warmed serving bowl and sprinkle over the pistachio nuts and shredded basil. Garnish with basil sprigs and serve with Italian bread.

Chilli & (Bell) Pepper Pasta

This roasted (bell) pepper and chilli sauce is sweet and spicy – the perfect combination!

NUTRITIONAL INFORMATION

Calories	423	Sugars	.........5g
Protein	.........9g	Fat	.........27g
Carbohydrate	...38g	Saturates	.......4g

 25 MINS 30 MINS

SERVES 4

I N G R E D I E N T S

2 red (bell) peppers, halved and deseeded

1 small red chilli

4 tomatoes, halved

2 garlic cloves

50 g/1¾ oz ground almonds

7 tbsp olive oil

675 g/1½ lb fresh pasta or 350 g/12 oz
 dried pasta

fresh oregano leaves, to garnish

  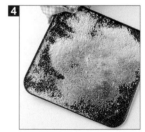

1 Place the (bell) peppers, skin-side up, on a baking tray (cookie sheet) with the chilli and tomatoes. Cook under a preheated grill (broiler) for 15 minutes or until charred. After 10 minutes turn the tomatoes skin-side up. Place the (bell) peppers and chillies in a polythene bag and leave to sweat for 10 minutes.

2 Remove the skin from the (bell) peppers and chillies and slice the flesh into strips, using a sharp knife.

3 Peel the garlic, and peel and deseed the tomatoes.

4 Place the almonds on a baking tray (cookie sheet) and place under the grill (broiler) for 2–3 minutes until golden.

5 Using a food processor, blend the (bell) pepper, chilli, garlic and tomatoes to make a purée. Keep the motor running and slowly add the olive oil to form a thick sauce. Alternatively, mash the mixture with a fork and beat in the olive oil, drop by drop.

6 Stir the toasted ground almonds into the mixture.

7 Warm the sauce in a saucepan until it is heated through.

8 Cook the pasta in a saucepan of boiling water for 8–10 minutes if using dried, or 3–5 minutes if using fresh. Drain the pasta thoroughly and transfer to a serving dish. Pour over the sauce and toss to mix. Garnish with the fresh oregano leaves.

VARIATION

Add 2 tablespoons of red wine vinegar to the sauce and use as a dressing for a cold pasta salad, if you wish.

Artichoke & Olive Spaghetti

The tasty flavours of artichoke hearts and black olives are a winning combination.

NUTRITIONAL INFORMATION

Calories	393	Sugars	........11g
Protein	........14g	Fat	...........11g
Carbohydrate	...63g	Saturates	.......2g

20 MINS   35 MINS

SERVES 4

I N G R E D I E N T S

2 tbsp olive oil

1 large red onion, chopped

2 garlic cloves, crushed

1 tbsp lemon juice

4 baby aubergines (eggplant), quartered

600 ml/1 pint/2½ cups passata (sieved
    tomatoes)

2 tsp caster (superfine) sugar

2 tbsp tomato purée (paste)

400 g/14 oz can artichoke hearts, drained
    and halved

125 g/4½ oz/¾ cup pitted black olives

350 g/12 oz wholewheat dried spaghetti

salt and pepper

sprigs of fresh basil, to garnish

olive bread, to serve

1 Heat 1 tablespoon of the oil in a large frying pan (skillet) and gently fry the onion, garlic, lemon juice and aubergines (eggplant) for 4–5 minutes or until lightly browned.

2 Pour in the passata (sieved tomatoes), season with salt and pepper to taste and add the sugar and tomato purée (paste). Bring to the boil, reduce the heat and simmer for 20 minutes.

3 Gently stir in the artichoke halves and olives and cook for 5 minutes.

4 Meanwhile, bring a large saucepan of lightly salted water to the boil, and cook the spaghetti for 8–10 minutes or until just tender. Drain well, toss in the remaining olive oil and season with salt and pepper to taste.

5 Transfer the spaghetti to a warmed serving bowl and top with the vegetable sauce. Garnish with basil sprigs and serve with olive bread.

Spaghetti with Ricotta Sauce

This makes a quick and easy starter, and is particularly ideal for the summer.

NUTRITIONAL INFORMATION

Calories 688	Sugars 5g
Protein 17g	Fat 51g
Carbohydrate ...43g	Saturates 16g

  15 MINS   20 MINS

SERVES 4

INGREDIENTS

350 g/12 oz spaghetti

3 tbsp olive oil

45 g/1½ oz/3 tbsp butter, cut into small
  pieces

2 tbsp chopped parsley

SAUCE

125 g/4½ oz/1 cup freshly ground almonds

125 g/4½ oz/½ cup Ricotta

large pinch of grated nutmeg

large pinch of ground cinnamon

150 ml/¼ pint/⅔ cup crème fraîche

125 ml/4 fl oz/½ cup hot chicken stock

1 tbsp pine kernels

pepper

coriander (cilantro) leaves, to garnish

COOK'S TIP

To toss spaghetti and coat
it with a sauce or dressing, use
the 2 largest forks you can find.
Holding one fork in each hand,
ease the prongs under the spaghetti
from each side and lift them
towards the centre. Repeat evenly
until the pasta is well coated.

1 Cook the spaghetti in a large pan of boiling salted water, to which you have added 1 tablespoon of the oil, for 8–10 minutes or until tender. Drain the pasta in a colander, return to the pan and toss with the butter and parsley. Cover the pan and keep warm.

2 To make the sauce, mix together the ground almonds, Ricotta, nutmeg, cinnamon and crème fraîche to make a thick paste. Gradually pour on the remaining oil, stirring constantly until it is well blended. Gradually pour on the hot stock, stirring all the time, until the sauce is smooth.

3 Transfer the spaghetti to warmed serving dishes, pour on the sauce and toss well. Sprinkle each serving with pine kernels (nuts) and garnish with coriander (cilantro) leaves. Serve warm.

Tagliatelle with Garlic Butter

Pasta is not difficult to make yourself, just a little time consuming. The resulting pasta only takes a couple of minutes to cook and tastes wonderful.

NUTRITIONAL INFORMATION

Calories	642	Sugars	.........2g
Protein	........16g	Fat	..........29g
Carbohydrate	...84g	Saturates	......13g

 45 MINS   5 MINS

SERVES 4

I N G R E D I E N T S

450 g/1 lb strong white flour,
   plus extra for dredging

2 tsp salt

4 eggs, beaten

3 tbsp olive oil

75 g/2¾ oz/5 tbsp butter, melted

3 garlic cloves, finely chopped

2 tbsp chopped, fresh parsley

pepper

1 Sift the flour into a large bowl and stir in the salt.

2 Make a well in the middle of the dry ingredients and add the eggs and 2 tablespoons of oil. Using a wooden spoon, stir in the eggs, gradually drawing in the flour. After a few minutes the dough will be too stiff to use a spoon and you will need to use your fingers.

3 Once all of the flour has been incorporated, turn the dough out on to a floured surface and knead for about 5 minutes, or until smooth and elastic. If you find the dough is too wet, add a little more flour and continue kneading. Cover with cling film (plastic wrap) and leave to rest for at least 15 minutes.

4 The basic dough is now ready; roll out the pasta thinly and create the pasta shapes required. This can be done by hand or using a pasta machine. Results from a machine are usually neater and thinner, but not necessarily better.

5 To make the tagliatelle by hand, fold the thinly rolled pasta sheets into 3 and cut out long, thin stips, about 1 cm/ ½ inch wide.

6 To cook, bring a pan of water to the boil, add 1 tbsp of oil and the pasta. It will take 2–3 minutes to cook, and the texture should have a slight bite to it. Drain.

7 Mix together the butter, garlic and parsley. Stir into the pasta, season with a little pepper to taste and serve immediately.

COOK'S TIP

Generally allow about 150 g/5½ oz fresh pasta or about 100 g/3½ oz dried pasta per person.

Pasta & Cheese Puddings

These delicious pasta puddings are served with a tasty tomato and bay leaf sauce.

 45 MINS   50 MINS

SERVES 4

I N G R E D I E N T S

15 g/½ oz/1 tbsp butter or margarine, softened

60 g/2 oz/½ cup dried white breadcrumbs

175 g/6 oz tricolour spaghetti

300 ml/½ pint/1¼ cups Béchamel Sauce (see page 28)

1 egg yolk

125 g/4½ oz/1 cup Gruyère (Swiss) cheese, grated

salt and pepper

fresh flat-leaf parsley, to garnish

T O M A T O   S A U C E

2 tsp olive oil

1 onion, chopped finely

1 bay leaf

150 ml/¼ pint/⅔ cup dry white wine

150 ml/¼ pint/⅔ cup passatta (sieved tomatoes)

1 tbsp tomato purée (paste)

1 Grease four 180 ml/6 fl oz/¾ cup moulds (molds) or ramekins with the butter or margarine. Evenly coat the insides with half of the breadcrumbs.

2 Break the spaghetti into 5 cm/2 inch lengths. Bring a saucepan of lightly salted water to the boil and cook the spaghetti for 5–6 minutes or until just tender. Drain well and put in a bowl.

3 Mix the Béchamel Sauce, egg yolk, cheese and seasoning into the cooked pasta and pack into the moulds (molds).

4 Sprinkle with the remaining breadcrumbs and place the moulds (molds) on a baking tray (cookie sheet). Bake in a preheated oven, 220°C/425°F/Gas Mark 7, for 20 minutes until golden. Leave to stand for 10 minutes.

5 Meanwhile, make the sauce. Heat the oil in a pan and fry the onion and bay leaf for 2–3 minutes or until just softened.

6 Stir in the wine, passata (sieved tomatoes), tomato purée (paste) and seasoning. Bring to the boil and simmer for 20 minutes or until thickened. Discard the bay leaf.

7 Run a palette knife (spatula) around the inside of the moulds (molds). Turn on to serving plates, garnish and serve with the tomato sauce.

Pasta & Bean Casserole

A satisfying winter dish, this is a slow-cooked, one-pot meal. The haricot (navy) beans need to be soaked overnight, so prepare well in advance.

NUTRITIONAL INFORMATION

Calories	323	Sugars	.........5g
Protein	........13g	Fat	..........12g
Carbohydrate	...41g	Saturates	.......2g

 25 MINS    3½ HOURS

SERVES 6

I N G R E D I E N T S

225 g/8 oz/generous 1 cup dried haricot
   (navy) beans, soaked overnight and
   drained

225 g/8 oz penne,
   or other short pasta shapes

6 tbsp olive oil

850 ml/1½ pints/3½ cups vegetable stock

2 large onions, sliced

2 cloves garlic, chopped

2 bay leaves

1 tsp dried oregano

1 tsp dried thyme

5 tbsp red wine

2 tbsp tomato purée (paste)

2 celery stalks, sliced

1 fennel bulb, sliced

125 g/4½ oz mushrooms, sliced

225 g/8 oz tomatoes, sliced

1 tsp dark muscovado sugar

4 tbsp dry white breadcrumbs

salt and pepper

T O   S E R V E

salad leaves

crusty bread

1 Put the beans in a large pan, cover them with water and bring to the boil. Boil the beans rapidly for 20 minutes, then drain them.

2 Cook the pasta for only 3 minutes in a large pan of boiling salted water, adding 1 tablespoon of the oil. Drain in a colander and set aside.

3 Put the beans in a large flameproof casserole, pour on the vegetable stock and stir in the remaining olive oil, the onions, garlic, bay leaves, herbs, wine and tomato purée (paste).

4 Bring to the boil, cover the casserole and cook in a preheated oven, 180°C/350°F/Gas Mark 4, for 2 hours.

5 Add the reserved pasta, the celery, fennel, mushrooms and tomatoes, and season with salt and pepper.

6 Stir in the sugar and sprinkle on the breadcrumbs. Cover the casserole and continue cooking for 1 hour. Serve hot, with salad leaves and crusty bread.

Spicy Tomato Tagliatelle

A deliciously fresh and slightly spicy tomato sauce which is excellent for lunch or a light supper.

NUTRITIONAL INFORMATION

Calories 306	Sugars 7g
Protein 8g	Fat 12g
Carbohydrate ...45g	Saturates 7g

15 MINS 35 MINS

SERVES 4

INGREDIENTS

50 g/1¾ oz/3 tbsp butter

1 onion, finely chopped

1 garlic clove, crushed

2 small red chillies,
    deseeded and diced

450 g/1 lb fresh tomatoes, skinned,
    deseeded and diced

200 ml/7 fl oz/¾ cup vegetable stock

2 tbsp tomato purée (paste)

1 tsp sugar

salt and pepper

675 g/1½ lb fresh green and white
    tagliatelle, or 350 g/12 oz dried

VARIATION

Try topping your pasta dish with 50 g/1¾ oz pancetta or unsmoked bacon, diced and dry-fried for 5 minutes until crispy.

1 Melt the butter in a large saucepan. Add the onion and garlic and cook for 3–4 minutes or until softened.

2 Add the chillies to the pan and continue cooking for about 2 minutes.

3 Add the tomatoes and stock, reduce the heat and leave to simmer for 10 minutes, stirring.

4 Pour the sauce into a food processor and blend for 1 minute until smooth.

Alternatively, push the sauce through a sieve.

5 Return the sauce to the pan and add the tomato purée (paste) sugar, and salt and pepper to taste. Gently reheat over a low heat, until piping hot.

6 Cook the tagliatelle in a pan of boiling water for 8–10 minutes or until it is tender, but still has 'bite'. Drain the tagliatelle, transfer to serving plates and serve with the tomato sauce.

Aubergine (Eggplant) Lasagne

This filling aubergine (eggplant), courgette (zucchini) and mozzarella lasagne is an Italian classic.

NUTRITIONAL INFORMATION

Calories . . . . . . .525 Sugars 14g
Protein . . . . .17g Fat 39g
Carbohydrate . . .28g Saturates 15g

  1¼ HOURS   1 HOUR

SERVES 6

I N G R E D I E N T S

1 kg/2 lb 4 oz aubergines (eggplant)

4 tsp salt

8 tbsp olive oil

25 g/1 oz/2 tbsp garlic and herb butter or
    margarine

500 g/1 lb 2 oz courgettes (zucchini), sliced

225 g/8 oz/2 cups grated Mozzarella

600 ml/1 pint/2½ cups passata (sieved
    tomatoes)

6 sheets pre-cooked green lasagne

600 ml/1 pint/2½ cups Béchamel Sauce
    (see page 28)

60 g/2 oz/½ cup Parmesan, grated

1 tsp dried oregano

pepper

1 Thinly slice the aubergines (eggplant). Layer the slices in a bowl, sprinkling with the salt as you go. Set aside for 30 minutes. Rinse well in cold water and pat dry with paper towels.

2 Heat 4 tbsp of oil in a frying pan (skillet) and fry half of the aubergine (eggplant) slices for 6–7 minutes or until lightly golden all over. Drain on paper towels. Repeat with the remaining aubergine (eggplant) slices and oil.

3 Melt the garlic and herb butter or margarine in the frying pan (skillet) and fry the courgettes (zucchini) for 5–6 minutes until golden. Drain thoroughly on paper towels.

4 Place half of the aubergine (eggplant) and courgette (zucchini) slices in a large ovenproof dish. Season with pepper and sprinkle over half of the Mozzarella. Spoon over half of the passata (sieved tomatoes) and top with 3 sheets of lasagne.

5 Arrange the remaining aubergine (eggplant) and courgette (zucchini) slices on top. Season with pepper and top with the remaining Mozzarella and passata (sieved tomatoes) and another layer of lasagne.

6 Spoon over the Béchamel Sauce and top with Parmesan and oregano. Put on a baking tray (cookie sheet) and bake in a preheated oven, 220°C/425°F/Gas Mark 7, for 30–35 minutes or until golden.

Pasta with Cheese & Broccoli

Some of the simplest and most satisfying dishes are made with pasta, such as this delicious combination of tagliatelle with two-cheese sauce.

NUTRITIONAL INFORMATION

Calories 624	Sugars 2g	
Protein 22g	Fat 45g	
Carbohydrate ...34g	Saturates 28g	

 5 MINS   15 MINS

SERVES 4

I N G R E D I E N T S

300 g/10½ oz dried tagliatelle tricolore
(plain, spinach- and tomato-flavoured
noodles)

225 g/8 oz/2½ cups broccoli, broken into
small florets

350g/12 oz/1½ cups Mascarpone cheese

125 g/4½ oz/1 cup blue cheese, chopped

1 tbsp chopped fresh oregano

25 g/1 oz/2 tbsp butter

salt and pepper

sprigs of fresh oregano, to garnish

freshly grated Parmesan, to serve

1 Cook the tagliatelle in plenty of boiling salted water for 8–10 minutes or until just tender.

2 Meanwhile, cook the broccoli florets in a small amount of lightly salted, boiling water. Avoid overcooking the broccoli, so that it retains much of its colour and texture.

3 Heat the Mascarpone and blue cheeses together gently in a large saucepan until they are melted. Stir in the oregano and season with salt and pepper to taste.

4 Drain the pasta thoroughly. Return it to the saucepan and add the butter, tossing the tagliatelle to coat it. Drain the broccoli well and add to the pasta with the sauce, tossing gently to mix.

5 Divide the pasta between 4 warmed serving plates. Garnish with sprigs of fresh oregano and serve with freshly grated Parmesan.

Pasta & Vegetable Sauce

A Mediterranean mixture of red (bell) peppers, garlic and courgettes (zucchini) cooked in olive oil and tossed with pasta.

NUTRITIONAL INFORMATION

Calories	341	Sugars	.........8g
Protein	........13g	Fat	..........20g
Carbohydrate	...30g	Saturates	.......8g

 15 MINS   20 MINS

SERVES 4

I N G R E D I E N T S

3 tbsp olive oil

1 onion, sliced

2 garlic cloves, chopped

3 red (bell) peppers, deseeded and cut
    into strips

3 courgettes (zucchini), sliced

400 g/14 oz can chopped tomatoes

3 tbsp sun-dried tomato paste

2 tbsp chopped fresh basil

225 g/8 oz fresh pasta spirals

125 g/4½ oz/1 cup grated Gruyère
    (Swiss) cheese

salt and pepper

fresh basil sprigs, to garnish

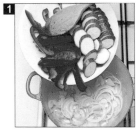

1 Heat the oil in a heavy-based saucepan or flameproof casserole. Add the onion and garlic and cook, stirring occasionally, until softened. Add the (bell) peppers and courgettes (zucchini) and fry for 5 minutes, stirring occasionally.

2 Add the tomatoes, sun-dried tomato paste, basil and seasoning, cover and cook for 5 minutes.

3 Meanwhile, bring a large saucepan of salted water to the boil and add the pasta. Stir and bring back to the boil.

Reduce the heat slightly and cook, uncovered, for 3 minutes, or until just tender. Drain thoroughly and add to the vegetables. Toss gently to mix well.

4 Put the mixture into a shallow ovenproof dish and sprinkle over the cheese.

5 Cook under a preheated grill (broiler) for 5 minutes until the cheese is golden. Garnish with basil sprigs and serve.

COOK'S TIP

Be careful not to overcook fresh pasta – it should be 'al dente' (retaining some 'bite'). It takes only a few minutes to cook as it is still full of moisture.

Tagliatelle with Pumpkin

This unusual pasta dish comes from the Emilia Romagna region of Italy.

NUTRITIONAL INFORMATION

Calories	454	Sugars	.........4g
Protein	.........9g	Fat	..........33g
Carbohydrate	...33g	Saturates	......12g

 15 MINS   35 MINS

SERVES 4

INGREDIENTS

500 g/1 lb 2 oz pumpkin or butternut
   squash

2 tbsp olive oil

1 onion, chopped finely

2 garlic cloves, crushed

4–6 tbsp chopped fresh parsley

good pinch of ground or freshly grated
   nutmeg

about 250 ml/9 fl oz/1 cup chicken or
   vegetable stock

125 g/4½ oz Parma ham (prosciutto), cut
   into narrow strips

275 g/9 oz tagliatelle, green or white (fresh
   or dried)

150 ml/¼ pint/⅔ cup double (heavy) cream

salt and pepper

freshly grated Parmesan, to serve

1 Peel the pumpkin or squash and scoop out the seeds and membrane. Cut the flesh into 1 cm/½ inch dice.

2 Heat the olive oil in a pan and gently fry the onion and garlic until softened. Add half of the parsley and fry for 1–2 minutes.

3 Add the pumpkin or squash and continue to cook for 2–3 minutes. Season well with salt, pepper and nutmeg.

4 Add half of the stock, bring to the boil, cover and simmer for about 10 minutes or until the pumpkin is tender, adding more stock as necessary. Add the Parma ham (prosciutto) and continue to cook for 2 minutes, stirring frequently.

5 Meanwhile, cook the tagliatelle in a large saucepan of boiling salted water, allowing 3–4 minutes for fresh pasta or 8–10 minutes for dried. Drain thoroughly and turn into a warmed dish.

6 Add the cream to the ham mixture and heat gently. Season and spoon over the pasta. Sprinkle with the remaining parsley and grated Parmesan separately.

Basil & Pine Nut Pesto

Delicious stirred into pasta, soups and salad dressings, pesto is available in most supermarkets, but making your own gives a concentrated flavour.

NUTRITIONAL INFORMATION

Calories 321	Sugars 1g	
Protein 11g	Fat 17g	
Carbohydrate . . .32g	Saturates 4g	

 15 MINS   10 MINS

SERVES 4

INGREDIENTS

about 40 fresh basil leaves,
  washed and dried

3 garlic cloves, crushed

25 g/1 oz pine nuts

50 g/1¾ oz Parmesan cheese, finely grated

2–3 tbsp extra virgin olive oil

salt and pepper

675 g/1½ lb fresh pasta or
  350 g/12 oz dried pasta

1 Rinse the basil leaves and pat them dry with paper towels.

2 Put the basil leaves, garlic, pine nuts and grated Parmesan into a food processor and blend for about 30 seconds or until smooth. Alternatively, pound all of the ingredients by hand, using a mortar and pestle.

3 If you are using a food processor, keep the motor running and slowly add the olive oil. Alternatively, add the oil drop by drop while stirring briskly. Season with salt and pepper to taste.

4 Cook the pasta in a saucepan of boiling water allowing 3–4 minutes for fresh pasta or 8–10 minutes for dried, or until it is cooked through, but still has

'bite'. Drain the pasta thoroughly in a colander.

5 Transfer the pasta to a serving plate and serve with the pesto. Toss to mix well and serve hot.

COOK'S TIP

You can store pesto in the refrigerator for about 4 weeks. Cover the surface of the pesto with olive oil before sealing the container or bottle, to prevent the basil from oxidising and turning black.

Pasta & Olive Omelette

Use any leftover cooked pasta you may have, such as penne, short-cut macaroni or shells, to make this fluffy omelette an instant success.

NUTRITIONAL INFORMATION

Calories	.521	Sugars	.3g
Protein	.18g	Fat	.34g
Carbohydrate	.38g	Saturates	.6g

 20 MINS   🕐 20 MINS

SERVES 2

INGREDIENTS

4 tbsp olive oil

1 small onion, chopped

1 fennel bulb, thinly sliced

125 g/4½ oz raw potato, diced and dried

1 garlic clove, chopped

4 eggs

1 tbsp chopped parsley

pinch of cayenne pepper

90 g/3 oz short pasta, cooked weight

1 tbsp stuffed green olives, halved, plus
    extra to garnish

salt and pepper

marjoram sprigs, to garnish

tomato salad, to serve

1 Heat 2 tablespoons of the oil in a heavy frying pan (skillet) over a low heat and fry the onion, fennel and potato for 8-10 minutes, stirring occasionally, until the potato is just tender. Do not allow it to break up. Stir in the garlic and cook for 1 minute. Remove the pan from the heat, lift out the vegetables with a slotted spoon and set aside. Rinse and dry the pan.

2 Break the eggs into a bowl and beat until frothy. Stir in the parsley and season with salt, pepper and cayenne.

3 Heat 1 tablespoon of the remaining oil in a pan over a medium heat. Pour in half of the beaten eggs, then add the cooked vegetables, the pasta and the olives. Pour on the remaining egg and cook until the sides begin to set.

4 Lift up the edges with a spatula to allow the uncooked egg to spread underneath. Continue cooking the omelette, shaking the pan occasionally, until the underside is golden brown.

5 Slide the omelette out on to a large, flat plate and wipe the pan clean with paper towels. Heat the remaining oil in the pan and invert the omelette. Cook the omelette on the other side until it is also golden brown.

6 Slide the omelette on to a warmed serving dish. Garnish with a few olives and sprigs of marjoram, and serve hot, cut into wedges, with a tomato salad, if wished.

Pasta with Green Vegetables

The different shapes and textures of the vegetables make a mouthwatering presentation in this light and summery dish.

NUTRITIONAL INFORMATION

Calories 517   Sugars 5g
Protein . . . . .17g   Fat 32g
Carbohydrate . . .42g   Saturates 18g

 10 MINS   25 MINS

SERVES 4

I N G R E D I E N T S

225 g/8 oz gemelli or other pasta shapes

1 tbsp olive oil

2 tbsp chopped fresh parsley

2 tbsp freshly grated Parmesan

salt and pepper

S A U C E

1 head of green broccoli, cut into florets

2 courgettes (zucchini), sliced

225 g/8 oz asparagus spears, trimmed

125 g/4½ oz mangetout (snow peas), trimmed

125 g/4½ oz frozen peas

25 g/1 oz/2 tbsp butter

3 tbsp vegetable stock

5 tbsp double (heavy) cream

large pinch of freshly grated nutmeg

1 Cook the pasta in a large pan of salted boiling water, adding the olive oil, for 8–10 minutes or until tender. Drain the pasta in a colander, return to the pan, cover and keep warm.

2 Steam the broccoli, courgettes (zucchini), asparagus spears and mangetout (snow peas) over a pan of boiling, salted water until just beginning to soften. Remove from the heat and plunge into cold water to prevent further cooking. Drain and set aside.

3 Cook the peas in boiling, salted water for 3 minutes, then drain. Refresh in cold water and drain again.

4 Put the butter and vegetable stock in a pan over a medium heat. Add all of the vegetables except for the asparagus spears and toss carefully with a wooden spoon to heat through, taking care not to break them up. Stir in the cream, allow the sauce to heat through and season with salt, pepper and nutmeg.

5 Transfer the pasta to a warmed serving dish and stir in the chopped parsley. Spoon the sauce over, and sprinkle on the freshly grated Parmesan. Arrange the asparagus spears in a pattern on top. Serve hot.

Italian Tomato Sauce & Pasta

Fresh tomatoes make a delicious Italian-style sauce which goes particularly well with pasta.

NUTRITIONAL INFORMATION

Calories 304	Sugars 8g
Protein 15g	Fat 14g
Carbohydrate . . .31g	Saturates 5g

 10 MINS   25 MINS

SERVES 2

I N G R E D I E N T S

1 tbsp olive oil

1 small onion, chopped finely

1–2 cloves garlic, crushed

350 g/12 oz tomatoes, peeled and chopped

2 tsp tomato purée (paste)

2 tbsp water

300–350 g/10½–12 oz dried pasta shapes

90 g/3 oz/¾ cup lean bacon,
   derinded and diced

40 g/1½ oz/½ cup mushrooms, sliced

1 tbsp chopped fresh parsley or 1 tsp
   chopped fresh coriander (cilantro)

2 tbsp soured cream or natural fromage
   frais (optional)

salt and pepper

COOK'S TIP

Sour cream contains
18–20% fat, so if you are
following a low fat diet you can leave
it out of this recipe or substitute a
low-fat alternative.

1 To make the tomato sauce, heat the oil in a saucepan and fry the onion and garlic gently until soft.

2 Add the tomatoes, tomato purée (paste), water and salt and pepper to taste to the mixture in the pan and bring to the boil. Cover and simmer gently for 10 minutes.

3 Meanwhile, cook the pasta in a saucepan of boiling salted water for 8–10 minutes, or until just tender. Drain the pasta thoroughly and transfer to warm serving dishes.

4 Heat the bacon gently in a frying pan (skillet) until the fat runs, then add the mushrooms and continue cooking for 3–4 minutes. Drain off any excess oil.

5 Add the bacon and mushrooms to the tomato mixture, together with the parsley or coriander (cilantro) and the soured cream or fromage frais, if using. Reheat and serve with the pasta.

Mushroom & Pasta Flan

Lightly cooked vermicelli is pressed into a flan ring and baked with a creamy mushroom filling.

NUTRITIONAL INFORMATION

Calories	557	Sugars	.........5g
Protein	........15g	Fat	..........36g
Carbohydrate	...47g	Saturates	......19g

10 MINS   1 HR 10 MINS

SERVES 4

I N G R E D I E N T S

225 g/8 oz vermicelli or spaghetti

1 tbsp olive oil

25 g/1 oz/2 tbsp butter, plus extra for greasing

salt and pepper

tomato and basil salad, to serve

S A U C E

60 g/2 oz/¼ cup butter

1 onion, chopped

150 g/5½ oz button mushrooms, trimmed

1 green (bell) pepper, cored, deseeded and sliced into thin rings

150 ml/¼ pint/⅔ cup milk

3 eggs, beaten lightly

2 tbsp double (heavy) cream

1 tsp dried oregano

pinch of finely grated nutmeg

1 tbsp freshly grated Parmesan

1 Cook the pasta in a large pan of salted boiling water, adding the olive oil, for 8–10 minutes or until tender. Drain the pasta in a colander, return to the pan, add the butter and shake the pan well.

2 Grease a 20 cm/8 inch loose-bottomed flan tin (pan). Press the pasta on to the base and around the sides to form a case.

3 Heat the butter in a frying pan (skillet) over a medium heat and fry the onion until it is translucent. Remove with a slotted spoon and spread in the flan base.

4 Add the mushrooms and (bell) pepper rings to the pan and turn them in the fat until glazed. Fry for 2 minutes on each side, then arrange in the flan base.

5 Beat together the milk, eggs and cream, stir in the oregano, and season with nutmeg and pepper. Pour the mixture carefully over the vegetables and sprinkle on the cheese.

6 Bake the flan in the preheated oven, 180°C/350°F/Gas Mark 4, for 40–45 minutes, or until the filling is set. Slide on to a serving plate and serve warm.

Three-Cheese Macaroni

Based on a traditional family favourite, this pasta bake has plenty of flavour. Serve with a crisp salad for a quick, tasty supper.

NUTRITIONAL INFORMATION

Calories	672	Sugars	........10g
Protein	........31g	Fat	..........44g
Carbohydrate	...40g	Saturates	......23g

 30 MINS   45 MINS

SERVES 4

I N G R E D I E N T S

600 ml/1 pint/2½ cups Béchamel Sauce
   (see page 28)

225 g/8 oz/2 cups macaroni

1 egg, beaten

125 g/4½ oz/1 cup grated mature
   (sharp) Cheddar

1 tbsp wholegrain mustard

2 tbsp chopped fresh chives

4 tomatoes, sliced

125 g/4½ oz/1 cup grated Red Leicester
   (brick) cheese

60 g/2 oz/½ cup grated blue cheese

2 tbsp sunflower seeds

salt and pepper

snipped fresh chives, to garnish

1 Make the Béchamel Sauce, put into a bowl and cover with cling film (plastic wrap) to prevent a skin forming. Set aside.

2 Bring a saucepan of salted water to the boil and cook the macaroni for 8–10 minutes or until just tender. Drain well and place in an ovenproof dish.

3 Stir the beaten egg, Cheddar, mustard, chives and seasoning into the Béchamel Sauce and spoon over the macaroni, making sure it is well covered. Top with a layer of sliced tomatoes.

4 Sprinkle over the Red Leicester (brick) and blue cheeses, and sunflower seeds. Put on a baking tray (cookie sheet) and bake in a preheated oven, 190°C/375°F/Gas Mark 5, for 25–30 minutes or until bubbling and golden. Garnish with chives and serve immediately.

Vegetable & Pasta Parcels

These small parcels are very easy to make and have the advantage of being filled with your favourite mixture of succulent mushrooms.

NUTRITIONAL INFORMATION

Calories 333   Sugars 1g
Protein . . . . .7g   Fat 30g
Carbohydrate . . .10g   Saturates 13g

20 MINS   20 MINS

SERVES 4

INGREDIENTS

FILLING

25 g/1 oz/3 tbsp butter or margarine

2 garlic cloves, crushed

1 small leek, chopped

2 celery sticks, chopped

200 g/7 oz/2⅓ cups open-cap
   mushrooms, chopped

1 egg, beaten

2 tbsp grated Parmesan cheese

salt and pepper

RAVIOLI

4 sheets filo pastry

25 g/1 oz/3 tbsp margarine

oil, for deep-frying

1 To make the filling, melt the butter or margarine in a frying pan (skillet) and sauté the garlic and leek for 2–3 minutes until softened.

2 Add the celery and mushrooms and cook for a further 4–5 minutes until all of the vegetables are tender.

3 Turn off the heat and stir in the egg and grated Parmesan cheese. Season with salt and pepper to taste.

4 Lay the pastry sheets on a chopping board and cut each into nine squares.

5 Spoon a little of the filling into the centre half of the squares and brush the edges of the pastry with butter or margarine. Lay another square on top and seal the edges to make a parcel.

6 Heat the oil for deep-frying to 180°C/350°F or until a cube of bread browns in 30 seconds. Fry the ravioli, in batches, for 2–3 minutes or until golden brown. Remove from the oil with a slotted spoon and pat dry on absorbent paper towels. Transfer to a warm serving plate and serve.

Rice & Grains

Rice dishes are particularly popular in the north of Italy as the people in this area are very fond of risottos. Milanese and other risottos are made with short-grain Italian rice,

the best of which is arborio rice. An Italian risotto is far moister than a pilau or other savoury rice dish, but it should not be soggy or sticky. Gnocchi are made with maize flour, cornmeal, potatoes or semolina, often combined with spinach or some sort of cheese. Gnocchi resemble dumplings and are either poached or baked. Polenta is made with cornmeal or polenta flour and can be served either as a soft porridge or a firmer cake which is then fried until crisp.

Golden Chicken Risotto

Long-grain rice can be used instead of risotto rice, but it won't give you the traditional, creamy texture that is typical of Italian risottos.

NUTRITIONAL INFORMATION

Calories	701	Sugars	.........7g
Protein	........35g	Fat	..........26g
Carbohydrate	...88g	Saturates	.......8g

10 MINS   30 MINS

SERVES 4

INGREDIENTS

2 tbsp sunflower oil

15 g/ ½ oz/1 tbsp butter or margarine

1 medium leek, thinly sliced

1 large yellow (bell) pepper, diced

3 skinless, boneless chicken breasts, diced

350 g/12 oz arborio (risotto) rice

a few strands of saffron

1.5 litres/2 ¾ pints/6 ¼ cups chicken stock

200 g/7 oz can sweetcorn
  (corn-on-the-cob)

60 g/2 oz/ ½ cup toasted unsalted peanuts

60 g/2 oz/ ½ cup grated Parmesan cheese

salt and pepper

COOK'S TIP

Risottos can be frozen, before adding the Parmesan cheese, for up to 1 month, but remember to reheat this risotto thoroughly as it contains chicken.

1 Heat the sunflower oil and butter or margarine in a large saucepan. Fry the leek and (bell) pepper for 1 minute, then stir in the chicken and cook, stirring until golden brown.

2 Stir in the arborio (risotto) rice and cook for 2–3 minutes.

3 Stir in the saffron strands and salt and pepper to taste. Add the chicken stock, a little at a time, cover and cook over a low heat, stirring occasionally, for about 20 minutes, or until the rice is tender and most of the liquid has been absorbed. Do not let the risotto dry out – add more stock if necessary.

4 Stir in the sweetcorn (corn-on-the-cob), peanuts and Parmesan cheese, then season with salt and pepper to taste. Serve hot.

Sun-dried Tomato Risotto

A Milanese risotto can be cooked in a variety of ways – but always with saffron. This version with sun-dried tomatoes has a lovely tangy flavour.

NUTRITIONAL INFORMATION

Calories	558	Sugars	.........2g
Protein	........16g	Fat	..........19g
Carbohydrate	...80g	Saturates	.......9g

10 MINS   30 MINS

SERVES 4

INGREDIENTS

1 tbsp olive oil

25 g/1 oz/2 tbsp butter

1 large onion, finely chopped

350 g/12 oz arborio (risotto) rice, washed

about 15 strands of saffron

150 ml/¼ pint/⅔ cup white wine

850 ml/1½ pints/3¾ cup hot vegetable or
  chicken stock

8 sun-dried tomatoes, cut into strips

100 g/3½ oz frozen peas, defrosted

50 g/1¾ oz Parma ham
  (prosciutto), shredded

75 g/2¾ oz Parmesan cheese, grated

1 Heat the oil and butter in a large frying pan (skillet). Add the onion and cook for 4–5 minutes or until softened.

2 Add the rice and saffron to the frying pan (skillet), stirring well to coat the rice in the oil, and cook for 1 minute.

3 Add the wine and stock slowly to the rice mixture in the pan, a ladleful at a time, stirring and making sure that all the liquid is absorbed before adding the next ladleful of liquid.

4 About half-way through adding the stock, stir in the sun-dried tomatoes.

5 When all of the wine and stock has been absorbed, the rice should be cooked. Test by tasting a grain – if it is still crunchy, add a little more water and continue cooking. It should take 15–20 minutes to cook.

6 Stir in the peas, Parma ham (prosciutto) and cheese. Cook for 2–3 minutes, stirring, until hot. Serve with extra Parmesan.

COOK'S TIP

The finished risotto should have moist but separate grains. This is achieved by adding the hot stock a little at a time, only adding more when the last addition has been absorbed. Don't leave the risotto to cook by itself: it needs constant checking to see when more liquid is required.

Rice-Filled Aubergines

An aubergine (eggplant) is halved and filled with a risotto mixture, topped with cheese and baked to make a snack or quick meal for two.

NUTRITIONAL INFORMATION

Calories 435   Sugars 17g
Protein . . . . .13g   Fat 23g
Carbohydrate . . .48g   Saturates 8g

20 MINS   1 HOUR

SERVES 2

INGREDIENTS

60 g/2 oz/¼ cup mixed long-grain and
  wild rice

1 aubergine (eggplant), about 350 g/12 oz

1 tbsp olive oil

1 small onion, chopped finely

1 garlic clove, crushed

½ small red (bell) pepper, cored, deseeded
  and chopped

2 tbsp water

25 g/1 oz/3 tbsp raisins

25 g/1 oz/¼ cup cashew nuts,
  chopped roughly

½ tsp dried oregano

45 g/1½ oz/⅓ cup mature (sharp) Cheddar
  or Parmesan cheese, grated

salt and pepper

fresh oregano or parsley, to garnish

1 Cook the rice in a pan of boiling salted water for 15 minutes or until tender. Drain, rinse and drain again.

2 Bring a large pan of water to the boil. Cut the stem off the aubergine (eggplant) and then cut in half lengthwise. Cut out the flesh from the centre, leaving a 1.5 cm/½ inch shell. Blanch the shells in the boiling water for 3–4 minutes. Drain.

3 Chop the aubergine (eggplant) flesh finely.

4 Heat the oil in a pan and fry the onion and garlic gently until just beginning to soften. Add the (bell) pepper and aubergine (eggplant) flesh and continue cooking for 2 minutes. Add the water and cook for 2–3 minutes.

5 Stir the raisins, cashew nuts, oregano and rice into the aubergine (eggplant) mixture and season with salt and pepper to taste.

6 Lay the aubergine (eggplant) shells in an ovenproof dish and spoon in the rice mixture, piling it up well. Cover and place in a preheated oven, at 190°C/375°F/Gas Mark 5, for 20 minutes.

7 Remove the lid and sprinkle the cheese over the rice. Place under a preheated moderate grill (broiler) for 3–4 minutes or until golden brown. Serve hot garnished with oregano or parsley.

Milanese Risotto

Italian rice is a round, short-grained variety with a nutty flavour, which is essential for a good risotto. Arborio is a good one to use.

NUTRITIONAL INFORMATION

Calories 631	Sugars 1g	
Protein 16g	Fat 29g	
Carbohydrate . . .77g	Saturates 17g	

10 MINS   35 MINS

SERVES 4

I N G R E D I E N T S

2 good pinches of saffron threads

1 large onion, chopped finely

1–2 garlic cloves, crushed

90 g/3 oz/6 tbsp butter

350 g/12 oz/1⅔ cups arborio (risotto) rice

150 ml/¼ pint/⅔ cup dry white wine

1.2 litres/2 pints/5 cups boiling stock
   (chicken, beef or vegetable)

90 g/3 oz/¾ cup Parmesan, grated

salt and pepper

1 Put the saffron in a small bowl, cover with 3–4 tablespoons of boiling water and leave to soak while cooking the risotto.

2 Fry the onion and garlic in 60 g/2 oz of the butter until soft but not coloured. Add the rice and continue to cook for 2–3 minutes or until all of the grains are coated in oil and just beginning to colour lightly.

3 Add the wine to the rice and simmer gently, stirring from time to time, until it is all absorbed.

4 Add the boiling stock a little at a time, about 150 ml/¼ pint/⅔ cup, cooking until the liquid is fully absorbed before adding more, and stirring frequently.

5 When all the stock has been absorbed (this should take about 20 minutes), the rice should be tender but not soft and soggy. Add the saffron liquid, Parmesan, remaining butter and salt and pepper to taste. Leave to simmer for 2 minutes until piping hot and thoroughly mixed.

6 Cover the pan tightly and leave to stand for 5 minutes off the heat. Give a good stir and serve at once.

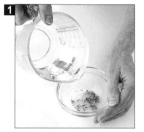

Green Risotto

A simple rice dish cooked with green vegetables and herbs. This recipe has been adapted for the microwave.

NUTRITIONAL INFORMATION

Calories	344	Sugars	.........4g
Protein	........13g	Fat	..........10g
Carbohydrate	...54g	Saturates	.......4g

15 MINS 20 MINS

SERVES 4

INGREDIENTS

1 onion, chopped

2 tbsp olive oil

225 g/8 oz/generous 1 cup risotto rice

700 ml/1¼ pints/3 cups hot
vegetable stock

350 g/12 oz mixed green vegetables, such
as asparagus, thin green beans,
mangetout (snow peas), courgettes
(zucchini), broccoli florets, frozen peas

2 tbsp chopped fresh parsley

60 g/2 oz/¼ cup fresh Parmesan cheese,
shaved thinly

salt and pepper

COOK'S TIP

For extra texture, stir in a few toasted pine kernels (nuts) or coarsely chopped cashew nuts at the end of the cooking time.

1 Place the onion and oil in a large bowl. Cover and cook on HIGH power for 2 minutes.

2 Add the rice and stir until thoroughly coated in the oil. Pour in about 75 ml/ 3 fl oz/⅓ cup of the hot stock. Cook, uncovered, for 2 minutes, until the liquid has been absorbed. Pour in another 75 ml/ 3 fl oz/⅓ cup of the stock and cook, uncovered, on HIGH power for 2 minutes. Repeat once more.

3 Chop or slice the vegetables into even-sized pieces. Stir into the rice

with the remaining stock. Cover and cook on HIGH power for 8 minutes, stirring occasionally, until most of the liquid has been absorbed and the rice is just tender.

4 Stir in the parsley and season generously. Leave to stand, covered, for almost 5 minutes. The rice should be tender and creamy.

5 Scatter the Parmesan cheese over the risotto before serving.

Genoese Seafood Risotto

This is cooked in a different way from any of the other risottos. First, you cook the rice, then you prepare a sauce, then you mix the two together.

NUTRITIONAL INFORMATION

Calories 424	Sugars 0g
Protein 23g	Fat 17g
Carbohydrate . . .46g	Saturates 10g

 10 MINS 25 MINS

SERVES 4

I N G R E D I E N T S

1.2 litres/2 pints/5 cups hot fish or
  chicken stock

350 g/12 oz arborio (risotto) rice, washed

50 g/1¾ oz/3 tbsp butter

2 garlic cloves, chopped

250 g/9 oz mixed seafood, preferably raw,
  such as prawns (shrimp), squid, mussels,
  clams and (small) shrimps

2 tbsp chopped oregano, plus extra
  for garnishing

50 g/1¾ oz pecorino or Parmesan
  cheese, grated

1 In a large saucepan, bring the stock to the boil. Add the rice and cook for about 12 minutes, stirring, or until the rice is tender. Drain thoroughly, reserving any excess liquid.

2 Heat the butter in a large frying pan (skillet) and add the garlic, stirring.

3 Add the raw mixed seafood to the pan (skillet) and cook for 5 minutes. If you are using cooked seafood, fry for 2–3 minutes.

4 Stir the oregano into the seafood mixture in the frying pan (skillet).

5 Add the cooked rice to the pan and cook for 2–3 minutes, stirring, or until hot. Add the reserved stock if the mixture gets too sticky.

6 Add the pecorino or Parmesan cheese and mix well.

7 Transfer the risotto to warm serving dishes and serve immediately.

COOK'S TIP

The Genoese are excellent cooks, and they make particularly delicious fish dishes flavoured with the local olive oil.

Mushroom & Cheese Risotto

Make this creamy risotto with Italian arborio rice and freshly grated Parmesan cheese for the best results.

NUTRITIONAL INFORMATION

Calories	.358	Sugars	.3g
Protein	.11g	Fat	.14g
Carbohydrate	.50g	Saturates	.5g

 20 MINS   40 MINS

SERVES 4

INGREDIENTS

2 tbsp olive or vegetable oil

225 g/8 oz/generous 1 cup arborio
    (risotto) rice

2 garlic cloves, crushed

1 onion, chopped

2 celery sticks, chopped

1 red or green (bell) pepper, deseeded
    and chopped

225 g/8 oz mushrooms, sliced

1 tbsp chopped fresh oregano or
    1 tsp dried oregano

1 litre/1¾ pints/4 cups vegetable stock

60 g /2 oz sun-dried tomatoes in olive oil,
    drained and chopped (optional)

60 g/2 oz/½ cup finely grated
    Parmesan cheese

salt and pepper

TO GARNISH

fresh flat-leaf parsley sprigs

fresh bay leaves

1 Heat the oil in a wok or large frying pan (skillet). Add the rice and cook, stirring, for 5 minutes.

2 Add the garlic, onion, celery and (bell) pepper and cook, stirring, for 5 minutes. Add the mushrooms and cook for 3–4 minutes.

3 Stir in the oregano and stock. Heat until just boiling, then reduce the heat, cover and simmer gently for about 20 minutes or until the rice is tender and creamy.

4 Add the sun-dried tomatoes, if using, and season to taste. Stir in half of the Parmesan cheese. Top with the remaining cheese, garnish with flat-leaf parsley and bay leaves and serve.

Chicken Risotto Milanese

This famous dish is known throughout the world, and it is perhaps the best known of all Italian risottos, although there are many variations.

NUTRITIONAL INFORMATION

Calories 857	Sugars 1g	
Protein 57g	Fat 38g	
Carbohydrate . . .72g	Saturates 21g	

 5 MINS   55 MINS

SERVES 4

INGREDIENTS

125 g/4½ oz/½ cup butter

900 g/2 lb chicken meat, sliced thinly

1 large onion, chopped

500 g/1 lb 2 oz/2½ cups risotto rice

600 ml/1 pint/2½ cups chicken stock

150 ml/¼ pint/⅔ cup white wine

1 tsp crumbled saffron

salt and pepper

60 g/2 oz/½ cup grated Parmesan cheese,
  to serve

1 Heat 60 g/2 oz/4 tbsp of butter in a deep frying pan (skillet), and fry the chicken and onion until golden brown.

2 Add the rice, stir well, and cook for 15 minutes.

3 Heat the stock until boiling and gradually add to the rice. Add the white wine, saffron, salt and pepper to taste and mix well. Simmer gently for 20 minutes, stirring occasionally, and adding more stock if the risotto becomes too dry.

4 Leave to stand for 2–3 minutes and just before serving, add a little more stock and simmer for 10 minutes. Serve the risotto, sprinkled with the grated Parmesan cheese and the remaining butter.

Wild Mushroom Risotto

This creamy risotto is flavoured with a mixture of wild and cultivated mushrooms and thyme.

NUTRITIONAL INFORMATION

Calories	364	Sugars	.........1g
Protein	........15g	Fat	..........16g
Carbohydrate	...44g	Saturates	.......6g

15 MINS 25 MINS

SERVES 4

INGREDIENTS

2 tbsp olive oil

1 large onion, finely chopped

1 garlic clove, crushed

200 g/7 oz mixed wild and cultivated
   mushrooms, such as ceps, oyster, porcini
   and button, wiped and sliced if large

250 g/9 oz arborio (risotto) rice, washed

pinch of saffron threads

700 ml/1¼ pints/scant 3 cups hot
   vegetable stock

200 ml/7 fl oz/¾ cup white wine

100 g/3½ oz Parmesan cheese, grated,
   plus extra for serving

2 tbsp chopped thyme

salt and pepper

COOK'S TIP

Wild mushrooms each have their own distinctive flavours and make a change from button mushrooms. However, they can be quite expensive, so you can always use a mixture with chestnut (crimini) or button mushrooms instead.

1 Heat the oil in a large frying pan (skillet). Add the onions and garlic and sauté for 3–4 minutes or until just softened.

2 Add the mushrooms to the pan and cook for 3 minutes or until they are just beginning to brown.

3 Add the rice and saffron to the pan and stir to coat the rice in the oil.

4 Mix together the stock and the wine and add to the pan, a ladleful at a time. Stir the rice mixture and allow the liquid to be fully absorbed before adding more liquid, a ladleful at a time.

5 When all of the wine and stock is incorporated, the rice should be cooked. Test by tasting a grain – if it is still crunchy, add a little more water and continue cooking. It should take at least 15 minutes to cook.

6 Stir in the cheese and thyme, and season with pepper to taste.

7 Transfer the risotto to serving dishes and serve sprinkled with extra Parmesan cheese.

Risotto-stuffed (Bell) Peppers

Sweet roasted (bell) peppers are delightful containers for a creamy risotto and especially good topped with Mozzarella cheese.

NUTRITIONAL INFORMATION

Calories	613	Sugars	.........7g
Protein	........17g	Fat	.........32g
Carbohydrate	...61g	Saturates	......15g

🍲 15 MINS   🕐 35 MINS

SERVES 4

I N G R E D I E N T S

4 red or orange (bell) peppers

1 tbsp olive oil

1 large onion, finely chopped

350 g/12 oz arborio (risotto) rice, washed

about 15 strands of saffron

150 ml/¼ pint/⅔ cup white wine

850 ml/1½ pints hot vegetable or
   chicken stock

50 g/1¾ oz/3 tbsp butter

50 g/1¾ oz pecorino cheese, grated

50 g/1¾ oz Italian sausage, such as
   felino salame or other coarse Italian
   salame, chopped

200 g/7 oz Mozzarella cheese, sliced

1 Cut the (bell) peppers in half, retaining some of the stalk. Remove the seeds.

2 Place the (bell) peppers, cut side up, under a preheated grill (broiler) for 12–15 minutes or until softened and charred.

3 Meanwhile, heat the oil in a large frying pan (skillet). Add the onion and cook for 3–4 minutes or until softened. Add the rice and saffron, stirring to coat in the oil, and cook for 1 minute.

4 Add the wine and stock slowly, a ladleful at a time, making sure that all of the liquid is absorbed before adding the next ladleful of liquid. When all of the liquid is absorbed, the rice should be cooked. Test by tasting a grain – if it is still crunchy add a little more water and continue cooking. It should take at least 15 minutes to cook.

5 Stir in the butter, pecorino cheese and the chopped Italian sausage.

6 Spoon the risotto into the (bell) peppers. Top with a slice of Mozzarella and grill (broil) for 4–5 minutes or until the cheese is bubbling. Serve hot.

VARIATION

Use tomatoes instead of the (bell) peppers, if you prefer. Halve 4 large tomatoes and scoop out the seeds. Follow steps 3–6 as there is no need to roast them.

Rice & Peas

If you can get fresh peas (and willing helpers to shell them), do use them: you will need 1 kg/2 lb 4 oz. Add them to the pan with the stock.

NUTRITIONAL INFORMATION

Calories 409	Sugars 2g
Protein 15g	Fat 23g
Carbohydrate ...38g	Saturates 12g

 10 MINS   50 MINS

SERVES 4

INGREDIENTS

1 tbsp olive oil

60 g/2 oz/¼ cup butter

60 g/2 oz/¼ cup pancetta
   (Italian unsmoked bacon), chopped

1 small onion, chopped

1.4 litres/2½pints/6¼ cups hot
   chicken stock

200 g/7 oz/1 cup risotto rice

3 tbsp chopped fresh parsley

225 g/8 oz/1¼ cups frozen or
   canned petits pois

60 g/2 oz/½ cup Parmesan, grated

pepper

1 Heat the oil and half of the butter in a saucepan.

2 Add the pancetta (Italian unsmoked bacon) and onion to the pan and fry for 5 minutes.

3 Add the stock (and fresh peas if using) to the pan and bring to the boil.

4 Stir in the rice and season to taste with pepper. Cook until the rice is tender, about 20–30 minutes, stirring occasionally.

5 Add the parsley and frozen or canned petits pois and cook for 8 minutes until the peas are thoroughly heated.

6 Stir in the remaining butter and the Parmesan. Serve immediately, with freshly ground black pepper.

Pesto Rice with Garlic Bread

Try this combination of two types of rice with the richness of pine kernels (nuts), basil, and freshly grated Parmesan.

NUTRITIONAL INFORMATION

Calories	.918	Sugars	.2g
Protein	.18g	Fat	.64g
Carbohydrate	.73g	Saturates	.19g

20 MINS   40 MINS

SERVES 4

INGREDIENTS

300 g/10½ oz/1½ cups mixed long-grain
   and wild rice

fresh basil sprigs, to garnish

tomato and orange salad, to serve

PESTO DRESSING

15 g/½ oz fresh basil

125 g/4½ oz/1 cup pine kernels (nuts)

2 garlic cloves, crushed

6 tbsp olive oil

60 g/2 oz/½ cup freshly grated Parmesan

salt and pepper

GARLIC BREAD

2 small granary or whole wheat
   French bread sticks

90 g/3 oz/½ cup butter or.
   margarine, softened

2 garlic cloves, crushed

1 tsp dried mixed herbs

1 Place the rice in a saucepan and cover with water. Bring to the boil and cook for 15–20 minutes. Drain well and keep warm.

2 Meanwhile, make the pesto dressing. Remove the basil leaves from the stalks and finely chop the leaves. Reserve 25 g/1 oz/¼ cup of the pine kernels (nuts) and finely chop the remainder. Mix with the chopped basil and dressing ingredients. Alternatively, put all the ingredients in a food processor or blender and blend for a few seconds until smooth. Set aside.

3 To make the garlic bread, slice the bread at 2.5 cm/ 1 inch intervals, taking care not to slice all the way through. Mix the butter or margarine with the garlic, herbs and seasoning. Spread thickly between each slice.

4 Wrap the bread in foil and bake in a preheated oven, 200°C/400°F/Gas Mark 6, for 10–15 minutes.

5 To serve, toast the reserved pine kernels (nuts) under a preheated medium grill (broiler) for 2–3 minutes until golden. Toss the pesto dressing into the hot rice and pile into a warmed serving dish. Sprinkle with toasted pine kernels (nuts) and garnish with basil sprigs. Serve with the garlic bread and a tomato and orange salad.

Green Easter Pie

This traditional Easter risotto pie is from Piedmont in northern Italy.
Serve it warm or chilled in slices.

NUTRITIONAL INFORMATION

Calories 392   Sugars 3g
Protein ....17g   Fat 17g
Carbohydrate ...41g   Saturates 5g

 25 MINS   50 MINS

SERVES 4

INGREDIENTS

2 tbsp olive oil

1 onion, chopped

2 garlic cloves, chopped

200 g/7 oz arborio (risotto) rice

700 ml/1¼ pints/scant 3 cups hot chicken
   or vegetable stock

125 ml/4 fl oz/scant ½ cup white wine

50 g/1¾ oz Parmesan cheese, grated

100 g/3½ oz frozen peas, defrosted

80 g/3 oz rocket (arugula)

2 tomatoes, diced

4 eggs, beaten

3 tbsp fresh marjoram, chopped

50 g/1¾ oz breadcrumbs

salt and pepper

1 Lightly grease and then line the base of a 23 cm/9 inch deep cake tin (pan).

2 Using a sharp knife, roughly chop the rocket (arugula).

3 Heat the oil in a large frying pan (skillet). Add the onion and garlic and cook for 4–5 minutes or until softened.

4 Add the rice to the mixture in the frying pan (skillet), mix well to combine, then begin adding the stock a ladleful at a time. Wait until all of the stock has been absorbed before adding another ladleful of liquid.

5 Continue to cook the mixture, adding the wine, until the rice is tender. This will take at least 15 minutes.

6 Stir in the Parmesan cheese, peas, rocket (arugula), tomatoes, eggs and 2 tablespoons of the marjoram. Season to taste with salt and pepper.

7 Spoon the risotto into the tin (pan) and level the surface by pressing down with the back of a wooden spoon.

8 Top with the breadcrumbs and the remaining marjoram.

9 Bake in a preheated oven, at 180°C/350°F/Gas Mark 4, for 30 minutes or until set. Cut into slices and serve immediately.

Aubergine & Rice Rolls

Slices of aubergine (eggplant) are blanched and stuffed with a savoury rice and nut mixture, and baked in a piquant tomato and wine sauce.

NUTRITIONAL INFORMATION

Calories	142	Sugars	.........3g
Protein	.........6g	Fat	...........9g
Carbohydrate	....9g	Saturates	.......3g

30 MINS   1HR 5 MINS

SERVES 8

I N G R E D I E N T S

3 aubergines (eggplants)
  (total weight about 750 g /1 lb 10 oz)

60 g/2 oz/⅓ cup mixed long-grain
  and wild rice

4 spring onions (scallions), trimmed and
  thinly sliced

3 tbsp chopped cashew nuts or toasted
  chopped hazelnuts

2 tbsp capers

1 garlic clove, crushed

2 tbsp grated Parmesan cheese

1 egg, beaten

1 tbsp olive oil

1 tbsp balsamic vinegar

2 tbsp tomato purée (paste)

150 ml/¼ pint/⅔ cup water

150 ml/¼ pint/⅔ cup white wine

salt and pepper

coriander (cilantro) sprigs, to garnish

1 Using a sharp knife, cut off the stem end of each aubergine (eggplant), then cut off and discard a strip of skin from alternate sides of each aubergine (eggplant). Cut each aubergine (eggplant) into thin slices to give a total of 16 slices.

2 Blanch the aubergine (eggplant) slices in boiling water for 5 minutes, then drain on paper towels.

3 Cook the rice in boiling salted water for about 12 minutes or until just tender. Drain and place in a bowl. Add the spring onions (scallions), nuts, capers, garlic, cheese, egg, salt and pepper to taste, and mix well.

4 Spread a thin layer of rice mixture over each slice of aubergine (eggplant) and roll up carefully, securing with a wooden cocktail stick (toothpick). Place the rolls in a greased ovenproof dish and brush each one with the olive oil.

5 Combine the vinegar, tomato purée (paste) and water, and pour over the aubergine (eggplant) rolls. Cook in a preheated oven, at 180°C/350°F/Gas Mark 4, for about 40 minutes or until tender and most of the liquid has been absorbed. Transfer the rolls to a serving dish.

6 Add the wine to the pan juices and heat gently until the sediment loosens and then simmer gently for 2–3 minutes. Adjust the seasoning and strain the sauce over the aubergine (eggplant) rolls. Leave until cold and then chill thoroughly. Garnish with sprigs of coriander (cilantro) and serve.

Polenta

Polenta is prepared and served in a variety of ways and can be served hot or cold, sweet or savoury.

NUTRITIONAL INFORMATION

Calories 661   Sugars 5g
Protein . . . . .15g   Fat 34g
Carbohydrate . . .68g   Saturates 12g

1¼ HOURS   1 HOUR

SERVES 4

INGREDIENTS

1.5 litres/2¾ pints/7 cups water

1½ tsp salt

300 g/10½ oz/2 cups polenta or
   cornmeal flour

2 beaten eggs (optional)

125 g/4½ oz/2 cups fresh fine white
   breadcrumbs (optional)

vegetable oil, for frying and oiling

2 quantities Basic Tomato Sauce (see
   page 28)

MUSHROOM SAUCE

3 tbsp olive oil

250 g/8 oz mushrooms, sliced

2 garlic cloves, crushed

150 ml/¼ pint/⅔ cup dry white wine

4 tbsp double (heavy) cream

2 tbsp chopped fresh mixed herbs

salt and pepper

1 Bring the water and salt to the boil in a large pan and gradually sprinkle in the polenta or cornmeal flour, stirring all the time to prevent lumps forming. Simmer the mixture very gently, stirring frequently, until the polenta becomes very thick and starts to draw away from the sides of the pan, about 30–35 minutes. It is likely to splatter, in which case partially cover the pan with a lid.

2 Thoroughly oil a shallow tin (pan), about 28 x 18 cm/11 x 7 inches, and spoon in the polenta. Spread out evenly, using a wet wooden spoon or spatula. Leave to cool, then leave to stand for a few hours at room temperature, if possible.

3 Cut the polenta into 30–36 squares. Heat the oil in a frying pan (skillet) and fry the pieces until golden brown all over, turning several times – about 5 minutes.

Alternatively, dip each piece of polenta in beaten egg and coat in breadcrumbs before frying in the hot oil.

4 To make the mushroom sauce: heat the oil in a pan and fry the mushrooms with the crushed garlic for 3–4 minutes. Add the wine, season well and simmer for 5 minutes. Add the cream and chopped herbs and simmer for 1–2 minutes.

5 Serve the polenta with either the tomato sauce or mushroom sauce.

Smoked Cod Polenta

Using polenta as a crust for a gratin dish gives a lovely crispy outer texture and a smooth inside. It works well with smoked fish and chicken.

NUTRITIONAL INFORMATION

Calories 616	Sugars 3g
Protein 41g	Fat 24g
Carbohydrate . . .58g	Saturates 12g

30 MINS   1¼ HOURS

SERVES 4

INGREDIENTS

350 g/12 oz instant polenta

1.5 litres/2¾ pints/6½ cups water

200 g/7 oz chopped frozen
   spinach, defrosted

50 g/1¾ oz/3 tbsp butter

50 g/1¾ oz pecorino cheese, grated

200 ml/7 fl oz/¾ cup milk

450 g/1 lb smoked cod fillet,
   skinned and boned

4 eggs, beaten

salt and pepper

1 Cook the polenta, using 1.5 litres/2¾ pints/6½ cups of water to 350 g/12 oz polenta, stirring, for 30–35 minutes.

2 Stir the spinach, butter and half of the pecorino cheese into the polenta. Season to taste with salt and pepper.

3 Divide the polenta among 4 individual ovenproof dishes, spreading the polenta evenly across the bottom and up the sides of the dishes.

4 In a frying pan (skillet), bring the milk to the boil. Add the fish and cook for 8–10 minutes, turning once, or until tender. Remove the fish with a perforated spoon.

5 Remove the pan from the heat. Pour the eggs into the milk in the pan and mix together.

6 Using a fork, flake the fish into smaller pieces and place it in the centre of the dishes.

7 Pour the milk and egg mixture over the fish.

8 Sprinkle with the remaining cheese and bake in a preheated oven, at 190°C/375°F/ Gas Mark 5, for 25–30 minutes or until set and golden. Serve hot.

VARIATION

Try using 350 g/12 oz cooked chicken breast with 2 tablespoons of chopped tarragon, instead of the smoked cod, if you prefer.

Polenta with Rabbit Stew

Polenta can be served fresh, as in this dish, or it can be cooled, then sliced and grilled (broiled).

NUTRITIONAL INFORMATION

Calories 726   Sugars 2g
Protein ....61g   Fat 25g
Carbohydrate ...55g   Saturates 6g

20 MINS   1³/₄ MINUTES

SERVES 4

INGREDIENTS

300 g/10½ oz/2 cups polenta or cornmeal

1 tbsp coarse sea salt

1.2 litres/2 pints/5 cups water

4 tbsp olive oil

2 kg/4 lb 8 oz rabbit joints (pieces)

3 garlic cloves, peeled

3 shallots, sliced

150 ml/¼ pint/⅔ cup red wine

1 carrot, sliced

1 celery stalk, sliced

2 bay leaves

1 sprig rosemary

3 tomatoes, skinned and diced

90 g/3 oz/½ cup pitted black olives

salt and pepper

1 Butter a large ovenproof dish. Mix the polenta, salt and water in a large pan, whisking well to prevent lumps forming. Bring to the boil and boil for 10 minutes, stirring vigorously. Turn into the buttered dish and bake in a preheated oven, 190°C/375°F/Gas Mark 5, for 40 minutes.

2 Meanwhile, heat the oil in a large saucepan and add the rabbit pieces, garlic and shallots. Fry for 10 minutes until browned.

3 Stir in the wine and cook for a further 5 minutes.

4 Add the carrot, celery, bay leaves, rosemary, tomatoes, olives and 300 ml/ ½ pint/1¼ cups water. Cover the pan and simmer for about 45 minutes or until the

rabbit is tender. Season with salt and pepper to taste.

5 To serve, spoon or cut a portion of polenta and place on each serving plate. Top with a ladleful of rabbit stew. Serve immediately.

Chilli Polenta Chips

Polenta is used in Italy in the same way as potatoes and rice. It has little flavour, but combined with butter, garlic and herbs, it is transformed.

NUTRITIONAL INFORMATION

Calories 365	Sugars 1g
Protein 8g	Fat 12g
Carbohydrate . . .54g	Saturates 5g

 5 MINS   20 MINS

SERVES 4

I N G R E D I E N T S

350 g/12 oz instant polenta

2 tsp chilli powder

1 tbsp olive oil

150 ml/¼ pint/⅔ cup soured cream

1 tbsp chopped parsley

salt and pepper

1 Place 1.5 litres/2¾ pints/6¼ cups of water in a saucepan and bring to the boil. Add 2 teaspoons of salt and then add the polenta in a steady stream, stirring constantly.

2 Reduce the heat slightly and continue stirring for about 5 minutes. It is essential to stir the polenta, otherwise it will stick and burn. The polenta should have a thick consistency at this point and should be stiff enough to hold the spoon upright in the pan.

3 Add the chilli powder to the polenta mixture and stir well. Season to taste with a little salt and pepper.

4 Spread the polenta out on to a board or baking tray (cookie sheet) to about 4 cm/1½ inch thick. Leave to cool and set.

5 Cut the cooled polenta mixture into thin wedges.

6 Heat 1 tablespoon of oil in a pan. Add the polenta wedges and fry for 3–4 minutes on each side or until golden and crispy. Alternatively, brush with melted butter and grill (broil) for 6–7 minutes until golden. Drain the cooked polenta on paper towels.

7 Mix the soured cream with parsley and place in a bowl.

8 Serve the polenta with the soured cream and parsley dip.

COOK'S TIP

Easy-cook instant polenta is widely available in supermarkets and is quick to make. It will keep for up to 1 week in the refrigerator. The polenta can also be baked in a preheated oven, at 200°C/400°F/Gas Mark 6, for 20 minutes.

Polenta Kebabs (Kabobs)

Here, skewers of thyme-flavoured polenta, wrapped in Parma ham (prosciutto), are grilled (broiled) or barbecued (grilled).

NUTRITIONAL INFORMATION

Calories 212	Sugars 0g	
Protein 8g	Fat 6g	
Carbohydrate . . .32g	Saturates 1g	

20 MINS   45 MINS

SERVES 4

INGREDIENTS

175 g/6 oz instant polenta

750 ml/1 pint 7 fl oz/scant 3¼ cups water

2 tbsp fresh thyme, stalks removed

8 slices Parma ham (prosciutto)
  (about 75 g/2¾ oz)

1 tbsp olive oil

salt and pepper

fresh green salad, to serve

1 Cook the polenta, using 750 ml/1 pint 7 fl oz/3¼ cups of water to 175 g/6 oz polenta, stirring occasionally, for 30–35 minutes. Alternatively, follow the instructions on the packet.

2 Add the fresh thyme to the polenta mixture and season to taste with salt and pepper.

COOK'S TIP

Try flavouring the polenta with chopped oregano, basil or marjoram instead of the thyme, if you prefer. You should use 3 tablespoons of chopped herbs to every 350 g/12 oz instant polenta.

3 Spread out the polenta, about 2.5 cm/ 1 inch thick, on to a board. Set aside to cool.

4 Using a sharp knife, cut the cooled polenta into 2.5 cm/1 inch cubes.

5 Cut the Parma ham (prosciutto) slices into 2 pieces lengthways. Wrap the Parma ham (prosciutto) around the polenta cubes.

6 Thread the Parma ham (prosciutto) wrapped polenta cubes on to skewers.

7 Brush the kebabs (kabobs) with a little oil and cook under a preheated grill (broiler), turning frequently, for 7–8 minutes. Alternatively, barbecue (grill) the kebabs (kabobs) until golden. Transfer to serving plates and serve with a salad.

Gnocchi with Herb Sauce

These little potato dumplings are a traditional Italian appetizer but, served with a salad and bread, they make a substantial main course.

🐚 🐚 🐚

🍚 30 MINS   🕐 30 MINS

SERVES 6

I N G R E D I E N T S

1 kg/2 lb 4 oz old potatoes, cut into
  1 cm/½ inch pieces

60 g/2 oz/¼ cup butter or margarine

1 egg, beaten

300 g/10½ oz/2½ cups plain
  (all-purpose) flour

salt

S A U C E

125 ml/4 fl oz/½ cup olive oil

2 garlic cloves, very finely chopped

1 tbsp chopped fresh oregano

1 tbsp chopped fresh basil

salt and pepper

T O   S E R V E

freshly grated Parmesan (optional)

mixed salad (greens)

warm ciabatta

1 Cook the potatoes in a saucepan of boiling salted water for about 10 minutes or until tender. Drain well.

2 Press the hot potatoes through a sieve (strainer) into a large bowl. Add 1 teaspoon of salt, the butter or margarine, egg and 150 g/5½ oz/1¼ cups of the flour. Mix well to bind together.

3 Turn on to a lightly floured surface and knead, gradually adding the remaining flour, until a smooth, soft, slightly sticky dough is formed.

4 Flour the hands and roll the dough into 2 cm/¾ inch thick rolls. Cut into 1 cm/½ inch pieces. Press the top of each piece with the floured prongs of a fork and spread out on a floured tea towel (dish cloth).

5 Bring a large saucepan of salted water to a simmer. Add the gnocchi and cook in batches for 2–3 minutes or until they rise to the surface.

6 Remove the gnocchi with a perforated spoon and put in a warmed, greased serving dish. Cover and keep warm.

7 To make the sauce, put the oil, garlic and seasoning in a pan and cook, stirring, for 3–4 minutes until the garlic is golden. Remove from the heat and stir in the herbs. Pour over the gnocchi and serve, sprinkled with Parmesan, and accompanied by salad and warm ciabatta.

Spinach Gnocchi

These gnocchi or small dumplings are made with potato and flavoured with spinach and nutmeg and served in a tomato and basil sauce.

NUTRITIONAL INFORMATION

Calories . . . . . . .337 Sugars 4g
Protein . . . . .9g Fat 10g
Carbohydrate . . .52g Saturates 4g

 25 MINS   1 HOUR

SERVES 4

I N G R E D I E N T S

450 g/1 lb baking potatoes

75 g/2¾ oz spinach

1 tsp water

25 g/1 oz/3 tbsp butter or margarine

1 small egg, beaten

150 g/5½ oz/¾ cup plain (all-purpose) flour

fresh basil sprigs, to garnish

T O M A T O   S A U C E

1 tbsp olive oil

1 shallot, chopped

1 tbsp tomato purée (paste)

225 g/8 oz can chopped tomatoes

2 tbsp chopped basil

85 ml/3 fl oz/6 tbsp red wine

1 tsp caster (superfine) sugar

salt and pepper

1 Cook the potatoes in their skins in a pan of boiling salted water for 20 minutes. Drain well and press through a sieve into a bowl.

2 Cook the spinach in 1 teaspoon of water for 5 minutes or until wilted. Drain and pat dry with paper towels. Chop and stir into the potatoes.

3 Add the butter or margarine, egg and half of the flour to the spinach mixture, mixing well. Turn out on to a floured surface, gradually kneading in the remaining flour to form a soft dough.

4 With floured hands, roll the dough into thin ropes and cut off 2 cm/¾ inch pieces. Press the centre of each dumpling with your finger, drawing it towards you to curl the sides of the gnocchi. Cover the gnocchi and leave to chill.

5 Heat the oil for the sauce in a pan and sauté the chopped shallots for 5 minutes. Add the tomato purée (paste), tomatoes, basil, red wine and sugar and season well. Bring to the boil and then simmer for 20 minutes.

6 Bring a pan of salted water to the boil and cook the gnocchi for 2–3 minutes or until they rise to the top of the pan. Drain well and transfer to serving dishes. Spoon the tomato sauce over the gnocchi. Garnish and serve.

Gnocchi Romana

This is a traditional Italian recipe but, for a less rich version, simply omit the eggs.

NUTRITIONAL INFORMATION

Calories	.709	Sugars	.9g
Protein	.32g	Fat	.41g
Carbohydrate	.58g	Saturates	.25g

1¼ HOURS   45 MINS

SERVES 4

INGREDIENTS

700 ml/1¼ pints/3⅛ cups milk

pinch of freshly grated nutmeg

90 g/3 oz/6 tbsp butter, plus extra
   for greasing

225 g/8 oz/1¼ cups semolina

125 g/4½ oz/1½ cups grated
   Parmesan cheese

2 eggs, beaten

60 g/2 oz/½ cup grated Gruyère (Swiss)
   cheese

salt and pepper

fresh basil sprigs, to garnish

1 Pour the milk into a pan and bring to the boil. Remove the pan from the heat and stir in the nutmeg, 25 g/ 1 oz/2 tbsp of butter and salt and pepper.

2 Gradually stir the semolina into the milk, whisking to prevent lumps forming, and return the pan to a low heat. Simmer, stirring constantly, for about 10 minutes, or until very thick.

3 Beat 60 g/2 oz/⅔ cup of Parmesan cheese into the semolina mixture, then beat in the eggs. Continue beating the mixture until smooth. Set the mixture aside for a few minutes to cool slightly.

4 Spread out the cooled semolina mixture in an even layer on a sheet of baking parchment or in a large, oiled baking tin (pan), smoothing the surface with a damp spatula – it should be 1 cm/½ inch thick. Set aside to cool completely, then chill in the refrigerator for 1 hour.

5 Once chilled, cut out rounds of gnocchi, measuring about 4 cm/1½ inches in diameter, using a plain, greased pastry cutter.

6 Grease a shallow ovenproof dish or 4 individual dishes. Lay the gnocchi

trimmings in the base of the dish or dishes and cover with overlapping rounds of gnocchi.

7 Melt the remaining butter and drizzle over the gnocchi. Sprinkle over the remaining Parmesan cheese, then sprinkle over the Gruyère (Swiss) cheese.

8 Bake in a preheated oven, at 200°C/400°F/Gas Mark 6, for 25-30 minutes, until the top is crisp and golden brown. Serve hot, garnished with the basil.

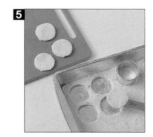

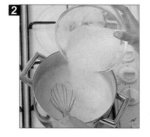

Spinach & Ricotta Gnocchi

Try not to handle the mixture too much when making gnocchi, as this will make the dough a little heavy.

NUTRITIONAL INFORMATION

Calories	.712	Sugars	.15g
Protein	.29g	Fat	.59g
Carbohydrate	.16g	Saturates	.33g

 20 MINS   15 MINS

SERVES 4

INGREDIENTS

1 kg/2 lb 4 oz spinach

350 g/12 oz/1½ cups Ricotta

125 g/4½ oz/1 cup Pecorino, grated

3 eggs, beaten

¼ tsp freshly grated nutmeg

plain (all-purpose) flour, to mix

125 g/4½ oz/½cup unsalted butter

25 g/1 oz/¼ cup pine kernels (nuts)

50 g/2 oz/⅓ cup raisins

salt and pepper

1 Wash and drain the spinach well and cook in a covered saucepan without any extra liquid until softened, about 8 minutes. Place the spinach in a colander and press well to remove as much juice as possible. Either rub the spinach through a sieve (strainer) or purée in a blender.

2 Combine the spinach purée with the Ricotta, half of the Pecorino, the eggs, nutmeg and seasoning to taste, mixing lightly but thoroughly. Work in enough flour, lightly and quickly, to make the mixture easy to handle.

3 Shape the dough quickly into small lozenge shapes, and dust lightly with a little flour.

4 Add a dash of oil to a large saucepan of salted water and bring to the boil. Add the gnocchi carefully and boil for about 2 minutes or until they float to the surface. Using a perforated spoon, transfer the gnocchi to a buttered ovenproof dish. Keep warm.

5 Melt the butter in a frying pan (skillet). Add the pine kernels (nuts) and raisins and fry until the nuts start to brown slightly, but do not allow the butter to burn. Pour the mixture over the gnocchi and serve sprinkled with the remaining grated Pecorino.

Gnocchi & Tomato Sauce

Freshly made potato gnocchi are delicious, especially when they are topped with a fragrant tomato sauce.

NUTRITIONAL INFORMATION

Calories	216	Sugars	.........5g
Protein	.........5g	Fat	..........6g
Carbohydrate	...39g	Saturates	.......1g

30 MINS   45 MINS

SERVES 4

I N G R E D I E N T S

350 g/12 oz floury (mealy) potatoes (those suitable for baking or mashing), halved

75 g/2¾ oz self-raising flour, plus extra for rolling out

2 tsp dried oregano

2 tbsp oil

1 large onion, chopped

2 garlic cloves, chopped

400 g/14 oz can chopped tomatoes

½ vegetable stock cube dissolved in 100 ml/3½ fl oz/⅓ cup boiling water

2 tbsp basil, shredded, plus whole leaves to garnish

salt and pepper

Parmesan cheese, grated, to serve

1 Bring a large saucepan of water to the boil. Add the potatoes and cook for 12–15 minutes or until tender. Drain and leave to cool.

2 Peel and then mash the potatoes with the salt and pepper, sifted flour and oregano. Mix together with your hands to form a dough.

3 Heat the oil in a pan. Add the onions and garlic and cook for 3–4 minutes.

Add the tomatoes and stock and cook, uncovered, for 10 minutes. Season with salt and pepper to taste.

4 Roll the potato dough into a sausage about 2.5 cm/1 inch in diameter. Cut the sausage into 2.5 cm/1 inch lengths. Flour your hands, then press a fork into each piece to create a series of ridges on one side and the indent of your index finger on the other.

5 Bring a large saucepan of water to the boil and cook the gnocchi, in batches, for 2–3 minutes. They should rise to the surface when cooked. Drain well and keep warm.

6 Stir the basil into the tomato sauce and pour over the gnocchi. Garnish with basil leaves and season with pepper to taste. Sprinkle with Parmesan and serve at once.

VARIATION

Try serving the gnocchi with Pesto Sauce (see page 377) for a change.

Gnocchi Piemontese

Gnocchi, a speciality from northern Italy, are small dumplings that are either poached or baked. Prepare the Espagnole Sauce well in advance.

NUTRITIONAL INFORMATION

Calories	643	Sugars	........4g
Protein	........25g	Fat	..........44g
Carbohydrate	...34g	Saturates	......21g

4³/₄ HOURS   15 MINS

SERVES 4

INGREDIENTS

450 g/1 lb warm mashed potato

75 g/2¾ oz/⅝ cup self-raising flour

1 egg

2 egg yolks

1 tbsp olive oil

150 ml/¼ pint/⅝ cup Espagnole Sauce
  (see page 29)

60 g/2 oz/4 tbsp butter

175 g/6 oz/2 cups freshly grated Parmesan
  cheese

salt and pepper

freshly chopped herbs, to garnish

1 In a large bowl, mix together the mashed potato and flour. Add the egg and egg yolks, season with salt and pepper and mix together to form a dough.

VARIATION

Serve with a tomato sauce. Mix 115 g/4 oz/1 cup chopped sun-dried tomatoes, 1 sliced celery stick, 1 crushed garlic clove and 6 tbsp red wine in a pan. Cook over a low heat for 15–20 minutes. Stir in 8 skinned, chopped plum tomatoes, season and simmer for 10 minutes.

2 Break off pieces of the dough and roll between the palms of your hands to form small balls the size of a walnut. Flatten the balls with a fork into the shape of small cylinders.

3 Bring a large pan of lightly salted water to the boil. Add the gnocchi and olive oil and poach for 10 minutes.

4 Mix together the Espagnole Sauce and the butter in a large saucepan over a gentle heat. Gradually blend in the grated Parmesan cheese.

5 Remove the gnocchi from the pan with a slotted spoon. Toss the gnocchi in the sauce, transfer to 4 serving plates, garnish and serve immediately.

Potato & Spinach Gnocchi

These small potato dumplings are flavoured with spinach, cooked in boiling water and served with a simple tomato sauce.

NUTRITIONAL INFORMATION

Calories	315	Sugars	. . . . .7g
Protein	. . . . .8g	Fat	. . . . .8g
Carbohydrate	. . .56g	Saturates	. . . . . . .1g

🍲 20 MINS   🕐 30 MINS

SERVES 4

I N G R E D I E N T S

300 g/10½ oz floury (mealy) potatoes, diced

175 g/6 oz spinach

1 egg yolk

1 tsp olive oil

125 g/4½ oz/1 cup plain (all-purpose) flour

salt and pepper

spinach leaves, to garnish

S A U C E

1 tbsp olive oil

2 shallots, chopped

1 garlic clove, crushed

300 ml/½ pint/1¼ cups passata (sieved tomatoes)

2 tsp soft light brown sugar

1 Cook the diced potatoes in a saucepan of boiling water for 10 minutes or until cooked through. Drain and mash the potatoes.

2 Meanwhile, in a separate pan, blanch the spinach in a little boiling water for 1-2 minutes. Drain the spinach and shred the leaves.

3 Transfer the mashed potato to a lightly floured chopping board and make a well in the centre. Add the egg yolk, olive oil, spinach and a little of the flour and quickly mix the ingredients into the potato, adding more flour as you go, until you have a firm dough. Divide the mixture into very small dumplings.

4 Cook the gnocchi, in batches, in a saucepan of boiling salted water for about 5 minutes or until they rise to the surface.

5 Meanwhile, make the sauce. Put the oil, shallots, garlic, passata (sieved tomatoes) and sugar into a saucepan and cook over a low heat for 10-15 minutes or until the sauce has thickened.

6 Drain the gnocchi using a perforated spoon and transfer to warm serving dishes. Spoon the sauce over the gnocchi and garnish with the fresh spinach leaves.

VARIATION

Add chopped fresh herbs and cheese to the gnocchi dough instead of the spinach, if you prefer.

Baked Semolina Gnocchi

Semolina has a similar texture to polenta, but is slightly grainier. These gnocchi, which are flavoured with cheese and thyme, are easy to make.

NUTRITIONAL INFORMATION

Calories	259	Sugars 0g
Protein	.........9g	Fat 16g
Carbohydrate	...20g	Saturates 10g

15 MINS   30 MINS

SERVES 4

INGREDIENTS

425 ml/¾ pint/1¾ cups vegetable stock

100 g/3½ oz semolina

1 tbsp thyme, stalks removed

1 egg, beaten

50 g/1¾ oz Parmesan cheese, grated

50 g/1¾ oz/3 tbsp butter

2 garlic cloves, crushed

salt and pepper

1 Place the stock in a large saucepan and bring to the boil. Add the semolina in a steady trickle, stirring continuously. Keep stirring for 3–4 minutes until the mixture is thick enough to hold a spoon upright. Set aside and leave to cool slightly.

VARIATION

Try adding ½ tablespoon of sun-dried tomato paste or 50 g/1¾ oz finely chopped mushrooms, fried in butter, to the semolina mixture in step 2. Follow the same cooking method.

2 Add the thyme, egg and half of the cheese to the semolina mixture, and season to taste with salt and pepper.

3 Spread the semolina mixture on to a board to about 12 mm/½ inch thick. Set aside to cool and set.

4 When the semolina is cold, cut it into 2.5 cm/1 inch squares, reserving any offcuts.

5 Grease an ovenproof dish, placing the reserved offcuts in the bottom. Arrange the semolina squares on top and sprinkle with the remaining cheese.

6 Melt the butter in a pan, add the garlic and season with pepper to taste. Pour the butter mixture over the gnocchi. Bake in a preheated oven, at 220°C/425°F/Gas Mark 7, for 15–20 minutes until puffed up and golden. Serve hot.

Potato Noodles

Potatoes are used to make a 'pasta' dough which is cut into thin noodles and boiled. The noodles are served with a bacon and mushroom sauce.

NUTRITIONAL INFORMATION

Calories 810	Sugars 5g	
Protein 21g	Fat 47g	
Carbohydrate . . .81g	Saturates 26g	

30 MINS   25 MINS

SERVES 4

I N G R E D I E N T S

450 g/1 lb floury (mealy) potatoes, diced

225 g/8 oz/2 cups plain (all-purpose) flour

1 egg, beaten

1 tbsp milk

salt and pepper

parsley sprig, to garnish

S A U C E

1 tbsp vegetable oil

1 onion, chopped

1 garlic clove, crushed

125 g/4½ oz open-capped
   mushrooms, sliced

3 smoked bacon slices, chopped

50 g/1¾ oz Parmesan cheese, grated

300 ml/½ pint/1¼ cups double
   (heavy) cream

2 tbsp chopped fresh parsley

1 Cook the diced potatoes in a saucepan of boiling water for 10 minutes or until cooked through. Drain well. Mash the potatoes until smooth, then beat in the flour, egg and milk. Season with salt and pepper to taste and bring together to form a stiff paste.

2 On a lightly floured surface, roll out the paste to form a thin sausage shape. Cut the sausage into 2.5 cm/1 inch lengths. Bring a large pan of salted water to the boil, drop in the dough pieces and cook for 3-4 minutes. They will rise to the surface when cooked.

3 To make the sauce, heat the oil in a pan and sauté the onion and garlic for 2 minutes. Add the mushrooms and bacon and cook for 5 minutes. Stir in the cheese, cream and parsley, and season.

4 Drain the noodles and transfer to a warm pasta bowl. Spoon the sauce over the top and toss to mix. Garnish with a parsley sprig and serve.

COOK'S TIP

Make the dough in advance, then wrap and store the noodles in the refrigerator for up to 24 hours.

Pizzas & Breads

There is little to beat the irresistible aroma and taste of a freshly-made pizza cooked in a wood-fired oven. The recipes for the homemade dough base and freshly made

tomato sauce in this chapter will give you the closest thing possible to an authentic Italian pizza. You can add any type of topping, from salamis and cooked meats, to vegetables and fragrant herbs – the choice is yours! The Italians make delicious bread, combining all of the flavours of the Mediterranean. You can use the breads in this chapter to mop up the juices from a range of Italian dishes, or you can eat them on their own as a tasty snack.

Bread Dough Base

Traditionally, pizza bases are made from bread dough; this recipe will give you a base similar to an Italian pizza.

NUTRITIONAL INFORMATION

Calories 182	Sugars 2g
Protein 5g	Fat 3g
Carbohydrate ...36g	Saturates 0.5g

   1½ HOURS   0 MINS

SERVES 4

INGREDIENTS

15 g/½ oz fresh yeast or 1 tsp dried or
    easy-blend yeast

90 ml/3½ fl oz/6 tbsp tepid water

½ tsp sugar

1 tbsp olive oil

175 g/6 oz plain (all-purpose) flour

1 tsp salt

1 Combine the fresh yeast with the water and sugar in a bowl. If using dried yeast, sprinkle it over the surface of the water and whisk in until dissolved.

2 Leave the mixture to rest in a warm place for 10–15 minutes until frothy on the surface. Stir in the olive oil.

3 Sift the flour and salt into a large bowl. If using easy-blend yeast, stir it in at this point. Make a well in the centre and pour in the yeast liquid, or water and oil (without the sugar for easy-blend yeast).

4 Using either floured hands or a wooden spoon, mix together to form a dough. Turn out on to a floured work surface and knead for about 5 minutes or until smooth and elastic.

5 Place the dough in a large greased plastic bag and leave in a warm place for about 1 hour or until doubled in size. Airing cupboards are often the best places for this process, as the temperature remains constant.

6 Turn out on to a lightly floured work surface and 'knock back' by punching the dough. This releases any air bubbles which would make the pizza uneven. Knead 4 or 5 times. The dough is now ready to use.

Scone (Biscuit) Base

This is a quicker alternative to the bread dough base. If you do not have time to wait for bread dough to rise, a scone (biscuit) base is ideal.

NUTRITIONAL INFORMATION

Calories	215	Sugars	.........3g
Protein	.........5g	Fat	...........7g
Carbohydrate	...35g	Saturates	.......4g

🥄 20 MINS 🕐 0 MINS

SERVES 4

INGREDIENTS

175 g/6 oz self-raising flour

½ tsp salt

25 g/1 oz butter

125 ml/4 fl oz/½ cup milk

1 Sift the flour and salt into a large mixing bowl.

2 Rub in the butter with your fingertips until it resembles fine breadcrumbs.

3 Make a well in the centre of the flour and butter mixture and pour in nearly all of the milk at once. Mix in quickly with a knife. Add the remaining milk only if necessary to mix to a soft dough.

4 Turn the dough out on to a floured work surface and knead by turning and pressing with the heel of your hand 3 or 4 times.

5 Either roll out or press the dough into a 25 cm/10 inch circle on a lightly greased baking tray (cookie sheet) or pizza pan. Push up the edge slightly all round to form a ridge and use immediately.

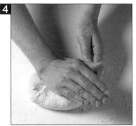

Potato Base

This is an unusual pizza base made from mashed potatoes and flour and is a great way to use up any leftover boiled potatoes.

NUTRITIONAL INFORMATION

Calories	170	Sugars	.........1g
Protein	.........4g	Fat	........3g
Carbohydrate	...34g	Saturates	.......1g

2¼ HOURS   0 MINS

SERVES 4

INGREDIENTS

225 g/8 oz boiled potatoes

60 g/2 oz/¼ cup butter or margarine

125 g/4½ oz/1 cup self-raising flour

½ tsp salt

1 If the potatoes are hot, mash them, then stir in the butter until it has melted and is distributed evenly throughout the potatoes. Leave to cool.

2 Sift the flour and salt together and stir into the mashed potato to form a soft dough.

3 If the potatoes are cold, mash them without adding the butter. Sift the flour and salt into a bowl.

4 Rub in the butter with your fingertips until the mixture resembles fine breadcrumbs, then stir the flour and butter mixture into the mashed potatoes to form a soft dough.

5 Either roll out or press the dough into a 25 cm/10 inch circle on a lightly greased baking tray (cookie sheet) or pizza pan, pushing up the edge slightly all round to form a ridge before adding the topping of your choice. This potato base is rather tricky to lift before it is cooked, so you will find it much easier to handle if you roll it out directly on to the baking tray (cookie sheet).

6 If the base is not required for cooking immediately, cover it with cling film (plastic wrap) and chill it for up to 2 hours.

Tomato Sauce

This is a basic topping sauce for pizzas. Using canned chopped tomatoes for this dish saves time.

NUTRITIONAL INFORMATION

Calories 41	Sugars 3g
Protein 1g	Fat 3g
Carbohydrate 3g	Saturates 0.4g

5 MINS   25 MINS

SERVES 4

INGREDIENTS

1 small onion, chopped

1 garlic clove, crushed

1 tbsp olive oil

200 g/7 oz can chopped tomatoes

2 tsp tomato purée (paste)

½ tsp sugar

½ tsp dried oregano

1 bay leaf

salt and pepper

1 Fry the onion and garlic gently in the oil for 5 minutes or until softened but not browned.

2 Add the tomatoes, tomato purée (paste), sugar, oregano, bay leaf and salt and pepper to taste. Stir well.

3 Bring the sauce to the boil, cover and leave to simmer gently for 20 minutes, stirring occasionally, until you have a thickish sauce.

4 Remove the bay leaf and season to taste. Leave to cool completely before using. This sauce keeps well in a screw-top jar in the refrigerator for up to 1 week.

Special Tomato Sauce

This sauce is made with fresh tomatoes. Use the plum variety whenever available and always choose the reddest ones for the best flavour.

NUTRITIONAL INFORMATION

Calories . . . . .81 Sugars 6g
Protein . . . . .1g Fat 6g
Carbohydrate . . . .6g Saturates 1g

 10 MINS   35 MINS

SERVES 4

INGREDIENTS

1 small onion, chopped

1 small red (bell) pepper, chopped

1 garlic clove, crushed

2 tbsp olive oil

225 g/8 oz tomatoes

1 tbsp tomato purée (paste)

1 tsp soft brown sugar

2 tsp chopped fresh basil

½ tsp dried oregano

1 bay leaf

salt and pepper

1 Fry the onion, (bell) pepper and garlic gently in the oil for 5 minutes until softened but not browned.

2 Cut a cross in the base of each tomato and place them in a bowl. Pour on boiling water and leave for about 45 seconds. Drain, and then plunge in cold water. The skins will slide off easily.

3 Chop the tomatoes, discarding any hard cores.

4 Add the tomatoes to the onion mixture with the tomato purée (paste), sugar, herbs and seasoning. Stir well. Bring to the boil, cover and leave to simmer gently for about 30 minutes, stirring occasionally, or until you have a thickish sauce.

5 Remove the bay leaf and adjust the seasoning to taste. Leave to cool completely before using.

6 This sauce will keep well in a screw-top jar in the refrigerator for up to 1 week.

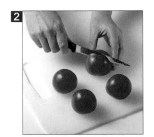

Pizza Margherita

Pizza means 'pie' in Italian. The fresh bread dough is not difficult to make but it does take a little time.

1 HOUR   45 MINS

SERVES 4

I N G R E D I E N T S

BASIC PIZZA DOUGH

7 g/½ oz dried yeast

1 tsp sugar

250 ml/9 fl oz/1 cup hand-hot water

350 g/12 oz strong flour

1 tsp salt

1 tbsp olive oil

TOPPING

400 g/14 oz can tomatoes, chopped

2 garlic cloves, crushed

2 tsp dried basil

1 tbsp olive oil

2 tbsp tomato purée

100 g/3½ oz Mozzarella cheese, chopped

2 tbsp freshly grated Parmesan cheese

salt and pepper

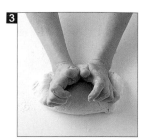

1 Place the yeast and sugar in a measuring jug and mix with 50 ml/2 fl oz/4 tbsp of the water. Leave the yeast mixture in a warm place for 15 minutes or until frothy.

2 Mix the flour with the salt and make a well in the centre. Add the oil, the yeast mixture and the remaining water. Using a wooden spoon, mix to form a smooth dough.

3 Turn the dough out on to a floured surface and knead for 4–5 minutes or until smooth.

4 Return the dough to the bowl, cover with an oiled sheet of cling film (plastic wrap) and leave to rise for 30 minutes or until doubled in size.

5 Knead the dough for 2 minutes. Stretch the dough with your hands, then place it on an oiled baking tray (cookie sheet), pushing out the edges until even. The dough should be no more than 6 mm/¼ inch thick because it will rise during cooking.

6 To make the topping, place the tomatoes, garlic, dried basil, olive oil and salt and pepper to taste in a large frying pan (skillet) and leave to simmer for 20 minutes or until the sauce has thickened. Stir in the tomato purée and leave to cool slightly.

7 Spread the topping evenly over the pizza base. Top with the Mozzarella and Parmesan cheeses and bake in a preheated oven, at 200°C/400°F/Gas Mark 6, for 20–25 minutes. Serve hot.

Tomato Sauce & (Bell) Peppers

This pizza is made with a pastry base flavoured with cheese and topped with a delicious tomato sauce and roasted (bell) peppers.

NUTRITIONAL INFORMATION

Calories	611	Sugars	.........8g
Protein	........14g	Fat	.........38g
Carbohydrate	...56g	Saturates	......21g

  1½ HOURS · 55 MINS

SERVES 4

INGREDIENTS

225 g/8 oz plain (all-purpose) flour

125 g/4½ oz butter, diced

½ tsp salt

2 tbsp dried Parmesan cheese

1 egg, beaten

2 tbsp cold water

2 tbsp olive oil

1 large onion, finely chopped

1 garlic clove, chopped

400 g/14 oz can chopped tomatoes

4 tbsp concentrated tomato purée (paste)

1 red (bell) pepper, halved

5 sprigs of thyme, stalks removed

6 black olives, pitted and halved

25 g/1 oz Parmesan cheese, grated

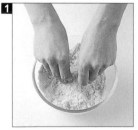  

1 Sift the flour and rub in the butter to make breadcrumbs. Stir in the salt and dried Parmesan. Add the egg and 1 tablespoon of the water and mix with a round-bladed knife. Add more water if necessary to make a soft dough. Cover with cling film (plastic wrap) and chill for 30 minutes.

2 Meanwhile, heat the oil in a frying pan (skillet) and cook the onions and garlic for about 5 minutes or until golden.

Add the tomatoes and cook for 8–10 minutes. Stir in the tomato purée (paste).

3 Place the (bell) peppers, skin-side up, on a baking tray (cookie sheet) and cook under a preheated grill (broiler) for 15 minutes until charred. Place in a plastic bag and leave to sweat for 10 minutes. Peel off the skin and slice the flesh into thin strips.

4 Roll out the dough to fit a 23 cm/ 9 inch loose base fluted flan tin (pan).

Line with foil and bake in a preheated oven, at 200°C/400°F/Gas Mark 6, for 10 minutes or until just set. Remove the foil and bake for a further 5 minutes until lightly golden. Leave to cool slightly.

5 Spoon the tomato sauce over the pastry base and top with the (bell) peppers, thyme, olives and fresh Parmesan. Return to the oven for 15 minutes or until the pastry is crisp. Serve warm or cold.

Vegetable & Goat's Cheese

Wonderfully colourful vegetables are roasted in olive oil with thyme and garlic. The goat's cheese adds a nutty, piquant flavour.

NUTRITIONAL INFORMATION

Calories	387	Sugars	.........9g
Protein	........10g	Fat	..........21g
Carbohydrate	...42g	Saturates	.......5g

 2¹/₂ HOURS   40 MINS

SERVES 4

INGREDIENTS

2 baby courgettes (zucchini), halved lengthways

2 baby aubergines (eggplant), quartered lengthways

½ red (bell) pepper, cut into 4 strips

½ yellow (bell) pepper, cut into 4 strips

1 small red onion, cut into wedges

2 garlic cloves, unpeeled

4 tbsp olive oil

1 tbsp red wine vinegar

1 tbsp chopped fresh thyme

Bread Dough Base (see page 416)

Tomato Sauce (see page 419)

90 g/3 oz goat's cheese

salt and pepper

fresh basil leaves, to garnish

1 Place all of the prepared vegetables in a large roasting tin (pan). Mix together the olive oil, vinegar, thyme and plenty of seasoning and pour over, coating well.

2 Roast the vegetables in a preheated oven, at 200°C/400°F/Gas Mark 6, for 15–20 minutes or until the skins have started to blacken in places, turning half-way through. Leave to rest for 5 minutes after roasting.

3 Carefully peel off the skins from the roast (bell) peppers and the garlic cloves. Slice the garlic.

4 Roll out or press the dough, using a rolling pin or your hands, into a 25 cm/ 10 inch circle on a lightly floured work surface. Place on a large greased baking tray (cookie sheet) or pizza pan and raise the edge a little. Cover and leave for 10 minutes to rise slightly in a warm place. Spread with the tomato sauce almost to the edge.

5 Arrange the roasted vegetables on top and dot with the cheese. Drizzle the oil and juices from the roasting tin (pan) over the pizza and season.

6 Bake in a preheated oven, at 200°C/ 400°F/Gas Mark 6, for 18–20 minutes, or until the edge is crisp and golden. Serve immediately, garnished with basil leaves.

Vegetable Calzone

These pizza base parcels are great for making in advance and freezing – they can be defrosted when required for a quick snack.

NUTRITIONAL INFORMATION

Calories ....499 Sugars 7g
Protein ....16g Fat 9g
Carbohydrate ...95g Saturates 2g

1¹⁄₂ HOURS   40 MINS

SERVES 4

INGREDIENTS

DOUGH

450 g/1 lb/3¹⁄₂ cups strong white flour

2 tsp easy-blend dried yeast

1 tsp caster (superfine) sugar

150 ml/¹⁄₄ pint/³⁄₄ cup vegetable stock

150 ml/¹⁄₄ pint/³⁄₄ cup passata (sieved tomatoes)

beaten egg

FILLING

1 tbsp vegetable oil

1 onion, chopped

1 garlic clove, crushed

2 tbsp chopped sun-dried tomatoes

100 g/3¹⁄₂ oz spinach, chopped

3 tbsp canned and drained sweetcorn

25 g/1 oz/¹⁄₄ cup French (green) beans, cut into 3

1 tbsp tomato purée (paste)

1 tbsp chopped oregano

50 g/1³⁄₄ oz Mozzarella cheese, sliced

salt and pepper

1 Sieve the flour into a bowl. Add the yeast and sugar and beat in the stock and passata (sieved tomatoes) to make a smooth dough.

2 Knead the dough on a lightly floured surface for 10 minutes, then place in a clean, lightly oiled bowl and leave to rise in a warm place for 1 hour.

3 Heat the oil in a frying pan (skillet) and sauté the onion for 2–3 minutes.

4 Stir in the garlic, tomatoes, spinach, corn and beans and cook for 3–4 minutes. Add the tomato purée (paste) and oregano and season with salt and pepper to taste.

5 Divide the risen dough into 4 equal portions and roll each on to a floured surface to form an 18 cm/7 inch circle.

6 Spoon a quarter of the filling on to one half of each circle and top with cheese. Fold the dough over to encase the filling, sealing the edge with a fork. Glaze with beaten egg. Put the calzone on a lightly greased baking tray (cookie sheet) and cook in a preheated oven, at 220°C/ 425°F/Gas Mark 7, for 25–30 minutes until risen and golden. Serve warm.

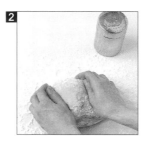  

Mushroom Pizza

Juicy mushrooms and stringy Mozzarella top this tomato-based pizza.
Use wild mushrooms or a combination of wild and cultivated mushrooms.

NUTRITIONAL INFORMATION

Calories ....302 Sugars 7g
Protein ....10g Fat 12g
Carbohydrate ...41g Saturates 4g

1¼ HOURS   45 MINS

SERVES 4

INGREDIENTS

1 portion Basic Pizza Dough (see page 421)

TOPPING

400g/14 oz can chopped tomatoes

2 garlic cloves, crushed

1 tsp dried basil

1 tbsp olive oil

2 tbsp tomato purée (paste)

200 g/7 oz mushrooms

150 g/5½ oz Mozzarella cheese, grated

salt and pepper

basil leaves, to garnish

  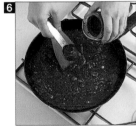

1 Place the yeast and sugar in a measuring jug and mix with 50 ml/2 fl oz/4 tbsp of the water. Leave the yeast mixture in a warm place for 15 minutes or until frothy.

2 Mix the flour with the salt and make a well in the centre. Add the oil, the yeast mixture and the remaining water. Using a wooden spoon, mix to form a smooth dough.

3 Turn the dough out on to a floured surface and knead for 4–5 minutes or until smooth. Return the dough to the bowl, cover with an oiled sheet of cling film (plastic wrap) and leave to rise for 30 minutes or until doubled in size.

4 Remove the dough from the bowl. Knead the dough for 2 minutes. Using a rolling pin, roll out the dough to form an oval or a circular shape, then place it on an oiled baking tray (cookie sheet), pushing out the edges until even. The dough should be no more than 6 mm/¼ inch thick because it will rise during cooking.

5 Using a sharp knife, chop the mushrooms into slices.

6 To make the topping, place the tomatoes, garlic, dried basil, olive oil and salt and pepper in a large pan and simmer for 20 minutes or until the sauce has thickened. Stir in the tomato purée (paste) and leave to cool slightly.

7 Spread the sauce over the base of the pizza, top with the mushrooms and scatter over the Mozzarella. Bake in a preheated oven, at 200°C/400°F/Gas Mark 6, for 25 minutes. Garnish with basil leaves.

Giardiniera Pizza

As the name implies, this colourful pizza should be topped with fresh vegetables from the garden, especially in the summer months.

NUTRITIONAL INFORMATION

Calories 362	Sugars 10g	
Protein 13g	Fat 15g	
Carbohydrate . . .48g	Saturates 5g	

  3¹/₂ HOURS   ⏱ 20 MINS

SERVES 4

I N G R E D I E N T S

6 spinach leaves

Potato Base (see page 418)

Special Tomato Sauce (see page 420)

1 tomato, sliced

1 celery stalk, sliced thinly

½ green (bell) pepper, sliced thinly

1 baby courgette (zucchini), sliced

25 g/1 oz asparagus tips

25 g/1 oz sweetcorn, defrosted if frozen

25 g/1 oz peas, defrosted if frozen

4 spring onions (scallions), trimmed and chopped

1 tbsp chopped fresh mixed herbs

60 g/2 oz Mozzarella, grated

2 tbsp freshly grated Parmesan

1 artichoke heart

olive oil, for drizzling

salt and pepper

1 Remove any tough stalks from the spinach and wash the leaves in cold water. Pat dry with paper towels.

2 Roll out or press the potato base, using a rolling pin or your hands, into a large 25 cm/10 inch circle on a lightly floured work surface. Place the round on a large greased baking tray (cookie sheet) or pizza pan and push up the edge a little. Spread with the tomato sauce.

3 Arrange the spinach leaves on the sauce, followed by the tomato slices. Top with the remaining vegetables and the herbs.

4 Mix together the cheeses and sprinkle over. Place the artichoke heart in the centre. Drizzle the pizza with a little olive oil and season.

5 Bake in a preheated oven, at 200°C/400°F/Gas Mark 6, for 18–20 minutes, or until the edges are crisp and golden brown. Serve immediately.

Tomato & Ricotta Pizza

This is a traditional dish from the Calabrian Mountains in southern Italy, where it is made with naturally sun-dried tomatoes and ricotta cheese.

NUTRITIONAL INFORMATION

Calories 274	Sugars 4g	
Protein 8g	Fat 11g	
Carbohydrate ...38g	Saturates 4g	

1¼ HOURS   30 MINS

SERVES 4

INGREDIENTS

1 portion Basic Pizza Dough (see page 421)

TOPPING

4 tbsp sun-dried tomato paste

150g/5½ oz ricotta cheese

10 sun-dried tomatoes

1 tbsp fresh thyme

salt and pepper

1 Place the yeast and sugar in a measuring jug and mix with 50 ml/2 fl oz/4 tbsp of the water. Leave the yeast mixture in a warm place for 15 minutes or until frothy.

2 Mix the flour with the salt and make a well in the centre. Add the oil, the yeast mixture and the remaining water. Using a wooden spoon, mix to form a dough.

3 Turn the dough out on to a floured surface and knead for 4–5 minutes or until smooth.

4 Return the dough to the bowl, cover with an oiled sheet of cling film (plastic wrap) and leave to rise for 30 minutes or until doubled in size.

5 Remove the dough from the bowl. Knead the dough for 2 minutes.

6 Using a rolling pin, roll out the dough to form a circle, then place it on an oiled baking tray (cookie sheet), pushing out the edges until even. The dough should be no more than 6 mm/¼ inch thick because it will rise during cooking.

7 Spread the sun-dried tomato paste over the dough, then add spoonfuls of ricotta cheese.

8 Cut the sun-dried tomatoes into strips and arrange these on top of the pizza.

9 Sprinkle the thyme, and salt and pepper to taste over the top of the pizza. Bake in a preheated oven, at 200°C/400°F/Gas Mark 6, for 30 minutes or until the crust is golden. Serve hot.

Florentine Pizza

A pizza adaptation of Eggs Florentine – sliced hard-boiled (hard-cooked) eggs on freshly cooked spinach, with a crunchy almond topping.

NUTRITIONAL INFORMATION

Calories 462   Sugars 6g

Protein . . . . .18g   Fat 26g

Carbohydrate . . .41g   Saturates 8g

3 HOURS   20 MINS

SERVES 4

INGREDIENTS

2 tbsp freshly grated Parmesan

Potato Base (see page 418)

Tomato Sauce (see page 419)

175 g/6 oz spinach

1 small red onion, sliced thinly

2 tbsp olive oil

¼ tsp freshly grated nutmeg

2 hard-boiled (hard-cooked) eggs

15 g/½ oz fresh white breadcrumbs

60 g/2 oz Jarlsberg, grated (or Cheddar or Gruyère, if not available)

2 tbsp flaked (slivered) almonds

olive oil, for drizzling

salt and pepper

1 Mix the Parmesan with the potato base. Roll out or press the dough, using a rolling pin or your hands, into a 25 cm/10 inch circle on a lightly floured work surface. Place on a large greased baking tray (cookie sheet) or pizza pan and push up the edge slightly. Spread the tomato sauce almost to the edge.

2 Remove the stalks from the spinach and wash the leaves thoroughly in plenty of cold water. Drain well and pat off the excess water with paper towels.

3 Fry the onion gently in the oil for 5 minutes or until softened. Add the spinach and continue to fry until just wilted. Drain off any excess liquid. Arrange on the pizza and sprinkle over the nutmeg.

4 Remove the shells from the eggs and slice. Arrange the slices of egg on top of the spinach.

5 Mix together the breadcrumbs, cheese and almonds, and sprinkle over. Drizzle with a little olive oil and season with salt and pepper to taste.

6 Bake in a preheated oven, at 200°C/ 400°F/Gas Mark 6, for 18–20 minutes, or until the edge is crisp and golden. Serve immediately.

Potato & Tomato Calzone

These pizza dough Italian pasties are best served hot with a salad as a delicious lunch or supper dish.

NUTRITIONAL INFORMATION

Calories 508	Sugars 8g
Protein 14g	Fat 7g
Carbohydrate ..104g	Saturates 2g

🍖 🍖 🍖

🥔 1½ HOURS   🕐 35 MINS

SERVES 4

INGREDIENTS

DOUGH

450 g/1 lb/4 cups white bread flour

1 tsp easy blend dried yeast

300 ml/½ pint/1¼ cups vegetable stock

1 tbsp clear honey

1 tsp caraway seeds

milk, for glazing

FILLING

225 g/8 oz waxy potatoes, diced

1 tbsp vegetable oil

1 onion, halved and sliced

2 garlic cloves, crushed

40 g/1½ oz sun-dried tomatoes

2 tbsp chopped fresh basil

2 tbsp tomato purée (paste)

2 celery sticks, sliced

50 g/1¾ oz Mozzarella cheese, grated

1 To make the dough, sift the flour into a large bowl and stir in the yeast. Make a well in the centre of the mixture.

2 Stir in the vegetable stock, honey and caraway seeds and bring the mixture together to form a dough.

3 Turn the dough out on to a lightly floured surface and knead for 8 minutes until smooth. Place the dough in a lightly oiled mixing bowl, cover and leave to rise in a warm place for 1 hour or until it has doubled in size.

4 Meanwhile, make the filling. Heat the oil in a frying pan (skillet) and add all of the remaining ingredients except for the cheese. Cook for 5 minutes, stirring.

5 Divide the risen dough into 4 pieces. On a lightly floured surface, roll them out to form four 18 cm/7 inch circles. Spoon equal amounts of the filling on to one half of each circle.

6 Sprinkle the cheese over the filling. Brush the edge of the dough with milk and fold the dough over to form 4 semi-circles, pressing to seal the edges.

7 Place on a non-stick baking (cookie) tray and brush with milk. Cook in a preheated oven, at 220°C/425°F/Gas Mark 7, for 30 minutes until golden and risen. Serve hot.

(Bell) Peppers & Red Onion

The vibrant colours of the (bell) peppers and onion make this a delightful pizza. Served cut into fingers, it is ideal for a party or buffet.

NUTRITIONAL INFORMATION

Calories 380	Sugars 19g
Protein 7g	Fat 17g
Carbohydrate ...53g	Saturates 2g

2¹/₂ HOURS   25 MINS

SERVES 8

I N G R E D I E N T S

Bread Dough Base (see page 416)

2 tbsp olive oil

¹/₂ each red, green and yellow (bell) pepper, sliced thinly

1 small red onion, sliced thinly

1 garlic clove, crushed

Tomato Sauce (see page 419)

3 tbsp raisins

25 g/1 oz pine kernels (nuts)

1 tbsp chopped fresh thyme

olive oil, for drizzling

salt and pepper

1 Roll out or press the dough, using a rolling pin or your hands, on a lightly floured work surface to fit a 30 x 18 cm/12 x 7 inch greased Swiss roll tin (pan). Place in the tin (pan) and push up the edges slightly.

2 Cover and leave the dough to rise slightly in a warm place for about 10 minutes.

3 Heat the oil in a large frying pan (skillet). Add the (bell) peppers, onion and garlic, and fry gently for 5 minutes until they have softened but not browned. Leave to cool.

4 Spread the tomato sauce over the base of the pizza almost to the edge.

5 Sprinkle over the raisins and top with the cooled (bell) pepper mixture. Add the pine kernels (nuts) and thyme. Drizzle with a little olive oil and season well.

6 Bake in a preheated oven, at 200°C/ 400°F/Gas Mark 6, for 18–20 minutes, or until the edges are crisp and golden. Cut into fingers and serve immediately.

Gorgonzola & Pumpkin Pizza

A combination of blue Gorgonzola cheese and pears combine to give a colourful pizza. The wholemeal base adds a nutty flavour and texture.

NUTRITIONAL INFORMATION

Calories 470	Sugars 5g
Protein 17g	Fat 15g
Carbohydrate . . .72g	Saturates 6g

1¼ HOURS   35 MINS

SERVES 4

INGREDIENTS

PIZZA DOUGH

7 g/¼ oz dried yeast

1 tsp sugar

250 ml/9 fl oz/1 cup hand-hot water

175 g/6 oz wholemeal flour

175 g/6 oz strong white flour

1 tsp salt

1 tbsp olive oil

TOPPING

400 g/14 oz pumpkin or squash,
   peeled and cubed

1 tbsp olive oil

1 pear, cored, peeled and sliced

100 g 3½ oz Gorgonzola cheese

1 sprig fresh rosemary, to garnish

1 Place the yeast and sugar in a measuring jug and mix with 50 ml/2 fl oz/4 tbsp of the water. Leave the yeast mixture in a warm place for 15 minutes or until frothy.

2 Mix both of the flours with the salt and make a well in the centre. Add the oil, the yeast mixture and the remaining water. Using a wooden spoon, mix to form a dough.

3 Turn the dough out on to a floured surface and knead for 4–5 minutes or until smooth.

4 Return the dough to the bowl, cover with an oiled sheet of cling film (plastic wrap) and leave to rise for 30 minutes or until doubled in size.

5 Remove the dough from the bowl. Knead the dough for 2 minutes. Using a rolling pin, roll out the dough to form a long oval shape, then place it on an oiled baking tray (cookie sheet), pushing out the edges until even. The dough should be no more than 6 mm/¼ inch thick because it will rise during cooking.

6 To make the topping, place the pumpkin in a shallow roasting tin (pan). Drizzle with the olive oil and cook under a preheated grill (broiler) for 20 minutes or until soft and lightly golden.

7 Top the dough with the pear and the pumpkin, brushing with the oil from the tin (pan). Sprinkle over the Gorgonzola. Bake in a preheated oven, at 200°C/400°F/ Gas Mark 6 for 15 minutes or until the base is golden. Garnish with rosemary.

Ratatouille & Lentil Pizza

Ratatouille and lentils on a wholemeal bread base are topped with cheese and sunflower seeds. The lentils need to be soaked so prepare in advance.

NUTRITIONAL INFORMATION

Calories	377	Sugars	.........6g
Protein	........11g	Fat	..........19g
Carbohydrate	...44g	Saturates	.......5g

2½ HOURS   55 MINS

SERVES 4

INGREDIENTS

60 g/2 oz green lentils

½ small aubergine (eggplant), diced

1 small onion, sliced

1 garlic clove, crushed

3 tbsp olive oil

½ courgette (zucchini), sliced

½ red (bell) pepper, sliced

½ green (bell) pepper, sliced

200 g/7 oz can chopped tomatoes

1 tbsp chopped fresh oregano or 1 tsp dried

Bread Dough Base (see page 416), made
  with wholemeal flour

60 g/2 oz Cheddar, sliced thinly

1 tbsp sunflower seeds

olive oil, for drizzling

salt and pepper

1 Soak the lentils in hot water for 30 minutes. Drain and rinse; then cover with fresh water and simmer over a low heat for 10 minutes.

2 Place the aubergine (eggplant) in a colander, sprinkle with a little salt and leave the bitter juices to drain for about 20 minutes. Rinse well and pat dry with paper towels.

3 Fry the onion and garlic gently in the oil for 3 minutes. Add the courgette (zucchini), (bell) peppers and aubergine (eggplant). Cover and leave to cook over a low heat for about 5 minutes.

4 Add the tomatoes, drained lentils, oregano, 2 tablespoons of water and seasoning. Cover and simmer for 15 minutes, stirring occasionally, adding more water if necessary.

5 Roll out or press the dough, using a rolling pin or your hands, into a 25 cm/10 inch circle on a lightly floured work surface. Place on a large greased baking tray (cookie sheet) or pizza pan and push up the edge slightly. Cover and leave the dough to rise slightly for 10 minutes in a warm place.

6 Spread the ratatouille over the dough base almost to the edge. Arrange the cheese slices on top and sprinkle over the sunflower seeds. Drizzle with a little olive oil and season with a little salt and pepper to taste.

7 Bake in a preheated oven, at 200°C/400°F/Gas Mark 6, for 18–20 minutes, or until the edge is crisp and golden brown. Serve immediately.

Cheese & Artichoke Pizza

Sliced artichokes combined with mature (sharp) Cheddar, Parmesan and blue cheese give a really delicious topping to this pizza.

NUTRITIONAL INFORMATION

Calories 424   Sugars 9g
Protein . . . . .16g   Fat 20g
Carbohydrate . . .47g   Saturates 8g

 1³/₄ HOURS   20 MINS

SERVES 4

I N G R E D I E N T S

Bread Dough Base (see page 416)

Special Tomato Sauce (see page 420)

60 g/2 oz blue cheese, sliced

125 g/4½ oz artichoke hearts in oil, sliced

½ small red onion, chopped

45 g/1½ oz mature (sharp) cheese, grated

2 tbsp freshly grated Parmesan

1 tbsp chopped fresh thyme

oil from artichokes for drizzling

salt and pepper

TO SERVE

salad leaves

cherry tomatoes, halved

1 Roll out or press the dough, using a rolling pin or your hands, to form a 25 cm/10 inch circle on a lightly floured work surface.

2 Place the pizza base on a large greased baking tray (cookie sheet) or pizza pan and push up the edge slightly. Cover and leave to rise for 10 minutes in a warm place.

3 Spread the tomato sauce almost to the edge of the base. Arrange the blue cheese on top of the tomato sauce, followed by the artichoke hearts and red onion.

4 Mix the Cheddar and Parmesan cheeses together with the thyme and sprinkle the mixture over the pizza. Drizzle a little of the oil from the jar of artichokes over the pizza and season to taste.

5 Bake in a preheated oven, at 200°C/ 400°F/Gas Mark 6, for 18–20 minutes, or until the edge is crisp and golden and the cheese is bubbling.

6 Mix the fresh salad leaves and cherry tomato halves together and serve with the pizza, cut into slices.

Cheese & Garlic Mushroom

This pizza dough is flavoured with garlic and herbs and topped with mixed mushrooms and melting cheese for a really delicious pizza.

NUTRITIONAL INFORMATION

Calories 541	Sugars 5g	
Protein 16g	Fat 15g	
Carbohydrate . . .91g	Saturates 6g	

 45 MINS 30 MINS

SERVES 4

INGREDIENTS

DOUGH

450 g/1 lb/3½ cups strong white flour

2 tsp easy-blend yeast

2 garlic cloves, crushed

2 tbsp chopped thyme

2 tbsp olive oil

300 ml/½ pint/1¼ cups tepid water

TOPPING

25 g/1 oz/2 tbsp butter or margarine

350 g/12 oz mixed mushrooms, sliced

2 garlic cloves, crushed

2 tbsp chopped parsley

2 tbsp tomato purée (paste)

6 tbsp passata (sieved tomatoes)

75 g/2¾ oz Mozzarella cheese, grated

salt and pepper

chopped parsley, to garnish

1 Put the flour, yeast, garlic and thyme in a bowl. Make a well in the centre and gradually stir in the oil and water. Bring together to form a soft dough.

2 Turn the dough on to a floured surface and knead for 5 minutes or until smooth. Roll into a 35 cm/14 inch round and place on a greased baking tray (cookie sheet). Leave in a warm place for 20 minutes or until the dough puffs up.

3 Meanwhile, make the topping. Melt the margarine or butter in a frying pan (skillet) and sauté the mushrooms, garlic and parsley for 5 minutes.

4 Mix the tomato purée (paste) and passata (sieved tomatoes) and spoon on to the pizza base, leaving a 1 cm/½ inch edge of dough. Spoon the mushroom mixture on top. Season well and sprinkle the cheese on top.

5 Cook the pizza in a preheated oven, at 190°C/ 375°F/Gas Mark 5, for 20–25 minutes or until the base is crisp and the cheese has melted. Garnish with chopped parsley and serve.

Tofu (Bean Curd), Corn & Peas

Chunks of tofu (bean curd) marinated in ginger and soy sauce impart something of an oriental flavour to this pizza.

NUTRITIONAL INFORMATION

Calories	596	Sugars	........17g
Protein	........33g	Fat	..........23g
Carbohydrate	...66g	Saturates	.......9g

 1 HOUR ⏱ 35 MINS

SERVES 4

I N G R E D I E N T S

1 litre/1¾ pints milk

1 tsp salt

225 g/8 oz semolina

1 tbsp soy sauce

1 tbsp dry sherry

½ tsp grated fresh ginger root

250 g/9 oz tofu (bean curd), cut into chunks

2 eggs

60 g/2 oz Parmesan, grated

Tomato Sauce (see page 419)

25 g/1 oz baby sweetcorn, cut into 4

25 g/1 oz mangetout (snow peas), trimmed
   and cut into 4

4 spring onions (scallions), trimmed and cut
   into 2.5 cm/1 inch strips

60 g/2 oz Mozzarella, sliced thinly

2 tsp sesame oil

salt and pepper

1 Bring the milk to the boil with the salt. Sprinkle the semolina over the surface, stirring all the time. Cook for 10 minutes over a low heat, stirring occasionally, taking care not to let it burn. Remove from the heat and leave to cool until tepid.

2 Mix the soy sauce, sherry and ginger together in a bowl, add the tofu (bean curd) and stir gently to coat. Leave to marinate in a cool place for 20 minutes.

3 Beat the eggs with a little pepper. Add to the semolina with the Parmesan and mix well. Place on a large greased baking tray (cookie sheet) or pizza pan and pat into a 25 cm/10 inch round, using the back of a metal spoon. Spread the tomato sauce almost to the edge.

4 Blanch the sweetcorn and mangetout (snow peas) in a saucepan of boiling water for 1 minute, drain and place on the pizza with the drained tofu (bean curd). Top with the spring onions (scallions) and slices of cheese. Drizzle over the sesame oil and season with salt and pepper.

5 Bake in a preheated oven, at 200°C/400°F/Gas Mark 6, for 18–20 minutes, or until the edge is crisp and golden. Serve immediately.

Wild Mushroom & Walnut

Wild mushrooms make a delicious pizza topping when mixed with walnuts and Roquefort cheese.

NUTRITIONAL INFORMATION

Calories	499	Sugars	.........9g
Protein	........13g	Fat	.......32g
Carbohydrate	...42g	Saturates	......11g

  1¼ HOURS   25 MINS

SERVES 4

I N G R E D I E N T S

Scone (Biscuit) Base (see page 417)

Special Tomato Sauce (see page 420)

125 g/4½ oz soft cheese

1 tbsp chopped fresh mixed herbs, such as
parsley, oregano and basil

225 g/8 oz wild mushrooms, such as oyster,
shiitake or ceps, or 125 g/4½ oz each
wild and button mushrooms

2 tbsp olive oil

¼ tsp fennel seeds

25 g/1 oz walnuts, chopped roughly

45 g/1½ oz blue cheese

olive oil, for drizzling

salt and pepper

sprig of flat-leaf parsley, to garnish

1 Roll out or press the scone (biscuit) base, using a rolling pin or your hands, into a 25 cm/10 inch circle on a lightly floured work surface. Place on a large greased baking tray (cookie sheet) or pizza pan and push up the edge a little with your fingers to form a rim.

2 Carefully spread the tomato sauce almost to the edge of the pizza base. Dot with the soft cheese and chopped fresh herbs.

3 Wipe and slice the mushrooms. Heat the oil in a large frying pan (skillet) or wok and stir-fry the mushrooms and fennel seeds for 2–3 minutes. Spread over the pizza with the walnuts.

4 Crumble the cheese over the pizza, drizzle with a little olive oil and season with salt and pepper to taste.

5 Bake in a preheated oven, at 200°C/ 400°F/Gas Mark 6, for 18–20 minutes, or until the edge is crisp and golden. Serve immediately, garnished with a sprig of flat-leaf parsley.

Tomato & Olive Pizzas

Halved ciabatta bread or baguettes are a ready-made pizza base. The colours of the tomatoes and cheese contrast beautifully on top.

NUTRITIONAL INFORMATION

Calories 181	Sugars 4g
Protein 7g	Fat 10g
Carbohydrate . . .18g	Saturates 4g

45 MINS   25 MINS

SERVES 4

I N G R E D I E N T S

2 loaves of ciabatta or 2 baguettes

Tomato Sauce (see page 419)

4 plum tomatoes, sliced thinly lengthways

150 g/5½ oz Mozzarella, sliced thinly

10 black olives, cut into rings

8 fresh basil leaves, shredded

olive oil, for drizzling

salt and pepper

1 Cut the bread in half lengthways and toast the cut side of the bread lightly. Carefully spread the toasted bread with the tomato sauce.

2 Arrange the tomato and Mozzarella slices alternately along the length.

3 Top with the olive rings and half of the basil. Drizzle over a little olive oil and season with salt and pepper.

4 Either place under a preheated medium grill (broiler) and cook until the cheese is melted and bubbling or bake in a preheated oven, 200°C/400°F/Gas Mark 6, for 15–20 minutes.

5 Sprinkle over the remaining basil and serve immediately.

Marinara Pizza

This pizza is topped with a cocktail of mixed seafood, such as prawns (shrimp), mussels, cockles and squid rings.

NUTRITIONAL INFORMATION

Calories . . . . .359 Sugars 9g
Protein . . . . .19g Fat 14g
Carbohydrate . . .42g Saturates 4g

 3¼ HOURS   20 MINS

SERVES 4

INGREDIENTS

Potato Base (see page 418)

Special Tomato Sauce (see page 420)

200 g/7 oz frozen seafood cocktail, defrosted

1 tbsp capers

1 small yellow (bell) pepper, chopped

1 tbsp chopped fresh marjoram

½ tsp dried oregano

60 g/2 oz Mozzarella, grated

15 g/½ oz Parmesan, grated

12 black olives

olive oil, for drizzling

salt and pepper

sprig of fresh marjoram or oregano, to garnish

1 Roll out or press out the potato dough, using a rolling pin or your hands, into a 25 cm/10 inch circle on a lightly floured work surface.

2 Place the dough on a large greased baking tray (cookie sheet) or pizza pan and push up the edge a little with your fingers to form a rim.

3 Spread the tomato sauce evenly over the base almost to the edge.

4 Arrange the seafood cocktail, capers and yellow (bell) pepper on top of the tomato sauce.

5 Sprinkle over the herbs and cheeses. Arrange the olives on top. Drizzle over a little olive oil and season with salt and pepper to taste.

6 Bake in a preheated oven, at 200°C/ 400°F/Gas Mark 6, for 18–20 minutes or until the edge of the pizza is crisp and golden brown.

7 Transfer to a warmed serving plate, garnish with a sprig of marjoram or oregano and serve immediately.

Onion & Anchovy Pizza

This tasty onion pizza is topped with a lattice pattern of anchovies and black olives. Cut the pizza into squares to serve.

NUTRITIONAL INFORMATION

Calories 373   Sugars 5g
Protein . . . . .12g   Fat 20g
Carbohydrate . . .39g   Saturates 4g

1¾ HOURS   30 MINS

MAKES 6

I N G R E D I E N T S

4 tbsp olive oil

3 onions, sliced thinly

1 garlic clove, crushed

1 tsp soft brown sugar

½ tsp crushed fresh rosemary

200 g/7 oz can chopped tomatoes

Bread Dough Base (see page 416)

2 tbsp freshly grated Parmesan

50 g/1¾ oz can anchovies

12–14 black olives

salt and pepper

1 Heat 3 tablespoons of the oil in a large saucepan and add the onions, garlic, sugar and rosemary. Cover and fry gently, stirring occasionally, for 10 minutes or until the onions are soft but not brown.

2 Add the tomatoes to the pan, stir and season with salt and pepper to taste. Leave to cool slightly.

3 Roll out or press the dough, using a rolling pin or your hands, on a lightly floured work surface to fit a 30 x 18 cm/ 12 x 7 inch greased Swiss roll tin (pan). Place in the tin (pan) and push up the edges slightly to form a rim.

4 Brush the remaining oil over the dough and sprinkle with the cheese. Cover and leave to rise slightly in a warm place for about 10 minutes.

5 Spread the onion and tomato topping over the base. Drain the anchovies, reserving the oil. Split each anchovy in half lengthways and arrange on the pizza in a lattice pattern. Place olives in between the anchovies and drizzle over a little of the reserved oil. Season to taste.

6 Bake in a preheated oven, at 200°C/ 400°F/Gas Mark 6, for 18–20 minutes, or until the edges are crisp and golden. Cut the pizza into 6 squares and serve immediately.

Salmon Pizza

You can use either red or pink salmon for this tasty pizza. Red salmon will give a better colour and flavour but it can be expensive.

NUTRITIONAL INFORMATION

Calories 321   Sugars 6g
Protein . . . . .12g   Fat 14g
Carbohydrate . . .39g   Saturates 6g

1¼ HOURS   20 MINS

SERVES 4

INGREDIENTS

1 quantity Scone (Biscuit) Base (see page 417)

1 quantity Tomato Sauce (see page 419)

1 courgette (zucchini), grated

1 tomato, sliced thinly

100 g/3½ oz can red or pink salmon

60 g/2 oz button mushrooms, wiped and sliced

1 tbsp chopped fresh dill

½ tsp dried oregano

45 g/1½ oz Mozzarella cheese, grated

olive oil, for drizzling

salt and pepper

sprig of fresh dill, to garnish

COOK'S TIP

If salmon is too pricy, use either canned tuna or sardines to make a delicious everyday fish pizza. Choose canned fish in brine for a healthier topping. If fresh dill is unavailable, you can use parsley instead.

1 Roll out or press the dough, using a rolling pin or your hands, into a 25 cm/10 inch circle on a lightly floured work surface (counter). Place on a large greased baking tray (cookie sheet) or pizza pan and push up the edge a little with your fingers to form a rim.

2 Spread the tomato sauce over the pizza base, almost to the edge.

3 Top the tomato sauce with the grated courgette (zucchini), then lay the tomato slices on top.

4 Drain the can of salmon. Remove any bones and skin and flake the fish. Arrange on the pizza with the mushrooms. Sprinkle over the herbs and cheese. Drizzle with a little olive oil and season with salt and pepper.

5 Bake in a preheated oven, at 200°C/400°F/Gas Mark 6, for 18–20 minutes or until the edge is golden and crisp.

6 Transfer to a warmed serving plate and serve immediately, garnished with a sprig of dill.

Pissaladière

This is a variation of the classic Italian pizza but is made with ready-made puff pastry (pie dough). It is perfect for outdoor eating.

NUTRITIONAL INFORMATION

Calories 612   Sugars 13g
Protein . . . . .12g   Fat 43g
Carbohydrate . . .47g   Saturates 11g

20 MINS   55 MINS

SERVES 8

INGREDIENTS

4 tbsp olive oil

700 g/1 lb 9 oz red onions, sliced thinly

2 garlic cloves, crushed

2 tsp caster (superfine) sugar

2 tbsp red wine vinegar

350 g/12 oz fresh ready-made puff pastry
    (pie dough)

salt and pepper

TOPPING

2 x 50 g/1¾ oz cans anchovy fillets

12 green stoned (pitted) olives

1 tsp dried marjoram

1 Lightly grease a swiss roll tin (pan). Heat the olive oil in a large saucepan. Add the red onions and garlic and cook over a low heat for about 30 minutes, stirring occasionally.

2 Add the sugar and red wine vinegar to the pan and season with plenty of salt and pepper.

3 On a lightly floured surface, roll out the pastry (pie dough) to a rectangle, about 33 x 23 cm/13 x 9 inches. Place the pastry (pie dough) rectangle on to the prepared tin (pan), pushing the pastry (pie dough) into the corners of the tin (pan).

4 Spread the onion mixture over the pastry (pie dough).

5 Arrange the anchovy fillets and green olives on top, then sprinkle with the marjoram.

6 Bake in a preheated oven, at 220°C/425°F/Gas Mark 7, for 20-25 minutes or until the pissaladière is lightly golden. Serve the pissaladière piping hot, straight from the oven.

VARIATION

Cut the pissaladière into squares or triangles for easy finger food at a party or barbecue (grill).

Mini Pizzas

Pizette, as they are known in Italy, are tiny pizzas. This quantity will make 8 individual pizzas, or 16 cocktail pizzas to go with drinks.

NUTRITIONAL INFORMATION

Calories 139	Sugars 1g	
Protein 4g	Fat 6g	
Carbohydrate ...18g	Saturates 1g	

1¼ HOURS · 15 MINS

SERVES 8

INGREDIENTS

1 portion Basic Pizza Dough (see page 421)

TOPPING

2 courgettes (zucchini)

100 g/3½ oz passata (sieved tomatoes)

75 g/2¾ oz pancetta, diced

50 g/1¾ oz black olives, pitted and
  chopped

1 tbsp mixed dried herbs

2 tbsp olive oil

1 Place the yeast and sugar in a measuring jug and mix with 50 ml/2 fl oz/4 tbsp of the water. Leave the yeast mixture in a warm place for 15 minutes or until frothy.

2 Mix the flour with the salt and make a well in the centre. Add the oil, the yeast mixture and the remaining water. Using a wooden spoon, mix to form a smooth dough.

3 Turn the dough out on to a floured surface and knead for 4–5 minutes or until smooth. Return the dough to the bowl, cover with an oiled sheet of cling film (plastic wrap) and leave to rise for 30 minutes or until the dough has doubled in size.

4 Knead the dough for 2 minutes and divide it into 8 balls.

5 Roll out each portion thinly to form circles or squares, then place them on an oiled baking tray (cookie sheet), pushing out the edges until even. The dough should be no more than 6 mm/¼ inch thick because it will rise during cooking.

6 To make the topping, grate the courgettes (zucchini) finely. Cover with paper towels and leave to stand for 10 minutes to absorb some of the juices.

7 Spread 2–3 teaspoons of the passata (sieved tomatoes) over the pizza bases and top each with the grated courgettes (zucchini), pancetta and olives. Season with pepper to taste, a sprinkling of mixed dried herbs and drizzle with olive oil.

8 Bake in a preheated oven at 200°C/ 400°F/Gas Mark 6 for 15 minutes or until crispy. Season with salt and pepper to taste and serve hot.

Four Seasons Pizza

This is a traditional pizza on which the toppings are divided into four sections, each of which is supposed to depict a season of the year.

NUTRITIONAL INFORMATION

Calories	313	Sugars	.........8g
Protein	.........8g	Fat	..........13g
Carbohydrate	...44g	Saturates	.......3g

2³/₄ HOURS   20 MINS

SERVES 4

INGREDIENTS

Bread Dough Base (see page 416)

Special Tomato Sauce (see page 420)

25 g/1 oz chorizo sausage, sliced thinly

25 g/1 oz button mushrooms, wiped and sliced thinly

45 g/1½ oz artichoke hearts, sliced thinly

25 g/1 oz Mozzarella, sliced thinly

3 anchovies, halved lengthways

2 tsp capers

4 pitted black olives, sliced

4 fresh basil leaves, shredded

olive oil, for drizzling

salt and pepper

1 Roll out or press the dough, using a rolling pin or your hands, into a 25 cm/10 inch circle on a lightly floured surface. Place on a large greased baking tray (cookie sheet) or pizza pan and push up the edge a little.

2 Cover and leave to rise slightly for 10 minutes in a warm place. Spread the tomato sauce over the pizza base, almost to the edge.

3 Put the sliced chorizo on to one quarter of the pizza, the sliced mushrooms on another, the artichoke hearts on a third, and the Mozzarella and anchovies on the fourth.

4 Dot with the capers, olives and basil leaves. Drizzle with a little olive oil and season. Do not put any salt on the anchovy section as the fish are very salty.

5 Bake in a preheated oven, at 200°C/ 400°F/Gas Mark 6, for 18–20 minutes, or until the crust is golden and crisp. Serve immediately.

Aubergine (Eggplant) & Lamb

An unusual fragrant, spiced pizza topped with minced (ground) lamb and aubergine (eggplant) on a bread base.

NUTRITIONAL INFORMATION

Calories	430	Sugars	........10g
Protein	........18g	Fat	..........22g
Carbohydrate	...44g	Saturates	.......7g

3 HOURS   30 MINS

SERVES 4

INGREDIENTS

1 small aubergine (eggplant), diced

Bread Dough Base (see page 416)

1 small onion, sliced thinly

1 garlic clove, crushed

1 tsp cumin seeds

1 tbsp olive oil

175 g/6 oz minced (ground) lamb

25 g/1 oz canned pimiento, thinly sliced

2 tbsp chopped fresh coriander (cilantro)

Special Tomato Sauce (see page 420)

90 g/3 oz Mozzarella, sliced thinly

olive oil, for drizzling

salt and pepper

1 Place the diced aubergine (eggplant) in a colander, sprinkle with the salt and let the bitter juices drain for about 20 minutes. Rinse thoroughly, then pat dry with paper towels.

2 Roll out or press the dough, using a rolling pin or your hands, into a 25 cm/10 inch circle on a lightly floured work surface. Place on a large greased baking tray (cookie sheet) or pizza pan and push up the edge to form a rim.

3 Cover and leave to rise slightly for 10 minutes in a warm place.

4 Fry the onion, garlic and cumin seeds gently in the oil for 3 minutes. Increase the heat slightly and add the lamb, aubergine (eggplant) and pimiento. Fry for 5 minutes, stirring occasionally. Add the coriander (cilantro) and season with salt and pepper to taste.

5 Spread the tomato sauce over the dough base, almost to the edge. Top with the lamb mixture.

6 Arrange the Mozzarella slices on top. Drizzle over a little olive oil and season with salt and pepper.

7 Bake in a preheated oven, at 200°C/ 400°F/Gas Mark 6, for 18–20 minutes, or until the crust is crisp and golden. Serve immediately.

Onion, Ham & Cheese Pizza

This pizza was a favourite of the Romans. It is slightly unusual because the topping is made without a tomato sauce base.

NUTRITIONAL INFORMATION

Calories 333	Sugars 8g	
Protein 12g	Fat 14g	
Carbohydrate ...43g	Saturates 4g	

 1 HOUR   40 MINS

SERVES 4

INGREDIENTS

1 portion of Basic Pizza Dough (see page 421)

TOPPING

2 tbsp olive oil

250 g/9 oz onions, sliced into rings

2 garlic cloves, crushed

1 red (bell) pepper, diced

100 g/3½ oz raw ham (prosciutto), cut into strips

100 g/3½ oz Mozzarella cheese, sliced

2 tbsp rosemary, stalks removed and roughly chopped

1 Place the yeast and sugar in a measuring jug and mix with 50 ml/2 fl oz/4 tbsp of the water. Leave the mixture in a warm place for 15 minutes or until frothy.

2 Mix the flour with the salt and make a well in the centre. Add the oil, the yeast mixture and the remaining water. Using a wooden spoon, mix to form a smooth dough.

3 Turn the dough out on to a floured surface and knead for 4–5 minutes or until smooth. Return the dough to the bowl, cover with an oiled sheet of cling film (plastic wrap) and leave to rise for 30 minutes or until doubled in size.

4 Remove the dough from the bowl. Knead the dough for 2 minutes. Using a rolling pin, roll out the dough to form a square shape, then place it on an oiled baking tray (cookie sheet), pushing out the edges until even. The dough should be no more than 6 mm/¼ inch thick because it will rise during cooking.

5 To make the topping, heat the oil in a pan. Add the onions and garlic and cook for 3 minutes. Add the (bell) pepper and fry for 2 minutes.

6 Cover the pan and cook the vegetables over a low heat for 10 minutes, stirring occasionally, until the onions are slightly caramelized. Leave to cool slightly.

7 Spread the topping evenly over the pizza base. Arrange the ham (prosciutto), Mozzarella and rosemary over the top.

8 Bake in a preheated oven, at 200°C/ 400°F/Gas Mark 6, for 20–25 minutes. Serve hot.

Tomato & Chorizo Pizza

Spicy chorizo sausage blends beautifully with juicy tomatoes and mild, melting Mozzarella cheese. This pizza makes a delicious light lunch.

NUTRITIONAL INFORMATION

Calories	574	Sugars 8g
Protein	........17g	Fat 38g
Carbohydrate	...43g	Saturates 8g

🍲 15 MINS   🕐 15 MINS

SERVES 2

INGREDIENTS

23 cm/9 inch ready-made pizza base

1 tbsp black olive paste

1 tbsp olive oil

1 onion, sliced

1 garlic clove, crushed

4 tomatoes, sliced

75 g/3 oz chorizo sausages, sliced

1 tsp fresh oregano

125 g/4½ oz Mozzarella cheese, sliced

6 black olives, pitted and halved

pepper

1 Put the pizza base on a baking tray (cookie sheet) and spread the black olive paste to within 1 cm/½ inch of the edge.

2 Heat the oil in a frying pan (skillet) and cook the onion for 2 minutes. Add the garlic and cook for 1 minute.

COOK'S TIP

There are several varieties of pizza base available. Those with added olive oil are preferable because the dough is much lighter and tastier.

3 Spread the onion mixture over the pizza base and arrange the tomato and chorizo slices on top. Sprinkle with the oregano, season with pepper to taste and arrange the Mozzarella cheese and olives on top.

4 Bake in a preheated oven, at 230°C/450°F/Gas Mark 8, for 10 minutes until the cheese is melted and golden. Serve immediately.

Smoky Bacon & Pepperoni

This more traditional kind of pizza is topped with peperoni, smoked bacon and (bell) peppers covered in a smoked cheese.

NUTRITIONAL INFORMATION

Calories	450	Sugars	.........6g
Protein	........19g	Fat	..........24g
Carbohydrate	...41g	Saturates	.......6g

1½ HOURS   20 MINS

SERVES 4

INGREDIENTS

Bread Dough Base (see page 416)

1 tbsp olive oil

1 tbsp freshly grated Parmesan

Tomato Sauce (see page 419)

125 g/4½ oz lightly smoked bacon, diced

½ green (bell) pepper, sliced thinly

½ yellow (bell) pepper, sliced thinly

60 g/2 oz pepperoni-style sliced spicy
   sausage

60 g/2 oz smoked Bavarian cheese, grated

½ tsp dried oregano

olive oil, for drizzling

salt and pepper

1 Roll out or press the dough, using a rolling pin or your hands, into a 25 cm/10 inch circle on a lightly floured work surface.

2 Place the dough base on a large greased baking tray (cookie sheet) or pizza pan and push up the edge a little with your fingers, to form a rim.

3 Brush the base with the olive oil and sprinkle with the Parmesan. Cover and leave to rise slightly in a warm place for about 10 minutes.

4 Spread the tomato sauce over the base almost to the edge. Top with the bacon and (bell) peppers. Arrange the pepperoni on top and sprinkle with the smoked cheese.

5 Sprinkle over the oregano and drizzle with a little olive oil. Season well.

6 Bake in a preheated oven, at 200°C/ 400°F/Gas Mark 6, for 18–20 minutes, or until the crust is golden and crisp around the edge. Cut the pizza into wedges and serve immediately.

Corned Beef Hash Pizza

A combination of corned beef and baked eggs on a soured cream and potato base makes a really unusual pizza.

NUTRITIONAL INFORMATION

Calories	563	Sugars	........16g
Protein	........36g	Fat	.........28g
Carbohydrate	...45g	Saturates	......12g

  1¼ HOURS   35 MINS

SERVES 4

INGREDIENTS

500 g/1 lb 2 oz potatoes

3 tbsp soured cream

325 g/11½ oz can corned beef

1 small onion, chopped finely

1 green (bell) pepper, chopped

3 tbsp tomato and chilli relish

Special Tomato Sauce (see page 420)

4 eggs

25 g/1 oz Mozzarella cheese, grated

25 g/1 oz Cheddar cheese, grated

paprika

salt and pepper

chopped fresh parsley, to garnish

1 Peel the potatoes and cut into even-sized chunks. Parboil them in a pan of boiling salted water for 5 minutes. Drain, rinse in cold water and cool.

COOK'S TIP

For extra colour, mix a grated carrot with the potato base. This will look and taste good, and will help to persuade children to eat their vegetables, if they are fussy eaters. Use the tomato and chilli relish sparingly if you are serving this to children.

2 Grate the potatoes and mix with the soured cream and seasoning in a bowl. Place on a large greased baking tray (cookie sheet) or pizza pan and pat out into a 25 cm/10 in circle, pushing up the edge slightly to form a rim.

3 Mash the corned beef roughly with a fork and stir in the onion, green (bell) pepper and relish. Season well.

4 Spread the tomato sauce over the potato base almost to the edge. Top with the corned beef mixture. Using a

spoon, make 4 wells in the corned beef. Break an egg into each.

5 Mix the cheeses together and sprinkle over the pizza with a little paprika. Season with salt and pepper.

6 Bake in a preheated oven, at 200°C/400°F/Gas Mark 6, for 20–25 minutes until the eggs have cooked but still have slightly runny yolks.

7 Serve immediately, garnished with chopped parsley.

Italian Calzone

A calzone is like a pizza in reverse – it resembles a large pasty with the dough on the outside and the filling on the inside.

NUTRITIONAL INFORMATION

Calories ....405 Sugars 7g
Protein ....19g Fat 17g
Carbohydrate ...48g Saturates 5g

1¼ HOURS   X MINS

SERVES 4

I N G R E D I E N T S

Bread Dough Base (see page 416)

1 egg, beaten

1 tomato, peeled and chopped

1 tbsp tomato purée (paste)

25 g/1 oz Italian salami, chopped

25 g/1 oz mortadella ham, chopped

25 g/1 oz Ricotta

2 spring onions (scallions), trimmed and chopped

¼ tsp dried oregano

salt and pepper

1 Roll out the dough to form a 23 cm/ 9 inch circle on a lightly floured work surface.

2 Brush the edge of the dough with a little beaten egg.

3 Spread the tomato purée (paste) over half of the circle nearest to you.

4 Scatter the salami, mortadella and chopped tomato on top.

5 Dot with the Ricotta and sprinkle over the spring onions (scallions) and oregano. Season with salt and pepper to taste.

6 Fold over the other half of the dough to form a half moon shape. Press the edges together well to prevent the filling from coming out.

7 Place the calzone on a baking tray (cookie sheet) and brush with beaten egg to glaze. Make a hole in the top in order to allow any steam to escape during the cooking time.

8 Bake in a preheated oven, at 200°C/ 400°F/Gas Mark 6, for 20 minutes, or until golden. Serve immediately.

Potato & Pepperoni Pizza

Potatoes make a great pizza base and this recipe is well worth making, rather than using a ready-made base, both for texture and flavour.

NUTRITIONAL INFORMATION

Calories	234	Sugars	.........5g
Protein	.........4g	Fat	..........12g
Carbohydrate	...30g	Saturates	.......1g

🥔 20 MINS   🕐 45 MINS

SERVES 4

INGREDIENTS

900 g/2 lb floury (mealy) potatoes, diced

15 g/½ oz/1 tbsp butter

2 garlic cloves, crushed

2 tbsp mixed chopped fresh herbs

1 egg, beaten

85 ml/3 fl oz/⅓ cup passata (sieved tomatoes)

2 tbsp tomato purée (paste)

50 g/1¾ oz pepperoni slices

1 green (bell) pepper, cut into strips

1 yellow (bell) pepper, cut into strips

2 large open-cap mushrooms, sliced

25 g/1 oz stoned (pitted) black olives, quartered

125 g/4½ oz Mozzarella cheese, sliced

1 Grease and flour a 23 cm/9 inch pizza tin (pan).

2 Cook the diced potatoes in a saucepan of boiling water for 10 minutes or until cooked through. Drain and mash until smooth. Transfer the mashed potato to a mixing bowl and stir in the butter, garlic, herbs and egg.

3 Spread the mixture into the prepared pizza tin (pan). Cook in a preheated oven, at 225°C/425°F/Gas6 Mark 7, for 7-10 minutes or until the pizza base begins to set.

4 Mix the passata (sieved tomatoes) and tomato purée (paste) together and spoon it over the pizza base, to within 1 cm/½ inch of the edge of the base.

5 Arrange the pepperoni, (bell) peppers, mushrooms and olives on top of the passata (sieved tomatoes).

6 Scatter the Mozzarella cheese on top of the pizza. Return to the oven for 20 minutes or until the base is cooked through and the cheese has melted on top. Serve hot.

COOK'S TIP

This pizza base is softer in texture than a normal bread dough and is ideal served from the tin (pan). Top with any of your favourite pizza ingredients that you have to hand.

Hot Chilli Beef Pizza

This deep-pan pizza is topped with minced (ground) beef, red kidney beans and jalapeño chillies, which are small, green and very hot.

NUTRITIONAL INFORMATION

Calories ....550 Sugars 5g
Protein ....24g Fat 26g
Carbohydrate ...60g Saturates 9g

 1½ HOURS   30 MINS

SERVES

INGREDIENTS

20 g/¾ oz fresh yeast or 1½ tsp dried or
   easy-blend yeast

125 ml/4 fl oz/½ cup tepid water

1 tsp sugar

3 tbsp olive oil

225 g/8 oz/2 cups plain (all-purpose) flour

1 tsp salt

TOPPING

1 small onion, sliced thinly

1 garlic clove, crushed

½ yellow (bell) pepper, chopped

1 tbsp olive oil

175 g/6 oz lean minced (ground) beef

¼ tsp chilli powder

¼ tsp ground cumin

200 g/7 oz can red kidney beans, drained

Tomato Sauce (see page 419)

25 g/1 oz jalapeño chillies, sliced

60 g/2 oz Mozzarella, sliced thinly

60 g/2 oz mature (sharp) Cheddar or
   Monterey Jack, grated

olive oil, for drizzling

salt and pepper

chopped parsley, to garnish

1 For the deep-pan dough base, use the same method as the Bread Dough Base recipe.

2 Roll out or press the dough, using a rolling pin or your hands, into a 23 cm/9 inch circle on a lightly floured work surface. Place on a large greased baking tray (cookie sheet) or pizza pan and push up the edge to form a small rim. Cover and leave to rise slightly for about 10 minutes.

3 Fry the onion, garlic and (bell) pepper gently in the oil for 5 minutes until soft but not browned. Increase the heat slightly and add the beef, chilli and cumin. Fry for 5 minutes, stirring occasionally. Remove from the heat and stir in the kidney beans. Season well.

4 Spread the tomato sauce over the dough, almost to the edge. Top with the meat mixture.

5 Top with the sliced chillies and Mozzarella and sprinkle over the grated cheese. Drizzle with a little olive oil and season with salt and pepper to taste.

6 Bake in a preheated oven, at 200°C/400°F/Gas Mark 6, for 18–20 minutes, or until the crust is golden. Serve immediately sprinkled with chopped parsley.

Folded-over Pizza

This recipe makes 4 large *calzones* (as these pizzas are known) or 8 small *calzones*.

NUTRITIONAL INFORMATION

Calories 402	Sugars 3g
Protein 16g	Fat 22g
Carbohydrate . . .37g	Saturates 5g

 1¼ HOURS   15 MINS

SERVES 4

I N G R E D I E N T S

1 portion of Basic Pizza Dough (see
  page 421)

freshly grated Parmesan cheese, to serve

T O P P I N G

75 g/2¾ oz mortadella or other Italian pork
  sausage, chopped

50 g/1¾ oz Italian sausage, chopped

50 g/1¾ oz Parmesan cheese, sliced

100 g/3½ oz Mozzarella, cut into chunks

2 tomatoes, diced

4 tbsp fresh oregano

salt and pepper

1 Place the yeast and sugar in a measuring jug and mix with 50 ml/ 2 fl oz/4 tbsp of the water. Leave the yeast mixture in a warm place for 15 minutes or until frothy.

2 Mix the flour with the salt and make a well in the centre. Add the oil, yeast mixture and remaining water. Using a wooden spoon, mix to form a dough.

3 Turn the dough out on to a floured surface and knead for 4–5 minutes or until smooth. Return the dough to the bowl, cover with an oiled sheet of cling film (plastic wrap) and leave to rise for 30 minutes or until doubled in size.

4 Knead the dough for 2 minutes and divide it into 4 pieces. Roll out each portion thinly to form circles. Place them on an oiled baking tray (cookie sheet). The dough should be no more than 6 mm/ ¼inch thick because it will rise during the cooking time.

5 To make the topping, place both Italian sausages, the Parmesan and the Mozzarella on one side of each circle. Top with the tomatoes and oregano. Season to taste with salt and pepper.

6 Brush around the edges of the dough with a little water then fold over the circle to form a 'pasty' shape. Squeeze the edges together to seal so that none of the filling leaks out during cooking.

7 Bake in a preheated oven, at 200°C/ 400°F/Gas Mark 6, for 10–15 minutes or until golden. If you are making the smaller pizzas, reduce the cooking time to 8–10 minutes. Garnish with freshly grated Parmesan cheese and serve with salad leaves, if liked.

Muffin Pizzas

Toasted muffins are topped with pineapple and Parma ham (prosciutto). Plain, wholemeal or cheese muffins will all make great pizza bases.

NUTRITIONAL INFORMATION

Calories	259	Sugars	.........7g
Protein	.........9g	Fat	..........15g
Carbohydrate	...24g	Saturates	.......3g

 45 MINS   5 MINS

SERVES 4

INGREDIENTS

4 muffins

1 quantity Tomato Sauce (see page 419)

2 sun-dried tomatoes in oil, chopped

60 g/2 oz Parma ham (prosciutto)

2 rings canned pineapple, chopped

½ green (bell) pepper, chopped

125 g/4½ oz Mozzarella cheese, sliced thinly

olive oil, for drizzling

salt and pepper

fresh basil leaves, to garnish

1 Cut the muffins in half and toast the cut side lightly.

2 Spread the tomato sauce evenly over the muffins.

3 Sprinkle the sun-dried tomatoes on top of the tomato sauce.

4 Cut the ham into thin strips and place on the muffins with the pineapple and green (bell) pepper.

5 Carefully arrange the Mozzarella slices on top.

6 Drizzle a little olive oil over each pizza, and season.

7 Place under a preheated medium grill (broiler) and cook until the cheese melts and bubbles.

8 Serve immediately garnished with small basil leaves.

COOK'S TIP

You don't have to use plain muffins for your base; wholemeal or cheese muffins will also make ideal pizza bases. Muffins freeze well, so always keep some in the freezer for an instant pizza.

Calabrian Pizza

Traditionally, this pizza has a double layer of dough to make it robust and filling. Alternatively, it can be made as a single pizza (as shown here).

NUTRITIONAL INFORMATION

Calories ....574 Sugars 6g
Protein ....20g Fat 30g
Carbohydrate ...60g Saturates 7g

2½ HOURS   55 MINS

SERVES 6

INGREDIENTS

400 g/14 oz/3½ cups plain (all-purpose) flour

½ tsp salt

1 sachet easy-blend yeast

2 tbsp olive oil

about 275 ml/9 fl oz/generous 1 cup warm water

FILLING

2 tbsp olive oil

2 garlic cloves, crushed

1 red (bell) pepper, cored, deseeded and sliced

1 yellow (bell) pepper, cored, deseeded and sliced

125 g/4½ oz Ricotta

175 g/6 oz jar sun-dried tomatoes, drained

3 hard-boiled (hard-cooked) eggs, sliced thinly

1 tbsp chopped fresh mixed herbs

125 g/4½ oz salami, cut into strips

150–175 g/5½–6 oz Mozzarella, grated

a little milk, to glaze

salt and pepper

1 Sift the flour and salt into a bowl and mix in the easy-blend yeast.

2 Add the olive oil and enough warm water to mix to a smooth, pliable dough. Knead for 10–15 minutes by hand, or process for 5 minutes in a mixer.

3 Shape the dough into a ball, place in a lightly oiled polythene bag and put in a warm place for 1–1½ hours or until doubled in size.

4 To make the filling, heat the oil in a frying pan (skillet) and fry the garlic and (bell) peppers slowly in the oil until softened.

5 Knock back the dough and roll out half to fit the base of a 30 x 25 cm/ 12 x 10 inch oiled roasting tin (pan).

6 Season the dough and spread with the Ricotta, then cover with sun-dried tomatoes, hard-boiled (hard-cooked) eggs, herbs and the (bell) pepper mixture. Arrange the salami strips on top and sprinkle with the grated cheese.

7 Roll out the remaining dough and place over the filling, sealing the edges well, or use to make a second pizza. Leave to rise for 1 hour in a warm place. An uncovered pizza will only take about 30–40 minutes to rise.

8 Prick the double pizza with a fork about 20 times, brush the top with milk and cook in a preheated oven, at 180°C/350°F/Gas Mark 4, for about 50 minutes or until lightly browned. The uncovered pizza will take only 35–40 minutes. Serve hot.

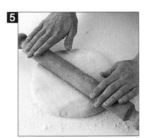

Funny Faces Pizza

These individual pizzas have faces made from sliced vegetables and pasta. Children love pizzas and will enjoy making their own funny faces.

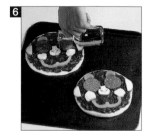

NUTRITIONAL INFORMATION

Calories 343	Sugars 5g	
Protein 10g	Fat 15g	
Carbohydrate ...45g	Saturates 2g	

2¹/₄ HOURS   30 MINS

SERVES 4

INGREDIENTS

Bread Dough Base (see page 416)

25 g/1 oz spaghetti or egg noodles

Tomato Sauce (see page 419)

8 slices pepperoni-style sausage

8 thin slices celery

4 slices button mushrooms

4 slices yellow (bell) pepper

4 slices Mozzarella

4 slices courgette (zucchini)

olive oil, for drizzling

8 peas

1 Divide the dough into 4 pieces. Roll each piece out into a 12 cm/5 inch diameter circle and place on greased baking trays (cookie sheets). Cover and leave to rise slightly in a warm place for about 10 minutes.

2 Cook the spaghetti or egg noodles in a pan of boiling water according to the packet instructions.

3 Divide the tomato sauce evenly between each pizza base and spread out almost to the edge.

4 To make the faces, use pepperoni slices for the main part of the eyes, celery for the eyebrows, mushrooms for the noses and (bell) pepper slices for the mouths.

5 Cut the Mozzarella and courgette (zucchini) slices in half. Use the cheese for the cheeks and the courgettes (zucchini) for the ears.

6 Drizzle a little olive oil over each pizza and bake in a preheated oven, at 200°C/ 400°F/Gas Mark 6, for 12–15 minutes or until the edges are crisp and golden.

7 Transfer the pizzas to serving plates and place the peas in the centre of the eyes.

8 Drain the spaghetti and arrange around the tops of the pizzas for hair. Serve immediately.

Avocado & Ham Pizza

A smoked ham and avocado salad is served on a pizza with a base enriched with chopped sun-dried tomatoes and black olives.

NUTRITIONAL INFORMATION

Calories . . . . . . .397 Sugars 9g
Protein . . . . .10g Fat 22g
Carbohydrate . . .43g Saturates 5g

2³/₄ HOURS   20 MINS

SERVES 4

INGREDIENTS

Bread Dough Base (see page 416)

4 sun-dried tomatoes, chopped

25 g/1 oz black olives, chopped

Special Tomato Sauce (see page 420)

4 small chicory (endive) leaves, shredded

4 small radicchio leaves, shredded

1 avocado, peeled, pitted and sliced

60 g/2 oz wafer-thin smoked ham

60 g/2 oz blue cheese, cut into small pieces

olive oil, for drizzling

salt and pepper

chopped fresh chervil, to garnish

1 Make the dough according to the instructions on page 416. Knead the dough gently with the sun-dried tomatoes and olives until well mixed.

2 Roll out or press the dough, using a rolling pin or your hands, into a 25 cm/10 inch circle on a lightly floured work surface. Place on a greased baking tray (cookie sheet) or pizza pan (tin) and push up the edge a little to form a rim.

3 Cover the dough and leave to rise slightly in a warm place for 10 minutes. Spread the tomato sauce almost to the edge of the pizza base.

4 Top the pizza with shredded lettuce leaves and avocado slices. Scrunch up the ham and add together with the blue cheese.

5 Drizzle with a little olive oil and season with salt and pepper to taste.

6 Bake in a preheated oven, at 200°C/ 400°F/Gas Mark 6, for 18–20 minutes, or until the edge is crisp and a golden brown colour.

7 Sprinkle with chervil to garnish and serve immediately.

Creamy Ham & Cheese Pizza

This traditional pizza uses a pastry case and Béchamel Sauce to make a type of savoury flan. Grating the pastry gives it a lovely nutty texture.

NUTRITIONAL INFORMATION

Calories 628	Sugars 5g
Protein 19g	Fat 47g
Carbohydrate . . .35g	Saturates 16g

20 MINS   40 MINS

SERVES 4

I N G R E D I E N T S

250 g/9 oz flaky pastry, well chilled

40 g/1½ oz/3 tbsp butter

1 red onion, chopped

1 garlic clove, chopped

40 g/1½ oz strong flour

300 ml/½ pint/1¼ cups milk

50 g/1¾ oz Parmesan cheese, finely grated,
  plus extra for sprinkling

2 eggs, hard-boiled (hard-cooked), cut
  into quarters

100 g/3½ oz Italian pork sausage, such as
  feline salame, cut into strips

salt and pepper

sprigs of fresh thyme, to garnish

1 Fold the pastry in half and grate it into 4 individual flan tins (pans), measuring 10 cm/4 inches across. Using a floured fork, press the pastry flakes down so they are even, there are no holes and the pastry comes up the sides of the tin (pan).

2 Line with foil and bake blind in a preheated oven, at 220°C/425°F/Gas Mark 7, for 10 minutes. Reduce the heat to 200°C/400°F/Gas Mark 6, remove the foil and cook for 15 minutes or until golden and set.

3 Heat the butter in a pan. Add the onion and garlic and cook for 5–6 minutes or until softened.

4 Add the flour, stirring well to coat the onions. Gradually stir in the milk to make a thick sauce.

5 Season the sauce with salt and pepper to taste and then stir in the Parmesan cheese. Do not reheat once the cheese has been added or the sauce will become too stringy.

6 Spread the sauce over the pastry cases. Decorate with the egg and strips of sausage.

7 Sprinkle with a little extra Parmesan cheese, return to the oven and bake for 5 minutes, just to heat through.

8 Serve immediately, garnished with sprigs of fresh thyme.

COOK'S TIP

This pizza is just as good cold, but do not prepare it too far in advance as the pastry will turn soggy.

Spicy Meatball Pizza

Small minced (ground) beef meatballs, spiced with chillies and cumin seeds, are baked on a scone (biscuit) base.

NUTRITIONAL INFORMATION

Calories	568	Sugars	.........5g
Protein	........24g	Fat	..........37g
Carbohydrate	...38g	Saturates	......15g

 2¼ HOURS   25 MINS

SERVES 4

INGREDIENTS

225 g/8 oz minced (ground) lean beef

25 g/1 oz jalapeño chillies in brine, chopped

1 tsp cumin seeds

1 tbsp chopped fresh parsley

1 tbsp beaten egg

3 tbsp olive oil

Scone (Biscuit) Base (see page 417)

Tomato Sauce (see page 419)

25 g/1 oz canned pimiento, sliced

2 rashers streaky bacon, cut into strips

60 g/2 oz mature (sharp) Cheddar, grated

olive oil, for drizzling

salt and pepper

chopped fresh parsley, to garnish

1 Mix the beef, chillies, cumin seeds, parsley and egg together in a bowl and season. Form into 12 small meatballs. Cover and chill for 1 hour.

2 Heat the oil in a large frying pan (skillet). Add the meatballs and brown all over. Remove with a perforated spoon or fish slice and drain on paper towels.

3 Roll out or press the dough into a 25 cm/ 10 inch circle on a lightly floured work surface. Place on a greased baking tray (cookie sheet) or pizza pan and push up the edge slightly to form a rim. Spread with the tomato sauce, almost to the edge.

4 Arrange the meatballs on the pizza with the pimiento and bacon. Sprinkle over the cheese and drizzle with a little olive oil. Season with salt and pepper.

5 Bake in a preheated oven, at 200°C/ 400°F/Gas Mark 6, for 18–20 minutes, or until the edge is crisp and a golden brown colour.

6 Serve immediately, garnished with chopped parsley.

Mini Pitta Bread Pizzas

Smoked salmon and asparagus make extra special party pizza canapés.
Mini pitta breads make great bases and are really quick to cook.

NUTRITIONAL INFORMATION

Calories . . . . .518 Sugars 10g
Protein . . . . .21g Fat 12g
Carbohydrate . . .87g Saturates 4g

  55 MINS   15 MINS

SERVES 4

INGREDIENTS

8 thin asparagus spears

16 mini pitta breads

1 quantity Special Tomato Sauce (see
  page 420)

25 g/1 oz mild Cheddar cheese, grated

25 g/1 oz Ricotta cheese

60 g/2 oz smoked salmon

olive oil, for drizzling

pepper

1 Cut the asparagus spears into 2.5 cm/
1 inch lengths; then cut each piece in
half lengthways.

2 Blanch the asparagus in a saucepan of
boiling water for 1 minute. Drain the
asparagus, plunge into cold water and
drain again.

3 Place the pitta breads on to 2
baking trays (cookie sheets). Spread
about 1 teaspoon of tomato sauce on
each pitta bread.

4 Mix the cheeses together and divide
between the 16 pitta breads.

5 Cut the smoked salmon into 16 long
thin strips. Arrange one strip on each
pitta bread with the asparagus spears.

6 Drizzle over a little olive oil and
season with pepper to taste.

7 Bake in a preheated oven, at 200°C/
400°F/Gas Mark 6, for 8–10 minutes.
Serve immediately.

COOK'S TIP

Smoked salmon is expensive,
so for a cheaper version, use
smoked trout. It is often half the
price of smoked salmon, and tastes
just as good. Try experimenting with
other smoked fish, such as smoked
mackerel, with its strong, distinctive
flavour, for a bit of variety.

Chicken & Peanut Pizza

This pizza is topped with chicken which has been marinated in a delicious peanut sauce.

NUTRITIONAL INFORMATION

Calories 418	Sugars 7g	
Protein 22g	Fat 19g	
Carbohydrate ...43g	Saturates 5g	

2³/₄ HOURS   20 MINS

SERVES 4

INGREDIENTS

2 tbsp crunchy peanut butter

1 tbsp lime juice

1 tbsp soy sauce

3 tbsp milk

1 red chilli, deseeded and chopped

1 garlic clove, crushed

175 g/6 oz cooked chicken, diced

1 quantity Bread Dough Base (see page 416)

1 quantity Special Tomato Sauce (see page 420)

4 spring onions (scallions), trimmed and chopped

60 g/2 oz Mozzarella cheese, grated

olive oil, for drizzling

salt and pepper

1 Mix together the peanut butter, lime juice, soy sauce, milk, chilli and garlic in a bowl to form a sauce. Season well.

2 Add the chicken to the peanut sauce and stir until well coated. Cover and leave to marinate in a cool place for about 20 minutes.

3 Roll out or press the dough, using a rolling pin or your hands, into a 25 cm/ 10 inch circle on a lightly floured work surface. Place on a large greased baking tray (cookie sheet) or pizza pan (tin) and push up the edge a little. Cover and leave to rise slightly for 10 minutes in a warm place.

4 When the dough has risen, spread the tomato sauce over the base, almost to the edge.

5 Top with the spring onions (scallions) and chicken pieces, spooning over the peanut sauce.

6 Sprinkle over the cheese. Drizzle with a little olive oil and season well. Bake in a preheated oven, at 200°C/400°F/Gas Mark 6, for 18–20 minutes, or until the crust is golden. Serve.

Cheese & Potato Plait

This bread has a delicious cheese, garlic and rosemary flavour, and is best eaten straight from the oven. This recipe makes a 450 g/1 lb loaf.

NUTRITIONAL INFORMATION

Calories 724	Sugars 4g	
Protein 22g	Fat 10g	
Carbohydrate ..147g	Saturates 4g	

2½ HOURS   40 MINS

SERVES 4

I N G R E D I E N T S

175 g/6 oz floury (mealy) potatoes, diced

2 x 7 g/1¼ oz sachets easy-blend dried
  yeast

675 g/1½ lb/6 cups white bread flour

1 tbsp salt

450 ml/16 fl oz/2 cups vegetable stock

2 garlic cloves, crushed

2 tbsp chopped fresh rosemary

125 g/4½ oz Gruyère cheese, grated

1 tbsp vegetable oil

1 Lightly grease and flour a baking tray (cookie sheet).

2 Cook the potatoes in a saucepan of boiling water for 10 minutes or until soft. Drain and mash the potatoes.

3 Transfer the mashed potatoes to a large mixing bowl.

4 Stir the yeast, flour, salt and stock into the mashed potatoes and mix to form a smooth dough.

5 Add the garlic, rosemary and 75 g/2¾ oz of the cheese and knead the dough for 5 minutes. Make a hollow in the dough, pour in the oil and knead the dough.

6 Cover the dough and leave it to rise in a warm place for 1½ hours or until doubled in size.

7 Knead the dough again and divide it into 3 equal portions. Roll each portion into a 35 cm/14 inch sausage shape.

8 Pressing one end of each of the sausage shapes together, plait the dough and fold the remaining ends underneath. Place the plait on the baking tray (cookie sheet), cover and leave to rise for 30 minutes.

9 Sprinkle the remaining cheese over the top of the plait and bake in a preheated oven, at 190°C/375°F/Gas Mark 5, for 40 minutes or until the base of the loaf sounds hollow when tapped. Serve warm.

VARIATION

Instead of making a plait, use the mixture to make a batch of cheesey rolls which would be ideal to serve with hot soup.

Roman Focaccia

Roman focaccia makes a delicious snack on its own or serve it with cured meats and salad for a quick supper.

NUTRITIONAL INFORMATION

Calories 119	Sugars 2g	
Protein 3g	Fat 2g	
Carbohydrate . . .24g	Saturates 0.3g	

 1 HOUR   45 MINS

Makes 16 squares

I N G R E D I E N T S

7 g/¼ oz dried yeast

1 tsp sugar

300 ml/½ pint/1¼ cups hand-hot water

450 g/1 lb strong white flour

2 tsp salt

3 tbsp rosemary, chopped

2 tbsp olive oil

450 g/1 lb mixed red and white onions,
  sliced into rings

4 garlic cloves, sliced

1 Place the yeast and the sugar in a small bowl and mix with 100 ml/3½ fl oz/8 tablespoons of the water. Leave to ferment in a warm place for 15 minutes.

2 Mix the flour with the salt in a large bowl. Add the yeast mixture, half of the rosemary and the remaining water and mix to form a smooth dough. Knead the dough for 4 minutes.

3 Cover the dough with oiled cling film (plastic wrap) and leave to rise for 30 minutes or until doubled in size.

4 Meanwhile, heat the oil in a large pan. Add the onions and garlic and fry for 5 minutes or until softened. Cover the pan and continue to cook for 7–8 minutes or until the onions are lightly caramelized.

5 Remove the dough from the bowl and knead it again for 1–2 minutes.

6 Roll the dough out to form a square shape. The dough should be no more than 6 mm/¼ inch thick because it will rise during cooking. Place the dough on to a large baking tray (cookie sheet), pushing out the edges until even.

7 Spread the onions over the dough, and sprinkle with the remaining rosemary.

8 Bake in a preheated oven, at 200°C/400°F/Gas Mark 6, for 25–30 minutes or until a golden brown colour. Cut the focaccia into 16 squares and serve immediately.

Mini Focaccia

This is a delicious Italian bread made with olive oil. The topping of red onions and thyme is particularly flavoursome.

NUTRITIONAL INFORMATION

Calories ....439 Sugars 3g
Protein ....9g Fat 15g
Carbohydrate ....71g Saturates 2g

  2¼ HOURS   25 MINS

SERVES 4

INGREDIENTS

350 g/12 oz/3 cups strong white flour

½ tsp salt

1 sachet easy blend dried yeast

2 tbsp olive oil

250 ml/9 fl oz tepid water

100 g/3½ oz green or black olives, halved

TOPPING

2 red onions, sliced

2 tbsp olive oil

1 tsp sea salt

1 tbsp thyme leaves

1 Lightly oil several baking trays (cookie sheets). Sieve (strain) the flour and salt into a large mixing bowl, then stir in the yeast. Pour in the olive oil and tepid water and mix everything together to form a dough.

2 Turn the dough out on to a lightly floured surface and knead it for about 5 minutes (alternatively, use an electric mixer with a dough hook and knead for 7-8 minutes).

3 Place the dough in a greased bowl, cover and leave in a warm place for about 1-1½ hours or until it has doubled in size. Knock back (punch down) the dough by kneading it again for 1-2 minutes.

4 Knead half of the olives into the dough. Divide the dough into quarters and then shape the quarters into rounds. Place them on the baking trays (cookie sheets) and push your fingers into the dough to achieve a dimpled effect.

5 To make the topping, sprinkle the red onions and remaining olives over the rounds. Drizzle the oil over the top and sprinkle with the sea salt and thyme leaves. Cover and leave to rise for 30 minutes.

6 Bake in a preheated oven, at 190°C/375°F/Gas Mark 5, for 20-25 minutes or until the focaccia are golden.

7 Transfer to a wire rack and leave to cool before serving.

VARIATION

Use this quantity of dough to make 1 large foccacia, if you prefer.

Italian Bruschetta

It is important to use a good quality olive oil for this recipe. Serve the bruschetta with kebabs (kabobs) or fish for a really summery taste.

NUTRITIONAL INFORMATION

Calories 415	Sugars 2g	
Protein 8g	Fat 24g	
Carbohydrate ...45g	Saturates 4g	

 10 MINS   10 MINS

Makes 1 loaf

INGREDIENTS

1 ciabatta loaf or small stick of
  French bread

1 plump clove garlic

extra virgin olive oil

fresh Parmesan cheese, grated (optional)

1 Slice the bread in half crossways and again lengthwise to give 4 portions.

2 Do not peel the garlic clove, but cut it in half.

3 Barbecue (grill) the bread over hot coals for 2–3 minutes on both sides or until golden brown.

4 Rub the garlic, cut side down, all over the toasted surface of the bread.

COOK'S TIP

As ready-grated Parmesan quickly loses its pungency and 'bite', it is better to buy small quantities of the cheese in one piece and grate it yourself as need-ed. Tightly wrapped in cling film (plastic wrap) or foil, it will keep in the refrigerator for several months.

5 Drizzle the olive oil over the bread and serve hot as an accompaniment.

6 If using Parmesan cheese, sprinkle the cheese over the bread.

7 Return the bread to the barbecue (grill), cut side up, for 1–2 minutes or until the cheese just begins to melt. Serve hot.

Roasted (Bell) Pepper Bread

(Bell) peppers become sweet and mild when they are roasted and make this bread delicious.

NUTRITIONAL INFORMATION

Calories 426	Sugars 4g
Protein 12g	Fat 4g
Carbohydrate ...90g	Saturates 1g

🥖 🥖 🥖

🍲 1³/₄ HOURS 🕐 1 HR 5 MINS

SERVES 4

I N G R E D I E N T S

1 red (bell) pepper, halved and deseeded

1 yellow (bell) pepper, halved and deseeded

2 sprigs of rosemary

1 tbsp olive oil

7 g/¼ oz dried yeast

1 tsp sugar

300 ml/½ pint/1¼ cups hand-hot water

450 g/1 lb strong white flour

1 tsp salt

1 Grease a 23 cm/9 inch deep round cake tin (pan).

2 Place the (bell) peppers and rosemary in a shallow roasting tin (pan). Pour over the oil and roast in a preheated oven, at 200°C/400°F/Gas Mark 6, for 20 minutes or until slightly charred. Remove the skin from the (bell) peppers and cut the flesh into slices.

3 Place the yeast and sugar in a small bowl and mix with 100 ml/3½ fl oz/8 tablespoons of hand-hot water. Leave to ferment in a warm place for 15 minutes.

4 Mix the flour and salt together in a large bowl. Stir in the yeast mixture and the remaining water and mix to form a smooth dough.

5 Knead the dough for about 5 minutes until smooth. Cover with oiled cling film (plastic wrap) and leave to rise for about 30 minutes or until doubled in size.

6 Cut the dough into 3 equal portions. Roll the portions into rounds slightly larger than the cake tin (pan).

7 Place 1 round in the base of the tin (pan) so that it reaches up the sides of the tin (pan) by about 2 cm/¾ inch. Top with half of the (bell) pepper mixture.

8 Place the second round of dough on top, followed by the remaining (bell) pepper mixture. Place the last round of dough on top, pushing the edges of the dough down the sides of the tin (pan).

9 Cover the dough with oiled cling film (plastic wrap) and leave to rise for 30–40 minutes. Return to the oven and bake for 45 minutes until golden or the base sounds hollow when lightly tapped. Serve warm.

Olive Oil Bread with Cheese

This flat cheese bread is sometimes called *foccacia*. It is delicious served with *antipasto* or simply on its own. This recipe makes one loaf.

NUTRITIONAL INFORMATION

Calories ....586 Sugars 3g
Protein ....22g Fat 26g
Carbohydrate ...69g Saturates 12g

🍲 1 HOUR   🕐 30 MINS

SERVES 4

INGREDIENTS

15 g/½ oz dried yeast

1 tsp sugar

250 ml/9 fl oz hand-hot water

350 g/12 oz strong flour

1 tsp salt

3 tbsp olive oil

200 g/7 oz pecorino cheese, cubed

½ tbsp fennel seeds, lightly crushed

1 Mix the yeast with the sugar and 100 ml/3½ fl oz/8 tbsp of the water. Leave to ferment in a warm place for about 15 minutes.

2 Mix the flour with the salt. Add 1 tablespoon of the oil, the yeast mixture and the remaining water to form a smooth dough. Knead the dough for 4 minutes.

COOK'S TIP

Pecorino is a hard, quite salty cheese, which is sold in most large supermarkets and Italian delicatessens. If you cannot obtain pecorino, use strong Cheddar or Parmesan cheese instead.

3 Divide the dough into 2 equal portions. Roll out each portion to a form a round 6 mm/¼ inch thick. Place 1 round on a baking tray (cookie sheet).

4 Scatter the cheese and half of the fennel seeds evenly over the round.

5 Place the second round on top and squeeze the edges together to seal so that the filling does not leak during the cooking time.

6 Using a sharp knife, make a few slashes in the top of the dough and brush with the remaining olive oil.

7 Sprinkle with the remaining fennel seeds and leave the dough to rise for 20–30 minutes.

8 Bake in a preheated oven, at 200°C/400°F/Gas Mark 6, for 30 minutes or until golden brown. Serve immediately.

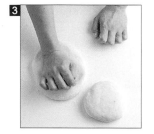

Sun-dried Tomato Loaf

This delicious tomato bread is great with cheese or soup or to make an unusual sandwich. This recipe makes one loaf.

NUTRITIONAL INFORMATION

Calories 403	Sugars 5g	
Protein 12g	Fat 2g	
Carbohydrate ...91g	Saturates 0.3g	

  1³/₄ HOURS 🕐 35 MINS

SERVES 4

I N G R E D I E N T S

7 g/¼ oz dried yeast

1 tsp sugar

300 ml/½ pint/1¼ cups hand-hot water

1 tsp salt

2 tsp dried basil

450 g/1 lb strong white flour

2 tbsp sun-dried tomato paste or tomato
   purée (paste)

12 sun-dried tomatoes, cut into strips

1 Place the yeast and sugar in a bowl and mix with 100 ml/3½ fl oz/ 8 tablespoons of the water. Leave to ferment in a warm place for 15 minutes.

2 Place the flour in a bowl and stir in the salt. Make a well in the dry ingredients and add the basil, the yeast mixture, tomato paste and half of the remaining water. Using a wooden spoon, draw the flour into the liquid and mix to form a dough, adding the rest of the water gradually.

3 Turn out the dough on to a floured surface and knead for 5 minutes or until smooth. Cover with oiled cling film (plastic wrap) and leave in a warm place to rise for about 30 minutes or until doubled in size.

4 Lightly grease a 900 g/2 lb loaf tin (pan).

5 Remove the dough from the bowl and knead in the sun-dried tomatoes. Knead again for 2–3 minutes.

6 Place the dough in the tin (pan) and leave to rise for 30–40 minutes or until it has doubled in size again. Bake in a preheated oven, at 190°C/375°F/Gas Mark 5, for 30–35 minutes or until golden and the base sounds hollow when tapped.

COOK'S TIP

You could make mini sun-dried tomato loaves for children. Divide the dough into 8 equal portions, leave to rise and bake in mini-loaf tins (pans) for 20 minutes. Alternatively, make 12 small rounds, leave to rise and bake as rolls for 12–15 minutes.

Sun-dried Tomato Rolls

These white rolls have the addition of finely chopped sun-dried tomatoes. The tomatoes are sold in jars and are available at most supermarkets.

NUTRITIONAL INFORMATION

Calories 214   Sugars 1g
Protein . . . . .5g   Fat 12g
Carbohydrate . . .22g   Saturates 7g

2¼ HOURS   15 MINS

SERVES 8

INGREDIENTS

225 g/8 oz/2 cups strong white bread flour

½ tsp salt

1 sachet easy-blend dried yeast

100 g/3½ oz/⅓ cup butter, melted and
   cooled slightly

3 tbsp milk, warmed

2 eggs, beaten

50 g/1¾ oz sun-dried tomatoes, well
   drained and chopped finely

milk, for brushing

1 Lightly grease a baking tray (cookie sheet).

2 Sieve (strain) the flour and salt into a large mixing bowl. Stir in the yeast, then pour in the butter, milk and eggs. Mix together to form a dough.

3 Turn the dough on to a lightly floured surface and knead for about 5 minutes (alternatively, use an electric mixer with a dough hook).

4 Place the dough in a greased bowl, cover and leave to rise in a warm place for 1-1½ hours or until the dough has doubled in size. Knock back (punch down) the dough for 2–3 minutes.

5 Knead the sun-dried tomatoes into the dough, sprinkling the work surface (counter) with extra flour as the tomatoes are quite oily.

6 Divide the dough into 8 balls and place them on to the baking tray (cookie sheet). Cover and leave to rise for about 30 minutes or until the rolls have doubled in size.

7 Brush the rolls with milk and bake in a preheated oven, at 230°C/450°F/Gas Mark 8, for 10-15 minutes or until the rolls are golden brown.

8 Transfer the rolls to a wire rack and leave to cool slightly before serving.

VARIATION

Add some finely chopped anchovies or olives to the dough in step 5 for extra flavour, if wished.

Garlic Bread

A perennial favourite, garlic bread is perfect with a range of barbecue (grill) meals.

NUTRITIONAL INFORMATION

Calories 261	Sugars 1g	
Protein 3g	Fat 22g	
Carbohydrate ...15g	Saturates 14g	

  10 MINS 🕐 15 MINS

SERVES 6

INGREDIENTS

150 g/5½ oz butter, softened

3 cloves garlic, crushed

2 tbsp chopped, fresh parsley

pepper

1 large or 2 small sticks of French bread

1 Mix together the butter, garlic and parsley in a bowl until well combined. Season with pepper to taste and mix well.

2 Cut the French bread into thick slices.

3 Spread the flavoured butter over one side of each slice and reassemble the loaf on a large sheet of thick kitchen foil.

4 Wrap the bread well and barbecue (grill) over hot coals for 10–15 minutes until the butter melts and the bread is piping hot.

5 Serve as an accompaniment to a wide range of dishes.

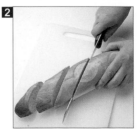

Desserts

The Italians love their desserts, but when there is an important gathering or celebration, then an extra special effort is made and a wide range of exquisite delicacies appear. The Sicilians are said to have the sweetest tooth of all, and many Italian desserts are thought to have originated there. Indeed, you have to go a very long way to

beat a Sicilian ice cream – they truly are the best in the world! Fresh fruit also features in many Italian desserts – oranges are often peeled and served whole, marinated in a fragrant syrup and liqueur. Chocolate, too, is very popular in Italy – try the different varieties of the classic Tiramisu that are included in this chapter. Whatever your dessert preference, there is sure to be an Italian dessert to tempt and satisfy you – you'll never be disappointed!

Tuscan Pudding

These baked mini-ricotta puddings are delicious served warm or chilled and will keep in the refrigerator for 3–4 days.

NUTRITIONAL INFORMATION

Calories	....	.293
Protein	....	.9g
Carbohydrate	...	.28g

Sugars	....	.28g
Fat	....	.17g
Saturates	....	.9g

20 MINS   15 MINS

SERVES 4

I N G R E D I E N T S

15 g/½ oz/1 tbsp butter

75 g/2¾ oz mixed dried fruit

250 g/9 oz ricotta cheese

3 egg yolks

50 g/1¾ oz caster (superfine) sugar

1 tsp cinnamon

finely grated rind of 1 orange,
    plus extra to decorate

crème fraîche (soured cream), to serve

1 Lightly grease 4 mini pudding basins or ramekin dishes with the butter.

2 Put the dried fruit in a bowl and cover with warm water. Leave to soak for 10 minutes.

COOK'S TIP

Crème fraîche (soured cream) has a slightly sour, nutty taste and is very thick. It is suitable for cooking, but has the same fat content as double (heavy) cream. It can be made by stirring cultured buttermilk into double (heavy) cream and refrigerating overnight.

3 Beat the ricotta cheese with the egg yolks in a bowl. Stir in the caster (superfine) sugar, cinnamon and orange rind and mix to combine.

4 Drain the dried fruit in a sieve set over a bowl. Mix the drained fruit with the ricotta cheese mixture.

5 Spoon the mixture into the basins or ramekin dishes.

6 Bake in a preheated oven, at 180°C/350°F/Gas Mark 4, for 15 minutes. The tops should be firm to the touch but not brown.

7 Decorate the puddings with grated orange rind. Serve warm or chilled with a dollop of crème fraîche (soured cream), if liked.

Tiramisu Layers

This is a modern version of the well-known and very traditional chocolate dessert from Italy.

NUTRITIONAL INFORMATION

Calories	798	Sugars	........60g
Protein	........12g	Fat	..........50g
Carbohydrate	...76g	Saturates	......25g

1¼ HOURS　　5 MINS

SERVES 6

INGREDIENTS

300 g/10½ oz dark chocolate

400 g/14 oz mascarpone cheese

150 ml/¼ pint/⅔ cup double (heavy) cream, whipped until it just holds its shape

400 ml/14 fl oz black coffee with 50 g/ 1¾ oz caster (superfine) sugar, cooled

6 tbsp dark rum or brandy

36 sponge fingers (lady-fingers), about 400 g/14 oz

cocoa powder, to dust

1 Melt the chocolate in a bowl set over a saucepan of simmering water, stirring occasionally. Leave the chocolate to cool slightly, then stir it into the mascarpone and cream.

2 Mix the coffee and rum together in a bowl. Dip the sponge fingers (lady-fingers) into the mixture briefly so that they absorb the coffe and rum liquid but do not become soggy.

3 Place 3 sponge fingers (lady-fingers) on 3 serving plates.

4 Spoon a layer of the mascarpone and chocolate mixture over the sponge fingers (lady-fingers).

5 Place 3 more sponge fingers (lady-fingers) on top of the mascarpone layer. Spread another layer of mascarpone and chocolate mixture and place 3 more sponge fingers (lady-fingers) on top.

6 Leave the tiramisu to chill in the refrigerator for at least 1 hour. Dust all over with a little cocoa powder just before serving.

VARIATION

Try adding 50 g/13/4 oz toasted, chopped hazelnuts to the chocolate cream mixture in step 1, if you prefer.

Orange & Almond Cake

This light and tangy citrus cake from Sicily is better eaten as a dessert than as a cake. It is especially good served after a large meal.

NUTRITIONAL INFORMATION

Calories	399	Sugars	........20g
Protein	.........8g	Fat	..........31g
Carbohydrate	...23g	Saturates	......13g

🍮 30 MINS 🕐 40 MINS

SERVES 8

INGREDIENTS

4 eggs, separated

125 g/4½ oz caster (superfine) sugar, plus
   2 tsp for the cream

finely grated rind and juice of 2 oranges

finely grated rind and juice of 1 lemon

125 g/4½ oz ground almonds

25 g/1 oz self-raising flour

200 ml/7 fl oz/¾ cup whipping (light) cream

1 tsp cinnamon

25 g/1 oz flaked (slivered) almonds, toasted

icing (confectioners') sugar, to dust

1 Grease and line the base of a 18 cm/ 7 inch round deep cake tin (pan).

2 Blend the egg yolks with the sugar until the mixture is thick and creamy. Whisk half of the orange rind and all of the lemon rind into the egg yolks.

VARIATION

You could serve this cake with a syrup. Boil the juice and finely grated rind of 2 oranges, 75 g/2¾ oz caster (superfine) sugar and 2 tbsp of water for 5–6 minutes until slightly thickened. Stir in 1 tbsp of orange liqueur just before serving.

3 Mix the juice from both oranges and the lemon with the ground almonds and stir into the egg yolks. The mixture will become quite runny at this point. Fold in the flour.

4 Whisk the egg whites until stiff and gently fold into the egg yolk mixture.

5 Pour the mixture into the tin (pan) and bake in a preheated oven, at 180°C/350°F/Gas Mark 4, for 35–40

minutes, or until golden and springy to the touch. Leave to cool in the tin (pan) for 10 minutes and then turn out. It is likely to sink slightly at this stage.

6 Whip the cream to form soft peaks. Stir in the remaining orange rind, cinnamon and sugar.

7 Once the cake is cold, cover with the almonds, dust with icing (confectioners') sugar and serve with the cream.

Panforte di Siena

This famous Tuscan honey and nut cake is a Christmas speciality. In Italy it is sold in pretty boxes, and served in very thin slices.

NUTRITIONAL INFORMATION

Calories ....257 Sugars 29g
Protein ....5g Fat 13g
Carbohydrate ...33g Saturates 1g

 10 MINS   1¹/₄ HOURS

SERVES 12

INGREDIENTS

125 g/4½ oz/1 cup split whole almonds

125 g/4½ oz/¾ cup hazelnuts

90 g/3 oz/½ cup cut mixed peel

60 g/2 oz/⅓ cup no-soak dried apricots

60 g/2 oz glacé or crystallized pineapple

grated rind of 1 large orange

60 g/2 oz/½ cup plain (all-purpose) flour

2 tbsp cocoa powder

2 tsp ground cinnamon

125 g/4½ oz/½ cup caster (superfine) sugar

175 g/6 oz/½ cup honey

icing (confectioners') sugar, for dredging

1 Toast the almonds under the grill (broiler) until lightly browned and place in a bowl.

2 Toast the hazelnuts until the skins split. Place on a dry tea towel (dish cloth) and rub off the skins. Roughly chop the hazelnuts and add to the almonds with the mixed peel.

3 Chop the apricots and pineapple fairly finely, add to the nuts with the orange rind and mix well.

4 Sift the flour with the cocoa and cinnamon, add to the nut mixture; mix.

5 Line a round 20 cm/8 inch cake tin or deep loose-based flan tin (pan) with baking parchment.

6 Put the sugar and honey into a saucepan and heat until the sugar dissolves, then boil gently for about 5 minutes or until the mixture thickens and begins to turn a deeper shade of brown. Quickly add to the nut mixture and mix evenly. Turn into the prepared tin (pan) and level the top using the back of a damp spoon.

7 Cook in a preheated oven, at 150°C/300°F/Gas Mark 2, for 1 hour. Remove from the oven and leave in the tin (pan) until cold. Take out of the tin (pan) and carefully peel off the paper. Before serving, dredge the cake heavily with sifted icing (confectioners') sugar. Serve in very thin slices.

Pear Cake

This is a really moist cake, deliciously flavoured with chopped pears and cinnamon.

NUTRITIONAL INFORMATION

Calories 119   Sugars 16g
Protein . . . . .2g   Fat 0.3g
Carbohydrate . . .29g   Saturates 0g

25 MINS   1½ HOURS

SERVES 12

INGREDIENTS

4 pears, peeled and cored

margarine, for greasing

2 tbsp water

200 g/7 oz/1½ cups plain (all-purpose) flour

2 tsp baking powder

100 g/3½ oz/½ cup soft light brown sugar

4 tbsp milk

2 tbsp clear honey, plus extra to drizzle

2 tsp ground cinnamon

2 egg whites

1 Grease and line the base of a 20 cm/ 8 inch cake tin (pan).

2 Put 1 pear in a food processor with the water and blend until almost smooth. Transfer to a mixing bowl.

3 Sieve in the plain (all-purpose) flour and baking powder. Beat in the sugar, milk, honey and cinnamon and mix well.

4 Chop all but one of the remaining pears and add to the mixture.

5 Whisk the egg whites until peaking and gently fold into the mixture until fully blended.

6 Slice the remaining pear and arrange in a fan pattern on the base of the tin (pan).

7 Spoon the cake mixture into the tin (pan) and cook in a preheated oven, at 150°C/300°F/Gas Mark 2, for 1¼ –1½ hours or until cooked through.

8 Remove the cake from the oven and leave to cool in the tin (pan) for 10 minutes.

9 Turn the cake out on to a wire cooling rack and drizzle with honey. Leave to cool completely, then cut into slices to serve.

COOK'S TIP

To test if the cake is cooked through, insert a skewer into the centre – if it comes out clean the cake is cooked. If not, return the cake to the oven and test at frequent intervals.

Pear & Ginger Cake

This deliciously buttery pear and ginger cake is ideal for tea-time or you can serve it with cream for a delicious dessert.

NUTRITIONAL INFORMATION

Calories 531	Sugars 41g
Protein 6g	Fat 30g
Carbohydrate . . .62g	Saturates 19g

15 MINS   40 MINS

SERVES 6

I N G R E D I E N T S

200 g/7 oz/14 tbsp unsalted butter, softened

175 g/6 oz caster (superfine) sugar

175 g/6 oz self-raising flour, sifted

3 tsp ginger

3 eggs, beaten

450 g/1 lb dessert (eating) pears, peeled, cored and thinly sliced

1 tbsp soft brown sugar

1 Lightly grease and line the base of a deep 20.5 cm/8 inch cake tin (pan).

2 Using a whisk, combine 175 g/6 oz of the butter with the sugar, flour, ginger and eggs and mix to form a smooth consistency.

3 Spoon the cake mixture into the prepared tin (pan), levelling out the surface.

4 Arrange the pear slices over the cake mixture. Sprinkle with the brown sugar and dot with the remaining butter.

5 Bake in a preheated oven, at 180°C/350°F/Gas Mark 4, for 35–40 minutes or until the cake is golden and feels springy to the touch.

6 Serve the pear and ginger cake warm, with ice cream or cream, if you wish.

COOK'S TIP

Soft, brown sugar is often known as Barbados sugar. It is a darker form of light brown soft sugar.

Italian Bread Pudding

This deliciously rich pudding is cooked with cream and apples and is delicately flavoured with orange.

NUTRITIONAL INFORMATION

Calories ....387 Sugars 31g

Protein ....8g Fat 20g

Carbohydrate ...45g Saturates 12g

  45 MINS   25 MINS

SERVES 4

INGREDIENTS

15 g/½ oz/1 tbsp butter

2 small eating apples, peeled, cored and sliced into rings

75 g/2¾ oz granulated sugar

2 tbsp white wine

100 g/3½ oz bread, sliced with crusts removed (slightly stale French baguette is ideal)

300 ml/½ pint/1¼ cups single (light) cream

2 eggs, beaten

pared rind of 1 orange, cut into matchsticks

1 Lightly grease a 1.2 litre/2 pint deep ovenproof dish with the butter.

2 Arrange the apple rings in the base of the dish. Sprinkle half of the sugar over the apples.

3 Pour the wine over the apples. Add the bread slices, pushing them down with your hands to flatten them slightly.

4 Mix the cream with the eggs, the remaining sugar and the orange rind and pour the mixture over the bread. Leave to soak for 30 minutes.

5 Bake the pudding in a preheated oven, at 180°C/350°F/Gas Mark 4, for 25 minutes until golden and set. Serve warm.

VARIATION

For a variation, try adding dried fruit, such as apricots, cherries or dates, to the pudding, if you prefer.

Baked Sweet Ravioli

These scrumptious little parcels are the perfect dessert for anyone with a really sweet tooth.

NUTRITIONAL INFORMATION

Calories ....765 Sugars 56g
Protein ....16g Fat 30g
Carbohydrate ...114g Saturates 15g

1½ HOURS   20 MINS

SERVES 4

INGREDIENTS

PASTA

425 g/15 oz/3¾ cups plain
(all purpose) flour

140 g/5 oz/10 tbsp butter, plus extra
for greasing

140 g/5 oz/¾ cup caster (superfine) sugar

4 eggs

25 g/1 oz yeast

125 ml/4 fl oz warm milk

FILLING

175 g/6 oz/⅔ cup chestnut purée (paste)

60 g/2 oz/½ cup cocoa powder

60 g/2 oz/¼ cup caster (superfine) sugar

60 g/2 oz/½ cup chopped almonds

60 g/2 oz/1 cup crushed amaretti
biscuits (cookies)

175 g/6 oz/⅝ cup orange marmalade

1 To make the sweet pasta dough, sift the flour into a mixing bowl, then mix in the butter, sugar and 3 eggs.

2 Mix together the yeast and warm milk in a small bowl and when thoroughly combined, mix into the dough.

3 Knead the dough for 20 minutes, cover with a clean cloth and set aside in a warm place for 1 hour to rise.

4 Mix together the chestnut purée (paste), cocoa powder, sugar, almonds, crushed amaretti biscuits (cookies) and orange marmalade in a separate bowl.

5 Grease a baking tray (cookie sheet) with butter.

6 Lightly flour the work surface (counter). Roll out the pasta dough into a thin sheet and cut into 5 cm/2 inch rounds with a plain pastry cutter.

7 Put a spoonful of filling on to each round and then fold in half, pressing the edges to seal. Arrange on the prepared baking tray (cookie sheet), spacing the ravioli out well.

8 Beat the remaining egg and brush all over the ravioli to glaze. Bake in a preheated oven, at 180°C/350°F/Gas Mark 4, for 20 minutes. Serve hot.

Mascarpone Cheesecake

The mascarpone gives this baked cheesecake a wonderfully tangy flavour. Ricotta cheese could be used as an alternative.

NUTRITIONAL INFORMATION

Calories	327	Sugars	........25g
Protein	.........9g	Fat	..........18g
Carbohydrate	...33g	Saturates	......11g

  15 MINS   50 MINS

SERVES 8

I N G R E D I E N T S

50 g/1¾ oz/1½ tbsp unsalted butter

150 g/5½ oz ginger biscuits (cookies), crushed

25 g/1 oz stem ginger (candied), chopped

500 g/1 lb 2 oz mascarpone cheese

finely grated rind and juice of 2 lemons

100 g/3½ oz caster (superfine) sugar

2 large eggs, separated

fruit coulis (see Cook's Tip), to serve

1 Grease and line the base of a 25 cm/10 inch spring-form cake tin (pan) or loose-bottomed tin (pan).

2 Melt the butter in a pan and stir in the crushed biscuits (cookies) and chopped ginger. Use the mixture to line the tin (pan), pressing the mixture about 6 mm/¼ inch up the sides.

COOK'S TIP

Fruit coulis can be made by cooking 400 g/14 oz fruit, such as blueberries, for 5 minutes with 2 tablespoons of water. Sieve the mixture, then stir in 1 tablespoon (or more to taste) of sifted icing (confectioners') sugar. Leave to cool before serving.

3 Beat together the cheese, lemon rind and juice, sugar and egg yolks until quite smooth.

4 Whisk the egg whites until they are stiff and fold into the cheese and lemon mixture.

5 Pour the mixture into the tin (pan) and bake in a preheated oven, at 180°C/350°F/Gas Mark 4, for 35–45 minutes until just set. Don't worry if it cracks or sinks – this is quite normal.

6 Leave the cheesecake in the tin (pan) to cool. Serve with fruit coulis (see Cook's Tip).

Zabaglione

This well-known dish is really a light but rich egg mousse flavoured with Marsala.

NUTRITIONAL INFORMATION

Calories 158	Sugars 29g	
Protein 1g	Fat 1g	
Carbohydrate ...29g	Saturates 0.2g	

5 MINS   15 MINS

SERVES 4

INGREDIENTS

5 egg yolks

100 g/3½ oz caster (superfine) sugar

150 ml/¼ pint/⅔ cup Marsala or
   sweet sherry

amaretti biscuits (cookies), to serve
   (optional)

1 Place the egg yolks in a large mixing bowl.

2 Add the caster (superfine) sugar to the egg yolks and whisk until the mixture is thick and very pale and has doubled in volume.

3 Place the bowl containing the egg yolk and sugar mixture over a saucepan of gently simmering water.

4 Add the Marsala or sherry to the egg yolk and sugar mixture and continue whisking until the foam mixture becomes warm. This process may take as long as 10 minutes.

5 Pour the mixture, which should be frothy and light, into 4 wine glasses.

6 Serve the zabaglione warm with fresh fruit or amaretti biscuits (cookies), if you wish.

Chocolate Zabaglione

As this recipe only uses a little chocolate, choose one with a minimum of 70 per cent cocoa solids for a good flavour.

NUTRITIONAL INFORMATION

Calories ....224 Sugars 23g
Protein ....4g Fat 10g
Carbohydrate ...23g Saturates 4g

 10 MINS   5 MINS

SERVES 4

INGREDIENTS

4 egg yolks

50 g/1¾ oz/4 tbsp caster (superfine) sugar

50 g/1¾ oz dark chocolate

125 ml/4 fl oz/1 cup Marsala wine

cocoa powder, to dust

1 In a large glass mixing bowl, whisk together the egg yolks and caster (superfine) sugar until you have a very pale mixture, using electric beaters.

2 Grate the chocolate finely and fold into the egg mixture.

3 Fold the Marsala wine into the chocolate mixture.

4 Place the mixing bowl over a saucepan of gently simmering water

and set the beaters on the lowest speed or swop to a balloon whisk. Cook gently, whisking continuously until the mixture thickens; take care not to overcook or the mixture will curdle.

5 Spoon the hot mixture into warmed individual glass dishes or coffe cups (as here) and dust with cocoa powder. Serve the zabaglione as soon as possible so that it is warm, light and fluffy.

COOK'S TIP

Make the dessert just before serving as it will separate if left to stand. If it begins to curdle, remove it from the heat immediately and place it in a bowl of cold water to stop the cooking. Whisk furiously until the mixture comes together.

Chocolate Chip Ice Cream

This marvellous frozen dessert offers the best of both worlds, delicious chocolate chip cookies and a rich dairy-flavoured ice.

NUTRITIONAL INFORMATION

Calories 238	Sugars 23g
Protein 9g	Fat 10g
Carbohydrate ...30g	Saturates 4g

6 HOURS   5 MINS

SERVES 6

INGREDIENTS

300 ml/½ pint/1¼ cups milk

1 vanilla pod (bean)

2 eggs

2 egg yolks

60 g/2 oz/¼ cup caster
   (superfine) sugar

300 ml/½ pint/1¼ cups natural
   (unsweetened) yogurt

125 g/4½ oz chocolate chip cookies,
   broken into small pieces

1 Pour the milk into a small pan, add the vanilla pod (bean) and bring to the boil over a low heat. Remove from the heat, cover the pan and set aside to cool.

2 Beat the eggs and egg yolks in a double boiler or in a bowl set over a pan of simmering water. Add the sugar and continue beating until the mixture is pale and creamy.

3 Reheat the milk to simmering point and strain it over the egg mixture. Stir continuously until the custard is thick enough to coat the back of a spoon. Remove the custard from the heat and stand the pan or bowl in cold water to prevent any further cooking. Wash and dry the vanilla pod (bean) for future use.

4 Stir the yogurt into the cooled custard and beat until it is well blended. When the mixture is thoroughly cold, stir in the broken cookies.

5 Transfer the mixture to a chilled metal cake tin (pan) or plastic container, cover and freeze for 4 hours. Remove from the freezer every hour, transfer to a chilled bowl and beat vigorously to prevent ice crystals from forming then return to the freezer. Alternatively, freeze the mixture in an ice-cream maker, following the manufacturer's instructions.

6 To serve the ice-cream, transfer it to the main part of the refrigerator for 1 hour. Serve in scoops.

Honey & Nut Nests

Pistachio nuts and honey are combined with crisp cooked angel hair pasta in this unusual dessert.

NUTRITIONAL INFORMATION

Calories . . . . . . .802 Sugars 53g
Protein . . . . .13g Fat 48g
Carbohydrate . . .85g Saturates 16g

10 MINS   1 HOUR

SERVES 4

INGREDIENTS

225 g/8 oz angel hair pasta

115 g/4 oz/8 tbsp butter

175 g/6 oz/1½ cups shelled pistachio nuts, chopped

115 g/4 oz/½ cup sugar

115 g/4 oz/⅓ cup clear honey

150 ml/¼ pint/⅔ cup water

2 tsp lemon juice

salt

Greek-style yogurt, to serve

1 Bring a large saucepan of lightly salted water to the boil. Add the angel hair pasta and cook for 8–10 minutes or until tender, but still firm to the bite. Drain the pasta and return to the pan. Add the butter and toss to coat the pasta thoroughly. Set aside to cool.

2 Arrange 4 small flan or poaching rings on a baking tray (cookie sheet). Divide the angel hair pasta into 8 equal quantities and spoon 4 of them into the rings. Press down lightly. Top the pasta with half of the nuts, then add the remaining pasta.

3 Bake in a preheated oven, at 180°C/350°F/Gas Mark 4, for 45 minutes, or until golden brown.

4 Meanwhile, put the sugar, honey and water in a saucepan and bring to the boil over a low heat, stirring constantly until the sugar has dissolved completely. Simmer for 10 minutes, add the lemon juice and simmer for 5 minutes.

5 Using a palette knife (spatula), carefully transfer the angel hair nests to a serving dish. Pour over the honey syrup, sprinkle over the remaining nuts and set aside to cool completely before serving. Serve the Greek-style yogurt separately.

COOK'S TIP

Angel hair pasta is also known as *capelli d'Angelo*. Long and very fine, it is usually sold in small bunches that already resemble nests.

Pear Tart

Pears are a very popular fruit in Italy. In this recipe from Trentino they are flavoured with almonds, cinnamon, raisins and apricot jam.

NUTRITIONAL INFORMATION

Calories ....629 Sugars 70g
Protein ....7g Fat 21g
Carbohydrate ..109g Saturates 13g

1½ HOURS   50 MINS

SERVES 6

INGREDIENTS

275 g/9½ oz/2¼ cups plain (all-purpose) flour

pinch of salt

125 g/4½ oz/½ cup caster (superfine) sugar

125 g/4½ oz/½ cup butter, diced

1 egg

1 egg yolk

few drops of vanilla essence (extract)

2–3 tsp water

sifted icing (confectioners') sugar, for sprinkling

FILLING

4 tbsp apricot jam

60 g/2 oz amaretti or ratafia biscuits (cookies), crumbled

850–1 kg/1¾–2 lb 4 oz pears, peeled and cored

1 tsp ground cinnamon

90 g/3 oz/½ cup raisins

60 g/2 oz/⅓ cup soft brown or demerara sugar

1 Sift the flour and salt on to a flat surface, make a well in the centre and add the sugar, butter, egg, egg yolk, vanilla essence (extract) and most of the water.

2 Using your fingers, gradually work the flour into the other ingredients to give a smooth dough, adding more water if necessary. Wrap in cling film (plastic wrap) and chill for 1 hour or until firm. Alternatively, put all the ingredients into a food processor and work until smooth.

3 Roll out three-quarters of the dough and use to line a shallow 25 cm/ 10 inch cake tin (pan) or deep flan tin (pan). Spread the jam over the base and sprinkle with the crushed biscuits (cookies).

4 Slice the pears very thinly. Arrange over the biscuits (cookies) in the pastry case. Sprinkle with cinnamon then with raisins, and finally with brown sugar.

5 Roll out a thin sausage shape using one-third of the remaining dough, and place around the edge of the pie. Roll the remainder into thin sausages and arrange in a lattice over the pie, 4 or 5 strips in each direction, attaching them to the strip around the edge.

6 Cook in a preheated oven, at 200°C/ 400°F/Gas Mark 6, for 50 minutes until golden and cooked through. Leave to cool, then serve warm or chilled, sprinkled with sifted icing (confectioners') sugar.

Quick Tiramisu

This quick version of one of the most popular Italian desserts is ready in minutes.

NUTRITIONAL INFORMATION

Calories ....387 Sugars 17g
Protein ....9g Fat 28g
Carbohydrate ...22g Saturates 15g

 15 MINS   0 MINS

SERVES 4

INGREDIENTS

225 g/8 oz/1 cup Mascarpone or full-fat
 soft cheese

1 egg, separated

2 tbsp natural yogurt

2 tbsp caster (superfine) sugar

2 tbsp dark rum

2 tbsp strong black coffee

8 sponge fingers (lady-fingers)

2 tbsp grated dark chocolate

1 Put the cheese in a large bowl, add the egg yolk and yogurt and beat until smooth.

2 Whisk the egg white until stiff but not dry, then whisk in the sugar and carefully fold into the cheese mixture.

COOK'S TIP

Mascarpone is an Italian soft cream cheese made from cow's milk. It has a rich, silky smooth texture and a deliciously creamy flavour. It can be eaten as it is with fresh fruits or flavoured with coffee or chocolate.

3 Spoon half of the mixture into 4 sundae glasses.

4 Mix together the rum and coffee in a shallow dish. Dip the sponge fingers (lady-fingers) into the rum mixture, break them in half, or into smaller pieces if necessary, and divide among the glasses.

5 Stir any remaining coffee mixture into the remaining cheese and spoon over the top.

6 Sprinkle with grated chocolate. Serve immediately or chill until required.

Raspberry Fusilli

This is the ultimate in self-indulgence – a truly delicious dessert that tastes every bit as good as it looks.

NUTRITIONAL INFORMATION

Calories	235	Sugars 20g
Protein	. . . . .7g	Fat 7g
Carbohydrate	. . .36g	Saturates 1g

5 MINS   20 MINS

SERVES 4

INGREDIENTS

175 g/6 oz/½ cup fusilli

700 g/1 lb 9 oz/4 cups raspberries

2 tbsp caster (superfine) sugar

1 tbsp lemon juice

4 tbsp flaked (slivered) almonds

3 tbsp raspberry liqueur

1 Bring a large saucepan of lightly salted water to the boil. Add the fusilli and cook for 8–10 minutes until tender, but still firm to the bite. Drain the fusilli thoroughly, return to the pan and set aside to cool.

2 Using a spoon, firmly press 225 g/ 8 oz/1⅓ cups of the raspberries through a sieve (strainer) set over a large mixing bowl to form a smooth purée (paste).

3 Put the raspberry purée (paste) and sugar in a small saucepan and simmer over a low heat, stirring occasionally, for 5 minutes.

4 Stir in the lemon juice and set the sauce aside until required.

5 Add the remaining raspberries to the fusilli in the pan and mix together well. Transfer the raspberry and fusilli mixture to a serving dish.

6 Spread the almonds out on a baking tray (cookie sheet) and toast under the grill (broiler) until golden brown. Remove and set aside to cool slightly.

7 Stir the raspberry liqueur into the reserved raspberry sauce and mix together well until very smooth. Pour the raspberry sauce over the fusilli, sprinkle over the toasted almonds and serve.

VARIATION

You could use any sweet, ripe berry for making this dessert. Strawberries and blackberries are especially suitable, combined with the correspondingly flavoured liqueur. Alternatively, you could use a different berry mixed with the fusilli, but still pour over raspberry sauce.

Rich Chocolate Loaf

Another rich chocolate dessert, this loaf is very simple to make and can be served as a tea-time treat as well.

NUTRITIONAL INFORMATION

Calories	180	Sugars	........16g
Protein	.........3g	Fat	...........11g
Carbohydrate	...18g	Saturates	.......5g

1¼ HOURS   5 MINS

MAKES 16 SLICES

I N G R E D I E N T S

150 g/5½ oz dark chocolate

75 g/2¾ oz/6 tbsp butter, unsalted

210 g/7¼ oz tin of condensed milk

2 tsp cinnamon

75 g/2¾ oz almonds

75 g/2¾ oz amaretti biscuits (cookies), broken

50 g/1¾ oz dried no-need-to-soak apricots, roughly chopped

1 Line a 675 g/1½ lb loaf tin (pan) with a sheet of kitchen foil.

2 Using a sharp knife, roughly chop the almonds.

3 Place the chocolate, butter, milk and cinnamon in a heavy-based saucepan.

COOK'S TIP

To melt chocolate, first break it into manageable pieces. The smaller the pieces, the quicker it will melt.

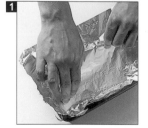

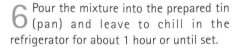

4 Heat the chocolate mixture over a low heat for 3–4 minutes, stirring with a wooden spoon, or until the chocolate has melted. Beat the mixture well.

5 Stir the almonds, biscuits and apricots into the chocolate mixture, stirring with a wooden spoon, until well mixed.

6 Pour the mixture into the prepared tin (pan) and leave to chill in the refrigerator for about 1 hour or until set.

7 Cut the rich chocolate loaf into slices to serve.

Caramelized Oranges

The secret of these oranges is to allow them to marinate in the syrup for at least 24 hours, so the flavours amalgamate.

NUTRITIONAL INFORMATION

Calories . . . . . . .235 Sugars 59g
Protein . . . . .2g Fat 0.2g
Carbohydrate . . .59g Saturates 0g

 3¼ HOURS   20 MINS

SERVES 6

INGREDIENTS

6 large oranges

225 g/8 oz/1 cup sugar

250 ml/9 fl oz/1 cup water

6 whole cloves (optional)

2–4 tbsp orange-flavoured liqueur
  or brandy

1 Using a citrus zester or potato peeler, pare the rind from 2 of the oranges in narrow strips without any white pith attached. If using a potato peeler, cut the peel into very thin julienne strips.

2 Put the strips into a small saucepan and barely cover with water. Bring to the boil and simmer for 5 minutes. Drain the strips and reserve the water.

3 Cut away all the white pith and peel from the remaining oranges using a very sharp knife. Then cut horizontally into 4 slices. Reassemble the oranges and hold in place with wooden cocktail sticks (toothpick). Stand in a heatproof dish.

4 Put the sugar and water into a heavy-based saucepan with the cloves, if using. Bring to the boil and simmer gently until the sugar has dissolved, then boil hard without stirring until the syrup thickens and begins to colour. Continue to

cook until a light golden brown, then quickly remove from the heat and carefully pour in the reserved orange rind liquid.

5 Place over a gentle heat until the caramel has fully dissolved again, then remove from the heat and add the liqueur or brandy. Pour over the oranges.

6 Sprinkle the orange strips over the oranges, cover with cling film (plastic wrap) and leave until cold. Chill for at least 3 hours and preferably for 24–48 hours before serving. If time allows, spoon the syrup over the oranges several times while they are marinating. Discard the cocktail stick (toothpick) before serving.

Cream Custards

Individual pan-cooked cream custards are flavoured with nutmeg and topped with caramelized orange strips.

NUTRITIONAL INFORMATION

Calories	406	Sugars	........38g
Protein	.........8g	Fat	.........26g
Carbohydrate	...38g	Saturates	......15g

2¼ HOURS   25 MINS

SERVES 4

INGREDIENTS

450 ml/16 fl oz/2 cups single (light) cream

100 g/3¾ oz caster (superfine) sugar

1 orange

2 tsp grated nutmeg

3 large eggs, beaten

1 tbsp honey

1 tsp cinnamon

1 Place the cream and sugar in a large non-stick saucepan and heat gently, stirring, until the sugar caramelizes.

2 Finely grate half of the orange rind and add it to the pan along with the nutmeg.

3 Add the eggs to the mixture in the pan and cook over a low heat for 10–15 minutes, stirring constantly. The custard will eventually thicken.

4 Strain the custard through a fine sieve into 4 shallow serving dishes. Leave to chill in the refrigerator for 2 hours.

5 Meanwhile, pare the remaining orange rind and cut it into matchsticks.

6 Place the honey and cinnamon in a pan with 2 tablespoons of water and heat gently. Add the orange rind to the pan and cook for 2–3 minutes, stirring, until the mixture has caramelized.

7 Pour the mixture into a bowl and separate out the orange strips. Leave to cool until set.

8 Once the custards have set, decorate them with the caramelized orange rind and serve.

COOK'S TIP

The cream custards will keep for 1–2 days in the refrigerator. Decorate with the caramelized orange rind just before serving.

Peaches in White Wine

A very simple but incredibly pleasing dessert, which is especially good for a dinner party on a hot summer day.

NUTRITIONAL INFORMATION

Calories 89   Sugars 14g
Protein . . . . .1g   Fat 0g
Carbohydrate . . .14g   Saturates 0g

 1¹/₄ HOURS   0 MINS

SERVES 4

I N G R E D I E N T S

4 large ripe peaches

2 tbsp icing (confectioners') sugar, sifted

1 orange

200 ml/7 fl oz/¾ cup medium or sweet
   white wine, chilled

1 Using a sharp knife, halve the peaches, remove the stones (pits) and discard them. Peel the peaches, if you prefer. Slice the peaches into thin wedges.

2 Place the peach wedges in a serving bowl and sprinkle over the sugar.

3 Using a sharp knife, pare the rind from the orange. Cut the orange rind into matchsticks, place them in a bowl of cold water and set aside.

4 Squeeze the juice from the orange and pour over the peaches together with the wine.

5 Let the peaches marinate and chill in the refrigerator for at least 1 hour.

6 Remove the orange rind from the cold water and pat dry with paper towels.

7 Garnish the peaches with the strips of orange rind and serve immediately.

Peaches & Mascarpone

If you prepare these in advance, all you have to do is pop the peaches on the barbecue (grill) when you are ready to serve them.

NUTRITIONAL INFORMATION

Calories 301	Sugars 24g	
Protein 6g	Fat 20g	
Carbohydrate ...24g	Saturates 9g	

 10 MINS   10 MINS

SERVES 4

INGREDIENTS

4 peaches

175 g/6 oz mascarpone cheese

40 g/1½ oz pecan or walnuts, chopped

1 tsp sunflower oil

4 tbsp maple syrup

1 Cut the peaches in half and remove the stones. If you are preparing this recipe in advance, press the peach halves together again and wrap them in cling film (plastic wrap) until required.

2 Mix the mascarpone and pecan or walnuts together in a small bowl until well combined. Leave to chill in the refrigerator until required.

VARIATION

You can use nectarines instead of peaches for this recipe. Remember to choose ripe but firm fruit which won't go soft and mushy when it is barbecued (grilled). Prepare the nectarines in the same way as the peaches and barbecue (grill) for 5–10 minutes.

3 To serve, brush the peaches with a little oil and place on a rack set over medium hot coals. Barbecue (grill) for 5–10 minutes, turning once, until hot.

4 Transfer the peaches to a serving dish and top with the mascarpone mixture.

5 Drizzle the maple syrup over the peaches and mascarpone filling and serve at once.

Sweet Mascarpone Mousse

A sweet cream cheese dessert that complements the tartness of fresh summer fruits rather well.

NUTRITIONAL INFORMATION

Calories 542	Sugars 31g	
Protein 14g	Fat 41g	
Carbohydrate ...31g	Saturates 24g	

 1½ HOURS   0 MINS

SERVES 4

INGREDIENTS

450 g/1 lb mascarpone cheese

100 g/3½ oz caster (superfine) sugar

4 egg yolks

400 g/14 oz frozen summer fruits, such as
   raspberries and redcurrants

redcurrants, to garnish

amaretti biscuits (cookies), to serve

1 Place the mascarpone cheese in a large mixing bowl. Using a wooden spoon, beat the mascarpone cheese until quite smooth.

2 Stir the egg yolks and sugar into the mascarpone cheese, mixing well. Leave the mixture to chill in the refrigerator for about 1 hour.

3 Spoon a layer of the mascarpone mixture into the bottom of 4 individual serving dishes. Spoon a layer of the summer fruits on top. Repeat the layers in the same order, reserving some of the mascarpone mixture for the top.

4 Leave the mousses to chill in the refrigerator for about 20 minutes. The fruits should still be slightly frozen.

5 Serve the mascarpone mousses with amaretti biscuits (cookies).

Panettone & Strawberries

Panettone is a sweet Italian bread. It is delicious toasted, and when it is topped with marscapone and strawberries it makes a sumptuous dessert.

NUTRITIONAL INFORMATION

Calories . . . . . . .227 Sugars 11g
Protein . . . . .5g Fat 13g
Carbohydrate . . .19g Saturates 8g

 35 MINS   2 MINS

SERVES 4

I N G R E D I E N T S

225 g/8 oz strawberries

25 g/1 oz caster (superfine) sugar

6 tbsp Marsala wine

½ tsp ground cinnamon

4 slices panettone

4 tbsp mascarpone cheese

1 Hull and slice the strawberries and place them in a bowl. Add the sugar, Marsala and cinnamon to the strawberries.

2 Toss the strawberries in the sugar and cinnamon mixture until they are well coated. Leave to chill in the refrigerator for at least 30 minutes.

3 When ready to serve, transfer the slices of panettone to a rack set over medium hot coals. Barbecue (grill) the panettone for about 1 minute on each side or until golden brown.

4 Carefully remove the panettone from the barbecue (grill) and transfer to serving plates.

5 Top the panettone with the mascarpone cheese and the marinated strawberries. Serve immediately.

Orange & Grapefruit Salad

Sliced citrus fruits with a delicious almond and honey dressing make an unusual and refreshing dessert.

NUTRITIONAL INFORMATION

Calories	217	Sugars	........33g
Protein	.........4g	Fat	..........9g
Carbohydrate	...33g	Saturates	.......1g

 2¼ HOURS 3 MINS

SERVES 4

I N G R E D I E N T S

2 grapefruit, ruby or plain

4 oranges

pared rind and juice of 1 lime

4 tbsp runny honey

2 tbsp warm water

1 sprig of mint, roughly chopped

50 g/1¾ oz chopped walnuts

1 Using a sharp knife, slice the top and bottom from the grapefruits, then slice away the rest of the skin and pith.

2 Cut between each segment of the grapefruit and remove the fleshy part only.

3 Using a sharp knife, slice the top and bottom from the oranges, then slice away the rest of the skin and pith.

4 Cut between each segment of the oranges to remove the fleshy part. Add to the grapefruit.

5 Place the lime rind, 2 tablespoons of lime juice, the honey and the warm water in a small bowl. Whisk with a fork to mix the dressing.

6 Pour the dressing over the segmented fruit, add the chopped mint and mix well. Leave to chill in the refrigerator for 2 hours for the flavours to mingle.

7 Place the chopped walnuts on a baking tray (cookie sheet). Lightly toast the walnuts under a preheated medium grill (broiler) for 2–3 minutes or until browned.

8 Sprinkle the toasted walnuts over the fruit and serve.

Vanilla Ice Cream

This home-made version of real vanilla ice cream is absolutely delicious and so easy to make. A tutti-frutti variation is also provided.

 5 MINS   15 MINS

SERVES 6

INGREDIENTS

600 ml/1 pint/2½ cups double
  (heavy) cream

1 vanilla pod

pared rind of 1 lemon

4 eggs, beaten

2 egg yolks

175 g/6 oz caster (superfine) sugar

1 Place the cream in a heavy-based saucepan and heat gently, whisking.

2 Add the vanilla pod, lemon rind, eggs and egg yolks to the pan and heat until the mixture reaches just below boiling point.

3 Reduce the heat and cook for 8–10 minutes, whisking the mixture continuously, until thickened.

VARIATION

For tutti frutti ice cream, soak 100 g/3½ oz mixed dried fruit in 2 tbsp Marsala or sweet sherry for 20 minutes. Follow the method for vanilla ice cream, omitting the vanilla pod, and stir in the Marsala or sherry-soaked fruit in step 6, just before freezing.

4 Stir the sugar into the cream mixture, set aside and leave to cool.

5 Strain the cream mixture through a sieve (strainer).

6 Slit open the vanilla pod, scoop out the tiny black seeds and stir them into the cream.

7 Pour the mixture into a shallow freezing container with a lid and freeze overnight until set. Serve the ice cream when required.

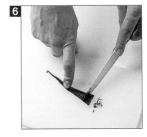

Ricotta Ice Cream

The ricotta cheese adds a creamy flavour, while the nuts add a crunchy texture. This ice cream needs to be chilled in the freezer overnight.

NUTRITIONAL INFORMATION

Calories	438	Sugars	........39g
Protein	........13g	Fat	.........25g
Carbohydrate	...40g	Saturates	.......9g

20 MINS   0 MINS

SERVES 6

I N G R E D I E N T S

25 g/1 oz/¼ cup pistachio nuts

25 g/1 oz/¼ cup walnuts or pecan nuts

25 g/1 oz/¼ cup toasted
  chopped hazelnuts

grated rind of 1 orange

grated rind of 1 lemon

25 g/1 oz/2 tbsp crystallized or stem ginger

25 g/1 oz/2 tbsp glacé cherries

25 g/1 oz/¼ cup dried apricots

25 g/1 oz/3 tbsp raisins

500 g/1 lb 2 oz/1½ cups Ricotta

2 tbsp Maraschino, Amaretto or brandy

1 tsp vanilla essence (extract)

4 egg yolks

125 g/4½ oz/½ cup caster (superfine)
  sugar

TO DECORATE

whipped cream

a few glacé cherries, pistachio nuts or

mint leaves

1 Roughly chop the pistachio nuts and walnuts and mix with the toasted hazelnuts, orange and lemon rind.

2 Finely chop the ginger, cherries, apricots and raisins, and add to the bowl.

3 Stir the Ricotta evenly through the fruit mixture, then beat in the liqueur and vanilla essence (extract).

4 Put the egg yolks and sugar in a bowl and whisk hard until very thick and creamy – they may be whisked over a saucepan of gently simmering water to speed up the process. Leave to cool if necessary.

5 Carefully fold the Ricotta mixture evenly through the beaten eggs and sugar until smooth.

6 Line a 18 x 12 cm/7 x 5 inch loaf tin (pan) with a double layer of cling film (plastic wrap) or baking parchment. Pour in the Ricotta mixture, level the top, cover with more cling film (plastic wrap) or baking parchment and chill in the freezer until firm – at least overnight.

7 To serve, carefully remove the ice-cream from the tin (pan) and peel off the paper. Place on a serving dish and decorate with whipped cream, glacé cherries, pistachio nuts and/or mint leaves. Serve in slices.

Lemon Granita

A delightful end to a meal or a refreshing way to cleanse the palate, granitas are made from slushy ice, so they need to be served very quickly.

NUTRITIONAL INFORMATION

Calories	102	Sugars	.......27g
Protein	.......0.1g	Fat	.......0g
Carbohydrate	...27g	Saturates	.......0g

5¼ HOURS   6 MINS

SERVES 4

INGREDIENTS

LEMON GRANITA

3 lemons

200 ml/7 fl oz/¾ cup lemon juice

100 g/3½ oz caster (superfine) sugar

500 ml/18 fl oz/2¼ cups cold water

VARIATION

To make coffee granita, place 2 tbsp instant coffee and 2 tbsp sugar in a bowl and pour over 2 tbsp hot water, stirring until dissolved. Stir in 600 ml/1 pint/ 2½ cups cold water and 2 tbsp rum or brandy. Pour into a shallow freezer container with a lid. Freeze for at least 6 hours, stirring occasionally, to create a grainy texture.

1 To make lemon granita, finely grate the lemon rind.

2 Place the lemon rind, juice and caster (superfine) sugar in a pan. Bring the mixture to the boil and leave to simmer for 5-6 minutes or until thick and syrupy. Leave to cool.

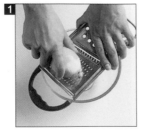

3 Once cooled, stir in the cold water and pour into a shallow freezer container with a lid.

4 Freeze the granita for 4–5 hours, stirring occasionally to break up the ice. Serve as a dessert or palate cleanser between dinner courses.

Rosemary Biscuits (Cookies)

Do not be put off by the idea of herbs being used in these crisp biscuits (cookies) – try them and you will be pleasantly surprised.

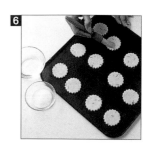

NUTRITIONAL INFORMATION

Calories 50	Sugars 2g
Protein 1g	Fat 2g
Carbohydrate 8g	Saturates 1g

 45 MINS   15 MINS

MAKES 25

I N G R E D I E N T S

50 g/1¾ oz/10 tsp butter, softened

4 tbsp caster (superfine) sugar

grated rind of 1 lemon

4 tbsp lemon juice

1 egg, separated

2 tsp finely chopped fresh rosemary

200 g/7 oz/1¾ cups plain (all-purpose)
   flour, sieved (strained)

caster (superfine) sugar, for sprinkling
   (optional)

1 Lightly grease 2 baking trays (cookie sheets).

2 In a large mixing bowl, cream together the butter and sugar until pale and fluffy.

3 Add the lemon rind and juice, then the egg yolk and beat until they are thoroughly combined. Stir in the chopped fresh rosemary.

4 Add the sieved (strained) flour, mixing well until a soft dough is formed. Wrap and leave to chill for 30 minutes.

5 On a lightly floured surface, roll out the dough thinly and then stamp out 25 circles with a 6 cm/2½ inch biscuit (cookie) cutter. Arrange the dough circles on the prepared baking trays (cookie sheets).

6 In a bowl, lightly whisk the egg white. Gently brush the egg white over the surface of each biscuit (cookie), then sprinkle with a little caster (superfine) sugar, if liked.

7 Bake in a preheated oven, at 180°C/ 350°F/Gas Mark 4, for about 15 minutes.

8 Transfer the biscuits (cookies) to a wire rack and leave to cool before serving.

COOK'S TIP

Store the biscuits (cookies) in an airtight container for up to 1 week.

Chocolate Biscotti

These dry biscuits (cookies) are delicious served with black coffee after your evening meal.

NUTRITIONAL INFORMATION

Calories 113	Sugars 9g
Protein 2g	Fat 5g
Carbohydrate . . .15g	Saturates 1g

🍴 20 MINS   🕐 40 MINS

MAKES 16

INGREDIENTS

1 egg

100 g/3½ oz/⅓ cup caster (superfine) sugar

1 tsp vanilla essence (extract)

125 g/4½ oz/1 cup plain (all-purpose) flour

½ tsp baking powder

1 tsp ground cinnamon

50 g/1¾ oz dark chocolate, chopped roughly

50 g/1¾ oz toasted flaked (slivered) almonds

50 g/1¾ oz pine kernels (nuts)

1 Lightly grease a large baking tray (cookie sheet).

2 Whisk the egg, sugar and vanilla essence (extract) in a mixing bowl with an electric mixer until it is thick and pale – ribbons of mixture should trail from the whisk as you lift it.

3 Sieve (strain) the flour, baking powder and cinnamon into a separate bowl, then sieve (strain) into the egg mixture and fold in gently. Stir in the chocolate, almonds and pine kernels (nuts).

4 Turn on to a lightly floured surface and shape into a flat log, 23 cm/ 9 inches long and 1.5 cm/¾ inch wide. Transfer to the baking tray (cookie sheet).

5 Bake in a preheated oven, at 180°C/ 350°F/Gas Mark 4, for 20-25 minutes or until golden. Remove from the oven and leave to cool for 5 minutes or until firm.

6 Transfer the log to a cutting board. Using a serrated bread knife, cut the log on the diagonal into slices about 1 cm/ ½ inch thick and arrange them on the baking tray (cookie sheet). Cook for 10-15 minutes, turning halfway through the cooking time.

7 Leave to cool for about 5 minutes, then transfer to a wire rack to cool completely.

Florentines

These luxury biscuits (cookies) will be popular at any time of the year, but make a particularly wonderful treat at Christmas.

NUTRITIONAL INFORMATION

Calories 186	Sugars 19g
Protein 2g	Fat 11g
Carbohydrate ...22g	Saturates 5g

20 MINS   🕐 15 MINS

MAKES 10

INGREDIENTS

50 g/1¾ oz/ 10 tsp butter

50 g/1¾ oz/¼ cup caster (superfine) sugar

25 g/1 oz/¼ cup plain (all-purpose) flour, sieved (strained)

50 g/1¾ oz/⅓ cup almonds, chopped

50 g/1¾ oz/⅓ cup chopped mixed peel

25 g/1 oz/¼ cup raisins, chopped

25 g/1 oz/2 tbsp glacé (candied) cherries, chopped

finely grated rind of ½ lemon

125 g/4½ oz dark chocolate, melted

1 Line 2 large baking trays (cookie sheets) with baking parchment.

2 Heat the butter and caster (superfine) sugar in a small saucepan until the butter has just melted and the sugar dissolved. Remove the pan from the heat.

3 Stir in the flour and mix well. Stir in the chopped almonds, mixed peel, raisins, cherries and lemon rind. Place teaspoonfuls of the mixture well apart on the baking trays (cookie sheets).

4 Bake in a preheated oven, at 180°C/ 350°F/Gas Mark 4, for 10 minutes or until lightly golden.

5 As soon as the florentines are removed from the oven, press the edges into neat shapes while still on the baking trays (cookie sheets), using a biscuit (cookie) cutter. Leave to cool on the baking trays (cookie sheets) until firm, then transfer to a wire rack to cool completely.

6 Spread the melted chocolate over the smooth side of each florentine. As the chocolate begins to set, mark wavy lines in it with a fork. Leave the florentines until set, chocolate side up.

VARIATION

Replace the dark chocolate with white chocolate or, for a dramatic effect, cover half of the florentines in dark chocolate and half in white.

Florentine Twists

These famous and delicious Florentine biscuits (cookies) are twisted into curls or cones and then just the ends are dipped in chocolate.

NUTRITIONAL INFORMATION

Calories 28   Sugars 15g
Protein ....1g   Fat 7g
Carbohydrate ...15g   Saturates 4g

20 MINS   20 MINS

MAKES 20

INGREDIENTS

90 g/3 oz/⅓ cup butter

125 g/4½ oz/½ cup caster (superfine) sugar

60 g/2 oz/½ cup blanched or flaked (slivered) almonds, chopped roughly

25 g/1 oz/3 tbsp raisins, chopped

45 g/1½ oz/¼ cup chopped mixed peel

45 g/1½ oz/scant ¼ cup glacé (candied) cherries, chopped

25 g/1 oz/3 tbsp dried apricots, chopped finely

finely grated rind of ½ lemon or ½ small orange

about 125 g/4½ oz/4 squares dark or white chocolate

1 Line 2–3 baking trays (cookie sheets) with non-stick baking parchment; then grease 4–6 cream horn tins (moulds) or a fairly thin rolling pin, or wooden spoon handles.

2 Melt the butter and sugar together gently in a saucepan and then bring to the boil for 1 minute. Remove the pan from the heat and stir in all the remaining ingredients, except for the chocolate. Leave to cool.

3 Put heaped teaspoonfuls of the mixture on to the baking sheets, keeping them well apart, only 3–4 per sheet, and flatten slightly.

4 Bake in a preheated oven, at 180°C/ 350°F/Gas Mark 4, for 10–12 minutes, or until golden. Leave to cool until they begin to firm up. As they cool, press the edges back to form a neat shape. Remove each one with a palette knife (spatula) and wrap quickly around a cream horn tin (mould), or lay over the rolling pin or spoon handles. If they become too firm to bend, return to the oven briefly to soften.

5 Leave until cold and crisp and then slip carefully off the horn tins (moulds) or remove from the rolling pin or spoons.

6 Melt the chocolate in a heatproof bowl over a saucepan of hot water, or in a microwave oven set on Full Power for about 45 seconds, and stir until smooth. Either dip the end of each Florentine twist into the chocolate or, using a pastry brush, paint chocolate to come about halfway up the twist. As the chocolate sets, it can be marked into wavy lines with a fork. Leave to set.

Mini Florentines

Serve these biscuits (cookies) at the end of a meal with coffee, or arrange in a shallow presentation box for an attractive gift.

NUTRITIONAL INFORMATION

Calories	75	Sugars	.........6g
Protein	.........1g	Fat	...........5g
Carbohydrate	....6g	Saturates	.......2g

🍴 20 MINS 🕐 20 MINS

MAKES 40

I N G R E D I E N T S

75 g/2¾ oz/⅓ cup butter

75 g/2¾ oz/⅓ cup caster (superfine) sugar

25 g/1 oz/2 tbsp sultanas (golden raisins) or raisins

25 g/1 oz/2 tbsp glacé (candied) cherries, chopped

25 g/1 oz/2 tbsp crystallised ginger, chopped

25 g/1 oz sunflower seeds

100 g/3½ oz/¾ cup flaked (slivered) almonds

2 tbsp double (heavy) cream

175 g/6 oz dark or milk chocolate

1 Grease and flour 2 baking trays (cookie sheets) or line with baking parchment.

2 Place the butter in a small pan and heat gently until melted. Add the sugar, stir until dissolved, then bring the mixture to the boil. Remove from the heat and stir in the sultanas (golden raisins) or raisins, cherries, ginger, sunflower seeds and almonds. Mix well, then beat in the cream.

3 Place small teaspoons of the fruit and nut mixture on to the prepared baking tray (cookie sheet), allowing plenty of space for the mixture to spread. Bake in a preheated oven, at 180°C/350°F/Gas Mark 4, for 10-12 minutes or until light golden in colour.

4 Remove from the oven and, whilst still hot, use a circular biscuit (cookie) cutter to pull in the edges to form a perfect circle. Leave to cool and crispen before removing from the baking tray (cookie sheet).

5 Melt most of the chocolate and spread it on a sheet of baking parchment. When the chocolate is on the point of setting, place the biscuits (cookies) flat-side down on the chocolate and leave to harden completely.

6 Cut around the florentines and remove from the baking parchment. Spread a little more chocolate on the coated side of the florentines and use a fork to mark waves in the chocolate. Leave to set. Arrange the florentines on a plate (or in a presentation box for a gift) with alternate sides facing upwards. Keep cool.

White Chocolate Florentines

These attractive jewelled biscuits (cookies) are coated with white chocolate to give them a delicious flavour.

NUTRITIONAL INFORMATION

Calories 235	Sugars 20g
Protein 3g	Fat 17g
Carbohydrate ...20g	Saturates 7g

20 MINS • 15 MINS

MAKES 24

INGREDIENTS

200 g/7 oz butter

225 g/8 oz caster sugar

125 g/4½ oz walnuts, chopped

125 g/4½ oz almonds, chopped

60 g/2 oz sultanas, chopped

25 g/1 oz glacé cherries, chopped

25 g/1 oz mixed candied peel,
    chopped finely

2 tbsp single (thin) cream

225 g/8 oz white chocolate

1 Line 3–4 baking trays (cookie sheets) with non-stick baking parchment.

2 Melt the butter over a low heat and then add the sugar, stirring until it has dissolved. Boil the mixture for exactly 1 minute. Remove from the heat.

COOK'S TIP

A combination of white and dark chocolate Florentines looks very attractive, especially if you are making them as gifts. Pack them in pretty boxes, lined with tissue paper and tied with some ribbon.

3 Add the walnuts, almonds, sultanas, glacé cherries, candied peel and cream to the saucepan, stirring well to mix.

4 Drop heaped teaspoonfuls of the mixture on to the baking trays (cookie sheets), allowing plenty of room for them to spread while cooking. Bake in a preheated oven, at 180°C/350°F/Gas Mark 4, for 10 minutes or until golden brown.

5 Remove the biscuits (cookies) from the oven and neaten the edges with a knife while they are still warm. Leave to cool slightly, and then transfer them to a wire rack to cool completely.

6 Melt the chocolate in a bowl placed over a pan of gently simmering water. Spread the underside of the biscuits (cookies) with chocolate and use a fork to make wavy lines across the surface. Leave to cool completely.

7 Store the Florentines in an airtight tin, kept in a cool place.